Ansels

House

1A BBy bR

Saint

Benebict

Ore

97373

9700

RAF
AT THE
CROSSROADS

RAF

AT THE

CROSSROADS

The Second Front and Strategic
Bombing Debate, 1942–1943

Greg Baughen

AIR WORLD

AIR WORLD

RAF AT THE CROSSROADS
The Second Front and Strategic Bombing Debate, 1942–1943

First published in Great Britain in 2021 by
Air World
An imprint of
Pen & Sword Books Ltd
Yorkshire – Philadelphia

Copyright © Greg Baughen, 2021

ISBN 978 1 52679 534 2

Typeset by SJmagic DESIGN SERVICES, India.

Printed and bound in the UK by CPI Group (UK) Ltd.

Pen & Sword Books Limited incorporates the imprints of Atlas, Archaeology,
Aviation, Discovery, Family History, Fiction, History, Maritime, Military, Military
Classics, Politics, Select, Transport, True Crime, Air World, Frontline Publishing, Leo
Cooper, Remember When, Seaforth Publishing, The Praetorian Press, Wharncliffe
Local History, Wharncliffe Transport, Wharncliffe True Crime and White Owl.

For a complete list of Pen & Sword titles please contact

PEN & SWORD BOOKS LIMITED
47 Church Street, Barnsley, South Yorkshire, S70 2AS, England
E-mail: enquiries@pen-and-sword.co.uk
Website: www.pen-and-sword.co.uk

Or

PEN AND SWORD BOOKS
1950 Lawrence Rd, Havertown, PA 19083, USA
E-mail: Uspen-and-sword@casematepublishers.com
Website: www.penandswordbooks.com

MIX
Paper from
responsible sources
FSC® C013604

Contents

Acknowledgements

My thanks to the staff of the National Archives, the Imperial War Museum and RAF Hendon for all their help over the years. Thanks also to Phil Butler for images provided and Les Whitehouse for the Boulton Paul images and line drawings. Thanks also to Stephen White for finding the time to provide me with some insights into more recent official British thinking on military doctrine. Finally thanks to all those who have kept this series going by buying the books.

Addendum to *RAF on the Offensive*.

Page 8, E.8/39 should be E.28/39.

Page 160, The comments credited to Hugh Trenchard were in fact made by John Slessor following a discussion with Trenchard.

Introduction

The year 1942 dawned with Britain facing a new enemy in the Far East and British forces yet again in headlong retreat. More defeats at the hands of the Japanese seemed inevitable. The short-term prospects looked bleak, but the future looked a lot brighter than it had eighteen months before. In the summer of 1940, Britain had stared defeat in the face and survived, but as summer gave way to autumn, and the German invasion barges dispersed, the long-term prospects still seemed poor. The threat of invasion and the danger of defeat were far from over and, even if this could be avoided, it was difficult to see how Britain could go on to win the war. The country was facing the mighty German war machine alone and defeating the German Army seemed beyond the means of Britain, even with the resources of an Empire.

The only route to victory appeared to be an entirely new method of warfare, one which would see an enemy dissected by precision strikes from the air. Its key industries would be picked out and eliminated and its people left terrorised, begging to be spared the continuous onslaught. It was the war-winning strategy the Air Staff had always believed in. The military defeat in France suddenly made it the only way Britain had of winning the war. In this scenario there would be no need to defeat the German Army. Bombing would destroy the ability and will of the German nation to continue the struggle. Germany would find herself in the same situation she had been in the autumn of 1918, willing to accept a ceasefire at any price to spare the country further destruction. The military reoccupation of the territories Germany had conquered would be a mere formality.

After a year of such wishful thinking, the Butt report in August 1941 left no one in any doubt about the stark reality: the bombing strategy was not working. Most bomber crews were not even finding their targets, never mind hitting them. Air Chief Marshal Charles Portal, the Chief of Air Staff, believed a staggering frontline strength of 4,000, perhaps even 6,000, heavy bombers would be required to achieve success. It was a demand that

vii

just seemed to prove that victory by bombing was well beyond the financial and industrial means of the country. The vision of victory through strategic bombing seemed to be a fantasy.

Winning by bombing alone had always been a speculative strategy. There had never been any evidence that the bomber could win wars on its own and none had emerged in the first two years of the current conflict. Contrary to pre-war expectations, it was not long-range bombing that had brought quick victories; it was mechanised armies with air support that were proving decisive. Was it too late to change tack? Should Britain be learning from the Wehrmacht rather than assembling huge bomber fleets to pound the enemy into submission?

Much had changed since Churchill had declared the bomber strategy was the only way Britain had of defeating Germany. Britain now had powerful new allies. Germany had invaded the Soviet Union in June 1941. No one had expected the Red Army to last any longer than the Wehrmacht's previous victims but, six months later, despite suffering many crushing defeats, Soviet forces were pushing the German Army back from the gates of Moscow. The United States was also now in the war. The new 'Big Three' coalition had more manpower and industrial resources than the Axis countries ranged against them. Churchill was fast losing faith in the bomber strategy and no longer saw it as the only route to victory. With these new powerful allies there was no longer any need to rely on the bomber. The Allies had the means to defeat the Axis armies on the field of battle.

Allied troops were already winning significant victories. It was not just the Soviet Army that was advancing. In the Western Desert, General Claude Auchinleck's Crusader offensive was driving Field Marshal Erwin Rommel's Afrika Korps back, using the sort of air support that German commanders had so often made such good use of. It was a work in progress but the practical problems of ground and air forces working together were being tackled.

On the Home Front, however, there had been far less progress. After more than two years of war, the air support Allied armies needed and the British Army would have needed to help repel an invasion had still not been put in place. It was a failure that left the country perilously vulnerable. Even the mighty Red Army, with an air force dedicated to supporting its ground forces, had struggled to hold the formidable Wehrmacht. The British had the English Channel to buttress the defence but, even so, the much smaller British Army would be bound to struggle if it had to fight the superbly equipped and led German Army without substantial and effective air support.

INTRODUCTION

It was very much a self-inflicted handicap. There was nothing new about battlefield air support. In 1918, Britain had led the world in using air power as a key element in the latest incarnation of the age-old combined arms approach to warfare. Nor was it that nobody thought close air support was needed. The War Office had tried to get the British Army the sort of air support the German Army enjoyed. The Air Ministry, however, simply did not believe air power should be used in this way. The Royal Navy and the English Channel might have proven adequate barriers to an invasion, but it was clearly not a good idea to expect the British Army to succeed without such a crucial element of any modern army.

Fortunately for Britain, an invasion never came and the lack of an effective tactical air force did not prove costly. But, as thoughts turned to taking the offensive on land, the failure to develop battlefield air support to defend the country meant there was no foundation to work on for the sort of air force that would be required to win the war. More than two years after the outbreak of war, there was still little agreement between Army and Air Force over how, or indeed if, the Army's air requirements should be met. But pressure was growing. It was not just the War Office demanding better air support. The leaders of the Commonwealth countries fighting alongside Britain were also making their views known and Churchill was beginning to side with them. Now a new brash ally had joined the Allied fold, one with army leaders who were not interested in long drawn out wars of attrition. The Americans wanted to end the war as quickly as possible and the shortest route to Berlin was through France. With the strategic bombing offensive stalled, the tide seemed to be turning against the Air Ministry's favoured strategy.

Bellmann

Biloti = m i ss

Schleswig

Germany

Chapter 1

Invasion of France 1942

Even before the American entry into the war, Britain was making the first tentative plans to take on the German Army in north-west Europe. With Rommel in retreat in the Western Desert, the German soldier no longer seemed so invincible. The bomber strategy had quite clearly failed to deliver the results the Air Staff had promised. Churchill had been as seduced as anyone by the apparently awesome destructive power of the bomber. He had spent the 1930s warning the nation about the cataclysmic consequences of bomber attack on the country, but the reality of war had shown those fears were vastly exaggerated. German bombing during the Blitz had caused much hardship and grief, but while the death toll had been grim it had never reached the apocalyptic proportions the pre-war doom-mongers had predicted. It had never come close to breaking the will of the people. At no point did the government find itself having to consider surrender.

Nor was bombing, German or British, able to inflict economic ruin. Despite some brutal Luftwaffe attacks, British production was increasing. The Butt report, issued in August 1941, made it clear that British bombers were having even less success. Long-range bombers were not the all-conquering weapon everyone imagined them to be. In the autumn of 1941, with the Soviet Army still fiercely resisting the German advance, Churchill asked his service chiefs to begin considering the possibility that the Wehrmacht might still be locked in combat on the Eastern Front in 1942, leaving Germany vulnerable to attack on her western front. Large-scale raids on the coast of Europe might be possible. The British Army should also be ready to move in should the Nazi regime show signs of collapsing (Operation Roundup). There was little enthusiasm for any of these operations among the service chiefs. Field Marshal John Dill, the Chief of the Imperial General Staff, was becoming more bullish in his attempts to get more priority for the Army and especially the tactical air support it would require, but he was not at all keen on attempting any major operations on mainland Europe in 1942.

British generals had many good reasons for fearing an early rematch with the German Wehrmacht, but high on the list was the lack of air support. German advances were spearheaded by the fearsome Stuka, but the British Army had nothing like it and the Air Ministry had shown little interest in developing anything similar. The War Office could at least begin to tackle the challenges the new era of mechanised warfare had thrown up, but air support was out of their hands. They had to rely entirely on Air Ministry goodwill and there was precious little of that between the leaders of the two services. With little sign they would get the air support the Army needed, the War Office was left hoping it would not have to defeat a German invasion and was extremely reluctant to even consider an invasion of France.

It was all hugely frustrating for the War Office. While the idea that bombers could win wars was a speculative theory with no track record of working, there was no shortage of evidence that air support on the battlefield worked extremely well. The Germany Army had used it to help conquer most of Europe. Commonwealth forces in Africa had used it to help defeat Italian forces and more recently Rommel's Afrika Korps. The lack of such support had been a major factor in British defeats in Norway, France and Greece. Yet, despite the mounting evidence to the contrary, the Air Staff were adamant that it was neither right nor necessary to give tactical air support more attention. Even the threat of an imminent German invasion could not induce any change of heart. Air support might work for armies on mainland Europe or in Africa, they argued, but it was not needed or necessary for Allied forces based in the United Kingdom.

In May 1941, in their latest demand for more air support, the War Office had wanted 109 specialist army support squadrons worldwide, 54 of which would be required in the UK to help the Army repel an invasion. Half these squadrons would be two- or three-seater bomber-reconnaissance and the other half single-seater fighter-reconnaissance aircraft. The former would be for reconnaissance, low-level ground attack and dive-bombing and should be capable of operating by day or night in any weather. The latter would be for daylight, fair weather reconnaissance and should be armed with cannon for ground strafing. As the fifty-four home-based squadrons would be solely for the use of the Army, the War Office wanted them to be controlled by the recently created Army Co-operation Command. This was headed by Air Marshal Arthur Barratt, who had led the RAF's tactical air forces in the 1940 French campaign. General Alan Brooke, commander of the Home Forces, saw these fifty-four squadrons as just the nucleus of the force that would support the Army; Fighter Command would provide fighter support and Bomber Command more bomber support.[1]

The War Office also wanted a transport fleet, with sufficient planes to carry a brigade of airborne troops. German operations in the Netherlands in 1940 and Crete in 1941 had left the War Office with an exaggerated idea of what airborne troops could achieve. In fact these operations had proven prohibitively costly, and both had come close to failure. Crete would be the last time Germany attempted to use airborne forces on a large scale. They were not the next step forward in warfare the War Office imagined them to be. Nevertheless, the War Office was right that the ability of transport planes to move troops and supplies to where they were needed was becoming an increasingly important factor in warfare.

The Air Staff rigidly stuck to their belief that close air support on the battlefield could not help defeat an invasion. Indeed, the Air Staff could not see the point of having an 'Army Co-operation Command' and had bitterly opposed its creation. Once created, they were determined to make sure it would never command anything. They became even more opposed to the organisation when its commander Barratt seemed incapable of explaining to the Army why the bomber offensive was more important than their requests for air support. If Britain was invaded, close air support would be a misuse of air power, the Air Ministry maintained. It could only be of any possible use if the Army in the UK went on to the offensive, always a very convenient argument when there were no such plans. The Air Staff insisted that, with Bomber Command engaged in intensive operations, it needed every aircraft it could get and since an invasion of mainland Europe was not on the agenda there was no point in preparing the air support it might require.

Things began to change in the second half of 1941. Churchill was beginning to take an interest in the army air support issue and was putting pressure on the Air Staff to meet War Office requirements. Portal was by no means as unsympathetic to the need for more specialised army support aircraft as he had once been. He saw the value of cannon-armed fighters for ground strafing and was particularly enthusiastic about Hurricane tank-busters armed with 40mm cannon. However, these were weapons the Air Force should use as they saw fit, not weapons the Army should have any control over. And the strategic air offensive would still always have priority.

With Churchill's support for the bomber strategy on the wane, Portal felt he had to concede ground. However, he hoped to limit the damage to his strategic air offensive by, as far as possible, reassigning squadrons that already existed to the army support role. Portal was already committed to increasing the number of army co-operation squadrons to twenty (half single-seater fighter-reconnaissance and half bomber-reconnaissance). To these Portal added the nine No. 2 Group light-bomber squadrons and fifteen fighter squadrons that Fighter Command was already planning to train in the ground attack role. This made forty-four in all. However, the bombers and fighters would remain with Bomber and Fighter Command respectively. Only the army co-operation squadrons, already attached directly to army corps, would be controlled by Barratt's Army Co-operation Command.[2] Portal insisted that as many aircraft as possible had to play their part in bombing Germany and defending Britain from German bombers, at least until they were needed for other roles. With the bomber still the country's chosen strategy for winning the war, it was not an unreasonable argument.

The War Office was not happy with the number and even less happy with the lack of control. Without control, it was extremely difficult to organise air involvement in army training exercises. Army commanders had to get used to using air support if they were ever to match the expertise of their German opponents. The Air Ministry had always been strongly opposed to delegating any operational units to army control, beyond the army co-operation squadrons. The argument had always been that the Army would treat bomber and fighter squadrons in the same way as their army co-operation squadrons and rigidly attach then to individual ground formations. Subdividing air capability into 'penny packets' just diluted the value of air power.

It sounded like a reasonable argument but it misrepresented army practice. The War Office had to have some basis for assessing and justifying how much air support it required and it used the number of units it planned to create as a guide. That did not necessarily mean it planned to permanently attach these squadrons to ground units, as Dill was not slow to explain.[3] Even when it did, it could just as easily un-attach them. In the First World War, squadrons attached to particular armies or army groups had been switched to completely different sectors of the front when required. In the German March 1918 spring offensive, even observation squadrons attached directly to army corps had been detached and used in a ground attack role against the advancing German Army.[4]

The Air Ministry should have been able to appreciate this, and probably did, but rather mischievously chose to credit its army colleagues with an improbably inflexible mind. The Air Ministry talked earnestly of the need to centralise air resources so they could be focused where they were needed. However, as the War Office was all too aware from their experience during the Battle of France, the Air Ministry was not concerned about the ability to focus air power tactically on any given sector of the front; it wanted the flexibility to switch resources away from the front line altogether and use them for strategic operations.

Both sides were after control; the Army wanted the ability to move squadrons where it wanted, not where the Air Ministry wanted them to go. Ironically, in the UK under RAF control, squadrons were not very capable of moving anywhere. They tended to be static formations tied to their home bases. Agility and adaptability were at this time not the RAF's strong points. The rigidity the Air Ministry was accusing the Army of was in fact an Air Force problem.

Portal argued it was not worth discussing the control issue further until after the Army Bumper exercises, due to be held in late September 1941. Portal was always very good at finding reasons for delaying discussion on army air support. Bumper was the first series of exercises where the War Office had managed to persuade the Air Ministry to provide a reasonable level of RAF support, although not without a struggle. Initially, only one squadron was going to take part. To get this increased to six required a meeting between the heads of the two services. It seemed a rather trivial matter for the chiefs of staff to be discussing and underlined what an uphill struggle it was to organise any proper air force/army training. By the time the Bumper exercises had taken place, the Butt report had revealed how unsuccessful the bombing campaign had been so far and Churchill was taking more interest in alternative ways of winning the war.

The Americans helped foster this change of heart. They were not yet in the war but were acting on the basis that they soon would be. At the Newfoundland conference in August 1941, where Churchill, Roosevelt and their respective service chiefs discussed future strategy, the Americans had made it clear that they were not happy with the British reliance on long-range bombing. The Americans were asked to commit their views to paper and their observations arrived in October 1941. The Americans did not accept that 'bomber offensives should be directed at general civil morale'. They could not understand how the British had so much faith in winning the war by this method when the German Blitz in the winter of 1940–1941 had clearly failed to break the will of the British people. In the American view:

> Naval and air power may prevent wars from being lost, and by weakening enemy strength, may greatly contribute to victory.

> The opinion is held that dependence cannot be placed on winning important wars by naval or air forces alone. It should be recognized as an almost invariable rule that wars cannot be finally won without the use of land armies.[5]

The Americans explained their plans for equipping and training land forces for 'eventual use wherever land offensive may ultimately appear to be profitable' and they assumed Britain was doing the same. This was just about true now that Churchill had told the War Office to begin thinking about more offensive operations in the European theatre. However, unlike the United States, Britain did not have the economic and manpower resources to build a powerful army and a large strategic bomber fleet. The United States might be able to afford the luxury of building a bomber force to make the task of its army easier, but Britain had to make choices. Mechanised armies and the air support they would need could only be created at the expense of the strategic bomber force.

American concerns were based on what the British position had been in August 1941. Events had moved on since then. The Butt report had forced a rethink on targeting, and policy was drifting even further in the direction of indiscriminate area bombing. This was not going to please the Americans. There was already concern amongst the British contingent in Washington that, unless the bomber policy was explained more clearly, the Americans might be reluctant to supply the aircraft Bomber Command needed. All Portal could manage was suggestions that the Americans simply did not understand the importance of bombing. Indeed, further clarification would have been counterproductive, as the Air Staff were moving even further in a direction the Americans clearly disapproved of.

It was not just the Americans who were questioning the British policy. The Admiralty was demanding far greater air support for its crucial struggle in the Atlantic and elsewhere and wanted bomber production to be cut to help achieve this. The problem for the Admiralty was that the Royal Navy could not win the war. It was fighting a defensive battle and, while the Admiralty would not agree with the policy, it could not deny there was a certain logic to devoting the minimum to defensive operations in order to maximise offensive options. Only the RAF and the Army were contenders to win the war.

With Churchill beginning to consider a more positive role for the Army, it seemed like a good time for the War Office to once more put the case for more air support. The aim now was not to defeat an invasion; the air support would be needed for amphibious landings on the continent and the campaigns on foreign soil that would follow. In the autumn of 1941, the War Office set about restating its need for an effective tactical air force.

Early drafts emphasised it was a 'change in heart' within the Air Ministry the Army wanted more than anything else.[6] Operations in the Middle East seemed to be showing the way forward. The Air Force there had been under-resourced and did not always get the aircraft it wanted or needed. Nevertheless, what was available was beginning to be used to provide air support that was becoming as flexible and effective as the support the Luftwaffe was providing. In overseas' theatres, it all seemed to evolve quite naturally. As one War Office assessment wearily noted, 'In the Middle East they are at war and away from such complications as War Offices and Air Ministries'.[7] The Army wanted air support to become one of the RAF's primary roles in the UK as it already was overseas. The Air Ministry had 'to devote time, energy and enthusiasm' to the task.[8] The unco-operative attitude adopted by the Air Ministry in preparing for a possible invasion had to change if the Army was to go onto the offensive.

There was much furious debate within the War Office about how much should be asked for. Some argued the previous demand for 109 squadrons worldwide was too ambitious. If army requirements were to be taken seriously they had to be possible with available production resources. Some tentatively suggested the War Office should emphasise that the fifty-four squadrons wanted in the UK could only be an ideal for a final phase of the war, not an immediate requirement.

There was also within the War Office much support for a softer line on who exactly should control these squadrons. There seemed no point in insisting that the bombers and fighters should be transferred to Army Co-operation Command if this was just going to antagonise the Air Ministry. As long as they were available for training with Army Co-operation Command, that would be enough. This rather appeasing attitude did not appeal to all. Others argued that the Air Ministry would always be obstructive when it came to allowing squadrons to take part in army exercises, as the problems getting the RAF involved in the recent Bumper exercises had underlined.

The problem for the War Office was that now that the talk was of invading France rather than defeating a German invasion, the Air Ministry case was far stronger. There had been no excuse for not preparing the RAF to help the Army deal with an invasion that might come any day. However, the War Office had not even thought about invading the continent and

Dill believed it would be some time before it would be possible. From the Air Ministry perspective, the War Office wanted to withdraw aircrews from a crucial battle in progress to train for a hypothetical battle that might occur many years hence. Having trained aircrews involved in army exercises was a waste of a resource. It was a powerful argument although, on this basis, all the army units in Britain training for a future invasion were an inactive, wasted resource. Indeed, extending their own logic, many in the Air Ministry did wonder why Britain was bothering with an army at all.

The War Office had always made it clear that any fighter and bomber squadrons transferred to Army Co-operation Command would be available for ongoing operations; it was in the Army's interests that the crews should keep their hands in. The control issue boiled down to whether Army Co-operation Command should be lending the squadrons to other RAF commands for operations, or those commands lending them to the Army for training. The War Office wanted to make sure Army Co-operation Command was doing the lending. Once ground operations were underway, these units would have to be under the operational control of the Army. War Office documents emphasised that there was no question of these squadrons being in an 'Army Air Arm', but they had to be an integral part of the Army.[9]

The word 'integral' was bound to raise Air Ministry hackles as it smacked of an Army attempt to take over the Air Force, a scenario the Air Ministry was somewhat paranoid about. In fact, it just meant air power had to be fully incorporated into army thinking, practice and operations. Whatever form of words was used, squadrons supporting the Army had to be permanently available to the Army. Commanders had to know that squadrons would not be whipped away in the middle of a battle. In terms of numbers, the War Office hoped that it might squeeze Portal's offer up to twenty squadrons from both Fighter and Bomber Command, making sixty in all with the twenty army co-operation squadrons.

This, however, was still seen by the War Office as merely an ideal which it accepted would take years to achieve. Indeed, as one assessment concluded, 'there is no possibility of this ideal being attained during the present war'.[10] It was just a reasonable initial bargaining position. Subsequent developments would demonstrate that this was a somewhat pessimistic and unambitious view. In June 1944, the Second Tactical Air Force started the Normandy campaign with fifty-six squadrons equipped with strike or reconnaissance planes. The problem was that, with Portal needing 1,300 heavy bombers a month to create and maintain his 4,000-strong force, and even the most optimistic forecast predicting Britain would struggle to produce half these, to the Air Ministry any War Office demand was going to look unreasonable.[11]

The War Office had identified the crux of the problem without appreciating the full implications. Unless Britain changed its production priorities, the War Office was not going to make much progress and these were only going to change if there was a definite plan to invade France. Britain's overall war strategy, with its reliance on the bomber, needed to be questioned and the autumn of 1941 seemed the right time to be doing this. The War Office was well aware of the problems the Air Ministry was having acquiring the bombers it needed. They knew about the problems Bomber Command was having finding and hitting its targets. They were also aware of the concerns the Americans had raised about the general direction British air policy and overall war strategy was taking. They knew the Admiralty was demanding that heavy bomber production be reduced.

The opportunity was there, but the War Office did not join those challenging the bomber strategy. Indeed, the War Office justifications for the bomber policy were sometimes more convincing than Air Ministry efforts. They were happy to accept the bomber policy as natural for an island state with no land frontiers to defend. There was a consensus within the War Office that any increase in tactical air support must not be at the expense of the bomber offensive; this would put the War Office in an 'untenable' position.[12] There was even sympathy for the problems disappointing American output was causing Bomber Command. At most, there was perhaps some tentative regret in middle-ranking War Office echelons about the way the bomber policy had been allowed to become so dominant. However, Dill had agreed that 'the heavy-bomber force will be our main preparatory weapon in bringing about the defeat of Germany' and there was a general acceptance that it was too late to change that policy now.[13] Even in private discussions within the confines of the War Office, attitudes seemed overly submissive. In fact, there was now less need for a lengthy preparatory bomber offensive. With the Soviet Union in the war and the full weight of American production behind the Allied cause, the Allied coalition was now stronger militarily, industrially and in manpower terms than the Axis forces ranged against them.

In his formal request, Dill emphasised that, whatever bombing might achieve, the war would ultimately have to be won by troops on the ground. This meant preparing the Army for offensive action and it would need properly organised air support. In terms of squadron numbers, the final War

Office submission wanted the 109 combat squadrons it had asked for the previous spring. These would be supplemented eventually by twelve artillery observation squadrons, three of which Dill wanted formed as soon as possible.

Dill pointed out that the proposed twenty army co-operation squadrons and the thirty-four bomber and reconnaissance squadrons were all in some form expected to undertake bombing and reconnaissance missions, and it was not efficient having aircraft performing similar roles under different commands. They should therefore all be an 'integral part of the Army' as the army co-operation squadrons already were. Dill mentioned the 'broader issue, namely the relative parts to be borne by land and air forces in their joint efforts to win the war, and in particular the part played by the heavy bomber', but did not challenge the bomber strategy. Indeed, he emphasised that the War Office welcomed the growing intensity of the bomber offensive and set no limits on its scale. The RAF had tended to neglect army air support because 'understandably' it tended to think in strategic terms because of its 'power and range'. With Home Forces not engaged, it was inevitable that RAF bombers would get ever larger and less suitable for army support and this was clearly a problem that had to be addressed. However, he had no desire to reduce current plans to expand the bomber force, Dill stressed. This was not just diplomatic talk to sooth Air Ministry fears; Dill genuinely believed the strategic air offensive was still necessary. Rather meekly, Dill suggested that the aircraft the Army needed could perhaps be found in the United States.[14]

Given the problems Bomber Command was encountering, Dill's appreciation of and support for the bomber offensive ran the risk of sounding ironic. It is possible that the War Office was not fully aware of the depth of the crisis Bomber Command was facing. It was not just that crews were not finding their targets; an increasing number were losing their lives in the attempt. On the night of 7/8 November 1941, thirty-seven bombers, nearly a tenth of the force despatched, failed to return. The weather was particularly bad that night and this was held responsible for a proportion of the losses, but poor weather over Europe was not uncommon. Flying by night in dubious weather was a dangerous business, even without any enemy defences to worry about. It was just another of the many problems Bomber Command had to overcome if the bomber strategy was to succeed. Churchill believed continuing the offensive in these circumstances was just a waste of brave crews. Following the disastrous mission on the night of the 7th/8th, Bomber Command was ordered to reduce the scale of its operations while ways of improving navigation and reducing losses were sought.

There would never be a better opportunity to reconsider the priority the bomber offensive was getting. However, instead of demanding that Britain start preparing for a return to the continent, Dill agreed with Churchill that any such action was unthinkable before 1943. The longer the decision to tackle the German Army in north-west Europe was delayed, the slower the preparations for invasion would be.

With Churchill siding with the War Office, Portal felt obliged to give more ground. He would not go beyond the fifteen ground attack fighter squadrons he had committed but agreed to expand No. 2 Group to twenty squadrons. However, there was no timescale for this, and both these and the fifteen fighter squadrons would remain part of Bomber Command and Fighter Command respectively. Dill might eventually get most of the squadrons he wanted, but there was no question of him getting the control.[15]

Interestingly, in its internal discussions the Air Ministry realised that there was a major element missing in the War Office request. The fifteen fighter squadrons the Air Ministry was offering were primarily for ground attack. An army fighting on the continent would also require fighters for air defence. For anti-invasion purposes, the War Office tended to assume that Fighter Command would cover this requirement. This was already a dubious assumption. When invasion threatened in 1940, air cover for the Army had been bottom of Fighter Command's list of priorities.

For an invasion of France, it might be reasonable to expect Fighter Command to protect the sea crossing and landing. However, as forces pushed inland, there would come a point where fighter operations could no longer be run from Fighter Command operations rooms in the UK. Nor was the static Fighter Command organisation right for squadrons that had to keep up with an advancing army. These were problems the War Office was well aware of. A fighter group of 'about twenty squadrons', attached to the Army on the same basis as the fifty-four bomber-reconnaissance squadrons had been suggested but did not appear in the final War Office proposal.[16] The War Office was anxious to keep its requirements as low as possible to make them seem more reasonable. At least fighter squadrons existed; ground attack squadrons did not exist and creating these was the more pressing need.

While the War Office was well aware of the disadvantages of asking for too much, the Air Ministry saw the advantages of making the War Office demand sound as unreasonable as possible. Although the twelve artillery observation squadrons only required cheap, light aeroplanes, the

Air Ministry insisted they would require the same support services, and therefore the same drain on resources, as any other squadron. By adding an arbitrary air defence element of twenty-four fighter squadrons, they raised the required total to ninety-one squadrons. This, the Air Ministry insisted, meant there would be ninety-one fewer squadrons for defending the UK and bombing Germany. Again events would demonstrate it was not in the least unreasonable; it was no more than the eventual strength of the Second Tactical Air Force. Both sides could see the problem. Creating the tactical air force the Army needed and the 4,000-strong heavy-bomber fleet Portal wanted was not possible.

To many in the War Office, Portal's offer of fifty-five squadrons seemed to be pretty much what they were asking for, at least in terms of numbers. They still did not have the control they required, but Churchill had decreed that in the Middle East the RAF must be at the disposal of the Army when operations on the ground were in progress. If there were definite plans for an invasion of France, presumably Churchill's decree would hold true in the United Kingdom as well, it was argued.

At this point, the debate was interrupted by dramatic events in the Far East where Japanese forces were sweeping south through Malaya towards Singapore. The need to focus attention on the unfolding crisis may have suspended the debate in the short-term, but in the long-term it added fuel to the flames. Once again the British Army was in retreat and being dive-bombed and strafed as it had been in Norway, France and Greece. The lack of adequate resources in the region was not difficult to explain; Commonwealth forces in action against German and Italian forces had to have priority. Nevertheless, the disparity between air and ground forces was striking. On the ground, the Commonwealth forces in Malaya had twice as many troops as the invading Japanese Army but only half as many aircraft. It was not so much a lack of resources as an absence of balance. As had happened so often in the Mediterranean, strength on the ground was not matched by strength in the air.

Quality was another problem. Again, it was inevitable that the Far East would be denied the latest equipment while there was no fighting in progress. However, by early 1942 the Far East should have been complaining about having to make do with 1939-vintage Spitfire Is instead of the more recent versions available to the RAF elsewhere. Instead, Spitfires of any mark were just a fanciful dream and Air Chief Marshal Robert Brooke-Popham, the commander of Commonwealth air forces in the Far East, was just grateful to be sent Hurricanes.

In Britain there was the inevitable criticism about misused resources. At the time, Britain was supplying 200 aircraft a month to the Soviet Union. In Parliament, Archibald Southby told his fellow MPs 'One month's supply of the aircraft sent to Russia would have saved Malaya'.[17] He might have been right, but the aircraft that had gone to the Soviet Union were at least making a significant contribution to the Allied cause. The far greater misdirected resource was the bombers being supplied to Bomber Command, which so far had contributed very little to the Allied cause. The fighters of Fighter Command had achieved a magnificent victory in the Battle of Britain, but with the Luftwaffe now fully engaged in the Soviet Union, there had to be a question mark over whether the United Kingdom still needed over a thousand for home defence.

The question was not whether resources should go to the Soviet Union, Libya or Malaya; the problem was with the more fundamental balance between the tactical (both naval and military) and strategic (offensive and defensive) air forces. By 1942, this imbalance had been around for so long it was becoming accepted as the norm. Britain seemed to be condemned to be forever fighting tactical air battles at a disadvantage, not because the country lacked the means to build the air resources required but because strategic air operations had to have priority. Portal explained that the little that was available had to be divided between the Middle East and the Far East, but it would be more accurate to say the two theatres had to make do with what was left after Fighter and Bomber Command had absorbed most of what was available. There were all the usual recriminations that followed British defeats. Portal blamed the Army for failing to protect RAF airfields.[18] Not for the first time, cause and effect were getting confused. One of the reasons the Army was in retreat and unable to hold the airfields was because there were so few aircraft operating from those airfields.

Meanwhile Dill had departed. He and Churchill had never got on. Dill had always opposed Churchill's policy of reinforcing the Army in the Middle East at the expense of the forces defending the United Kingdom. Churchill had long considered his army chief unimaginative and obstructive. Brooke took over from Dill, who moved to the United States where he did invaluable work co-ordinating Allied strategy. Brooke, however, was even less enthusiastic about offensive action in Europe than his predecessor. He had spent the last eighteen months desperately trying to create an army that might fend off an invasion, and defending Britain would remain his focus in his new post. For anything more offensive, he, too, was quite happy to fall in line with Air Ministry thinking and wait for the bomber offensive to weaken

German military power. Perhaps by 1944 a landing would be possible. For more immediate offensive action on land, he believed Britain should look to the Middle East.

This rather unambitious time frame was not how Britain's new American ally saw it. It had always been Roosevelt's intention to enter the war against Germany. It was just a question of judging when the mood of the American people was ready for such a move. The attack on Pearl Harbor brought the United States into the war on Britain's side against Japan but not against Germany and, with a nation baying for revenge against the Japanese aggressor, it was probably not the best time to ask the American people to take on the Nazis as well. However, any difficulties Roosevelt might have had persuading the American people otherwise were swept aside when both Germany and Italy chose to declare war on the United States.

Despite the humiliation suffered at Pearl Harbor and the rapid defeat of US forces in the Philippines, Roosevelt immediately made it clear that the European theatre and the defeat of Hitler would have priority. It was a bold decision that accelerated a fundamental transformation in the strategic balance of power in Europe. Germany and Italy now faced in the west an enemy with even greater industrial and manpower resources than those of her still undefeated Soviet enemy in the east. With the United States actively engaged in the war there was even less need for the rebalancing of forces that the War Office was expecting Bomber Command to achieve.

With German forces in retreat in the Western Desert and falling back from Moscow, the Americans saw no reason for delay. The war would be won by taking Berlin and the quickest way to Berlin was across the Channel and through France. A cross-Channel invasion was also the most obvious way of helping the Soviets. Roosevelt wanted this to happen quickly. There was enormous pressure from many quarters in the United States to avenge American defeats in the Pacific. It would be deeply embarrassing for the President if resources were diverted away from the Pacific to Europe and were then not used. The demands of General Douglas MacArthur, the US land commander in the Far East, and Admiral Ernest King, the US Navy chief, to give the Pacific theatre priority might become impossible to counter.

Roosevelt and his army chief, General George Marshall, had no intention of waiting until 1944 to invade mainland Europe; both wanted to act in 1942. Even General 'Hap' Arnold, the United States Army Air Corps commander, wanted an invasion in 1942, so confident was he of the mayhem Allied bombers could wreak on the enemy.[19] Weeks after the disaster at Pearl Harbor and with American troops in retreat on every front, it was an impressively confident approach. In the Far East, despite the lower priority the theatre was getting, they were soon backing their aggressive talk with action. Just seven months after Pearl Harbor and ignominious eviction from the Philippines, the Americans were on the offensive, landing forces on the island of Guadalcanal. Two years after a similarly ignominious defeat and retreat from Dunkirk, and the defensive victory in the Battle of Britain, it did not seem, from the American perspective, to be too soon for the British, too, to be considering going on to the offensive in north-west Europe. They were after all the battle-hardened veterans of more than two years of war. Indeed, the Americans did not see why Britain need wait for American support to arrive before acting.

The American desire to strike quickly in Europe put more pressure on the British to come up with concrete proposals. Operation Roundup, a full-scale invasion should the Germans suddenly show signs of collapse, was already on the agenda. No one thought this remotely likely before 1943, but at least some preliminary planning for such an operation was underway. Churchill was also suggesting large-scale raids. Some of these involved large numbers of troops and tanks staying on the continent for weeks or even months, before conducting an orderly withdrawal. The bridgeheads would be large enough for RAF squadrons to operate from within them. Such operations were not so different to a full-scale invasion.

The United States' entry into the war did not change Churchill and Brooke's ideas about the feasibility of a full-scale cross-Channel invasion in 1942. Brooke was put off by the technical problems and materiel shortages, while Churchill's objections were more to do with grand strategy. The Prime Minister saw the Middle East, with its lines of communication to the Far East, as central to British interests. Indeed, both Churchill and Brooke saw the preservation of the British Empire as a key war aim. The first priority of the new alliance, they believed, should be to clear North Africa of Axis troops. They hoped that the successful Crusader offensive would be followed by Operation Acrobat, an advance into Libya. The defeat of the Axis forces in North Africa would be hastened by Operation Gymnast, a British plan involving the landing of 55,000 British troops in Vichy French-controlled Algeria in the rear of Rommel's forces. Initially, Churchill was able to persuade Roosevelt to commit American troops to this operation, rather than a cross-Channel venture.

However, far from pushing the Germans back further into Libya, it was the Commonwealth forces who were soon in retreat. The island base of

Malta had been playing a key role in enabling the Commonwealth forces to retain the upper hand. Aircraft and submarines operating from the island fortress had been inflicting heavy losses on the convoys carrying supplies to the Axis forces in Africa. However, in December 1941, the Luftwaffe returned to Maltese skies and the Hurricanes immediately started to struggle against the German Bf 109F and Italian Macchi C.202. German bombers began breaking through the defences with disconcerting frequency and losses on the ground, as well as in the air, rapidly mounted. The effects were immediate. Anti-convoy strikes from the island became less effective and adequate supplies began getting through to Rommel's Afrika Korps. Rommel only had about sixty tanks, but this did not deter him from taking the offensive. Rommel ordered a limited advance, but what was little more than a raid soon turned into a full-scale offensive.

Air Marshal Arthur Tedder was in overall charge of the RAF in the theatre, with Air Vice-Marshal Arthur Coningham commanding front-line Commonwealth squadrons in the Western Desert. Following the recent successful Crusader operation, Commonwealth forces were overstretched and short of supplies. Some, like 7th Armoured Division, had been pulled back to rest and refit. Air units had also been withdrawn. Aircraft were in short supply. Deliveries of the American Maryland had ceased as the Martin factories switched production to the improved Baltimore. Spares for the Maryland were scarce and squadrons equipped with those planes would have to wait for Baltimore deliveries before they became operational again. The Boston squadrons had also been withdrawn because of problems with the Wright Cyclone engines. Deliveries of Tomahawks had also stopped as its successor, the Kittyhawk, replaced it on the Curtiss production lines. The first Kittyhawks were only just arriving.[20]

Events in the Far East were a further major complication. The entry of Japan into the war exposed how reliant Britain was on the United States for the aircraft needed for army support. The American priority now had to be her own armed forces. To make matters worse, the situation in the Far East was desperate and the Middle East was the nearest source of reinforcement. Tedder would comply with the requests for help with far less protest than similar requests to send aircraft to Greece provoked from his predecessor, Air Chief Marshal Arthur Longmore, the year before. If the Air Ministry felt any twinge of guilt about keeping substantial air resources in the United Kingdom while both the Middle East and Far East struggled, the dutiful Tedder helped ease their conscience. The first batch of fifty crated Hurricanes left Port Sudan on 15 January. Three Blenheim squadrons were soon on their way and the strength of these squadrons was raised to twenty-four, which could only be done at the expense of the units that remained. As a result, there were now just two Blenheim squadrons available for operations over the Libyan front.[21]

Tedder's relaxed attitude was not likely to accelerate the delivery of replacements. Indeed Tedder's willingness to co-operate encouraged further demands. When Portal asked him whether the transfer of three or four Hurricane squadrons would interfere with Operation Acrobat (the plan to clear Axis forces from the rest of North Africa), the ever compliant Tedder assured Portal it would not. They might prove inadequate if Vichy French forces proved unco-operative when Commonwealth forces reached the frontier with Tunisia, he warned. His weakened forces would also struggle to deal with a German offensive through the Caucasus or an attack on Turkey, but these were even more speculative scenarios.[22] The real danger was somewhat closer at hand. However, Tedder and his fellow commanders can hardly be blamed for not seeing it. The Axis supply situation in North Africa was so precarious that Rommel had been given very strict instructions to stay on the defensive. Unfortunately for the Commonwealth forces, Rommel was not very good at obeying orders.

On paper at least, a substantial force of fighters was still based in western Cyrenaica. Ten Hurricane and Tomahawk/Kittyhawk squadrons were using the airfields at Antelat, 40 miles north-west of Agedabia, either as their main or forward bases. Pilots were not in short supply, but fighters for them to fly were. Even so, they were opposed by even fewer German fighters. If the Commonwealth fighters had not been so inferior in quality, they would have been more than capable of holding their own.

With more petrol getting through to Luftwaffe squadrons, German pilots were able to take full advantage of the technical superiority of their equipment. On 9 January 1942, ten Hurricanes of No. 229 Squadron on escort duty were bounced by six Bf 109s and four British fighters were lost. On the 14th it was the turn of No. 94 Squadron, two Bf 109s shooting down no fewer than seven Hurricanes.[23] To make matters worse, on the day Rommel struck, 21 January, the airfields at Antelat were waterlogged and Ju 87s took the opportunity to pound British positions unopposed. Axis air effort was not huge; around 260 sorties were flown on the 21st and 230 on the 22nd, but it was applied where it would have most effect. Not expecting any sort of Axis attack, Commonwealth troops fell back in some disorder. So successful was this initial raid, Rommel pushed on further. From the 22nd, Allied air units were back in action, although one of their first tasks

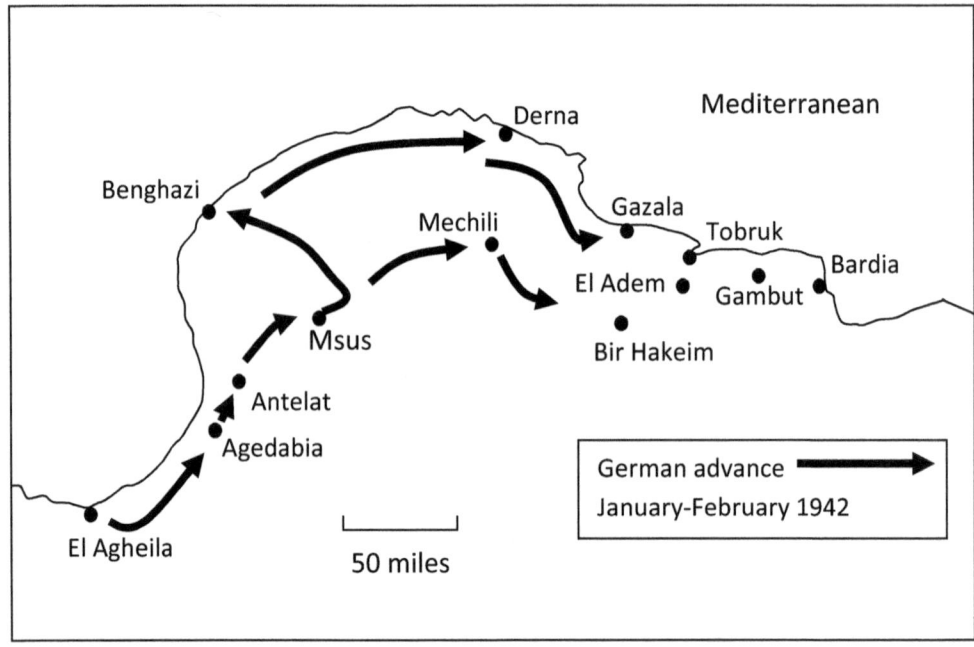

was to abandon Antelat. German armour was fast approaching the airfield, the last planes scampering away under enemy fire. During the day, just twenty-two fighters flew offensive sweeps; twelve attacked ground targets and twenty escorted the two Blenheim squadrons. Including defensive patrols in the rear, little more than a hundred fighter sorties were flown from a force that had recently been managing 300 a day.[24]

Bomber operations were stepped up by using Wellingtons to attack tactical targets by night. On the 23rd, Commonwealth fighters, now operating from Msus, were, according to the official Air Ministry narrative, able to re-establish air superiority, although in reality this appears to mean that the seventy-five fighter sorties flown over the front did not encounter any major German formations. The Army was also denied the support of the two Blenheim squadrons, as these were needed to attack an Italian convoy heading for Tripoli. On the 24th, the Hurricanes of No. 274 Squadron showed the fighter could still be effective if it could fight its way past the enemy escorts. The squadron intercepted a formation of thirty enemy planes and claimed four Ju 87s destroyed and four probably destroyed, along with three Italian fighters.[25]

In an effort to stem the German tide, Allied fighters were switched to ground attack missions. This sort of flexible use of fighter resources was becoming standard practice in the African campaigns. Fighter pilots are never happy about conceding the altitude advantage to the enemy, especially when the enemy is flying superior planes. Flying low just increased the risk of being surprised from above. It was not the sort of risk Group Captain Kenneth Cross, commanding No. 258 Wing, would have been happy about taking. He had been commanding No. 252 Wing, responsible for rear defence in Egypt, until just before the Crusader offensive, when he had taken over No. 258 Wing at the front. He entered the battle with the standard Air Ministry belief that the primary role of the fighter pilot was to seek out the enemy and establish air superiority, not support ground forces directly, and this meant flying as high as possible to gain an advantage.[26] However, having been compelled by circumstances to use his fighters low down to support ground forces, Cross discovered that his pilots actually coped better with the enemy opposition than when they attempted to take on Luftwaffe fighters at higher altitudes.[27] This was particularly true of the Tomahawk and Kittyhawk, both of which performed best at lower altitudes, which, to some extent, offset the height advantage conceded.

Despite the efforts of the Commonwealth squadrons, Rommel continued to advance. On 25 January, squadrons had to abandon Msus and head for Mechili. Anxious to avoid another close shave as had occurred at Antelat, the Army rather prematurely announced that this airfield could not be held either and on the 28th the squadrons were pulled back to Gazala. As it turned out, Rommel's move on Mechili was a feint and he turned west to strike at Benghazi. Coningham's squadrons were too far away to help and the port fell on 29 January. Mechili was not abandoned until 3 February, but by this time some of Coningham's squadrons had fallen back as far as El Adem or even Gambut on the Egyptian frontier. As the Commonwealth forces streamed back to the Gazala-Bir Hakeim line, they once more came within the range of air support. Rommel's advance was so rapid the Luftwaffe could not keep up and it was reduced to using a few long-range bombers to hit Commonwealth troops. Temporarily spared the intervention of German fighters, Commonwealth squadrons were able to concentrate on strafing the advancing German columns. The advance was finally brought to a halt, but half of the Crusader gains had been lost.[28]

The setbacks in the Middle East, coming on top of more defeats in the Far East, were stoking the growing criticism back home in the press and Parliament to Churchill's war policy. In the first six months of 1942 Churchill faced two votes of no confidence. The lack of air support for the Army and Navy was a frequently mentioned issue. British efforts in the air were in stark contrast to the support German and Japanese armies were getting and there was much talk in political circles of the need to give the Army its own air arm in order to rectify this shortcoming.

The problems Bomber Command was encountering were scarcely a secret. Nobody in Parliament was arguing that the bomber offensive should be abandoned, but some were saying there was a case for reviewing the priority it was getting and a very strong case for improving air support for the Army and Navy. Leslie Hore-Belisha, who had been Secretary of State for War from 1937 to 1940, spoke of the need for the 'striking of a new balance between the strategical and tactical functions of the Royal Air Force'. He wanted the Army and Navy to have more control over the air forces they required, but he emphasised that he was not talking about splitting the RAF up. He wanted integration, not co-operation. In a remarkable piece of progressive thinking he suggested, 'The ideal is not three separate Services but to integrate all Services.'[29] It is an ideal British armed forces were still trying to achieve the best part of a century later.

Sir Stafford Cripps, the Lord Privy Seal and seen by some as a potential successor to Churchill, felt obliged to demonstrate the government was willing to be flexible. He reminded his Parliamentary colleagues that the bomber strategy had been devised when Britain stood alone. With the Soviet Union and United States now in the war, he conceded the situation was very different. Stafford Cripps assured the House that the government was aware of the new circumstances and that 'the original policy has come under review … and the moment they arrive at a decision that the circumstances warrant a change, a change in policy will be made'.[30] The need for change in air policy was very much on the political agenda.

Despite the setbacks in the Middle and Far East, there was in Britain still a lot of popular support for a second front in France. Stalin had been putting pressure on Churchill to act ever since the German invasion. Now there was also plenty of interest from the other side of the Atlantic. With Rommel's recent advance in North Africa, Churchill's hopes of pushing the Axis forces out of North Africa had suddenly disappeared. His idea of landing troops in north-west Africa ceased to be an attractive option and the Americans reverted to their original plan of building up US forces in the United Kingdom for a cross-Channel invasion, which they wanted to take place as soon as possible, preferably in 1942.

Nor were Britain's Joint Planning Staff put off by recent military defeats. The committee brought together the planning departments of the three services, with Captain Charles Lambe representing the Navy, Brigadier Guy

Stewart the Army and Air Commodore William Dickson, a future Chief of Air Staff, heading the Air Ministry team. At Churchill's request, they had been investigating operations against mainland Europe since the previous autumn. By March 1942, the Soviet winter counter-offensive was running out of steam and evidence was mounting that, once the weather improved, the Germans would attempt to renew their advance eastwards. Once again the fear was that, without General Winter to help them, the Soviet Union might struggle to contain the Wehrmacht. The Joint Planning Staff were clear that a Soviet defeat would be disastrous for the Allied cause and that on purely military grounds the case for a 'major diversion' in the west was overwhelming. The committee pointed out that the Americans were thinking along the same lines.

The Joint Planning Committee argued that Britain had to do more than just drop bombs on German cities and fly occasional offensive fighter patrols over France. The Soviet and German forces were engaged in a titanic battle, and the outcome of the war hung in the balance. Yet, in the United Kingdom there were substantial military forces playing no part in this struggle, forces indeed that were becoming increasingly demoralised by the lack of any action. A Soviet collapse would enable the Germans to threaten the Middle East from the north and lines of communication to the Far East might be cut. The release of the German forces tied up on the Russian front would once more threaten the United Kingdom and certainly rule out any possibility of mounting an invasion of France even in 1943. The committee felt that the only way of giving the Soviets real assistance was 'the seizure and retention of a bridgehead on the continent', with the operation taking place as early as mid-May 1942.[31]

It might seem extraordinary that anyone should consider cobbling together a makeshift invasion fleet in two months, given that it eventually took two years, but it was no more extraordinary than German efforts to improvise an invasion fleet in the summer of 1940. As a major naval power, Britain was certainly in a stronger position than Germany to contemplate such an operation. Even so, it was a tall order. The purely military grounds for an invasion might be overwhelming but, as the committee readily conceded, this did not mean it could be done.

A landing on the Cherbourg peninsula was the initial proposal. By 1 May 1942, there ought to be sufficient specialist landing craft to put ashore nearly 8,000 troops, 200 tanks and some 400 guns and vehicles in a first wave. An improvised fleet of 1,500 trawlers and other small craft would transport another 60,000 troops. Following the initial assault, around 4,000 troops an hour could be landed on the first day, subsequently dropping to 8,000 a day.

The force would reach its target strength of two armoured divisions, two tank brigades and seven infantry divisions after four weeks.

Fighter cover was the most worrying problem. It was assumed fighters would only be able to patrol for ten minutes over the peninsula on internal fuel, which was a little pessimistic compared to later Air Ministry estimates. With thirty to thirty-six squadrons flying three-squadron-strength patrols and each plane flying three sorties a day, only five hours' cover could be provided. Airfields within the bridgehead could initially only be used as advanced landing grounds as they were unlikely to be beyond enemy artillery range. The capture of an airfield on the Channel Islands was one suggestion for easing the problem. Despite the difficulties, the committee felt it was a feasible operation and wanted an overall commander appointed immediately so that planning could begin.[32]

The Joint Planning Committee's ideas were presented to the Chiefs of Staff on 10 March 1942 and the Joint Planners were instructed to come up with some more detailed proposals, with, slightly less ambitiously, a landing taking place as early as 1 June, the operation acquiring the codename Sledgehammer. From the outset, Brooke and General Bernard Paget, who had taken over from Brooke as commander of Home Forces, were strongly against any cross-Channel adventure, but there was plenty of support for the operation from the War Office Military Operations Directorate. They emphasised that British and Canadian forces gathering in the UK could not be kept inactive indefinitely. A major operation against mainland Europe would not just raise the morale of the Army, it would lift the entire nation. An invasion of France might be risky, but it was feasible, the Directorate insisted. Even in the worst case scenario of the entire invasion force being wiped out, the failure would not fatally compromise Britain's ability to defeat a German invasion. This was perhaps reassuring but scarcely encouraging. An interesting advantage mentioned was that airfields on the continent would allow Bomber Command to operate by day over Germany with escorts.[33] It was scarcely the Army's area of expertise, but even to the War Office, fighter escorts seemed like an obvious solution to Bomber Command's problems.

Unsurprisingly, plenty of objections soon emerged as the planners began to look into the options more closely. Getting ashore and establishing a beachhead was not seen as a major problem and in 1942 this was probably the case. Very little effort had been put into fortifying the French coastline. In March 1942, Hitler ordered the coastal defences along the English Channel to be strengthened, but initially effort was focused on defending the ports. The main danger to the operation was that German reserves would arrive faster than troops could be landed. One of the advantages of a landing in the Cherbourg region was that it was quite far west and there would, perhaps, be fewer reserves in the vicinity. The Admiralty also preferred a landing in this region because it was close to Southampton and Portsmouth and the sea lanes would be relatively short and easier to protect. However, with the limited endurance of RAF fighters, providing effective fighter cover seemed an insuperable problem. Capturing one of the Channel Islands would help and might be easier than establishing a bridgehead on the mainland, but even capturing an island was a risky operation and it could only provide a base for a handful of fighter squadrons.

A landing in the Pas de Calais region solved the fighter cover problem. Not only was the coast well within range of even the RAF's short-range interceptors, but, it was noted, squadrons would still be well placed to block any air assault on London.[34] Even in 1942, the spectre of the much-feared knockout blow still hung over British planning. However, the nearest major ports were still Portsmouth and Southampton with London just as distant, presenting the Navy with long lines of communication to defend. The Pas de Calais region was also where German defences were expected to be strongest and enemy reinforcements were more likely to arrive sooner.

Having boldly proposed a landing, the Joint Planners now rather meekly decided that carrying it out was not feasible. Nevertheless, the Chiefs of Staff felt that if the Soviet Union was on the brink of collapse, something would have to be done. A landing in France was unlikely to cause ground forces to move from the Eastern Front, but there was a good chance that Luftwaffe squadrons would be moved westwards. Even Portal could see that air support was a key factor in the German Army's success and reducing the level of that air support might make all the difference. Diverting and engaging the Luftwaffe now became the principal purpose of the operation. For the British, there was no question of liberating France and driving on to Berlin; it would just be a bridgehead which would force a reaction from the Luftwaffe.

Key commanders were brought into the discussions. These included Admiral Louis Mountbatten, who had been put in charge of the Combined Operations Command, whose tasks included trying to get the three services to work together in a reasonably co-operative manner. Vice-Admiral Bertram Ramsay represented the Navy, and Paget the Army. The obvious candidate to represent the Air Force at this level might seem to be Barratt, the commander of Army Co-operation Command. This was, after all, the Air

Force command that had been set up to support the Army. However, Army Co-operation Command was very much the unwanted black sheep of the Air Ministry family and Barratt's attempts to develop army/air co-operation were seen as almost an act of outright disloyalty to the Air Staff.

Instead of Barratt, Air Marshal Sholto Douglas, the head of Fighter Command, represented the Air Force. It was by no means an unsuitable appointment; Douglas had shown more interest than most RAF commanders in army air support and was keen to develop his command into much more than a home defence interceptor force. Fighters operating over northern France were being increasingly used for ground attack and Douglas was enthusiastic about creating the fifteen specialist ground attack fighter squadrons that Portal had offered the War Office. Even so, the decision to give the commander of Fighter Command the task reflected the Air Ministry view that the main purpose of the operation was to attract and shoot down enemy planes.

With the air battle now the central feature, the landing had to be in the Pas de Calais. An outline plan was drawn up, envisaging landings north and south of Le Touquet, where German defences were expected to be less well developed. The invading forces would push 20 miles inland, the eventual bridgehead encompassing the ports of Boulogne and Calais. It would be large enough to have RAF squadrons operating from within it.

Neither Douglas nor Paget were particularly impressed by such ideas. Douglas did not see any reason why air action alone would not do. Portal disagreed and indeed there was very little evidence that the operations the RAF had been flying over France for more than a year had forced the Germans to transfer any air units from the Eastern Front. Portal believed there had to be a threat on the ground to draw the Luftwaffe into battle. Paget thought it might be possible to establish the bridgehead but an orderly retreat would be impossible and, as at Dunkirk, the Army would lose all its heavy equipment. However, he conceded that the operation might have to be risked if the Soviet Union was about to go under.

Paget and Douglas were asked to reconsider their pessimistic prognosis for the operation. Their response opened with some encouraging talk of there being an opportunity which 'if resolutely seized, might lead to far-reaching results'.[35] However, defeat would inevitably expose Britain to the danger of a German counter invasion and a landing in France could only succeed if Germany was at least 'fully' extended on the Eastern Front and preferably in headlong retreat. As the operation was supposed to bolster a Soviet Union on the brink of defeat, this conclusion was not particularly helpful.

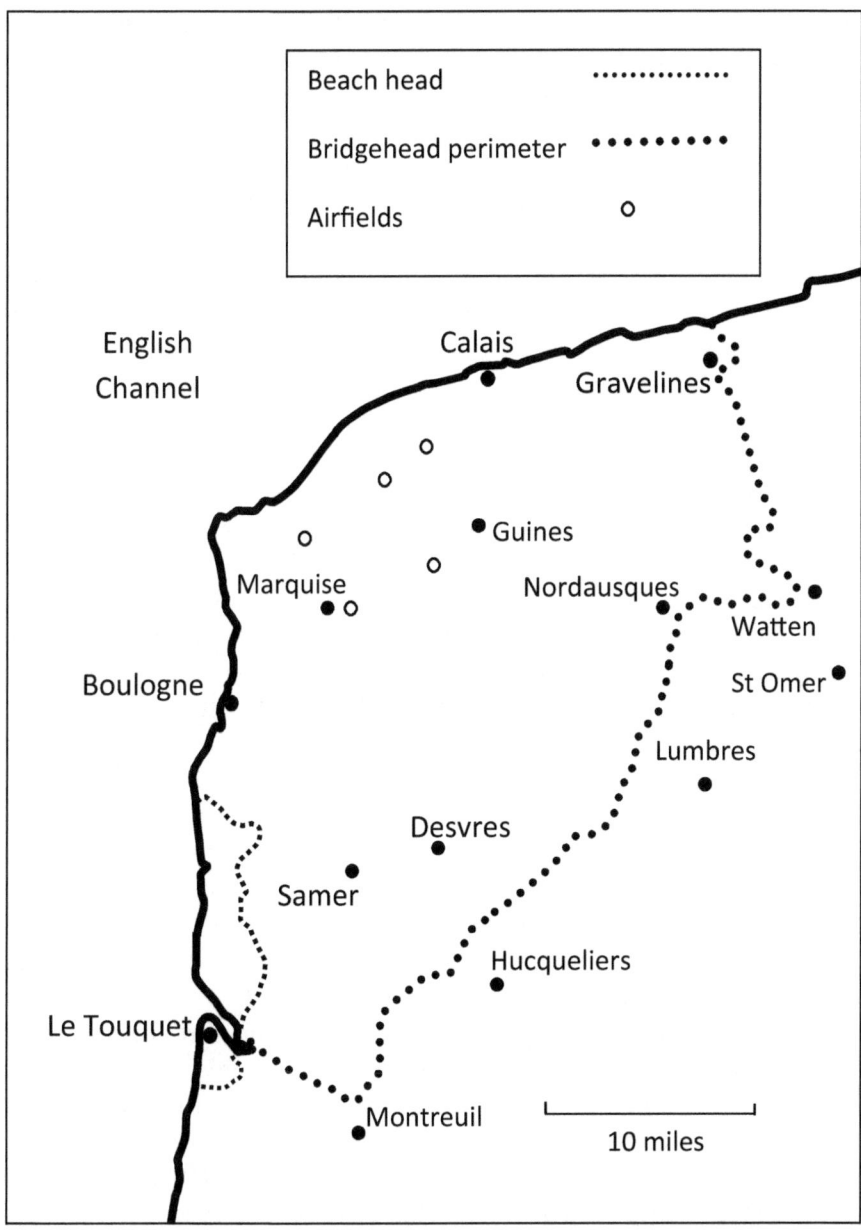

There was no shortage of scepticism about the operation, especially at the highest level, but talk of an invasion was on the agenda. The Americans were very keen and even in British circles there was a consensus that as a last ditch effort to keep the Soviet Union in the war, something might have to be attempted. A British Army might be fighting in France far sooner than either the Air Ministry or War Office imagined. The need to provide the Army with air support might not be so distant. Once again, it seemed the ideal time for the War Office to restate its demands for a powerful tactical air force.

In the early spring of 1942, the War Office still seemed to have the backing from Churchill it had secured in 1941. The evidence from every front was that air power was playing a key role on the battlefield. In February, Churchill and his war cabinet learned how British Army observers on the Moscow front had watched Soviet close air support in action. Soviet Air Force units were attached directly to army units and regimental commanders could request air strikes. Aircraft were engaging the enemy within an hour of a request being made, with low-level attacks using bombs, cannon and anti-tank rockets.[36] Nor was it just the War Office that was interested in this sort of support. Even Portal was talking enthusiastically about creating a fleet of Hurricane tank-busters by the spring of 1943 to support ground operations.

In March, the Prime Minister, in typically robust form, wanted to know from Portal what had happened to the American dive-bombers that the Army had been promised in 1940. How many were on order? When were they due to arrive?[37] Churchill was also defending the under-siege Barratt. The Air Minister, Archibald Sinclair, was trying to get the recalcitrant Army Co-operation commander replaced by Air Marshal Guy Garrod, currently holding a training post, which was what the Air Staff saw as the Command's proper function. Sinclair told Churchill that Dill, Brooke and David Margesson, the recently departed Secretary of State for War, had all wanted Garrod to replace Barratt.

This was not Churchill's understanding of the situation and he asked his top military adviser, General Hastings Ismay, to find out what the War Office really thought. Ismay reported back that both Brooke and Paget wanted Barratt to stay. Sinclair was not deterred by this contradiction of his claim. He expressed surprise that they had apparently changed their minds but insisted that the promises he had recently made to Parliament to improve inter-service co-operation all depended on Barratt going. He continued to persist, even after Churchill demanded documentary proof of War Office discontent and Sinclair had to admit there was none. In Air Ministry circles the knives were out for Barratt, but Churchill overruled his minister and ensured Barratt stayed.[38]

Things seem to be going the War Office way. In March 1942, as the Joint Planning Staff worked on their invasion plans, Brooke renewed

War Office attempts to get the air support those plans would require. In a blistering attack on the Air Ministry's unco-operative attitude, he declared that no serious progress had been made in the previous nine months. Only fifteen of the promised twenty army co-operation squadrons had been formed and the fighter-reconnaissance squadrons only had on average just four serviceable planes. The Army had been promised that No. 2 Group's day bombers would always be available to support the Army but this Group had 'practically disintegrated'. Brooke pointed out that recent defeats in the Far East had once again demonstrated the crucial role air power had to play in modern warfare. 'The outstanding lesson of the war has been that land forces inadequately supported from the air are doomed to failure when opposed by a modern enemy equipped with suitable types of aircraft and adequate forces trained for close co-operation with land forces.'[39] Air support was as essential as artillery or tanks and it was no good relying on second best with types designed for something else or ones that 'have proved unsuitable for other roles'.

The War Office accepted that naval air and strategic bombing requirements had also to be met and Brooke insisted that he was therefore only asking for an absolute minimum, but, 'Up to the present this irreducible minimum has not been found in any theatre'. Brooke wanted a worldwide army support force of sixty fighter-reconnaissance, thirty light-bomber reconnaissance, twelve artillery observation, four ambulance and five intercommunication squadrons, 111 squadrons in total. He also wanted sufficient transport planes and gliders to carry an airborne division into battle. Although Brooke was happy for existing aircraft to be converted into transports, he was anxious that development of a purpose-built transport, designed for parachutists and with large doors that would allow rapid loading and unloading, should begin as soon as possible.[40]

The non-combat requirements were all forward-looking proposals that would become standard features of any modern army. Commanders needed communication planes to keep in touch. The knowledge that, if wounded, a soldier could expect to be rapidly evacuated to first-class medical facilities was an enormous boost to morale, especially in difficult mountainous and jungle terrain. Air transport would become vital for all armies, as its value in the recent British retreat in Burma was demonstrating.[41] However, to an Air Ministry transfixed by the bomber's destructive power, communication, ambulance aircraft and transports were not the way to win a war.

In other ways, Brooke's demands were a step backwards. Brooke was sticking with the fighter-reconnaissance and bomber-reconnaissance mix that he had been demanding back in May 1941 and Dill had reiterated the previous autumn. There was no mention of Portal's offer of fifty-five squadrons. Many in the War Office believed this essentially gave the Army what it was asking for and was in fact a more specialised and versatile mix. Brooke insisted that squadrons supporting the Army had to be 'an integral part of the Army', ideally within an 'Army Command', analogous to the existing Fighter, Bomber and Coastal Commands, over which army commanders would have real operational control. There was a very real warning that if the Air Ministry could not do better in this regard, the only option would be the far more extreme measure of having an Army Air Arm like the Navy's Fleet Air Arm.

Nine months earlier, similar threats had helped trigger a reassessment by Churchill of the Air Staff's preoccupation with strategic bombing. This time the results would be somewhat different. One of the reasons was the fate of the small Baltic port of Lübeck.

Chapter 2

Bomber Revival

As 1942 dawned, Bomber Command and its bomber strategy seemed to be in deep crisis. The force was still reeling from the revelations of the Butt report. Operations had been scaled back to prevent crews being lost on what were now seen as pointless missions. If strategic bombing had a future it might just be as a much smaller, more specialised force, a useful rather than a decisive war-winning weapon. A force that could pin down German resources on defensive duties without requiring half the British aircraft industry to sustain it; 'a heavy and I trust a seriously increasing annoyance', as Churchill put it in 1941.[1]

Portal and the Air Staff, however, had no intention of allowing their bomber strategy to be downgraded to a mere 'annoyance'. The Air Staff remained convinced that the bomber was a war-winning weapon. For more than two decades the Air Ministry had been developing the theory and the hardware to deliver it, and the defeat of the French Army in 1940 had swept away the only alternative way of winning the war. The bomber strategy reigned supreme. It was soon proving more difficult to put into practice than anyone had imagined, but the more the problems with the strategic air offensive mounted, the more determined the bomber advocates became to prove they had been right all along. That the strategic air offensive would win the war had become an article of faith, and with the War Office not offering bold alternative strategies to go with the aircraft they were demanding, the Air Staff believed they had time to get the bomber offensive back on track.

Politicians of all nationalities and persuasions were fascinated by the destructive power of the bomber and Churchill was no exception. He no longer believed the bomber could win the war, but he was still in awe of its power and it was still the only immediate way of striking Germany. Politically, it was very useful in persuading Stalin that Britain was doing some real fighting and not just supplying the Soviets with arms so they could do all the fighting for them. Crucially, Portal's belief in strategic bombing was far greater than Dill and Brooke's belief in the likelihood of landings in France succeeding. In the bomber strategy's darkest hour these factors helped sustain the policy. Portal got assurances from Churchill that he had no intention of changing existing policy; it was a rather lukewarm endorsement – the strategic bombing offensive was on probation – but it was enough for Portal to push on with his plans.

It helped Portal's cause that the bomber policy had acquired considerable momentum. British industry was geared up to deliver the bombers the Air Ministry was demanding, and reversing this priority would be extremely disruptive. Indeed, despite all the doubts, the December 1941 production programme envisaged a substantial expansion of bomber production. Overall output would increase to around 2,500 planes per month by the middle of 1943, of which 1,000 would be bombers. It was not exactly what Portal wanted; the increase was only achieved by substantially increasing the number of medium bombers. By the end of 1943, bomber output would settle down at just 80 light bombers, 300 medium and 625 heavy a month. It was not nearly enough to create and maintain the 4,000 heavy-bomber force Portal needed.

There was not even any certainty that Bomber Command would get the extra bombers being built. The Admiralty and War Office were hovering over the incapacitated Bomber Command like vultures. More bomber crews were being sent to the Middle East where even Portal conceded they could contribute more than they could over Germany. In February, eight and a half squadrons were transferred to Coastal Command for anti-submarine patrols over the Atlantic and long-range reconnaissance in the Indian Ocean. More followed in March. The vice-like grip the bomber policy had on British strategy seemed to be loosening.

The Air Staff and their Air Minister, Archibald Sinclair, vainly continued to insist it was far more efficient to destroy the dockyards building submarines than hunting for them in the Atlantic. The Air Ministry always liked to give the impression this involved the hopeless task of scanning the vast oceans in the hope of coming across an enemy vessel, a veritable hunt for a needle in a haystack. In fact the Navy just wanted patrols where the U-boats were likely to be and that meant in the vicinity of the convoys.[2] It was Bomber Command's attempts to find the dockyards building the submarines in blacked-out Germany that more closely resembled the hunt for the proverbial needle.

Commanders in the Far East also believed they could make much better use of the bombers being sent over Germany. General Archibald Wavell, commanding Allied forces in India and Burma, complained that while Bomber Command could put 200 heavy bombers over a German city on a single night, he could not even put twenty light bombers in the air to counter an attack on British shipping that cost three warships and 100,000 tons of merchant shipping. In Britain, calls for more Bomber Command squadrons to be deployed elsewhere were growing. Serious questions were being asked about the priority the strategic bombing was getting and with American pressure to open a second front in western Europe, alternative strategies were threatening the future of the bomber offensive.

The entry of the United States into the war was a mixed blessing for the bomber advocates. There would now be very little hope of the United States making up the shortfall in British heavy bomber production. The Americans would also be an even stronger influence on Allied strategy and their army commanders had made it clear they did not believe the bomber could win the war on its own. However, although the United States Army Air Corps (soon to become the United States Army Air Forces – USAAF) was still a part of the American Army, its air force commanders were imbued with the strategic bombing ideology and were already gently guiding their country's air policy in a more strategic direction. The RAF might not be able to build a bomber force of four to six thousand aircraft, but it seemed a reasonable target for a joint Anglo-American force.

For the Americans, cost was not such a huge obstacle. The United States had the financial and industrial resources to build and develop both tactical and strategic air forces simultaneously, and indeed still have plenty of spare production capacity to arm her allies. The Americans could afford to experiment with long-range bombing without fatally damaging the prospects of the other branches of their armed forces. However, for Arnold, bomber theory was no experiment. He, too, was a believer. During Arnold's visit to Britain in April 1941, the Air Ministry and RAF commanders had taken every opportunity to encourage the American Air Forces chief's belief in the power of independent bombing. Coming from an air force with two years' experience of war, it was for Arnold welcome confirmation that his views of how air power should be used were correct.[3]

When, in the autumn of 1941, Roosevelt asked his military to draw up plans for a war with Germany, Arnold insisted a massive aerial offensive would be required before any attempt could be made to engage the enemy on the battlefield. Indeed this might be so successful, the follow up land operations on the continent might be a mere formality.[4] Although provision would be made for the tactical bombers an eventual invasion of France might require, many within the Air Forces believed heavy bombers could provide this support. The Americans were not copying RAF strategy; it was the direction USAAF commanders had always wanted to take their air forces. But the British seemed to be providing the proof the theory was correct. The RAF was pursuing an independent bombing policy and, unlike many other enemies of Germany, Britain remained undefeated.

By the time the United States entered the war, Bomber Command had abandoned any attempt at precision bombing. Portal rather hoped he could save the Americans time by persuading them to join Bomber Command in its area bombing by night, but he was never likely to succeed. The American confidence in their Fortresses and Liberators was as unshakeable as British confidence had been at the outbreak of war that Wellingtons and Stirling could defeat any attempts to intercept them. When it entered service, the Stirling had proven no more capable of operating unescorted by day than the Wellington. Any hopes that the arrival of the Avro Lancaster might change the situation were quickly dashed when, in April 1942, seven out of twelve were shot down by fighters and flak in a low-level daylight raid on a submarine engine factory in Augsburg. The Americans, however, were still convinced that the defensive firepower of their Fortresses and Liberators could beat off German fighters and, with their revolutionary Norden bombsight, the Americans were convinced they could hit targets with precision from altitudes that would be beyond the reach of anti-aircraft guns.

Enemy morale would not be the target. The USAAF was part of the Army. The whole point of the bomber force was that it would make the task of the ground forces easier. There was no place for an air force that was just going to try and win the war on its own by breaking enemy morale. The Army generals did not share their air force colleagues' faith that bombing alone might prove decisive, but anything the long-range bombers could do to weaken German resistance would clearly help. They might not agree on where it would lead but American air and land commanders were pulling in the same direction.

Arnold gave control of the Eighth Air Force gathering in the United Kingdom to General Carl Spaatz, with instructions to prepare the force for the dual role of conducting a daylight strategic air offensive against Germany and preparing for the support of land forces in a cross-Channel invasion. However, Spaatz was also a firm believer in the power of the bomber and it would always be the former that would have priority. The bomber element of the force, VIII Bomber Command, would be commanded by Brigadier General Ira Eaker, another staunch advocate of the bombing strategy. There was plenty of lip service to the needs for army support. The Americans were impressed by British Army Air Support Controls, the communication systems the RAF and Army had developed for requesting and delivering air support on the battlefield, and were quite happy to adopt them. The system was incorporated into *US Army Field Manual FM 31-35*, issued in April 1942. This instruction was later mocked by those seeking a more independent role for the USAAF, but it was a reasonable, if somewhat vague, description of how ground and air forces should work together. It emphasised that air units were not subordinate to ground forces and only if centralised control broke down would air units be attached to specific ground units. Its main crime seems to have been to emphasise that, for effective air support, ground and air forces have to be integrated.[5] This was not to the liking of many in the USAAF. Like their RAF counterparts, American air force commanders did not see battlefield air support as their central role.

The stance adopted by the USAAF was a huge boost for the Air Ministry's bomber strategy. However, if the bomber was to prove its worth, Bomber Command had to start finding a way of achieving some concrete results. Clearly a new approach was required. Lowering enemy morale had always been one of Bomber Command's aims, but now it became the primary aim. For some time, Bomber Command had been moving away from attempting precision bombing and focusing more on indiscriminate area bombing. So far, this had been a last resort, forced on the RAF by poor weather or moonless nights, but now it would become the standard approach. The aim was no longer to hit individual factories; the aim was simply to hit a city. The aiming point would be city centres and the surrounding residential areas rather than industries which tended to be located on the outskirts of towns and cities. Full use was to be made of incendiary bombs and the 'primary object' was 'the morale of the civil population and, in particular, of the industrial workers'.[6] It was back to the Trenchard doctrine of the 1920s.

There was no great moral dilemma involved in this change of emphasis; the destruction of cities and the accompanying heavy loss of civilian life had for decades been what everyone had expected future wars to be about. The RAF could at least claim to have attempted to apply a more refined, discriminate approach. It had done its best and failed. At least it had tried. By adopting indiscriminate area bombing, the Air Ministry was not plumbing new depths of inhumane methods of waging war; it was just returning to a former policy.

With the new 'no holds barred' approach, and people rather than factories the target, there was no reason why all weapons of mass destruction should not be back on the table. Chemical weapons were a very obvious way of attacking people and undermining their morale. In the inter-war years it had always been assumed that gas would be used by both sides. The British government had vowed it would only use gas in retaliation, as indeed it had vowed it would only bomb cities in response to German attacks on Allied cities. However, whereas in 1940 the Air Ministry had been keen to find evidence that the Luftwaffe was attacking civilian targets in order to get its own bomber offensive going, there was no such desire to find evidence of chemical weapons being used.

Coincidently, the question of using gas was on the political agenda in the spring of 1942. The Soviets had discovered what they suspected to be a poison-gas container in a German Ju 88 bomber they had shot down. They asked the British government to announce Britain would retaliate with gas if the Germans used similar weapons against the Soviets. It turned out that the suspect device was in fact just a normal component of the fuel system in a long-range version of the Ju 88. Nevertheless, on 10 May 1942, the British government issued the warning the Soviets had requested.

The discussions of the Chiefs of Staff that preceded the announcement were revealing. In 1940, RAF poison gas stocks were low, and a gas war was scarcely in Britain's interests. Even so, Churchill saw no great moral dilemma over using poison gas, and it probably would have been used against German forces if Britain had been invaded. By 1942, Churchill had made sure that there were substantial stocks of mustard and phosgene gas. There were no doubts about the effectiveness of such weapons; assessments at the time concluded that 'owing to the psychological effect due to its lethal nature, phosgene is eminently suitable for use against the civil population'.[7]

However, in their discussions on the Soviet request, Portal and his fellow Chiefs of Staff were certainly not looking for an excuse to use chemical weapons. Indeed, they warned Churchill that any Soviet claim should be thoroughly checked. The Soviet Union was less vulnerable to chemical attack than the more densely populated United Kingdom and the Soviets might be deviously trying to draw Britain into an unwarranted use of gas to draw German resources away from the Eastern Front. They also pointed out that an Allied beachhead in any invasion of France would be very vulnerable to gas attack.[8] On other matters, Portal would insist it was not British policy to forgo the use of a weapon for fear of retaliation but gas was different. The Air Staff had been very keen to start a bombing war with high explosives, but no one wanted a gas war.

The Air Staff might claim the area bombing policy was still paving the way for an invasion, but a demoralised civilian population was not necessarily going to make it any easier to defeat the German Army on the battlefield. The move to the area bombing policy was a gradual one over the course of many months. Perhaps for this reason the Admiralty and War Office did not pick up on the full significance. Under the new policy the aim was not to help the Army and Navy win the war, it was now an undisguised attempt to win the war by bombing alone.

Air Marshal Richard Peirse, in charge of Bomber Command, was blamed for the poor results so far achieved. He had been an ardent supporter of strategic bombing, but the difficulties of delivering on the promises made had worn down his enthusiasm. Peirse was hastily moved on even before a successor was ready to take his place. It was more than a month before the forthright Air Marshal Arthur Harris took over. An intense man of few words but strong opinions, Harris had an extraordinary presence which had a galvanising effect on not just those in his High Wycombe headquarters but on his entire command. His no-nonsense approach to bombing had already been exercised in colonial conflicts. In the 1920s, his squadron became the first to be equipped for the transport role. For Harris, transporting troops was not what air forces were for and he took it upon himself to convert his transports into bombers. He took pride in the ability of his ex-transports to wipe out a village in forty-five minutes.[9] In Palestine in the 1930s his preferred policy for dealing with discontent was 'a bomb in each village that speaks out of turn'.[10] Portal knew exactly what he was getting when he appointed Harris.

The new commander was not responsible for the area bombing policy. The policy was decided before Harris took over. Harris was just the ideal person to implement the policy. Harris, however, was not just following orders; he believed passionately in the strategy and saw it as his personal responsibility to persuade any doubters that it was the right path to follow. It was a crusade, which Harris would pursue with religious fervour. The target list he was given included industrial towns like Schweinfurt, with its important ball bearing plants, but it also included less important targets like Lübeck, a Baltic port with very little industry.[11]

Harris set about making his force more effective. There would be fewer operations but effort would be more focused. Rather than bombers attacking throughout the course of the night, all bombs would be delivered in a limited time span in order to make the task of the emergency services as difficult as possible. The initial wave would carry high explosive bombs to blow off roofs and shatter windows. This would allow the incendiaries that followed to find materials that burned and air flow to feed the fires. There was nothing new about the process; the RAF had had similar plans in 1918.[12]

Aiming a bomb at a city was a lot easier than aiming it at a factory, but the bombers still had to find the city and the Butt report had made it clear many crews were not even managing that. Even before the Butt report, the need to improve navigation was recognised and the Telecommunications Research Establishment (TRE), Britain's radio and radar research centre, was already working on various navigational aids. Before the Butt report, no one appreciated just how urgent the need was. Indeed, some were dismissive of such technical aids. Peirse had always been more aware than most of the difficulties of operating bombers by night but even he had warned Arnold that there would be no place for new-fangled American navigational aids in a real war. American crews would have to learn to navigate properly like RAF crews. Before the Butt report, the navigational devices under development were just seen as useful additional aids. Butt changed all that. They were now required to rescue the bomber offensive.

The first of these new aids, GEE, was already up and running. The idea had been around since 1938 but serious development only began in June 1940. The bomber picked up two pulsed signals from transmitters 200 miles apart and a cathode-ray tube displayed the time difference between those and a third transmission. The figures corresponded to two of the grid lines on the navigator's GEE map and where they intersected was the position of the bomber. Since the system relied on signals transmitted from Britain, range was limited by the curvature of the earth to around 300-400 miles, but this was enough for the system to be used over the Ruhr, where the permanent industrial haze made finding targets particularly difficult. Accuracy depended on range and conditions. It could be as accurate as half a mile, or as inaccurate as 5 miles. The system was tried out over Germany for the first time in August 1941 – with potentially disastrous consequences. A Wellington carrying it was shot down and there could be no certainty that the device had not fallen into German hands. As it turned out, the Germans had not recovered the equipment from the wreck, but it would be a nervous six months while sufficient sets were available to justify full-scale use.

Oboe was another navigational aid already being developed. This made use of the fact that radar could measure distance very accurately. Instead of flying straight towards the target, the bomber flew along the circumference of a circle defined by radar signals transmitted by a station in the United Kingdom and retransmitted by the plane. When the circular path intersected the intended target, a signal from a second station triggered the release of the bombs. This system could bomb blind with accuracies of the order of hundreds of yards. As early as December 1941 an early prototype was used in a rather ambitious attempt to bomb the *Scharnhorst* and *Gneisenau* battle-cruisers sheltering in the French port of Brest. The two German ships were far too small and survived, but the system was good enough to allow city centres or even large factories to be bombed blind. Only one plane at a time could use the system, so its main use was to mark targets for those following. Like GEE, it could only be used over western Germany.

A third development, H2S, was a spin-off from the airborne radar night-fighters used. Again the idea had been around for some time. The earliest 1.5-metre sets had picked up the reflections from coastlines and given an indication of whether the aircraft was flying over sea or land, but at this wavelength it was difficult to tell much more. Centimetric radar, with 10-cm wavelengths, created a much clearer idea of the terrain below and, with a rotating beam, actually swept out a crude map with water, countryside and urban sprawl giving reasonably distinctively different images on the radar screen.

Whether Bomber Command would be allowed to use this over Germany was another matter. The cavity magnetron that powered centimetric radar was a closely guarded secret. The latest radars using the technology had a vital role to play in the air defence of Britain. Royal Navy warships were using centimetric Type 271 radar, which was so sensitive it could even detect the periscope of a submerged submarine. Using the cavity magnetron over Germany would mean it would be bound to fall into German hands. If the Germans discovered the Allies had mastered 10-cm wavelength radar, they would immediately begin investigating ways of jamming it or at least develop receivers that would warn of the presence of its probing transmissions. It was a measure of how ruthless the Air Staff were willing to be that the Air Ministry took very little notice of these objections. Nothing would be allowed to stand in the way of making the bomber offensive work.

Whether Bomber Command would want to use H2S was also an issue. It was a system that transmitted a signal, and as the scientists were constantly warning the Air Ministry, any such active system could betray the position of the plane transmitting the signal. Using it might cause more problems than it solved. Again the Air Ministry preferred to disregard these warnings. It was a very cavalier approach to take just to give bombers a better chance of hitting town centres.

The ingenuity scientists were showing in their efforts to overcome the problems Bomber Command faced was quite remarkable. It was all in rather stark contrast to the rigid thinking that ensured the bomber strategy had to be pursued come what may. The technology required just to keep the bomber strategy afloat was many orders of magnitude more sophisticated than the technology required to provide the Army with effective air support on the battlefield.

GEE was the first of the new navigational systems to become available. Assuming the Germans had not recovered the GEE equipment in the crashed Wellington and did not already have counter-measures in place, at best the effective life of GEE was expected to be about six months. By early March 1942, sufficient GEE sets were available to make its use by Bomber Command worthwhile. March also saw the operational debut of the four-engined Lancaster, which was a vast improvement on its twin-engined Manchester predecessor and indeed superior to the Stirling and Halifax. The restrictions imposed on the Command the previous November were lifted and Harris was ordered to resume the offensive at maximum effort.[13]

Ironically, the new phase of bombing started with a precision attack on a specific target. The Renault factory in Paris was building trucks for the German Army and Bomber Command was asked to attempt to destroy it without inflicting heavy civilian casualties in the surrounding residential areas. Given its previous record, it was a tall order. However, because the target was French, anti-aircraft defences would be minimal and the bombers would at least be able to fly as low as they liked. On the night of 3/4 March 1942, 235 bombers headed for the factory. It was the largest Bomber Command raid of the war up to that time and turned out to be by far the most accurate. A large number of flares were used to illuminate the target and the attack was delivered in less than two hours. The factory was very heavily damaged and output ceased for a month. Just one bomber was lost. Compared to Bomber Command's previous efforts, it was an outstanding success.

However, not all the bombs found their target; some hit residential areas nearly 10 miles away. The civilian death toll was nearly 400, more than twice the casualties inflicted on any raid on a German town. The long casualty list just emphasised another fundamental flaw in the bomber strategy.

The industries of occupied countries were an important source of war material for the Wehrmacht, but those factories could only be bombed at huge risk to the local population. The Renault raid cost the German Army 2,500 trucks, but 400 French lives was a very heavy price to pay.

On the night of 8/9 March, GEE was used for the first time, but three unsuccessful efforts to bomb Essen demonstrated that, even with this aid, bombing the Ruhr was not easy. The first successful GEE-led raid was the 13/14 March attack on Cologne. One hundred and thirty-five bombers took part. A cable factory, two rubber factories, five churches and a cinema were hit: 1,500 homes were damaged or destroyed and sixty-two civilians killed. Forty-six of the deaths occurred when 4,000lb bombs demolished two blocks of flats. The death toll would have been two higher, but miraculously, two children were rescued after being buried under the rubble for nearly three days.[14]

Harris needed something much more dramatic than this level of damage to demonstrate he was getting the results expected of him. It was, he argued, far better to destroy a small unimportant town than cause minimal damage to a more important, larger target. He was not the first to suggest targets need not have any great economic value. Churchill had been constantly demanding more random bombing and Air Vice-Marshal John Slessor, a strident advocate of the bomber policy, had suggested that the bombing of provincial towns should coincide with local fairs, when the town would be full of visitors, to maximise the terror.[15] It was to apply this level of ruthlessness that Harris had been brought in.

The Baltic port of Lübeck was on Harris's list of potential targets and this small medieval city seemed ideal. There was an important U-boat shipyard nearby and this would also be targeted, but it was the city, 6 miles further inland, that would be the main focus off the attack. It was a port and therefore not entirely devoid of military significance, but there were no major industries or military targets within the town. Its main attraction as a target was that it was on the coast and therefore easy to find and its historic wooden buildings could be guaranteed to burn. It was to be an undisguised terror attack. British air policy had gone from one of precision attacks on economic targets, to aiming bombs in the general direction of where factories might be, to choosing a town that would burn. This was how far the Air Staff were willing to go to prove their bomber policy worked.

On the night of 28/29 March 1942, 234 bombers, carrying a high proportion of incendiaries, struck the port. Thirty per cent of the town was devastated. Two-thirds of all buildings were destroyed or damaged and over

300 civilians were killed. This was nearly twice the death toll in any previous raid on Germany. German leaders were taken aback by the target chosen and the ruthlessness of the attack. There were serious concerns about the ability of the civilian population to withstand such an assault. The aim of Bomber Command was to terrorise and, in this respect, the raid seemed to have succeeded.

It was the first time Bomber Command could claim to have caused widespread damage and Harris had the photographic evidence to back it up. 'What we did to Lübeck' screamed the headline of the *Daily Mirror*, with photos of the burnt-out city centre. There was little to indicate what had been there, but propaganda posters urging factory workers to ever greater efforts showed bombs raining down on the port and nearby factories. However, there were no important factories. The raid was used by those defending the bomber strategy in Parliament as an example of the support the RAF was providing the Navy, but the U-boat yard was many miles away from the devastated city centre.[16]

The Lübeck raid came at a calamitous time for the British and Commonwealth forces in every theatre. In the Middle East, Rommel was advancing. In the Far East, 85,000 troops in Singapore had surrendered and the *Prince of Wales* and *Repulse* had been sunk by Japanese bombers. The *Scharnhorst, Gneisenau* and *Prinz Eugen* had sailed up the English Channel in broad daylight to safety in Germany. In all these disastrous failures the ineffectiveness of the RAF was a major contributory, common factor, but the defeats were seen as army and naval failures. In sharp contrast, Lübeck was an RAF success.

With Churchill under pressure from his opponents in Parliament, any victory on any front was welcome and Lübeck gave him that victory. This was not just a politician cynically exploiting the situation; in Churchill's eyes this was a very real victory. It was the scale of indiscriminate destruction he had been urging on Portal for some time. It was not second best to destroying oil plants and aircraft factories; for Churchill it was at least as good. He was not going to change his mind about bombers winning wars, but if bombing could cause this much destruction, then the offensive would have his full backing.

Churchill's scientific adviser, Frederick Lindemann (Lord Cherwell), was soon reinforcing Churchill's revived interest in bombing. Two days after the raid, Lindemann sent Churchill a note based on an investigation that was already underway on the effects of German bombing on British cities during the Blitz. The investigation was being carried out by Solly

Zuckerman and John Bernal, two scientists working for the Ministry of Home Security. Their report, based on raids on Hull and Birmingham, would not be issued until April, but Lindemann thought Churchill should be aware of what he claimed were their preliminary findings.

Lindemann explained to the Prime Minister that 'careful analysis' of the Luftwaffe attacks on Birmingham and Hull provided ample evidence bombing could be decisive. Current plans called for 10,000 bombers to be delivered to the RAF by mid-1943. If each flew on average fourteen missions, carrying an average of 3 tons of bombs and half of these fell on residential areas, they could inflict ten times more damage on the fifty-eight largest German cities than the Luftwaffe had inflicted on Birmingham and Hull. A tenth of the houses in Hull had been destroyed, so it followed that ten times this level of destruction would result in the great majority of the population of these fifty-eight German cities being made homeless.

Losing one's home was a devastating blow, Lindemann explained. 'People seem to mind it more than having their friends or even relatives killed ... . There seems little doubt that this [scale of attack] would break the spirit of the German people,' Lindemann concluded.[17] Lindemann steered clear of any mention of human casualties, although clearly a large number of those who had lost their homes would no longer be around to feel demoralised. Lindemann, however, did point out that, as a bonus, German war industries would be bound to suffer some damage. In a perverse twist of normal usage, German factories would suffer collateral damage.

Professor Patrick Blackett, who was the Admiralty's scientific adviser, and Henry Tizard, at the Ministry of Aircraft Production (MAP), were not convinced. Blackett claimed Lindemann was exaggerating the weight of attack by 600 per cent. Tizard wondered where he had got the 10,000 bomber production target from. The actual figure was under 9,000, and around 800 of these were destined for Coastal Command. It was also unlikely that these production targets would be met; the Air Ministry customarily knocked off 15 per cent for lost production through enemy action or other problems. According to Tizard, seven thousand bombers was a more reasonable figure and 25 per cent a more likely estimate of the number of bombers that would find their target.

Lindemann seemed surprised that there could be anything wrong with his 'simple calculation' and the 'self-evident' conclusion it led to. The 10,000 figure was simply rounded up to make the arithmetic easier for Churchill to understand, he explained. Tizard, however, believed Lindemann's analysis was dangerous; the possible scale of attack could not be decisive and in the meantime 'we may lose the war in other ways'.[18] These 'other ways' Tizard referred to included the Battle of the Atlantic and indeed the Royal Navy's struggle worldwide. Tizard agreed with the Admiralty that this was where long-range bombers could be more usefully employed.

In fact, when the Zuckerman-Bernal report was issued in April 1942, the overall conclusion was that the bombing on Hull and Birmingham had less effect on civilian morale than many had feared. The bombing had been traumatising, but there was no sign of society collapsing. The report did not feel able to say precisely what scale of attack would cause the breakdown of society. It guessed that it might have to be at least five times greater, but this was more to emphasise how difficult it might be to achieve rather than a sensible target to aim for. Zuckerman was rather annoyed that Lindemann had used his findings to support the case for indiscriminate bombing.

However, Lindemann was telling Churchill what he wanted to hear. The Air Ministry was quick to add their support; Sinclair and Portal thought Lindemann's arguments were 'simple, clear and convincing'.[19] They claimed the recent attacks on Lübeck, Cologne and the Ruhr had already achieved more than the 50 per cent bombing accuracy that Lindemann was assuming. Provided the bombers were built and there were no major diversions of bomber effort away from Germany, before the end of 1943 the degree of destruction predicted by Lindemann would be achieved. One of those diversions was, of course, the 111 squadrons Brooke was insisting the Army needed.

Brooke had put in his demand three weeks before the Lübeck raid. As with all War Office demands, it was greeted within the Air Ministry with a mixture of anger and incredulity. It was a measure of the divide that separated the two services that the Air Ministry not only rejected the War Office demands, it also took offence. The sense of hurt is very apparent in private letters Air Chief Marshal Wilfred Freeman, Portal's deputy and a hard-line supporter of the bomber offensive, wrote to Lieutenant General Archibald Nye, Brooke's deputy in the War Office. Initially unaware that Nye had been responsible for much of the document outlining army needs, Freeman expressed his grave displeasure at its offensive tone. Although the War Office document was entirely concerned with resources, Freeman chose to take the Army criticism as one directed at aircrews.[20] It was a highly questionable tactic. Attempting to discredit criticism by claiming it was directed at the courageous aircrews who had to risk their lives implementing the policy rather than the decision makers who shaped the policy is difficult to justify.

A puzzled Nye pointed out there was not a single word of criticism of aircrews in the report. He could see nothing that was in any way offensive; it was just a blunt request that the Army get better tools for close air support. The discovery that Nye was one of the authors did little to temper Freeman's criticism. Even after aides had advised removing the accusation that 'the War Office could not have done more if they had tried to make future co-operation as difficult and unpleasant as possible', it was still a fiercely worded response. As Freeman saw it, the War Office document began with accusations of bad faith and ended with threats. In between, every defeat 'from Narvik to Singapore are linked, if not due, to the Air Ministry's refusal to recognise and fulfil the Army's need for air support'.[21] Freeman offered no apology for dragging aircrews into the argument. They could not be blamed for thinking that the unfair criticism they had been subjected to had been inspired by the War Office.

Freeman's passion for the bomber cause is clear, but, as was the case with so many of his fellow bomber advocates, this passion was blinding him to the repercussions the bomber policy was having on land and sea operations. There were many reasons for the string of defeats the Army had suffered since the outbreak of war, but no one could deny that one of the more obvious explanations was the inability to match the air support British and Allied troops were up against. Freeman, the Air Staff and the Air Ministry were in denial about how dearly the bomber priority had handicapped the Army in its operations.

Portal also took exception to the War Office attitude. On 1 April 1942, the Chief of Air Staff's stinging riposte was delivered to Churchill and his cabinet Defence Committee. Brooke's original paper was very forward thinking in many ways, but it also presented Portal with some easy opportunities to score points. Portal could quite correctly point out that the War Office had not even bothered to respond to his November fifty-five squadron offer (twenty No. 2 Group bomber, fifteen ground attack fighter and twenty army co-operation squadrons). Totting up Army demands, the Air Ministry calculated the War Office wanted 4,100 planes supporting the Army. This was, they claimed, 850 more than the Luftwaffe had ever used along the entire Eastern Front.

It was a mischievous comparison. Portal arrived at his 4,100 figure by including 2,900 non-combat planes (transports, glider tugs, communication and ambulance planes) and was comparing this with the number of combat planes the Luftwaffe was believed to have on the Eastern Front. Portal then compared the 1,200 ground attack, dive-bombing and reconnaissance planes Brooke wanted attached to the British Army to the 400 tactical reconnaissance planes attached to individual German Army units, leaving out of the calculation the centrally controlled German tactical bomber force. Portal claimed the War Office wanted the 2,500 transport planes to be of a specially designed type which would take four years to develop. In fact the War Office had made it clear that the purpose-built transport was a long-term requirement and for the time being they would be perfectly happy with types that already existed.[22]

Portal had also received a demand from the Admiralty for 2,000 planes, in addition to the 400 already in the Fleet Air Arm, for the 'Coastal Commands' they wanted around the world. The total demand was therefore for an additional 6,000 planes for what the Air Ministry considered to be 'limited and specialised roles'. These 'limited and specialised roles' were in fact what was required to fight the war being fought around the globe, as opposed to the parallel bomber war the Air Ministry had immersed itself in.

Portal suggested that the Luftwaffe was successful precisely because it did not allocate particular air units to Army or Navy. It was a multi-purpose flexible force and Portal insisted that was what the RAF was. Unfortunately that was precisely what the UK-based RAF was not. The huge fleet of four-engined bombers the Air Ministry was trying to assemble could not match the greater versatility of the smaller light and medium bombers equipping the Luftwaffe.

Portal took exception to Brooke's statement that the Air Ministry had it in its power to do something about the lack of air support in the Far East and had deliberately chosen not to. It was an intentionally confrontational way of putting the War Office argument but, in the case of fighters, it was essentially true. The Air Ministry had the resources in the United Kingdom and had always had it within its power to send more to all the campaigns the Army had been involved in. As many critics of the Air Ministry were pointing out at the time, by holding back such large numbers of fighters and, in particular, refusing to deploy Spitfire squadrons outside the UK, the Air Staff were over-insuring on home defence at the expense of armies in the field. The same was not true of tactical bombers; there was no readily available supply of these. Nevertheless, this shortage was by choice. Restricting the production of light bombers and indeed fighters to maximise heavy bomber output was the Air Ministry's preferred policy. More significantly perhaps, it was the government's chosen policy. If the War Office wanted effort switched to tactical bombers, they had to challenge the bomber policy that was responsible for the shortage of tactical aircraft.

That the Army had not got the air support it needed in the first three years of war could scarcely be disputed, but Portal pounced on Brooke's assertion that in no campaign so far had the Army had the 'irreducible minimum' of air support required for success. Portal triumphantly pointed out that in the recently concluded Crusader offensive, the RAF had established air superiority and had been universally acclaimed for the support it had provided the Army. To hammer home the point, he listed every quote he could find (eighteen of them), mostly from Auchinleck, praising in some way the air support provided.

Not for the first time, Portal's eagerness to prove he was right, only succeeded in highlighting the failure of Air Staff policy. After two years of war, Crusader was the only operation Portal felt he could point to as an example of where the RAF had provided effective air support. What he did not mention was that this happy state of affairs had only been achieved after a titanic and acrimonious struggle between the army commanders in the region and the Air Ministry. By emphasising RAF success in this operation, Portal was merely drawing attention to the failure to provide adequate air support in the many other crucial battles the Army had been involved in, both past and ongoing.

As for providing the Army in the UK with more air support, Portal rather scornfully suggested that it was up to the Cabinet Defence Committee to decide if priority should go to the air force units fighting on the Eastern Front, in Malaya or North Africa or inactive army co-operation squadrons in the United Kingdom waiting for an invasion, the probability of which was 'negligible'.

The Air Ministry view on the likelihood of an invasion tended to depend on circumstances; it was a serious danger if it was a question of moving fighter squadrons overseas but a negligible risk if the Army in Britain wanted air support. In fact the likelihood of an invasion had never been an Air Ministry consideration; even in the summer of 1940 when invasion seemed imminent the Air Ministry had been just as reluctant to meet army requirements. No matter what the circumstances, the Air Ministry did not want to waste resources on a tactical air force.

In truth, there should never have been a time when such a force was not required. As soon as the threat of invasion passed, thoughts should have been turning to how the Air Force would support offensive action across the Channel. War Office policy was clearly not helping the Army cause. Brooke's extreme reluctance to consider seriously going onto the offensive in north-west Europe was creating a policy vacuum in which it seemed a tactical air force was not needed. The War Office was making it very easy for the Air Ministry to argue that a UK-based tactical air force was a waste of resources. On the other hand, the failure to get adequate air support scarcely encouraged a more aggressive army policy.

Not making provision for the air support the Army needed to defend Britain might have been fatal for the country. Not making provision for the air support it needed to go onto the offensive could only extend the war. Portal saw it somewhat differently. He believed giving the Army and Navy the air resources they wanted as the fatal error. It would delay victory, or even put victory beyond the country's grasp. Playing on War Office fears, he suggested:

> It is vain to imagine any major operations in Western Europe can develop until the resistance of Germany is undermined by the cumulative and combined effect of sea and air pressure. With the help of the United States of America we are well placed to subject the Axis powers to the full rigour of an overwhelming air superiority which will be decisive in the struggle ahead.[23]

The 'overwhelming air superiority' he was talking about was not the sort of superiority gained by fighters over the battlefield in the Crusader campaign; it was still the old Trenchardian concept of air superiority gained by having more bombers. In Portal's war, air superiority still meant bomber superiority. Portal's assertion that 'War experience shows that the primary need of an army in battle is the achievement of general air superiority' misunderstood Army needs. The Army wanted air support; air superiority just provided the ideal circumstances in which this air support could be provided. If air superiority was not achievable, a way still had to be found of giving the Army the best possible air support. Too often the failure to achieve air superiority had been used as an explanation for the absence of air support. Not having air superiority made it more difficult to support the Army; it did not make it impossible.

Given that the first two years of the bomber offensive had achieved so little, there was not much basis for Portal's predictions that the bomber could undermine German powers of resistance anytime soon. Ironically, it was the Soviet Army that was achieving what Bomber Command had set out to achieve. By engaging the bulk of the German Army on the Eastern Front, the Soviets had slashed what was available to defend the Western

Front to an extent that was far in excess of anything Bomber Command could ever possibly hope to achieve. Unfortunately, Brooke was only too happy to concur with Portal's belief that the forces assembling in Britain would have to wait until Bomber Command had succeeded before they went on to the offensive.

Between Brooke's initial demand and Portal's response much had happened. Lübeck had been devastated and Churchill's most trusted adviser was claiming Germany could be defeated by making the German population homeless. The Prime Minister was not completely uncritical of Portal's response. He saw a great future for airborne forces and was suspicious of Portal's claim that developing a specialist transport aircraft would take so long. It would surely not be so different to existing civil transports, Churchill insisted. It was an observation that suggested Churchill was not rushing off a hasty response. He had given Portal's objections careful consideration. It makes the uncritical reaction to Portal's other observations all the more significant.

Just days before, Churchill had been pushing Portal for news on the dive-bomber question and defeating Air Ministry efforts to sack Barratt. Suddenly, Churchill was taking a completely different tack. The success of the Lübeck raid and Lindemann's dehousing memo were pushing Churchill on a path he was more than happy to follow. The covering note Churchill sent Brooke attached to Portal's comments was terse and uncompromising. The Prime Minister railed at Brooke's pointless 'truism' that armies inadequately supported from the air are doomed when faced with armies that are supported in this way. If it was so self-evidently true, however, perhaps Churchill should have pondered why it had been happening so often in the first three years of war and why Britain seemed unable to do anything about it. Churchill insisted that 'the requirements of the General Staff for the Army appear to be out of all proportion to existing or prospective resources' and if satisfied would mean the end of an independent RAF.[24] In fact what the Army wanted was nowhere near as unreasonable as the 4,000-6,000 heavy bombers Portal was insisting he needed.

Churchill expected the War Office to respond to three specific points. (1) Why did the War Office want to decentralise the RAF when the centrally controlled Luftwaffe was so successful? (2) Why did the War Office want 1,080 planes for 'intimate support' for fifty divisions when the Luftwaffe only had 400 planes for 300 divisions? (3) Why were the British Army's total air requirements for fifty divisions 850 more aircraft than the Luftwaffe had deployed on the Eastern Front to support 178 divisions?

The flaws in Churchill's specific criticisms were so obvious that the War Office must have realised that they had lost the battle. Brooke did his best but, if Churchill's sharp mind chose not to spot the fallacies, no additional explanation from the War Office was likely to make much difference. Churchill was going to believe what he wanted to believe.

Brooke carefully explained that while it was true that the RAF and Luftwaffe were both centralised organisations, they were centralised with completely different aims in mind. The Luftwaffe existed to support the German Army and Navy, whereas the RAF existed to pursue an independent bombing policy. The RAF, unlike the Luftwaffe, was not trained or equipped to support the army.

Brooke explained that Portal's figures were not comparing like with like. Most of the aircraft Portal had included in his estimate of army requirements were non-combat and he had no idea where the Air Ministry had got the 2,500-transport aircraft figure from. The threat of invasion had scarcely been 'negligible'; indeed, he pointedly reminded Churchill, even now the Air Ministry was holding back a large number of fighter squadrons to deal with such a contingency. Brooke emphasised that it was 'a real and true spirit of collaboration' that the War Office really wanted but once again meekly accepted that the bomber offensive had to have priority.[25] If Brooke had accompanied his requests for better air support with bold, clear plans for how he would use it, it might have received a more favourable reaction from Churchill. Instead, Churchill's rebuff can only have increased Brooke's pessimism about a cross-Channel invasion ever succeeding.

In a rather humiliating climb-down, Brooke meekly accepted the fifty-five-squadron force that was already on the table, with few assurances about when they would be available and none about who would control them. The Air Ministry promised to have twenty army co-operation squadrons (fourteen Mustang, three Tomahawk, two Blenheim and one Lysander) in place by 1 September. More vaguely, Portal assured Brooke that the twenty light-bomber squadrons would be formed as soon as aircraft deliveries made it possible.[26] Given Portal's urgent need for as many heavy bombers as possible, this was not likely to be soon. In the battle for the heart and mind of the Prime Minister, the Air Ministry was winning. The Air Ministry and RAF offered boldness and victories. All the War Office and Army could offer was pessimism and defeats.

Brooke had failed to get the air support his Army needed, yet the military operations they would be required for were more imminent than Brooke was anticipating. Ironically it was the Air Ministry now urging the War Office to prepare for a landing in France in 1942.

Chapter 3

More Invasion Plans

While Churchill focused on accelerating the expansion of Bomber Command and ensuring it got all the new technology it needed, support for the operation that might require an expansion of a parallel tactical air force, Operation Sledgehammer, was growing. The three Chiefs of Staff had reluctantly conceded a landing might have to be risked if the Soviet Union was on the brink of defeat, but this might not be enough to satisfy Roosevelt. In April, the American president despatched Marshall and Harry Hopkins, his personal adviser, to the United Kingdom to urge Churchill to establish a second front on mainland Europe as soon as possible.

Roosevelt was scarcely in a strong position to insist on a 1942 operation. American ground troops would only start arriving in the autumn of 1942 and in the air the best the Americans could offer was 400 fighters and 300 'other combat planes' by 15 September 1942. Nevertheless, the Americans hoped the British would be willing to go it alone in 1942 and assured their ally that, if they did, everything they had would be made available. If a 1942 operation was not possible, Roosevelt and Marshall wanted a definite plan in place for the spring of 1943, by which time far more substantial American force would have arrived. This would include 1,450 American fighters and 1,800 'other combat planes'. Operation Roundup, a move into France if the Germans appeared to be close to collapse, was now upgraded to 'Operation Super-Roundup', a full-scale invasion of France in the spring of 1943 regardless of Germany's military situation. The 'super' prefix was soon dropped, but Operation Roundup was now a very different affair.

There was, in American and British circles, much optimistic talk of the Allies having air superiority by 1943, if not before. Portal was claiming his bomber offensive would be in full swing by then. Marshall confidently spoke of the Germans getting a taste of what it was like to fight without air support.[1] Once again, the 'air superiority' both were talking about was based on having large numbers of heavy bombers. The 'other combat planes' the Americans spoke of were going to be largely four-engined bombers.

Portal was thinking along similar lines. The Americans were told how crucial American aircraft deliveries would be if the British were to attempt an invasion on their own, but Portal made it clear that it was heavy bombers that would be particularly useful.[2] It was not what the assaulting forces would need, nor was it what Harris planned to do with any American heavy bombers delivered to his command.

It was not just the Americans who were pushing for a 1942 invasion. As Portal moved to quash War Office efforts to acquire the air support an invasion of France would require, support from within the Air Ministry for such an operation was growing. Indeed Portal was leading it. He had already made it clear he believed some sort of landing was needed, even if it was only a temporary stay on the continent. More support for landing in France came from the unlikeliest of sources – none other than Air Vice-Marshal John Slessor, one of the hardcore supporters of the bomber policy.

Slessor was about to take over No. 11 Group Fighter Command after a stint at No. 5 Group Bomber Command when he was told he would be filling an entirely new post: Assistant Chief of Air Staff responsible for policy. His firm belief in the bomber policy seemed to make him the ideal candidate for the post. So convinced was he that the bomber would win the war, he had in the past often ridiculed any idea of the Army playing any significant role in the current conflict.[3] However, during his career Slessor would often show a capacity to lurch from one policy position to another, sometimes diametrically, opposed position. Despite his views on the diminishing role of ground forces, it was Slessor who, in the spring of 1939, had foreseen that holding fighters back in Britain while Allied armies were fighting a critical battle in France might not be in the country's best interest.[4] On taking over his new role, Slessor was suddenly rather keen for the Army to get involved in another crucial battle in France.

Slessor was soon getting plenty of reasons from the Air Ministry plans department on why a landing in France should be launched in 1942. Slessor was persuaded, and amplified the arguments in a note to Portal. In this he explained that ultimate victory was certain, provided the Soviet Army prevented a German victory in 1942 and the only way of ensuring this was for the British Army to intervene in the west, however risky the operation might be. The note was full of contempt for Army objections. Brooke had not the slightest intention of acting. The Army was always frightened of what might go wrong. The idea that a failed invasion would leave Britain vulnerable to a counter-invasion was 'bunkum'. The Army seemed to be trying to fight a war without suffering any casualties.

Slessor was quite emphatic about what was required. 'We must and can do Sledgehammer this summer not later than July. This is probably the most important and far reaching decision yet to be made in this war,' he declared. 'I believe it would be worth facing the loss of every man and tank we put ashore in France rather than sit back and do nothing,' he added, but would probably not have accepted so readily losing every pilot and plane.[5] It was perhaps not the sort of sentiment that was likely to encourage Brooke.

Slessor wanted Portal to get the Joint Planning Committee to revisit their previous pessimistic conclusions about any attempted cross-Channel operation. Portal did not need much persuading. The importance of keeping the Soviet Union in the war was underlined by a rather bleak intelligence assessment. If the Soviet Union was defeated in 1942, by 1944, Russian aircraft factories would be producing vast numbers of bombers for the Luftwaffe, and an Allied victory might become forever impossible. An invasion in 1942 would be a very risky undertaking, the assessment continued, but if Fighter Command could destroy 250 German fighters a month and if Bomber Command could hit German aircraft factories, both somewhat optimistic expectations, air superiority would inevitably follow and the German Air Force would be unable to interfere with the landings. 'It is within our power to defeat Germany this winter,' the report confidently proclaimed. Showing a Slessoresque disregard for the fate of the ground forces, even if the landing force was eventually defeated, it would have served its purpose of keeping Russia in the war.[6]

Not many shared this belief in victory this winter. For the bomber lobby, any landing in France was just a way of facilitating the strategic bombing victory they still firmly believed in. Armies might not be required to win the war but they might be required to enable the bomber to win the war. The Soviet Army had to halt the German Army and it might require the sacrifice of the British Army in a doomed invasion attempt to achieve this. Once the British and Soviet armies had prevented the Germans from taking over the Soviet aircraft industry, the Air Staff could revert to the original plan of winning the war by bombing.

It was the reverse of what was supposed to be the existing policy. Instead of bomber fleets paving the way for a victory on land, armies would be paving the way for a victory in the air. It was a very Trenchardian approach. Everything revolved around the needs of the bomber offensive. The war raging on land and at sea was only relevant to the extent that it helped or hindered this aerial offensive. The Air Staff might have ulterior motives for the operation, but an early invasion of France now had growing Air Ministry backing.

The appointment of commanders was giving the operation a very concrete feel. Vice-Admiral Bertram Ramsay would lead the naval force, General Edmund Schreiber, the commander of V Corps, the ground forces and Air Vice-Marshal Trafford Leigh-Mallory, commander of No. 11 Group Fighter Command, would command the RAF element. Leigh-Mallory had been involved in developing air/tank co-operation in the First World War and one of his inter-war posts was commander of the Army Co-operation School. He was more sympathetic than most to the need for army air support. However, it was the importance of the air battle rather than army air support that ensured he would be the commander of the air forces involved. Who would provide overall control was not clear. Slessor believed a supreme commander was needed, but neither Douglas, Paget nor the Admiralty thought it necessary, which scarcely augured well for the operation.[7]

When staff talks between the Americans and British got going in April, the Americans were dismayed at the lack of any planning on the British side for offensive action. Brooke and Paget were still insisting that a German invasion of the United Kingdom could not be ruled out and this should remain the priority.[8] The Americans desperately tried to persuade their new ally that, with substantial American forces soon arriving to deal with such a scenario, Britain could afford to take risks and plan more aggressively. Brooke and Paget found themselves in an increasingly uncomfortable situation. The brash Americans did not seem to see the problems of crossing the Channel as insurmountable. Calls for offensive action from an increasingly senior partner in a new coalition were difficult to counter. The British were forced to consider many basic issues for the first time in front of their new Allies. The differences of opinion that emerged on the British side left, according to one observer, the Americans 'bored and puzzled'.[9] Even Dill, now working in Washington with the Americans on the Joint Chiefs of Staff, could see that the fresh minds the Americans could provide were needed to shake up British ideas, moulded by three years of trying to avoid defeat, although this was perhaps easier to say from the other side of the Atlantic.[10]

The need to do something to help the Russians was soon to become much more urgent. In May 1942, a Russian offensive around Kharkov went disastrously wrong and a German counter-offensive smashed though the Soviet defences. German forces were soon advancing rapidly towards the Caucasus and Stalingrad. Churchill was still arguing the 'second front' should be landings in French North-West Africa, with the invasion of

France following in 1943. Roosevelt made it very clear that there had to be landings somewhere in 1942 to fend off the pressure he was under to switch the main American effort to the Pacific. The troops he was sending to Europe had to be in action by the end of the year.

In July, Roosevelt despatched Hopkins, along with the American Army and Navy commanders, Marshall and King, to London in a renewed attempt to urge 'immediate all out preparation' for an invasion of France which should be executed 'whether or not Russian collapse becomes imminent'.[11] It would still have to be an entirely Commonwealth operation, although American divisions would soon be arriving to reinforce any bridgehead established. If there was no full-scale cross-Channel invasion, there would at least have to be some sort of major raid, possibly even establishing a bridgehead on the continent, which might be held through the winter, providing the base for more extensive operations in the spring of 1943.[12] One thing was certain: the British and Canadian troops based in Britain were going to be landing somewhere in 1942, and they would need all the air support they could get. The Air Ministry needed to turn its enthusiasm for a cross-Channel operation into practical ways of supporting it.

The Joint Planning Committee emphasised that time was short even for the spring 1943 Operation Roundup invasion. There was much to put right. Existing arrangements for air support, with squadrons in three separate commands (Fighter Command, Bomber Command and Army Co-operation Command) were not going to work. They recommended that an 'Air Striking Command', capable of air defence, strike and reconnaissance should be created. This was the sort of multi-role BAFF (British Air Forces in France) that had supported the British Army in 1940 in the French campaign.[13] It would in effect be an upgraded Army Co-operation Command with an air defence as well as strike and reconnaissance capability.

Again it was the bomber arch-advocate Slessor, with the conviction of the converted, who was leading the demand for a change of attitude. It was, he insisted, a crucial time for the RAF. 'The transition stage from our present organization to one suited for an entirely different type of war to that we have been waging for 3 years in this theatre will be very difficult,' he warned. No time should be lost in 'planning and preparing for what amounts to a complete re-organisation of the Metropolitan Air Force'.[14] Slessor was sure the transition could be achieved speedily. 'If we took on this job by the methods, at tempo and in the spirit in which we took the Army off at Dunkirk and prepared to meet invasion in 1940, we could put them back again in 1942.' Slessor feared the summer of 1942 might be the last chance to strike in the west. If Britain did not act, the Soviet Union might be defeated and then 'we should then have to settle down to the job of bombing'.[15] It was a remarkable statement from the champion of the bomber strategy. For Slessor, bombing was becoming a fallback option.

The 'entirely different type of war' Slessor wanted the RAF to prepare for was in fact no more than the war that had been raging round the planet since 1939. In 1940, remarkable energy had been shown in re-equipping the troops plucked from the Dunkirk beaches with the weapons they needed to beat off an invasion, but there had been no similar drive about giving the RAF the tools to support them. The 'complete re-organisation of the Metropolitan Air Force' had been as necessary in 1940 to defeat a German invasion as it was in 1942 to support an Allied invasion. It was not, as Slessor seemed to be suggesting, some new requirement that had suddenly emerged.

Slessor was not short of suggestions about what the Army should do to prepare for invasion. Troops should immediately begin training for the assault role, but there were no parallel suggestions that RAF squadrons should begin training to support them. Slessor was quick to back the 'Air Striking Command' proposal because he appreciated army air support had to be focused and he felt there was no one big enough to co-ordinate the existing independent Fighter, Bomber and Army Co-operation Commands. The last of these still seemed the obvious starting point for the co-ordinated air support the Army required, but for reasons which Slessor did not elaborate on, using this was 'manifestly impossible'. Indeed, Slessor believed the proposed invasion put the very existence of Army Co-operation Command in question.

To Slessor it was obvious that the commander of Fighter Command would lead the new Air Striking Command because air defence would be its most important task.[16] Fighter squadrons were also all that was readily available. When the air support the RAF might provide was listed, it comprised forty-five day fighter squadrons but just six close support bomber, five army co-operation and four night-fighter squadrons. Nevertheless, the very fact that the line-up included specialist support squadrons was a major step forward. For the first time, British forces in north-west Europe would be going into battle with a dedicated close air support element. In addition, ten to fifteen of the fighter squadrons would be available for ground attack.[17] The UK-based RAF was becoming a far more flexible force.

Even so, while the bomber and fighter squadrons remained part of Bomber and Fighter Command, how they would be used were decisions that would be out of the Army's control. The War Office needed these squadrons under the control of Barratt's more Army-friendly Army Co-operation Command. Commodore Henry Thorold, the Senior Air Staff Officer at Army Co-operation Command, and Brigadier Claude Oxborrow, from Home Forces command, were working together to try and come up with a compromise that would keep everyone happy. Both had been deeply involved in army air support. Thorold had been a staff officer in Barratt's BAFF in 1940. Oxborrow had worked closely with Lieutenant Colonel Charles Carrington, the Army's liaison officer at Bomber Command, on organising the air support No. 2 Group would have provided in the event of a German invasion.

It was clear to Thorold that current equipment was not suitable for close air support. The Blenheims of No. 2 Group were too large for low-level operations, while the Hurricanes of Fighter Command lacked firepower. Both were too vulnerable to ground fire. He saw the need for a more specialist plane, armed and armoured for the close support role. Initially, these would have to be adaptations of existing types, but eventually specialist ground attack planes would have to be developed. To decide on exactly what was required, the Army needed aircraft to trial the various available options. The full thirty-five fighter and bomber squadrons the Air Ministry had agreed to commit was perhaps too much to expect, so, as a first step, Thorold and Oxborrow suggested just twelve squadrons should be created and attached to Army Co-operation Command for aircrew training and aircraft trials. Since No. 2 Group was currently thirteen squadrons short of the twenty Portal promised, creating these twelve squadrons involved no new Air Ministry commitment, they pointed out.

To try out the main existing options, they suggested the twelve squadrons should comprise four squadrons of anti-tank fighters with 40mm cannon, four fighter squadrons with four 20mm cannon and four squadrons with the American Bermuda dive-bombers that were about to arrive. This Army Air Support Group would be trained and equipped to be fully mobile. This meant a force that was comfortable operating from more primitive temporary airstrips behind an advancing army rather than the better-equipped permanent bases RAF squadrons in the UK were used to. The squadrons would be available for Bomber and Fighter Command operations, thus allowing crews to keep their hands in. Their specially modified planes would be particularly useful against the small, well-defended targets the RAF were sometimes called upon to attack. The remaining twenty-three squadrons the War Office had been promised would at times be temporarily attached to the group for training. Once ground operations were underway, these twenty-three squadrons would be transferred permanently to Army Co-operation Command.[18] It was all very late in the day for a capability that might soon be required. The proposal was put to the Air Staff under Thorold's name only, lest the mere mention of an Army officer prejudice the reaction.[19]

Portal was no happier about transferring twelve squadrons to Army Co-operation Command than he had been about the original thirty-five. However, like Slessor, he, recognised the advantage of the squadrons supporting the Army being in a single command and Slessor came up with an alternative proposal. He suggested for invasion purposes an 'Eastern Air Force' within No. 11 Group Fighter Command. This would have the twelve army support fighter squadrons Thorold's proposal required, all newly created, together with the bombers of No. 2 Group. No. 11 Group would become a multi-functional formation with three mixed groups to provide support for three armies. American air units would be based farther west, forming 'the Western Air Force'.[20]

Slessor suggested that No. 11 Group would extend across the Channel in much the same way as a German *Luftflotte*. It was always a good tactic to compare any army support proposal to German practice. This was, after all, what the War Office was continually insisting on having. Slessor's proposal had Portal's full backing, but even within the Air Ministry there were concerns that this involved a lengthy chain of command, with no fewer than five links between the Army Air Support Units requesting air support from within the beachhead and No. 11 Group headquarters at Uxbridge. Commanders closer to the front, it was argued, had to have more executive power.[21]

Portal and Douglas used some interesting arguments for basing the force within Fighter Command. The command was set up to direct fighters towards bombers; directing aircraft towards ground targets was essentially the same process.[22] There was something in this. In the Battle of France, sector controls based in France designed to vector fighters towards bombers had been used to direct fighters on patrol against ground targets. Indeed, one might wonder why the Air Ministry had not thought of using UK sector controls in this way when invasion threatened in the summer of 1940.

Meanwhile, Fighter Command was already setting about the task of acquainting its squadrons with the ground attack role. The commitment to the Army involved fifteen squadrons, but Douglas eventually wanted all his squadrons to be equally proficient in air combat and ground attack. Douglas was keen to get the ball rolling and Portal was encouraging squadron commanders to go out and sell the idea to local army commanders.[23] This was not universally popular within Fighter Command. Air Vice-Marshal Richard Saul, commanding No. 12 Group, felt strongly that pilots needed to focus on their primary air combat role. 'Our pilots will neither be fully efficient fighters nor competent Army co-operators,' he protested.[24] Elsewhere, however, there seemed to be plenty of enthusiasm for getting to grips with this new challenge.

In April, Paget issued a directive which had as its aim 'To train Army and RAF formations to work together in battle with the fullest knowledge of each other's possibilities, limitations and procedures'.[25] Topics to be covered included moving squadrons with all their equipment and personnel to forward aerodromes and getting pilots used to rapid briefing on targets Army Air Support Controls wanted attacked. Douglas was keen to encourage closer Air Force/Army links. Group commanders were ticked off for not organising enough air force/army officer exchanges.[26] After some prompting, No. 9 Group enthusiastically set about ways of speeding up the response time to army requests for support.[27] By the end of May 1942, fifty-seven fighter squadrons had received some training in ground attack, during the course of 128 exercises.[28] There were complaints reaching the War Office that their involvement in some army exercises was rather 'perfunctory', but the process of getting the two services to work together was underway.[29]

The problem for the War Office was that, however much air force enthusiasm there was for co-operating with the Army, Fighter Command's priority would always be the air defence of Great Britain. Indeed, Leigh-Mallory's No. 11 Group had the crucial role of defending London. The German bomber threat still loomed large and the Army had every reason to fear that it might just take one raid on London for the fighters supporting the Army to be switched to home defence. In 1940, it had taken no raids on Britain to ensure the majority of fighters were deployed in home defence while the Army was taking a hammering in France. Brooke had been one of the commanders in France and he had not forgotten the experience.

At the very least, building army air support around No. 11 Group would over-emphasise the importance of air defence. It perhaps also placed too much reliance on Fighter Command's integrated air defence system. The War Office was impressed by the Air Ministry argument that maximum use should be made of the sophisticated radar and communication systems Fighter Command had developed. However, as useful as these were for defending the ports the invasion would set off from, covering the landings required fighters on standing patrols. Radar could provide useful information for fighters already on these patrols, but fighters could not be scrambled from one side of the English Channel to intercept a raid taking place on the other.

At some point, an army advancing on the continent would have to have its own air force. Brooke argued the Air Ministry was just creating an air force for a specific operation, the invasion of France, rather than getting to grips with the problem of providing the air support the Army needed wherever it was fighting. The fixed, static nature of No. 11 Group was not a sound basis for developing the highly mobile force the Army required.[30] The tactical air element had to train with the Army. RAF commanders in distant operations rooms would not work. There had to be face to face contact between army commanders and air force officers with the latter having full executive powers to order RAF squadrons into action. Brooke wanted Thorold's twelve-squadron Army Support Group formed immediately within Army Co-operation Command to get this training going.[31]

Bridging the gulf between the UK-based Army and Air Force was proving a slow process, which the possible imminent need for joint action was not hastening. There was plenty of enthusiasm from some for the army air support role but the process was being held up by the Air Ministry's determination to ensure RAF independence was not violated in any way. Air assets had to be kept completely separate from any sort of army influence. The RAF would support the Army, but from a distance, both in spirit and physical location.

While the Air Ministry battled to keep the RAF free of army influence, on every front from the Russian steppes and the North African desert to the jungles of the Far East, key battles were being fought by armies and air forces working closely together. In the summer of 1942, with Soviet forces reeling back towards Stalingrad, the need for an invasion was increasing. Even a reluctant Churchill urged the preparation of plans for Sledgehammer with 'all possible speed, energy and ingenuity', and Slessor for one was taking this very much to heart.[32] A 1942 major landing of some sort somewhere was almost certain. The argument that developing and building the specialist aircraft the Army needed could be put off until a future date was becoming increasingly more difficult to sustain.

Chapter 4

Aircraft for Army Support

Developing specialist aircraft for any sort of army air support had never been a priority for the Air Ministry and developing a specialist ground attack plane to strike targets on the battlefield had always been something to be avoided at all costs. The Air Ministry had always argued that such targets should be dealt with by ground-based weapons, not expensive aircraft and highly trained crews. It seemed a reasonable enough argument, but the closing stages of the First World War had demonstrated how valuable air support on the battlefield could be. The ability to switch air resources rapidly from one front to another, either for defensive or offensive purposes, was priceless. Often the first reinforcements to reach an unexpected enemy advance was the Air Force. Even when ground forces were to hand, there would also always be targets too close to friendly forces to be engaged safely by distant artillery, or linear targets such as movement along roads that were more vulnerable to air attack than artillery.

In both world wars, the actual damage inflicted on battlefield targets was often overstated, but the positive and negative psychological impact on friend and foe respectively more than made up for this. This aspect was often mockingly dismissed as pointless 'flying the flag' by critics, but it was arguably the greatest contribution air power made to success on the battlefield. The German Stuka was a prime example of the demoralising impact battlefield air support can have. Whether for its psychological or physical impact, close air support was an invaluable extra string to the bow of any army commander. During the inter-war years, the Air Staff could not, or chose not, to see this.

For the Air Ministry, however, it was more than just a tactical objection. There was the straightforward economic argument. Any sort of tactical aircraft could only be built at the expense of long-range bombers. Even more fundamental, however, was the fear that battlefield air support necessarily required close co-ordination and co-operation, and the more integrated air and ground forces were, the easier providing air support became. This was a

59

dangerous path for the Air Ministry to go down as it seemed to undermine the need for a separate air force. The independence of the RAF could best be guaranteed by having a distinct independent role, which strategic bombing provided. If the Air Force had to support the Army it should be as distant from the battlefield as possible. Interdiction in the enemy rear was ideal. This gave the RAF a quasi-independent role and the deeper the interdiction was, the more independent it felt.

Nevertheless, no one could deny the Army had to have some basic battlefield air capability, even if it was only reconnaissance. If the Army insisted on anything beyond this, then these additional roles would have to be performed by the same aircraft. In the inter-war years, the 'army co-operation' plane was the vehicle for doing this. This was supposed to meet every army battlefield requirement from short-range artillery observation to medium-range reconnaissance, low-level attack and dive bombing. For this the Air Ministry gave the Army the Lysander. The Army wanted an air force, but all it got was an aircraft.

By the outbreak of war it was becoming clear one design would not suffice. No. 1 Group with its single-engined Battles and No. 2 Group with its twin-engined Blenheims were roped in to provide more offensive punch, at least until they could be re-equipped with bombers that could contribute to the strategic bombing campaign. No. 1 Group converted to Wellingtons, but No. 2 Group continued to be available for army support. It was expected to provide indirect and close air support for the Army. However, it was also expected to make a contribution to the air offensive against Germany. It was where the idea of a return to large-scale daylight strategic bombing could be kept alive.

The twin-engined Blenheim was supposed to provide close air support. It was scarcely ideal. It was too large for low-level bombing over the battlefield, and not what the Army wanted. However, from the Air Ministry point of view, it had the great advantage that it could carry plenty of fuel and therefore could also be used for long-range bombing if required. When the War Office demanded something more suitable, all they got was the armoured Blenheim V or Bisley. Although this was supposed to be a quick-fix way of giving the army an armoured close support plane in time for the battles of 1940, it did not reach the squadrons until the summer of 1942. By this time, it had lost most of its armour and was just another conventional, rather slow, light bomber of rather dated origin.

The War Office demands for something more like the Stuka brought Lord Beaverbrook into the story. In May 1940, he had just been put in charge of the new Ministry of Aircraft Production and this provided the War Office with a way of bypassing the Air Ministry. Beaverbrook met War Office demands by ordering single-engined Vultee Vengeance and Brewster Bermuda dive-bombers from the United States. These were supposed to begin arriving late in 1940 but in early 1942 there was still no sign of them.

With both the army co-operation and No. 2 Group squadrons having close air support among their roles, aircraft like the Bisley and the American dive-bombers were lined up to equip both sets of squadrons. Although the idea of a single 'army co-operation' aircraft was fast fading the Air Ministry was anxious to keep the idea of the 'army co-operation' squadron alive as having multi-role squadrons helped keep army requirements to a minimum. At the beginning of 1942, both the 'army co-operation' and No. 2 Group squadrons were surviving for the most part on obsolete aircraft or rejects from other RAF commands. Fortunately, aircraft like the Tomahawk and Boston were rather useful rejects. The Boston was one of the world's best light bombers and the low-level performance of the Tomahawk made it an excellent tactical reconnaissance fighter.

At the beginning of 1942, the existing fourteen army co-operation squadrons consisted of eight Tomahawk, four Lysander and two Blenheim squadrons. The force was supposed to be expanded to ten bomber-reconnaissance and ten fighter-reconnaissance squadrons. The American Bermuda dive-bomber was lined up for the former. In the latter role, the Allison-powered Mustang was to replace the Tomahawk. The Army had wanted the ten fighter-reconnaissance squadrons to be cannon armed so that they could be used for ground attack, but with Fighter Command providing fifteen ground attack fighter squadrons they could now focus on their reconnaissance role.

Fighter photo-reconnaissance had developed rapidly in the Middle East through sheer operational necessity. Hurricanes were soon being fitted with sideways-pointing cameras for low-level reconnaissance and vertical cameras for high-altitude work. With no operations in progress and an uninterested Air Ministry it was a much slower process in the UK. Indeed, fitting cameras to the Tomahawk seemed to conjure up all sorts of difficulties. Initially, it was decided fitting vertical cameras was quite impossible and flights of Lysanders had to be retained for this. It was January 1942 before it was agreed the fighter could carry both vertical and sideways-looking cameras. Even then, modifying the planes was a torturously slow process. Despite the talk of a possible cross-Channel venture, only twenty modified Tomahawks had been delivered by November 1942 and some squadrons were still having to use Lysanders.[1]

The first Mustangs were delivered to Army co-operation squadrons in April 1942 and the same cycle of events was repeated. In February 1942, the Air Ministry had announced it was quite impracticable to fit cameras for high-altitude vertical photography in the Mustang and now it would be the Tomahawk flights that would have to be retained to do this. Then in September 1942 it was discovered the Americans were using Mustangs taken over from British contracts for high-altitude photography and the Air Ministry had to drop its objections.[2]

The Mustang was quite some acquisition for the army co-operation squadrons. Rejected as a fighter because of the poor performance of its Allison engine at higher altitudes, Fighter Command's loss was Army Co-operation Command's gain. At medium and low altitudes it was a superb fighter. Mustang pilots need fear no one and they were to grow increasingly aggressive in their reconnaissance missions over northern France. With aircraft like the Mustang, the future for the tactical reconnaissance squadrons was bright, but in the spring and summer of 1942 there were only a handful of Mustangs and Tomahawks with the squadrons and many of these were grounded through a lack of spares. It was not a force-ready to support an invasion.

High-speed single-seater fighters were not ideal for directing artillery fire. This was one task the faithful Lysander was perfectly capable of performing – it was just that it was a rather expensive way of doing it. Powerful, supercharged engines were not needed for aircraft that only had to fly a few hundred feet into the air. The War Office considered cheap, low-powered, light sports planes perfectly adequate. The Air Ministry was totally puzzled by the idea. Planes flying in the combat zone had to be fast and well armed; using an unarmed sports plane just seemed ludicrous. The Air Ministry only agreed because what the Army wanted required far fewer resources than the Lysander and freed more production capacity for what the Air Ministry considered to be more useful types.

Again the process was torturously slow, with both War Office and Air Ministry to blame. Although the idea had been tried out in France in 1940, it was August 1941 before the first Air Observation Post (AOP) squadron, No. 651, began forming.[3] Part of the delay was caused by the late arrival of the Stinson Vigilants ordered in 1940 from the United States. When they finally arrived, it was decided a modified version of the Taylorcraft plane used in the original French trials was a better option.[4] Some early versions of what now became the Taylorcraft Auster I were rushed through to the forming AOP squadrons in July 1942, soon followed by the production version, the more powerful Auster III. The first squadron would eventually become operational in the autumn of 1942, again too late for a 1942 invasion.[5]

As far as specialist bombers were concerned, Portal had promised the War Office that No. 2 Group would be built up to twenty squadrons, but in reality the force was being run down. Transfers to other Bomber Command groups and overseas had seen strength reduced from a peak of thirteen Blenheim squadrons in the summer of 1940 to just three by January 1942. These were joined by two Boston squadrons in February, but by this time the ageing Blenheims could only be risked under cover of darkness. A third squadron converted to the Boston but in the summer of 1942 only these were available for daylight army support missions, and, because of their size, they were best suited for more distant indirect support beyond the battlefield.

With possible land operations in France in the offing, whether in the form of a raid or full-scale invasion, even Portal conceded that No. 2 Group could no longer just be considered as bait for fighter operations; it had to become an effective bomber force.[6] This was easier said than done. The supply of Boston IIIs would soon dry up as all new deliveries were going straight to the Middle East. There were no plans to re-equip more than three squadrons with the type in the UK.

No. 2 Group was told that it would eventually have fifteen Mosquito bomber squadrons, although where these were to come from was not clear.[7] The Mosquito, along with the Spitfire, was the outstanding British design of the war years, but it was not a major part of MAP production plans. In 1942, only about fifty a month were being built at the de Havilland Hatfield plant and these were wanted as Coastal Command strike planes, night-fighters and photo-reconnaissance aircraft as well as light bombers. It was also another rather large twin-engined plane that was scarcely ideal for attacking small battlefield targets. One No. 2 Group squadron had converted to the Mosquito, but this was mainly to try the unarmed Mosquito on long-range, daylight harassing raids over Germany in support of the strategic air offensive. No decisions had been taken about how quickly further squadrons might convert.

No. 2 Group was also supposed to be getting the American Bermuda dive-bomber. When these were delayed, the Air Ministry offered the group the twin-engined American Lockheed Ventura as a substitute.

It was scarcely a like-for-like replacement. Like its Lockheed Hudson predecessor, the bomber was a converted airliner, on order as a replacement for Coastal Command's Hudsons. Deliveries were supposed to begin in 1941 but by the end of the year none had arrived. With less range than the Hudson it was scarcely ideal for maritime patrolling and Coastal Command objected to having the plane thrust upon them without any consultation.[8] If Coastal Command did not want it, No. 2 Group seemed like a good alternative destination.[9] It may have lacked range but, in terms of speed and bomb load, it was a vast improvement on its Hudson predecessor. It was over 50 mph faster than the Bisley and had similar speed, bomb load and defensive armament to the B-25 Mitchell. As a short-range medium bomber, it was perhaps not as unsuitable as is sometimes claimed, but by no stretch of the imagination was it suitable for battlefield air support.

It was easy for the Air Ministry to draw up expansion plans. A March 1942 scheme envisaged some sixty-eight light-bomber and bomber/reconnaissance squadrons worldwide by March 1944. This would comprise thirteen Mosquito, six Blenheim, five Boston, six Ventura, thirteen Baltimore, ten Bermuda, and fifteen Vengeance squadrons.[10] Air Chief Marshal Christopher Courtney, the Air Staff member responsible for supply and organisation, noted that only two of these were British designs, the Blenheim and Mosquito, and both of these had been designed with long-range strategic missions in mind. The Blenheim was obsolete and not many Mosquitoes were being built. Courtney feared that soon the only planes that Britain would be producing would be four-engined heavy bombers and single-engined fighters and questioned whether the Air Ministry was genuinely meeting the needs of the Army and Navy by such a programme.[11] That such a question should be asked demonstrated that ideas were changing.

Portal argued that the Hurribomber was the new Blenheim and in the army support role Portal was right. The single-engined fighter-bomber was far more suitable for many of the missions the twin-engined light bomber had been expected to perform and it was already proving a success in the Middle East. Armed first with 40lb bombs and later with 250lb bombs and, with later versions of the Hurricane II, four 20mm cannon, the Hurricane provided the Army with an effective alternative to the dive-bomber, with the added advantage that it could double as a fighter.

In the UK, the fifteen fighter squadrons Douglas had allocated to the ground attack role (eleven Hurricane II squadrons, the two Whirlwind squadrons and two Spitfire squadrons) were a sound basis for a ground attack force. The cannon these aircraft were equipped with were effective against exposed targets. More would be needed against better protected targets but only the two Hurribomber squadrons could carry bombs. Leigh-Mallory and Douglas were both pushing for more fighter-bombers and wanted the Typhoon modified to carry bombs, just as soon as that plane's technical problems were overcome.[12] However, in the summer of 1942 there were still only the two Hurribomber squadrons. Portal might see it as the new Blenheim, but he was no more enthusiastic about creating Hurribomber squadrons than he was Blenheim squadrons.

The problem with the Typhoon and Hurricane as fighter-bombers was that there were doubts about both as pure fighters. The Hurricane was obsolete and the Typhoon, which was supposed to replace the Spitfire, was not living up to expectations. A lot of the advantages of the fighter-bomber were lost if it could not perform its fighter role. Using obsolete fighters as fighter-bombers was a common practice in many air forces and it was a sensible way of using aircraft like the Hurricane that were readily available, but they needed as much escorting as any other bomber.

The American Kittyhawk also carried bombs and was a more capable fighter than the Hurricane, although now that the Americans were in the war these were more difficult to come by. The Bell P-39 Airacobra was a more plentiful option. This could carry bombs and came armed with a 37mm cannon or a 20mm cannon preferred by the RAF. It was fast and manoeuvrable enough at low altitude to be useful in the low-level attack role and could more than hold its own as a low/medium altitude fighter. The Soviets considered it one of the best fighters the Allies were sending them. Ironically, when fifteen Fighter Command squadrons were assigned the army support role in January 1942, the lone Airacobra squadron, No. 601, was not one of them. Indeed, the Air Ministry was happy to get rid of the type. British orders were packed off to the Russians, in place of the supposedly more valuable Hurricanes. On arrival in the Soviet Union the Russians rushed them off to the front as quickly as possible to replace Hurricanes.

Even fighter-bombers that could double as fighters had their limitations. They could not be heavily armoured without making them less suitable for air combat. Without protection, pilots would not want to spend too long within range of enemy ground fire. The aim was to deliver the attack as quickly as possible, sacrificing accuracy for safety and making sure they lived to fight another day. There were also limits to the armament fighters could carry and still be useful as fighters. Fixed guns were far more accurate than bombs and the 40mm cannon that Portal had done so much to promote was powerful enough to destroy a tank. Ideally, because of its low rate of fire, the weapon needed a slow-flying plane and the slow-speed handling of the Hurricane was just about good enough. The first Hurricanes (Mark IId) armed with this cannon were beginning to reach the squadrons in mid-1942 and Portal was hoping five hundred 40mm cannon-armed Hurricanes would have arrived in the Middle East by April 1943.[13] However, the hefty slow-firing 40mm cannon greatly reduced performance and was useless for fighter-versus-fighter combat.

The 3-inch rocket projectile was another ground attack weapon that affected an aircraft's fighter capabilities. Early in 1942, a Hurricane carrying three of these below each wing successfully completed trials. There was no shortage of scepticism about the value of the weapon. After seeing it in action, Brooke doubted they would be much good against targets as small as a tank.[14] Douglas wanted trials to go ahead but also had his doubts about a weapon its supporters had spent years trying to get to work as an anti-aircraft weapon and now suddenly expected to be successful in an air-to-ground role.[15] The doubts about the weapon's accuracy would prove to be well founded but, as the Soviets were discovering on the Eastern Front, the psychological impact the screeching rockets had on enemy morale went a long way towards making up for this deficiency. However, the rockets needed launching rails, so even after the weapons were launched the fighter was severely handicapped.

There was a case for a more specialist ground attack aircraft that would not be expected to operate as a fighter, a better protected plane that could fly at lower speeds and carry more specialist weapons, something more akin to the Soviet Sturmovik. So far, the only aircraft used for close air support were those designed for other purposes. Starting with a blank sheet of paper, something entirely different might emerge. Air Vice-Marshal Ralph Sorley, the Assistant Chief of Air Staff responsible for framing requirements, seemed to be thinking along these lines. Edgar Percival, an Australian aircraft designer renowned for his air racing exploits, had sent Sorley a design for a novel, specialist low-level ground attack plane. It was armoured against 0.5-inch bullets and, in order to give the pilot the best possible view forward, it was a twin-boom design with a pusher engine mounted behind the pilot. Armament would be an impressive two 40mm cannon and four 20mm cannon. It was precisely the sort of fresh approach that Thorold and Oxborrow would soon be demanding.

On 1 January 1942, Sorley informed the Ministry of Aircraft Production that the Air Staff required the development of an armoured, single-seater ground attack plane, along the lines of the Percival design. Sorley saw it as a replacement for the Hurricane, which, he emphasised, was a purely interim solution to the ground attack problem. He wanted its replacement to have a better view forward, heavier armament, more ammunition and armour protection. As an alternative to the cannon Percival was proposing, Sorley suggested a battery of 3-inch rockets could be mounted in the nose. He also wanted it to have more range than the Hurricane. This seemed an odd stipulation. The Soviet Sturmovik could not even fly as far as a Hurricane, but the Soviets did not see this as a problem for a plane only expected to operate over the battlefield. Sorley seemed to have targets further afield than the battlefield in mind. Nevertheless what Sorley was suggesting was, for the Air Ministry, quite revolutionary. There was no question of such a plane playing any part in a strategic air offensive. Nor was it expected to have any air combat capability. It was to be a specialist ground attack plane. The Air Ministry seemed finally to be willing to give the Army what it had always wanted.[16]

At this stage Sorley saw no immediate need for the plane. He knew that present engine output was taken up by the existing production programme and therefore an immediate order would not be possible. Nevertheless, he suggested that airframes could be built and stored away to be equipped with engines at some future date when they were required.[17] It was a strange suggestion. Sometimes Air Ministry officials in their London cocoon seemed to forget there was a war raging in the rest of the world. If the sort of plane Sorley had in mind was going to be useful for some future campaign in Europe, it would also be useful on the various fronts where British forces were already engaged.

With the armour and proposed weapons it was not going to be a high performance plane. For the War Office this was not a problem, they saw low speed as an advantage, even suggesting that the ideal ground attack plane might fly as slowly as 100 mph.[18] The Army did not need aircraft that could fly fast, far and high; slow, near and low was their maxim. As with the artillery observing Auster, this was a difficult concept for the Air Ministry to grasp. Their goal was always precisely the opposite. As the helicopter would later demonstrate, the slow-flying, short-range combat aircraft was a perfectly valid concept. Sorley, however, could not break free from Air Ministry conventional wisdom. He saw the advantages of a plane that could fly slowly but still wanted to combine this with good range and a top speed that was as high as possible.

Although the Ministry of Aircraft Production was responsible for building aircraft rather than deciding what aircraft should be built, its ministers, Beaverbrook and his successor, John Moore-Brabazon, and civilian staff like Tizard, had traditionally sided with the War Office in their appeals for a specialist ground attack plane. It had been the MAP that had ordered the American Bermuda and Vengeance dive-bombers. Back in 1939, before becoming the Minister for Aircraft Production, Moore-Brabazon had put forward his own proposal for a ground attack plane which was remarkably similar to Percival's pusher.[19] However, the Ministry was under constant pressure from the Air Ministry and Churchill to meet their bomber targets, which tended to dull enthusiasm for anything that was not a heavy bomber.

The bomber priority now prompted an interesting reversal of roles. When Sorley's suggestion reached the MAP there was little sympathy for the idea. It was too late to introduce an entirely new type into the December 1941 production schedule, with or without engine. If the Air Ministry wanted this specialist close support plane, it would have to tell the MAP what it wanted cut from the existing programme. 'Much as one would like to see the best possible design in use for this limited role', the MAP preferred 'to adhere to the present policy of using the older types of operational aircraft for these duties', which indeed mirrored the feelings of many of Sorley's colleagues in the Air Ministry.[20]

The MAP staff doubted that there had been any serious discussion within the Air Staff about a specialist close support plane. Indeed, there was no specification number associated with the requirement, and it was suspected that Sorley's request was more to do with some lobbying by Percival. The fact that repeated requests for more details about what exactly the 'Air Staff' actually wanted brought no reply tended to support this theory. It was scarcely the sort of plane one might suspect the 'Air Staff' of wanting. Nor does there appear to be any record of any formal discussion, although as a member of the Air Staff, Sorley could legitimately claim he was acting on their behalf.

A fresh face at the Ministry of Aircraft Production seemed to revive interest in the project. In February 1942, Brabazon made some unfortunate remarks about hoping Germany and the Soviet Union would destroy each other and was forced to resign. He was replaced by John Llewellin, an ex-Army officer, who seemed more concerned about the lack of low-level ground attack planes.[21] In March, Sorley put forward a more detailed idea of what he felt was needed. The aircraft was to be a small, light, single-seater which was more manoeuvrable, more heavily armed and had a better view than the Hurricane. He still wanted greater range, some 750 miles, which was 50 per cent more than the Soviet Sturmovik. The plane had to be able to take off in 700 yards and land in 600 yards on a grass airfield. A maximum speed of 280 mph would be required and it had to be capable of delivering attacks at 200 mph by day, but just 90 mph by night. Various combinations of armament were proposed including four 40mm cannon and two 20mm cannon, a single 47mm cannon, rocket projectiles or two 500lb bombs.[22]

The speed requirement was tricky; 280 mph does not seem much but combining it with an attacking speed of less than 100 mph is not easy. Generally speaking, the faster a plane flies, the higher its minimum speed has to be. The rather excessive range requirement was another complication. Captain Roger Norman Liptrot, in the MAP Research and Development Department, investigated the options. To provide the excellent forward view required, the aircraft had to be either twin-engined or a pusher like Percicval's original proposal. Liptrot sketched out various possibilities, but the results were far heavier and two to three times larger than the Hurricane. Norbert Rowe, the MAP Director of Technical Development, believed the only way of providing more power and good forward vision was the twin-engined approach and the end result would probably be bigger than a Mosquito. History seemed to be repeating itself as the MAP found itself going down the same path as the Air Ministry with the Blenheim/Bisley. The MAP proposals were bound to be too large and unwieldy and much too vulnerable to ground fire for low-level work over the battlefield.

Sorley was not impressed with these suggestions and told Liptrot to start with a small, simple design and see what it could carry. Liptrot triumphantly announced the answer was none. The payload was taken up entirely by the fuel required to strike at targets 300 miles beyond the front line.[23] If Sorley had just wanted an aircraft that could operate over the battlefield, the requirements would not have been so impossible to meet.

The MAP again questioned whether such a plane was really needed at all. The Hurricane was still perfectly satisfactory in this role, they argued, and with improvements, including more armour, could continue to serve satisfactorily for some time. If a better view forward was required, then the twin-engined Mosquito might be a possible successor.[24] Perhaps surprisingly, given his forthright views on the overriding importance of strategic bombing, Freeman insisted the project should go ahead as it would be 'of great assistance to the War Office'.[25] It was perhaps another sign of Air Staff movement on the army air support question, although equally his motive may have been simply to counter the growing criticism from the War Office and elsewhere over Air Ministry intransigence on the army support issue.

Again the MAP wanted to know what should be cut from the existing programme to make room for the new aircraft. Freeman was not short of ideas; the Fleet Air Arm could not possibly want 140 Fairey Barracuda torpedo-bombers a month and he could not see why they needed the obsolete Fairey Swordfish at all. There was plenty of spare capacity there, he insisted.[26] Reducing bomber output was not on Freeman's agenda. Tactical army support would have to come at the expense of tactical navy support. Sorley dropped the 90 mph attack requirement and extended permissible take-off run. Even so, anything meeting Sorley's requirements was going to require some pretty imaginative design work. Despite the difficulties the MAP had in imagining what sort of aircraft might meet the requirement, various companies were asked to see what they could come up with.

It had the potential to be a turning point in the history of British air power. It was the first time the Air Ministry had asked designers to start with a blank sheet of paper and design a plane solely for battlefield ground attack. Even the Sopwith Salamander of 1918 had just been a heavily armoured version of the Sopwith Snipe fighter. It was, however, a very tentative new beginning. Only relatively small companies not already involved in any major projects (Boulton Paul, Airspeed, Phillips and Powis) were asked to put forward proposals. Also, there was still no official specification number attached to the programme, which cannot have been encouraging for the design teams.

The emphasis was on simplicity of design and it was hoped to have something ready for production by January 1944. With Brooke not believing an invasion of France would be possible until 1944, it was not necessarily too late for the current conflict. Nevertheless, when it would be available should not have been an issue. This was not a replacement for an existing type; this was an entirely new line of aircraft development. Victory in the Second World War would not end the need for such a plane. The lack of a specialist close support plane was a longstanding deficiency and would have to be dealt with at some stage. This was as good a time as any to make a start.

The specialist ground attack plane would involve even more fracturing of the multi-role 'army co-operation' concept. The armoured ground attack

70

plane joined the fighter-bomber, light-bomber, fighter-reconnaissance and artillery observation plane as yet another specialist type required by the Army. What the Air Ministry hoped could be restricted to a handful of multi-purpose squadrons was becoming a fully fledged air force. However, in the summer of 1942, it was an air force that was in a rather sorry state. Only half of the light-bomber and army co-operation squadrons even existed. Most of these were ill-equipped and/or understrength. Fifteen fighter squadrons had been nominated for ground attack duties, but how available these would be was far from clear. These and the bomber and army co-operation squadrons were spread across three different commands. Instead of the prospect of Allied troops landing on the continent in 1942 galvanising efforts, progress in creating the air force the Army needed had almost ground to a halt. The Air Ministry had no stake in accelerating the process and Churchill was once again totally absorbed by the strategic bombing project.

Two years after it might have been called upon to deal with a German invasion, the attack and reconnaissance elements of the RAF were still in no fit state to help the Army defend the country, never mind support landings in France. Nor was there any urgency about tackling the shortcomings. When discussing with the Americans why an invasion in 1942 was not possible, the lack of adequate bomber and reconnaissance support for the invading land forces was not mentioned. The Americans were, however, fully briefed on the problems concerning fighter cover.

Chapter 5

Fighter Crisis

While the lack of a suitable reconnaissance and ground attack planes had always been a concern to the War Office, they had always assumed there was no need to worry about the quality and suitability of the available fighters. Controlling the skies above the Army was a task that could safely be left in the hands of the formidable Fighter Command. Following its victory in the Battle of Britain, this was surely one element of Britain's armed forces that need not raise any concerns. However, all was not well within the force. Fighter Command was not as formidable as the War Office imagined.

Fighter Command had been set up to defend British cities in a bomber war. Since the outbreak of war, it had been adapting to a very different war but it was a slow process. This was partly because the need for change was not clearly identified. Even though fighter-versus-fighter combat had been so crucial in the 1940 battles on the continent and over Britain, it was still the bomber threat that was dominating Air Ministry thinking. No one would deny the fighter was playing a crucial role in the defensive struggle but the consensus was still that the bomber, not the fighter, was the primary means of taking the offensive and establishing air superiority. The fixation with the German bomber threat and the much-feared knockout blow distracted attention from the need to rethink the bomber interceptor approach to developing fighters and the tactics pilots used.

Radical change was needed in both. Pilots were trained to fly in tight formations for mass attacks on unescorted bombers. There was little direction from above about how these tactics should change now that they were having to deal with fighter escorts; pilots had to figure it out for themselves. Only slowly were squadrons adopting the more spaced-out pairs and finger four formations German pilots used. Nor were the fighters they flew intended for fighter-versus-fighter combat. British fighters were designed to fly fast and straight; they were not designed to perform the violent manoeuvres required for dog-fighting. In the war that had materialised, much more than a simple bomber interceptor was required.

Much had been done to turn the Spitfire into a more versatile fighter. Constant speed propellers helped improve acceleration and metal ailerons were introduced to improve control at high speed. The 'Tilly orifice', the work of Miss 'Tilly' Shilling at the Royal Aircraft Factory, Farnborough, stopped the Merlin engine's unfortunate habit of cutting out in negative-g manoeuvres. Nevertheless, the Spitfire was still essentially a modified bomber interceptor and it was still the bomber threat that was shaping future fighter development.

The grim civilian casualties suffered during the Blitz, and the exaggerated expectations of what British bombers might achieve, led to the parallel expectation that Germany would continue to rely on the bomber as its main means of defeating Britain. Germany was known to be developing high-altitude bombers and there was a real fear that these might deliver devastating blows from altitudes RAF fighters could not reach. The only new fighters required after the Battle of Britain were twin-engined, heavily armed, bomber destroyers capable of climbing to great heights, like the piston-engined Westland Welkin and jet-powered Meteor. The re-emergence of dog-fighting as an important element of aerial warfare had not triggered the development of an air superiority fighter specifically designed to deal with enemy fighters.

The need for such a fighter was becoming more apparent with each passing month. Unlike squadrons overseas, Fighter Command was at least getting the best that was available. However, even Spitfires were struggling to deal with the latest German fighters. The heavy losses suffered by Fighter Command during 1941 in its fighter sweeps over France were evidence of this inferiority. The Air Ministry was forced to accept that the Spitfire V was inferior to the latest Bf 109F and totally outclassed by the FW 190. Winter and poor flying weather had come as a very welcome relief to Douglas's hard-pressed squadrons.

In February 1942, the inadequacies of Fighter Command and indeed British air forces in general, were embarrassingly exposed by the break out of the *Scharnhorst, Gneisenau* and *Prinz Eugen* from their Brest base. The warships had been the subject of repeated but unsuccessful Bomber Command attempts to sink them and Hitler decided they were of more use guarding against an invasion of Norway. Rather than take them around the United Kingdom, and risk a clash with the Royal Navy, they decided on a daring dash through the English Channel. To achieve maximum surprise, the ships set off under cover of darkness, but this meant passing through the Straits of Dover around midday. The German fighter force was given the task of ensuring the RAF did not intervene.

Throughout the day, the Bf 109s and FW 190s flew constant patrols over the warships. Disorganised attempts by the RAF and Fleet Air Arm to intervene included the despatch of no fewer than 248 bombers, of which only 45 actually managed to find their target. No serious damage was inflicted by air attack and the German warships reached Germany with only slight damage from mines they struck. Some 400 Luftwaffe defensive fighter sorties had held the RAF and Fleet Air Arm at bay. Fifteen RAF bombers and seventeen fighters were lost, along with all six Fleet Air Arm Swordfish despatched by No. 825 Squadron, while German losses amounted to just one Bf 109 and three FW 190s.

It was a dramatic and rather disturbing display of just how dominant the Luftwaffe still was in the west, despite its numerical inferiority. The Luftwaffe was capable not just of maintaining air superiority over the continent but also of establishing air superiority over the Channel. Even in 1942, with most of the German Air Force deployed on other fronts, the English Channel still belonged to the Luftwaffe. This hardly augured well for any attempt to invade France. Indeed, it did not auger well should Hitler decide to go on the defensive in the east and invade the United Kingdom. The failure to make any impression on warships sailing though the Straits of Dover in broad daylight scarcely suggested a German invasion fleet had much to fear from the RAF.

The one-sided air battle once more underlined the inferiority of British fighters. The Spitfire V was far and away the best fighter available to the RAF, yet it was clearly struggling. The Hurricane was totally outclassed. Outside Air Ministry circles there was a presumption that the Spitfire and Hurricane were essentially comparable fighters with different strengths and weaknesses. With Hurricanes pouring off the production lines, it was not a misconception the Air Ministry was in a hurry to correct. Those within the Air Ministry and RAF were very aware the Hurricane was far inferior to the Spitfire. Its inferiority in the Battle of Britain was so marked, the superb Spitfire III had to be dropped so that Hurricane pilots could benefit from the latest Merlin XX in an attempt to give them at least some chance. However, Douglas at Fighter Command made it clear that even the upgraded Hurricane II was also hopelessly inadequate almost as soon as it entered service and was demanding that Hurricane production end.

Although the Air Ministry often blamed the MAP for the RAF's continued reliance on the fighter, it was a problem long before this ministry came into existence. Doubts about the value of the Hurricane had existed ever since the Spitfire had first flown in 1936.[1] The problem was that there always seemed to be a perfectly good reason for keeping it in production. It was easier to build than the Spitfire, although not that much easier; 1,000 Hurricanes could be built for the man-hours 900 Spitfires required. During the 1940 crisis, Britain had little choice but to build as many as possible of whatever was in production. When the Soviets were promised help, Hurricanes were the easiest way of providing it. The Typhoon had for some time been due to replace it on the Hawker production lines, but technical problems with the engine and airframe were delaying full-scale production. There was little point in halting Hurricane production until the Typhoon was ready to replace it.

There might be short-term advantages in building Hurricanes but long-term the policy was trapping the RAF in a vicious circle. The less numerous Spitfires were reserved for home defence which meant the Hurricane had to be used overseas to take on superior Italian, German and Japanese fighters. Unsurprisingly, Hurricane losses were heavy, which negated the advantage of it being easier to build. More had to be built just to compensate for the higher loss rate. In the final analysis, 900 Spitfires were far more useful than 1,000 Hurricanes. Continued production of the Hurricane was causing more problems than it was solving.

It was not just the quality of the available fighters. The fighter production targets the Hurricane helped meet were far too low. Air Staff policy had always been to build as few fighters as possible. Fighters were seen as purely defensive weapons and building too many was considered defeatist. Bombers won wars, not fighters. Throughout Beaverbrook's reign at the Ministry of Aircraft Production, the Air Staff constantly criticised his ministry for trying to build too many fighters. The October 1940 production schedule envisaged fighter production rising to over 1,000 a month by the middle of 1941 and up to 1,150 by the end of the year. This compared to just 200 heavy bombers a month by the end of 1941. This was not the balance the Air Ministry wanted and there was no regret that the fighter target was never achieved.

When Moore-Brabazon took over at the MAP in 1941, the fighter target was lowered, with a peak of 866 a month required in 1942, dropping to a steady 777, while heavy bomber production would rise to 500 a month. The December 1941 programme envisaged fighter output reaching nearly 950 by the end of 1943, with heavy bomber output rising to 625. The fighter target was still lower than Beaverbrook's October 1940 target, and a large proportion of the increase merely compensated for the 100 British-built fighters a month that had been promised to the Soviets. (The other 100 were redirected American Lend Lease aircraft.) To make matters worse, fighters were increasingly required for tactical reconnaissance and ground attack and these had to come out of the fighter allocation. Heavy bomber production, by comparison, was to increase threefold, and none of these were going to the Soviets.[2] Bomber production had absolute priority and, while this was the case, RAF fighter forces on all fronts were going to struggle.

Nor were the prospects of solving the quality problem particularly bright. The Typhoon was lined up to replace both the Spitfire and Hurricane. It was originally supposed to enter service in the spring of 1940 but, two years later, aerodynamic problems were still causing excessive buffeting and vibrations and its Napier Sabre II engine was still proving unreliable. Production of the airframe had begun but only on a small scale and most of these had to be stored away engineless while Napier tried to resolve the problems with the engine. Hawker hoped to get round the aerodynamic problems by introducing a new, much thinner, wing and replacing the chin radiator with one built into the leading edge of the wing, but development of this 'thin-wing' Typhoon II (the future Tempest) was running behind schedule. The production version of the Typhoon II was supposed to have the improved Sabre IV engine with direct fuel injection, but this was not expected to be available until 1943 at the earliest.

However, with growing fears that the problems with the thick-wing Typhoon would never be resolved, in December 1941, out of sheer desperation, first deliveries of the Typhoon II were brought forward four months to October 1942, which seemed improbably soon to the Air Ministry and indeed many in the MAP. After six years of trying, Napier had not yet got the Sabre II working properly. Three hundred engineless Typhoon airframes in storage stood testament to this failure. It seemed scarcely credible that the more advanced Sabre IV would be up and running ahead of schedule. Perhaps some new information on the experimental Sabre IV engine had suddenly come to light, an exasperated MAP official ironically speculated.[3] The Typhoon problem, however, had a silver lining for the MAP. The Hurricane had to stay in production and these were far easier to build than Typhoons. The Typhoon took even more man-hours than the Spitfire. One thousand Hurricanes could be built for 650 Typhoons, making it much easier for the MAP to hit its fighter production targets.

The Japanese attack in the Far East had immediately increased the demand for fighters and the easiest way to meet this demand was to build more Hurricanes. Even the Air Ministry dropped its criticisms of the fighter and appealed for yet more, at least to tide the Air Force over the next critical six months. It was assumed that the Hurricane would still be more than useful against the supposedly inferior Japanese fighters. There was even talk of new production lines being set up.[4]

The problems with the Typhoon were now seen by the MAP as even more of a blessing in disguise. Perhaps it would be better to abandon the Typhoon I entirely and wait for the Typhoon II. This, it was calculated, would enable an extra 1,985 Hurricanes to be built.[5] The final plan did not quite go this far. In February 1942, it was decided to keep the Typhoon in production but at a much reduced rate until the Typhoon II became available. An extra 1,250 Hurricanes could then be built up to the end of 1943 at the expense of 843 Typhoon Is. Since sufficient engines were unlikely to be available for these airframes, it was scarcely a difficult decision and the possibility of further increasing Hurricane production at the expense of the Typhoon was not ruled out.[6]

It seemed extraordinary, but once again, with fighters urgently needed everywhere, increasing Hurricane production was a quick and easy way of providing them. Problem-free Hurricanes had to be more useful than engineless Typhoons. The MAP took up the Air Ministry suggestion that new Hurricane production lines should be set up. The Cunliffe-Owen company, based in Eastleigh near Southampton, was already supplying components for Hawker, and the MAP proposed expanding its facilities so the plant could build complete airframes.

The Air Ministry pointed out that the Cunliffe-Owen factory was close to the Supermarine works in Southampton. Would it not be possible to build Spitfires instead of Hurricanes, they suggested. The MAP was adamant; the plant had been involved in Hurricane production and switching it to any other design would in the short term only reduce output. Such was the immediate need for more fighters, the Air Ministry was forced to concede the MAP had a point.[7] Less than a year after the Air Ministry had been demanding that Hurricane production be brought to an end as quickly as possible, the type was going from strength to strength, with the Air Ministry's blessing. The Cunliffe-Owen contribution would enable Hurricane monthly output to remain at 240 throughout 1942 and 1943, making available an extra 1,780 Hurricanes.

There were some dissenting voices within the Air Ministry, although not so much about the way Hurricane production was outpacing Spitfire production. The greater concern was the apparent pre-occupation with defensive fighters at the expense of more offensive aircraft. At a meeting with the MAP, Air Ministry 'representatives' (Freeman, Sorley and

Courtney were present) expressed some surprise that after claiming that the December 1941 plans represented the absolute limits of the British aero-industry and nation, it seemed that the MAP had suddenly found the capacity to build another 2,000 fighters. It seemed that when more fighters were required the MAP had no problem coming up with them, but for any other type there was never any spare production capacity.[8] The MAP was told 'single-seater fighters were required less than any other class' and more torpedo-bombers, twin-engined fighters, trainers and target-towers were needed more than Hurricanes and even Spitfires.[9] For some, the First World War idea of the single-seater fighter being the key to success in the air war was a distant fading memory.

Compared to the December 1941 programme, in total nearly 3,000 more Hurricanes would now be built with production continuing well into 1944.[10] Some were wondering what exactly the RAF was going to do with them all, once the immediate crisis in the Far East had passed. Nobody in the UK wanted them as fighters. Tedder in the Middle East still seemed reasonably happy with the Hurricane, although discontent seeping through had led to a decision to send a couple of Spitfire squadrons, with initially twenty, increased to seventy in January 1942, being delivered each month to cover losses.[11] However, the Hurricane would remain the numerically most important British fighter in the region.

How long this could continue remained to be seen. Pilots who flew the Hurricane in combat had to believe they were flying the best that was available, but there was only so long the facade could be maintained. As soon as squadrons converted to Spitfires, it became obvious that they had not been flying the best. There were no Spitfire pilots demanding their squadrons should revert to Hurricanes. It was difficult to imagine the Middle and Far East wanting Hurricanes as fighters in 1944, if Douglas did not want them for Fighter Command in 1941.

The Hurricane was useful in other roles. The Air Ministry wanted to keep the two Hurribomber squadrons, but there were no plans for any more. Hurricane squadrons might help meet Portal's commitment to have fifteen squadrons trained in Army support duties. Night-fighting was another option. The latest innovation in this field was the Turbinlite Havoc (the night-fighter version of the Douglas Boston). This was an unarmed night-fighter with a searchlight in the nose to illuminate the enemy bomber while accompanying single-seater fighters delivered the attack. There were huge hopes that this would revolutionise night-fighting and ten Hurricane squadrons were earmarked for this role.

Tactical reconnaissance was another possibility. The Air Ministry was promising the War Office ten fighter-reconnaissance squadrons. However, there were already excellent American fighters lined up for this role and, in any case, as one assessment gloomily pointed out, there would be enough Hurricanes coming off the production line to equip fifty such squadrons. Hurricanes would still be useful for meeting the 200 fighters a month the Soviet Union had been promised. As these were gifts from Britain, surely the Soviets would not be so ungracious as to complain about the quality.

In April 1942, however, the Air Ministry was alarmed by reports in *The Times* that the Soviets were 'turning up their noses' at the prospect of more Hurricanes. Their correspondent reported that the Russians considered the fighter obsolete, and only useful for second-line fighter duties well behind the front line.[12] Deliveries to the Soviet Union would continue, whether they wanted them or not. Eventually, some 3,000 examples of the fighter would find their way to the Soviet Union.

With Hurricane being phased out as a day fighter on the home front, Douglas would seem to have little to complain about. However, even he was from happy with his lot. His command, he complained, was entering 1942 with only sixty-eight of the seventy-five day fighter squadrons he was supposed to have and only fifty-one of them were equipped with the Spitfire. Of these only forty-one had the latest Spitfire V. Between 250 and 270 Spitfires were being built a month but the decision to send 70 of these to the Middle East would be bound to slow down even further his attempts to complete re-equipment with the Spitfire V. Douglas was noticeably more strident in his demands than Tedder in the Middle East, where crucial battles were being fought and the need for the best fighters was far greater.

Indeed, Fighter Command seemed almost embarrassingly well equipped. After more than two years of war it was still the only RAF fighter force that had Spitfires. Fighter Command was without doubt the most powerful concentration of day fighters on any Allied front, east or west. Indeed, this had been the case throughout the war. Yet it was also the greatest unused Allied resource. For most of the war, its ample resources were simply not in the right place to have any influence on the course of the war. From the frozen wastes of the Arctic Circle, to the deserts of the Middle East and the jungles of Malaya, RAF fighter squadrons were having to fight critical battles with second-rate equipment. The only time the enemy had encountered Spitfires was when they came within range of Fighter Command airfields in Britain. The command had fought one major battle, and they did not come any more important than the Battle of Britain, but even that battle had only happened because of the unexpected collapse of France. The attack Fighter Command had been designed to deal with, the dreaded knockout blow, had never come. If France had not collapsed, Fighter Command's day fighters would have stayed on the side-lines and played no part in the war whatsoever. In 1942, with only the occasional hit-and-run daylight raid to deal with, Douglas needed a major role to justify the huge resources that were locked into his Command.

In the spring of 1942 that major role might be covering an invasion. Given that Douglas had 800 Spitfires in the front line it might seem strange that there were fears that Fighter Command might lack the strength to do this. However, there were genuine concerns that Spitfire production was not sufficient to sustain this force, and these fears grew during the course of 1942 as Spitfires finally began to be deployed overseas. Demand from the Middle East increased, Spitfires were going to Australia to defend Darwin and plans were being laid to deploy them in Burma. The Fleet Air Arm also wanted them. The 1940 Norwegian campaign had demonstrated that aircraft carriers had to have fighters that could compete with land-based single-seaters and this had led to the development of the Blackburn Firebrand. However, until this was available, a proportion of Spitfire production was having to go to the Fleet Air Arm in the form of the navalised Seafire.

Any military operations on the Channel front would be bound to provoke a fierce Luftwaffe reaction and it was predicted monthly losses might be as high as 330 Spitfires a month. One estimate had monthly losses supporting an invasion peaking at no less than 600 in August, with the entire reserve of 500 Spitfires available in May being wiped out by September.[13] In the spring of 1942, average monthly Spitfire production had risen to around 350 a month. Even with an additional 100 repaired machines arriving each month, output was less than predicted wastage plus planned deliveries overseas.[14] Even so, with a frontline strength of some 800 Spitfires and a reserve of 500, these concerns might bring a wry smile to the face of commanders on other fronts around the world where they were still waiting for their first Spitfire.

Slessor feared that a Spitfire shortage might scupper any plans for an invasion. More had to be found from somewhere and he was short of ideas about where they might come from. Deliveries to the Middle East could be halved and the Fleet Air Arm could make do with Hurricanes rather than the Seafires. It was very much a case of robbing Peter to pay Paul. The additional Hurricanes that would be needed for the Navy and Middle East could come from the deliveries currently going to the Soviet Union. The Soviets would surely gladly forgo these if it meant a second front, Slessor reasoned. Indeed getting a second front in exchange for fighters that they did not want would look like a very good deal to the Soviets.

Despite the heavy losses suffered the year before, Douglas was keen to renew his fighter offensive over the Pas de Calais. The primary aim was still to try and divert Luftwaffe units from the Eastern Front, but the possibility of a cross-Channel operation gave the offensive a little more purpose than it had in 1941. Whether it would be any more successful was another matter. Douglas knew he faced a Luftwaffe that was struggling to meet the demands being made of it. RAF intelligence had picked up the movement of fighter formations from France to Norway to escort attacks on the convoys heading for the Soviet Union, further depleting their defences in the west.[15] However, as Douglas had discovered the year before, all the advantages were with the defence. The Luftwaffe only had to defend a narrow coastal strip along the Pas de Calais and Lowlands coast and there was nothing there crucial to the German cause. There was no need to intervene unless circumstances were favourable. These were the worst possible circumstances in which to take on arguably the best fighters and some of the most experienced pilots in any air force.

Not much was expected from the offensive but, even if Fighter Command victories could just match losses, Churchill thought it would be worthwhile.[16] At least it would demonstrate to the Soviets that Britain was doing some fighting. On 24 March, Fighter Command resumed its fighter sweeps over France. At the beginning of April, Portal was assuring the Prime Minister the offensive was going well. In the first week Fighter Command pilots had claimed fifty-five German fighters and only lost thirty-four. This was much better than Churchill had feared. Unfortunately, actual German losses were only twelve fighters.[17]

In the first two weeks of April, not even the exaggerated claims of Fighter Command could disguise the one-sided nature of the battle. Fighter Command lost forty planes while only twenty-one German fighters could even be claimed. Actual German losses were just eleven. As was always the case with offensive missions, an RAF loss usually meant the loss of the pilot as well, whereas a German pilot baling out was soon back with his squadron. It was Fighter Command that was being worn down, not the Luftwaffe. Nevertheless, fighter operations were stepped up. On 15 April more than 500 sorties were flown by Fighter Command. In an effort to reduce losses, operations were restricted to targets on the coast, but the result was the same. In the second half of the month, Fighter Command lost sixty-four planes but could only claim forty-four enemy fighters. Again it was an exaggeration; German losses were just ten fighters.[18]

Douglas convinced himself that the Luftwaffe was making a huge effort to scare off the RAF before summer weather meant it had to turn its full attention back to Russia. Douglas planned to call the enemy bluff. He would maintain the offensive at the current intensity and then, as soon as the Germans went on to the offensive in the east, expected at the end of May, he would step up Fighter Command effort by 50 per cent and overwhelm any remaining Luftwaffe fighters. An extra Spitfire squadron was to be moved into each sector of No. 11 Group in readiness.

Douglas reckoned that if the Luftwaffe lost 200 fighters a month, the German fighter force would go into decline. If this could be increased to 250, the Germans would be forced to bring in reinforcements from other fronts. It was an ambitious target, but if his pilots could knock down half this figure in combat, losses through other causes, he believed, would account for the rest. It was a somewhat optimistic estimate of German accident rates, but it made the target seem obtainable. Only sixty-five fighters had been claimed in April, but 100 a month did not seem that many more.

However, if the offensive was to be maintained, Douglas insisted that Fighter Command had to have priority over other theatres. In April, six of Douglas's Spitfire squadrons were despatched to the Mediterranean. A furious Douglas accused Freeman of yielding to piecemeal demands from overseas instead of sticking with agreed policy.[19] The Air Ministry could not have it both ways, he argued, expecting Fighter Command to take the offensive in Europe and provide reinforcements for the Middle East. It was scarcely an argument that was likely to cut much ice with overseas commanders. They had far more to complain about than Douglas. The protests were ignored and Douglas was told to maintain the offensive as a priority, with his existing squadrons.[20]

Heavy losses continued in the first two weeks of May. In the second half of the month it seemed Fighter Command might have turned the corner, in the loss victory ratio at least; twenty-seven enemy fighters were claimed for the loss of twenty-five. Perhaps Douglas had been right and that with a full-scale German offensive on the Eastern Front under way, the Luftwaffe had lowered its guard in the west. It proved to be a false dawn. In the first two days of June the German fighters savaged Fighter Command; twenty fighters were lost and only two enemy planes were even claimed.[21]

In the four months March to June, Fighter Command lost 264 fighters compared to German losses of 58. It was an even more one-sided balance sheet in terms of pilot losses. Even with the excessive claiming of British pilots concealing the true scale of Fighter Command's inferiority, it was still obvious to Douglas and Leigh-Mallory it was a battle his pilots were losing. It did not seem to bode well for a possible invasion of France.

It was perhaps surprising that results were so poor, given that Fighter Command was so much better equipped than Commonwealth squadrons facing the same enemy in the Western Desert. There were no FW 190s in the desert until late 1942 and Axis squadrons were often plagued by a lack of fuel. Even so, the gap in fighter quality was far greater in the Middle East. Commonwealth squadrons had admittedly paid a high price in terms of losses, yet the Hurricanes and Tomahawks had still been able to contribute effectively to the Allied cause, as demonstrated in the recent successful Crusader offensive, despite their inferiority.

There were reasons. The constant combat in the desert probably produced battle-hardened, experienced pilots more quickly. However, perhaps the crucial difference was that over France there was no ground offensive to contribute to. The RAF was taking on the Luftwaffe in an air-only campaign at medium and high altitudes where the Bf 109F in particular had the edge and German pilots need only engage if they felt they had the advantage. As Commonwealth squadrons were discovering in the Western Desert, a low-level tactical air battle in support of ground forces, where German pilots could not pick and choose when to intervene, favoured Allied pilots more. Flying in support of an invasion might bring Fighter Command more success than aimless fighter sweeps.

Pilots on the Channel front might be much better off in terms of the fighters they flew than their Desert compatriots, but there was no disguising the inferiority of the Spitfire V when compared to the Bf 109F and FW 190. The RAF needed better fighters and hopes rested with the Merlin 61-powered Spitfire and the long overdue Typhoon. In the spring of 1942, Fighter Command was expecting to have four squadrons with the former and three with the latter by 1 July.[22] Despite all the problems with the Typhoon, much was still expected of the fighter. Leigh-Mallory had convinced himself that both the Typhoon and the Merlin 61 Spitfire were 'considerably superior' to the Bf 109F and FW 190. The effect on German morale of even a small number of superior fighters ought, he felt, to give the RAF a 'reasonable chance of gaining a measure of air superiority'.[23] Fighter Command operations were cut back by 50 per cent in July in an effort to conserve resources until these fighters were ready to operate in reasonable numbers.

It was with enormous relief that, on 22 May 1942, the MAP was finally able to announce that the Typhoon's aerodynamic and its Sabre engine reliability problems had been 'eradicated'.[24] Modified versions had been issued to the three squadrons converting to the fighter and they had flown 600 hours without any problems. On 28 May, nearly two years after the type was originally supposed to enter service and ten months after the first had been delivered to a squadron, the fighter was scrambled for the first time to intercept an intruder. In what proved to be an anti-climax, the enemy turned out to be a friendly Spitfire.

An anxious Air Ministry was urging Douglas to try out the Typhoon on more offensive operations as soon as possible to see if it really would give Fighter Command the edge.[25] The pilots were not quite so keen. Sufficient flying was taking place to discover that the problems with the Napier engine were far from resolved. The aerodynamic problems also persisted with excessive vibration at high speed putting enormous strain on the airframe. On 29 July a pilot of No. 257 Squadron was killed when the tail of his Typhoon broke off in a dive. Little more than a week later, a test pilot was killed in a similar incident. An investigation had hardly got underway when a pilot of No. 56 Squadron was a third victim.[26] The cause of the structural failure was a complete mystery; the part of the fuselage that was fracturing was, in theory, supposed to be one of the stronger elements of the airframe.[27] In these circumstances there was reluctance to use the fighter for anything. Offensive patrols over enemy territory were out of the question.

This left all hopes resting on the Merlin 61-powered Spitfire. The new Merlin, with its two superchargers in tandem driving even more oxygen into the engine, had been tried out in the Spitfire III airframe, achieving an impressive 414 mph and a service ceiling of nearly 42,000 feet. The version that eventually went into production was an even more radical redesign, including a completely new wing. It came in two versions, the Spitfire VII, with pressurised cockpit to take full advantage of the plane's impressive ceiling, and the Mark VIII with a standard cockpit. Both of these second-generation Spitfires were due to become available in the summer of 1942, but the desire for ever greater ceiling, for fighter combat and the need to deal with high-altitude bombers, meant the Spitfire VII had priority. As a precaution against delays, Supermarine were asked to try out the Merlin 61 in a standard Spitfire V airframe, making the minimum of modifications to accommodate the heavier, more powerful engine. Trials were due to take place in April.

Deliveries of the Merlin 61 engine were soon falling behind schedule. It was supposed to be a specialist high-altitude engine that might only be needed in relatively small numbers. The engine's unexpectedly high output at medium altitudes meant the Air Ministry now wanted as many as possible. However, its two-stage supercharger made it a complicated engine to build. Rolls Royce was doing its best and perhaps had been too keen to promise too much too soon. It was already committed to the delivery of large numbers of the Merlin XX for the Lancaster and the increased orders for Hurricanes, and was already struggling to meet these demands. The Griffon, the Merlin's much larger successor, was also about to enter production. On top of all these requirements, they were now expected to mass produce the Merlin 61. It did not help that Rolls Royce were notoriously dismissive of mass-production techniques. The company took pride in the individual care that went into the construction of each engine. Instead of ensuring components were sufficiently standardised to be slotted together by semi-skilled labour, Rolls Royce relied on the judgement and skills of their craftsmen to assemble their engines. It was May 1942 before the first production version of the Merlin 61 emerged.

However, production of the Spitfire VII and VIII airframes was even more behind schedule. The first Spitfire VII was not now expected until July and the first Mark VIII two months later.[28] Douglas was horrified when he discovered the version with the pressurised cockpit had been given priority over the standard version. For Douglas, the struggle his fighters were engaged in over France was a far more immediate problem than a hypothetical high-altitude bombing offensive. His pilots urgently needed better equipment and something had to be done to speed up the process. In a rather desperate move, instructions were issued to fit Merlin 61 engines to Spitfire V airframes as they came off the production lines, even though trials with a prototype had not yet been completed. In this way, perhaps, one hundred of this makeshift version, the Spitfire IX, would be available before the end of June.[29]

Official trials demonstrated the risk had been worth taking. Compared to the Spitfire V, the plane was 'outstandingly better' especially at heights over 20,000 feet. The airframe was only just about strong enough to take the heavier engine. By peacetime standards the plane might not have been considered safe to fly, but pilots facing the FW 190 would feel a lot safer in a Spitfire IX, whose strength was just about adequate, than the inadequate Spitfire V. As it turned out, structural strength was never a problem.

In June 1942, the first Spitfire IX was delivered and the following month it flew its first operational sortie. Soon, no less than a thousand of this supposedly interim version would be on order. However, the low Merlin 61 production rate meant getting versions of the Spitfire powered by this engine into service was going to be a painfully slow affair. Output of Merlin 61-powered Spitfires was not expected to exceed Spitfire V output until April 1943.[30] Home-based squadrons would only convert at about a rate of one a month; even by the spring of 1943 it was only planned to have ten Spitfire IX and three Spitfire VII squadrons, compared to forty-one Spitfire V and one Spitfire VI (the high-altitude version of the Spitfire V) squadrons.[31] Relying so heavily on the Spitfire V in 1943 was a disquieting prospect. A depressed Freeman feared, 'We shall fight the next Battle of Britain with aircraft seriously inferior to those of our opponents.'[32] It was interesting that even in 1942 Freeman was still thinking in terms of another 'Battle of Britain'.

Far from closing the gap, the RAF seemed to be falling ever further behind. Before the Spitfire IX even reached the squadrons yet another version of the Bf 109 appeared. With hindsight it would become clear that the Bf 109 development had peaked with the Bf 109F. From this point on, the price paid for increased performance would be deteriorating handling qualities. This, however, did not stop the Bf 109G being a formidable opponent, especially at altitude. With nitrous oxide boost the Bf 109G-2 was 45 mph faster than the Spitfire V at 28,000 feet. The fighter was the perfect foil for the FW 190. The Messerschmitt had outstanding performance at higher altitudes, whereas the FW 190 was at its best at low and medium altitudes. It was a formidable combination.

In the first six months of 1942 there was very little good news about what might follow the Merlin 61 Spitfire. The entire fighter development programme seemed to be unravelling. The troublesome Sabre scarcely seemed to be an engine on which the future of the fighter force should depend, yet the Sabre IV-powered 'thin-wing' Typhoon II was still an important part of future plans. Tizard insisted that the sleeve-valve technology used by engines like the Sabre and the huge new 54-litre Bristol Centaurus radial were the only way of achieving speeds in excess of 400 mph. With the Merlin 61-powered Spitfire already exceeding 400 mph, it was a claim that was beginning to look a little suspect. Despite the Sabre's many problems, in the spring of 1942 there were plans to expand the London Napier factory and allocate more shadow factory space to Sabre production. Rolls Royce were even approached about the possibility of turning over some of their production capacity to the Napier engine, which must have produced some puzzled faces at Rolls Royce as they struggled to meet the huge demands being made of their immaculate Merlin.[33]

The rate at which Typhoon airframes were being stockpiled, even with the new reduced production schedules, was alarming. Even if Napier solved the problems with their engine, it would be some time before Sabre production could catch up with the backlog. For this reason alone, alternative sources of power for the Typhoon had to be considered. Tizard favoured the Centaurus radial, which was already being lined up to power the Buckingham high-speed bomber (the replacement for the interim Bisley), the Warwick II (the Wellington's geodetic successor) and the B.8/41 Super Stirling. Production of this engine was supposed to get underway in the autumn of 1942.[34]

Camm had been thinking about using the Centaurus with the Typhoon/ Tornado since before the war. A prototype had been ordered early in 1941 and a Tornado first flew, with a 2,200 hp Centaurus engine, in October of that year. The plane topped 400 mph and it was hoped 430 mph might eventually be possible. Tizard thought this was a bit optimistic but even if it was only as fast as the Sabre II Typhoon, the Centaurus version would still be well worth having given the shortage of Sabres. It also seemed unlikely that the temperamental Sabre would ever be reliable enough for use in more demanding conditions overseas.

Planned Centaurus production, 350 a month, would not be sufficient for all the aircraft that were supposed to use it. Tizard, always anxious to try and move the Air Ministry away from its bomber strategy, suggested dropping the Warwick II and Super Stirling long-range bombers in favour of the high-speed Buckingham light bomber and the Centaurus/Typhoon combination.[35] Freeman was not so keen, believing that the Centaurus-powered Typhoon would be no more than 'an acceptable substitute for the Hurricane' in a ground attack role.[36] Despite these doubts, Camm was instructed to give the Centaurus/Typhoon top priority.[37] Six prototypes were to be built and, to demonstrate the importance attached to the project, an initial batch of 500 was ordered. Deliveries were expected to begin as early as November 1942, with production rising to sixty per month.[38] This version would still be using the thick-wing Typhoon I airframe.

Meanwhile, the thin-wing Typhoon II and Sabre IV engine were so far behind schedule, in March 1942 the MAP dropped the Typhoon II entirely from its future production plans and inserted the Sabre II-powered Typhoon I at a rate of 230 a month up to the end of 1944. The disappearance of the Sabre IV was a major concern for Camm. He was building his prototype Typhoon II to take either the Sabre II or IV, but feared the plane would lose most of its performance advantage with the earlier version of the engine. It would seem he was expecting the Sabre IV to generate considerably more power, presumably on the basis of the rather ambitious long-term plans Napier had to introduce three-speed, two-stage superchargers. In fact, the proposed Sabre IV was just a Sabre II with fuel injection instead of a carburettor and this version was not going to offer any substantial increase in power.

As a substitute for the Sabre IV, Camm proposed two more variations of his Typhoon II, one with the Rolls Royce Griffon IIb and another with the Griffon 61. The Griffon was the 37-litre big brother of the Merlin. In its IIb form it only had a single-stage supercharger and performed best at low and medium altitudes. The Griffon 61 used the same two-stage supercharging that had made the Merlin 61 so successful. The Griffon IIb version was expected to have a top speed of 400 mph and ceiling of 31,000 feet, while the Griffon 61 version would be capable of a more impressive 430 mph and a ceiling of 40,000 feet. The former, with its good low-level performance, was seen by Camm as a Hurricane replacement in the army support role and would be armed with four 20mm or two 40mm cannon and carry up to 1,000lb of bombs. The two-stage Griffon 61 version was intended as a genuine pure fighter replacement for the Spitfire.

However, the engine and airframe were scarcely a perfect match. As Camm conceded, according to his own calculations the Typhoon airframe was 'a little too strong' for the Griffon engine, or in other words unnecessarily heavy, by a factor of 500lb.[39] Nor was it a quick fix; the Griffon 61 had not yet been cleared for production and was unlikely to become available until 1943. As the thin-wing Typhoon II airframe was also behind schedule, there was a suggestion the initial Griffon version might have to use the thick wing Typhoon I airframe.[40] A Typhoon powered by this engine was quickly added to the spring 1942 production programme, even though work had not even started on a prototype.

The plethora of engine/airframe combinations was confusing to say the least. It is not even clear if the Griffon-powered Typhoon that was ordered was a thick-wing or thin-wing version. The first was supposed to come off the production line in July 1943 with production rising to a hundred a month by April 1944. There was no shortage of ideas about how to take the Typhoon project forward but little certainty about which might prove successful or when they might become available.

Even Spitfire development was going awry. The 27-litre Merlin seemed to be coming to the end of its useful life and Supermarine were relying on the larger 37-litre Griffon to keep their Spitfire competitive. The Air Ministry was indeed very impressed by the potential of the Griffon-powered Spitfire XX. Mounting the larger engine involved a major redesign but, unlike the Typhoon, at least the Supermarine team had a sound basis to work on. Rolls Royce's recent track record was much better than Napier's so there was good reason to believe this third-generation Spitfire would be a success. There was scepticism that the two-stage Griffon 61 would be ready for the Spitfire XX as early as January 1943 but, so promising was the combination, Supermarine were told to prepare drawings for the Castle Bromwich site so that production of the airframe could go ahead even if the engines to power them were not yet available.

Much of the documentation on the Spitfire/Griffon combination was rather loosely worded, frequently failing to distinguish between the versions with the single-stage Griffon IIb and the much more advanced two-stage Griffon 61. This lack of clarity would have disastrous consequences. In March 1942 the MAP was astonished to discover that Supermarine had prepared drawings for a Griffon IIb-powered Spitfire and passed these on to Castle Bromwich and this was the plane they were preparing to mass produce.[41]

New drawings were hurriedly prepared but the case for the Griffon 61 version was fading fast. The engine was still suffering from teething problems and there was still no definite date for production to begin. Plans at Castle Bromwich for the Griffon IIb version were so well advanced it did not seem worth changing everything for an engine that might not be ready for some time. The MAP found itself committed to the mass production of a fighter it had never asked for. To avoid further confusion, the Griffon IIb version was re-designated Spitfire XII and the Griffon 61-powered version the Spitfire XXI. The horse, however, had bolted. Production of the Spitfire XII would continue at Castle Bromwich until the Griffon 61 became available. This, it was gloomily concluded, might now be as late as January 1944.[42] The spring 1942 production schedule included nearly two thousand Spitfire XIIs.

With proposals to power both the Spitfire and Typhoon with the same Griffon engines, the development paths of these two fighters had crossed, making direct comparisons easier. It was not a comparison that would give Camm much pleasure. Although the Typhoon was supposed to be a second-generation monoplane replacement for the Spitfire, it was clearly inferior, even with the new thinner wings. Both fighters were expected to achieve the same top speed, but the proposed Griffon 61 Typhoon was expected to be no less than 2,000lb heavier than the Griffon 61 Spitfire, and would have nothing like the same manoeuvrability, acceleration, rate of climb or ceiling. Both the MAP and Air Ministry now began to view the Typhoon Griffon 61, like the Griffon IIb-powered version, as no more than a Hurricane replacement in the ground attack role.[43] This was good news for the Army; there seemed to be no shortage of fighters going into production that would only be capable of army air support. It was not such good news for pilots seeking an answer to the latest Messerschmitts and Focke-Wulfs. Since the clearly superior performance of the Spitfire would ensure the Supermarine fighter got priority, it was difficult to see any Griffon 61s being available for Typhoon production before the end of 1944.[44]

All this left Air Vice-Marshal Francis Linnell, in charge of Research and Development at the MAP, wondering 'how we managed to live, as late as the beginning of November 1941, in such a world of optimism!'[45] The Air Ministry was not impressed either; 1943 would see the large-scale production of a number of fighters of extremely dubious value, chief among these being the Griffon IIb-powered Spitfire XII. The Air Ministry could see the justification for a small number as a pre-production run before the Griffon 61 Spitfire became available but not the 2,000 on order.

As for Camm's proposals, the Air Ministry felt that the only justification for the Centaurus and Griffon IIb-powered Typhoon seemed to be that they were an improvement on the Hurricane, which was not saying very much. The Griffon Typhoon might prove satisfactory as an anti-tank weapon if it could be adapted to fly slowly enough to use 40mm cannon and this might allow the Hurricane to 'die out', but that was about all.[46] The Air Ministry certainly did not want 230 Sabre II Typhoons a month. The Air Ministry was now convinced that, even with the Sabre IV, the thin-wing Typhoon II would be inferior to German fighters.

In June 1942, MAP plans for the summer of 1943 involved the production of around 250 Typhoons (Sabre II, Centaurus and Griffon IIb) a month, nearly a hundred Griffon IIb/Spitfire XIIs, over one hundred Hurricanes and around 300 Merlin 61/Spitfires. Only the Merlin 61 Spitfires inspired any confidence. More than half of the output would be very dubious Typhoons, obsolescent Hurricanes and mistakenly ordered Spitfire XIIs.

Even by the end of 1944, fighter production would have an unhealthy air about it. There would be 280 Griffon 61 Spitfires and 200 Merlin 61 Spitfires rolling off the production lines each month. However, there would also be 230 Sabre II Typhoons, 100 Griffon IIb Typhoons, and 60 Hurricanes. 'If we persist in a policy of production of types inferior to those of the enemy our defeat in the air is certain', the Air Ministry warned.[47] This stark message set the MAP thinking. If even the Sabre IV/Typhoon II was going to be so inferior, then perhaps it was not worth persisting with the Napier engine.[48]

Camm was told to get the 'thin-wing' Typhoon II to the squadrons by March 1943, with the Sabre II rather than the Sabre IV if necessary. To speed things up, the first prototype would fly with the Typhoon I's chin radiator rather than the new wing-embedded radiators. This prototype took to the air in September 1942 and was immediately suffering the same sort of aerodynamic problems that had plagued its thick-wing predecessor.[49]

In June 1942 the MAP finally got some good news. Rolls Royce announced that the teething problems with the Griffon 61 had been sorted out and the engine was ready to go into production. Deliveries could begin in the spring of 1943 but only if their production facilities were expanded. This announcement coincided with news that, far from becoming available in October 1942, the Sabre IV would not now be ready until 1944. It was the final straw. The Griffon had a two-stage supercharger, the Napier engine did not. Although serious development of the Griffon had started four years after the Sabre, the Rolls Royce team had proven sleeveless valves were not as necessary as the experts had claimed. Their engine had overtaken the Napier engine in terms of performance, reliability and availability.

Plans for another Napier factory were scrapped and the Rolls Royce plants in Derby and Crewe expanded to accommodate Griffon production with deliveries expected early in 1943.[50] From this point on it would be Rolls Royce that would benefit from government investment in expanded production capacity. Castle Bromwich was told to abandon the Spitfire XII and prepare to build the Spitfire XXI instead. Just one hundred Spitfire XIIs would be built, enough to equip and maintain a couple of squadrons. The first Griffon 61 Spitfire XXI was now expected to start rolling off the production lines in June 1943.[51]

Meanwhile, the MAP had changed its mind about the Centaurus-powered Typhoon I and told Camm to use the Centaurus powerplant in the 'thin-wing' Typhoon II airframe instead. Even this more advanced version was not expected to have the rate of climb and performance at altitude

91

the Air Ministry required for a pure fighter. At best it would still only be a replacement for the Hurricane in the low-level ground attack role.[52] Tizard, with a different outlook on the war and in particular the way the air war was evolving, took a rather different view. What the Air Ministry saw as disadvantages, Tizard saw as advantages. Tizard believed a fighter with good low/medium altitude performance was precisely what would soon be needed. In the land fighting taking place in the Western Desert it was this sort of fighter that was proving so valuable. It might not be what the UK-based RAF wanted for air defence, but, he suggested, by 1944 the RAF might be involved in intensive Army support operations in north-west Europe. With its air-cooled engine, and therefore no cooling system for ground fire to puncture, Tizard believed the Typhoon/Centaurus combination could well be the ideal high-performance ground attack fighter to support these operations.[53]

As a Spitfire replacement, however, these were desperate times for the Typhoon. The MAP was frantically thrashing around for ways of turning the design into a reasonable fighter. The unpalatable truth seemed to be that the Typhoon in any form was inferior to the Spitfire. Still there was a determination to get something out of the Typhoon project. If all the permutations and combinations were investigated, surely something would emerge. The order for six Centaurus Typhoon prototypes was replaced by one for six 'thin-wing' Typhoon IIs with different engines. Four of them would be powered by the Sabre II, Sabre IV, Griffon IIb and Griffon 61 and the remaining two would have the Centaurus, one for Hawker and one for Bristol to use as a test bed. Camm protested that he did not have the resources to build so many different prototypes. The only relief he got was the dropping of one of the Centaurus prototypes. He was told the others were all needed to ensure no stone was left unturned in the search for a Typhoon that worked.[54] Confusion reigned. The MAP seemed to be expecting the Centaurus-powered Typhoon II before the more straightforward Sabre II-powered version. This, Camm insisted, was not possible. Even if the Tornado/Centaurus trials were successful, work on modifying the Typhoon II airframe to take the larger radial could not begin until much later in the year.[55]

The proliferation of Typhoon variants was confusing everyone. Production programmes were appearing with 'Centaurus Typhoon' and 'Griffon Typhoon', with plenty of scope for misunderstanding over which version of the Griffon was being referred to and whether the thick-wing Typhoon I or the thin-wing Typhoon II was intended. Another Spitfire/Griffon fiasco was looming. To make things clearer, the thin-wing Tyhoon II was renamed the Tempest. The Tempest I would have the Sabre IV, the Tempest II the Centaurus, the Tempest III the Griffon IIb and the Tempest IV the Griffon 61. The new nomenclature reduced the confusion but not the workload on the struggling Hawker design office.[56]

May 1942 brought good and bad news on American fighter development. The British Aircraft Commission, responsible for ordering American aircraft, passed a damning judgement on the turbo-supercharged twin-engined Lockheed P-38 fighter. The plane had a very respectable speed of 390 mph at 25,000 feet, matching the top speed of the Merlin 61 Spitfire at this altitude. However, it was a handful to fly and suffered from serious buffeting and vibrations. Limits on diving speeds had been imposed for safety reasons. Furthermore, the twin-boom arrangement, necessary to accommodate the turbo-superchargers, reduced manoeuvrability. All in all, the fighter seemed to have very little going for it. 'We cannot of course prevent the Americans equipping their fighter squadrons with this type, but I hope there will be no question of British fighter squadrons having to fight on the Lightning,' a less than impressed Douglas informed the Air Staff.[57]

The good news was the North American Mustang. This was not being built for the USAAF; it had been ordered by the British in the panic of 1940. At that time the plane had not even flown, but the British were so desperate they were willing to order anything. By the time production began, the Air Ministry had been so unimpressed with previous American fighters that the North American offering had been relegated to the army co-operation role before it even reached the country. The first arrived in November 1941. The report on official trials, issued in May 1942, revealed that, even in its original Allison-powered form, this was no ordinary fighter. The plane was extremely fast, thanks partly to its low-drag laminar airflow wings. Although equipped with exactly the same Allison engine as the Kittyhawk, it was some 30 mph quicker. It was also 30 to 35 mph faster than the Spitfire Vb up to 15,000 feet. Up to 20,000 feet it was even faster than the Merlin 61 Spitfire. It was slightly less manoeuvrable but could accelerate much faster in the dive.

There was no doubt that Mustang was an outstanding airframe. However, like the Tomahawk and Kittyhawk before it, its performance at altitude was limited by its Allison engine. The fighter's relatively high weight did not help either. The climbing performance of the Mustang was inferior to the Spitfire's at all altitudes. Above 25,000 feet the plane really struggled and flight above 30,000 feet was impossible. Poor ceiling and climb had been one of the main reasons for the Air Ministry's low opinion of all previous American fighters and in this respect the Mustang was no different.

One interesting feature that initially did not attract much attention was its fuel capacity. All American fighters tended to carry more fuel than contemporary British designs but the Mustang, with internal tanks holding 150 gallons compared to the 85 gallons of the Spitfire V, carried more fuel than any previous American single-engined fighter. Furthermore, its higher cruising speed ensured it went further on the same quantity of fuel. At its most economical cruising speed, the Mustang could fly an impressive 1,000 miles. The fighter may not have had the required performance at altitude, but it was an excellent low and medium altitude fighter and, according to those who tested it, 'certainly the best American fighter that has so far reached this country'.[58] These qualities might have been more appreciated if the Air Ministry had not attached so much importance to high-altitude performance. With its excellent endurance the Mustang would have been invaluable for providing the low-level cover a cross-Channel expedition would require.

The Mustang's qualities were not enough to change the decision to use it to equip army co-operation squadrons. Deliveries began in April 1942 and the first operational sortie was flown in May 1942, a far more rapid deployment than was the case with most previous American fighters. The Army co-operation squadrons were delighted with their latest acquisition. The only problem appeared to be that production of the plane was about to come an end. The fighter had only been ordered by the British and, now the United States was at war, all American effort had to be focused on the fighters the USAAF had ordered. An urgent appeal went out to try and get the Americans to change their minds.

The Mustang was a valuable asset simply as a low-level fighter-reconnaissance plane. There were soon even more compelling reasons to persuade the Americans to keep the plane in production. Late in April 1942, Ronnie Harker, a Rolls Royce test pilot, tried out the fighter. He was extremely impressed and his thoughts soon turned to what the plane might be capable of if it was powered by a Merlin 61. Rolls Royce engineers calculated that with this engine, the speed of the Mustang would be increased from 390 mph at 20,000 feet to a sensational 441 mph at 26,000 feet and work began on adapting a Mustang for its new engine.[59] Rolls Royce were in close touch with their counterparts at North American, who were equally enthusiastic about a Merlin-powered version and began work on their own prototype. It was a far from straightforward task; it would take the North American design team and engineers longer to make the modifications than it had taken to build the original prototype. So radical were the changes the plane briefly became the P-78, before the Americans settled on the P-51B.

Why the basic Mustang airframe should be so superior to the Spitfire was a mystery to the aerodynamicists at Farnborough. The low-drag laminar-flow wing could only explain part of the performance differential. If a similar wing was fitted to a Tempest, it was predicted it would only be 8 mph faster.[60] To match the performance of the Merlin 61/Mustang, the Spitfire needed the much more powerful Griffon 61. Even before the Merlin 61 version flew, the predicted performance had Portal convinced that the Merlin 61/Mustang combination was a better option than the Merlin 61/Spitfire. Indeed, not surprisingly, Portal was soon wondering what a Griffon 61-powered Mustang might be capable of.

The Americans extended Mustang production, but not as a fighter or to supply the RAF. The Americans had taken over fifty-seven of the final British contract and converted them for photo-reconnaissance and ordered another 500 for dive-bombing as the A-36 Apache. The preferred fighters for the USAAF remained the P-47 Thunderbolt and the P-38 Lightning. The British suggested the Americans build 1,200 Merlin 61-powered Mustang P-51s by October 1943, with the two countries sharing them, but the Americans were not easily convinced.[61] The P-38 Lightning and P-47 Thunderbolt were flying and had not even had a chance to prove their capabilities in combat. The Americans were somewhat puzzled by the quirky British faith in a version of a fighter that had not even flown yet.

For the British, it was extremely frustrating to see what was potentially the best fighter available to the Allies side-lined in the American production programme. Nevertheless, the British could hardly criticise, given their reluctance to devote more production space to the Spitfire instead of inferior Hurricanes and Typhoons. This might have crossed British minds when fears of the Tempest being as great a failure as the Typhoon, had them mulling over the possibility of getting Hawker to build Spitfires or indeed Mustangs.[62] So desperate were the British for the fighter, there was even a suggestion that Rolls Royce refit all the existing Allison-powered Mustangs in the United Kingdom with Merlin engines.

While the Merlin 61-powered Mustang P-51B and Griffon 61-powered Spitfire offered some hope for the future, the one first-class fighter available to the RAF in 1942 would be the Merlin 61 Spitfire IX, and these were only arriving in small numbers. It was not an ideal position to be in with possible landings in France in the offing. Even so, given the situation on other fronts, the quality of the fighters available to Douglas was scarcely a reason for not invading France. The range of the available fighters seemed a far more legitimate concern. When explaining to the Americans why an invasion was impossible, the British chiefs of staff gave two reasons: the shortage of landing craft and the inadequate range of RAF fighters.[63] Both were serious problems, but the former was merely a production issue. The latter was seen as a more fundamental technical problem with no obvious solution.

British fighters were designed as bomber interceptors and defending fixed points did not require much range. Ever since landings in France had been first seriously considered late in 1941, the range of the fighters available to the RAF had been recognised as a major problem. With a major landing on the continent now more likely, Paget made sure Fighter Command understood it was a problem that needed resolving quickly. More aerodromes would have to be available in the south of the country for fighters to operate from. Captured airfields on the continent would need to be put back into operation as quickly as possible and radar early warning and effective light anti-aircraft guns would have to be in place to defend them. Most of all, however, a longer-range fighter was required in quantity, to operate over the invading forces from airfields in the UK. Paget was encouraged by his understanding that it was already Air Ministry policy to develop such a capability.[64] This was perhaps more a gentle prod than anything else.

Long range was not a new requirement for British fighters; there had always been plenty of excellent reasons for increasing fighter range. The Admiralty needed fighters to protect naval forces from land bases and escort long-range Coastal Command air strikes and had been pushing for a long-range fighter for some time.[65] The Air Staff should perhaps have been more interested as it provided a means of continuing the strategic bomber offensive by day. For the Air Staff the long-range fighter had always been a fantasy. In opposing the idea, however, they were fighting a losing battle. As cruising speeds increased, fighters with the same endurance would inevitably be able to fly further. Time was on the side of the long-range fighter.

The Air Ministry had always argued that long-range fighter escort was intrinsically impossible because the extra fuel an escort fighter had to carry would always make them inferior to a short-range interceptor that did not have to carry so much fuel. The efforts made to develop long-range escorts seemed designed to prove the Air Staff were right. Spitfires had been fitted with a clumsy bulbous fixed tank protruding from one wing, which drastically reduced performance and made the fighter perilously dangerous to fly. There were much more straightforward ways of increasing internal fuel, which, when forced to, the Air Ministry was quite willing to adopt. Photo-reconnaissance Spitfires already carried an additional 29 gallons in a rear fuselage tank. The Spitfire was not so easy to fly while the tank was full, but this fuel could be used first on the outward flight and the empty tank weighed the same as the lead ballast the Spitfire had to carry anyway. The Merlin 61 had a higher rate of fuel consumption than earlier Merlins, so, to compensate, room was found in the wing leading edge and lower fuselage of the Spitfire VII and VII for an extra 38 gallons. It seemed that where there was a will there was a way.

The most obvious method of increasing range was to use drop tanks. For ferry purposes the Spitfire was already carrying 30- and 90-gallon slipper drop tanks and there were plans for a huge 170-gallon tank to enable Spitfires to fly direct from Gibraltar to Malta. However, even with the 90-gallon tank, basic manoeuvring was impossible; the Spitfire could only fly straight and level. This, the Air Ministry insisted, meant it could only be used for ferrying. This was scarcely the case since the tank could be jettisoned as soon as the enemy appeared. The full 90 gallons could not be used by the Spitfire V for long-range escort as this exceeded the 85 gallons carried internally. Combat and the return flight had to be on internal fuel. However, it could be used for extending patrol time in areas closer to home, such as the French coast. The Air Ministry, however, insisted that 30 gallons was the maximum that could be carried on combat missions.[66]

Even the 30-gallon tanks were slow to arrive. Supermarine had been instructed to modify Spitfires to carry a drop tank in the summer of 1941, but it was late December before the first was produced and initially only six a week were being delivered.[67] Douglas did his best to chivvy things along, but it would be May 1942 before all Spitfires coming off the Supermarine and Castle Bromwich plans were modified to carry the slipper tank.

With just an extra 30 gallons, British fighters would struggle to protect a cross-Channel operation anywhere other than the Pas de Calais. On internal fuel, a Spitfire could patrol for twenty minutes at a distance of 85 miles, which would enable the Dieppe coastline or the northern tip of the Cherbourg peninsula to be covered. With a 30-gallon drop tank the Spitfire could patrol for the same time at a distance of 140 miles, which would bring the more distant Normandy coastline west of Le Havre into range, or patrol for more than twice as long at the shorter distance of 85 miles.[68] Even this might not be possible with Merlin 61-powered Spitfires. While the Spitfire VII and VIII had additional fuel to compensate for the Merlin 61's higher fuel consumption, the makeshift Spitfire IX did not.

As far as the Air Ministry was concerned no more was possible. However, events in the Far East were soon suggesting this was not the case. Japanese single-seater fighters seemed to be ranging far and wide, establishing air superiority many hundreds of miles from their bases, as British commanders in the region were soon pointing out. On 22 February 1942, General Wavell, commanding Allied forces in the Far East, reported that the extraordinary range of Japanese fighters was causing severe problems and wanted to know if anything was being done about developing something similar.[69] An irate Churchill wanted an explanation from Portal as to how Japanese fighters were able to do this when the Air Ministry had assured him that 'no important advance in range was likely to be made'.[70]

On 15 March, Wavell renewed his complaint, claiming in a note to Churchill that, while his own fighters could only manage 350 miles, Japanese fighters had a range of 1,500 miles.[71] 'This is very grave. You have repeatedly assured me that ranges of this kind were impossible for fighters,' a disgruntled Churchill informed Portal.[72] The Chief of Air Staff rather lamely replied that he had not said it was impossible, merely impossible to operate effectively over such ranges. Unfortunately for Portal the Japanese fighters were operating very effectively. While British planners considering an invasion of France had to make do with fighters that could operate 100 miles from the United Kingdom, the Japanese were operating up to 400 miles from their bases and still outperforming the opposing fighters in the target area.

Portal's claim that the Japanese had only managed to do this because Allied air defences were weak did not explain why Japanese fighters were able to fly so far to expose this weakness. Lindemann, Churchill's scientific advisor, chipped in with the observation that British fighters had sacrificed range for speed and that Japanese fighters were 100 mph slower than British designs. Lindemann claimed that once jettisonable tanks had been fitted to British fighters they would have the same range but greater speed and firepower, precisely what Portal insisted was impossible.

Commonwealth pilots at the front would not be impressed by the claim that Japanese fighters were 100 mph slower, with Mitsubishi Zeros and

Nakajima Oscars running rings round their Hurricanes. Indeed, given the low power of the engines available to the Japanese, their fighters were remarkably fast. They were not even carrying particularly huge quantities of fuel. The Mitsubishi Zero, the most impressive of the Japanese fighters, only carried 114 gallons internally. The Air Ministry was under no illusions about this; indeed their intelligence believed it could only carry 95 gallons, only slightly more than the Spitfire V and much less than the 123 gallons the Spitfire VII and VIII could carry.[73] Much of the Zero's range was down to the low fuel consumption of its Sakae engine, but the drop tank carried another 72 gallons, and it was this willingness to carry more fuel externally that the RAF needed to copy.

The Japanese had put the long-range fighter back on the agenda and Portal now felt obliged to demonstrate that Britain was not as far behind as Wavell was suggesting. In figures he supplied to Churchill, he claimed the Hurricane IIB would soon carry two 90-gallon jettisonable tanks giving it a range of 1,380 miles. The Spitfire V with a single jettisonable 30-gallon tank had a range approaching 700 miles and with a jettisonable 90-gallon tank could manage around 1,000 miles. This was a ferry range, but an internal memo made very clear to Portal that there was nothing to stop the larger tank being used on operations.[74]

Portal assured Churchill that the plan was for all Spitfires to be capable of using both these tanks and, rather ambiguously, that a stockpile was being created in Britain and overseas.[75] Portal immediately ordered production to be stepped up, but only for the 30-gallon tank. Even this was running behind schedule; instead of the planned 7,000 by the end of May, only 1,600 had been delivered by mid-May. More companies were brought into the production programme and it was hoped to have over 8,000 30-gallon drops tanks in the UK by 1 September, sufficient to keep seventeen squadrons going for a month.[76]

However, Portal still did not really believe long-range single-engined fighters were the answer; only twin-engined fighters like the Beaufighter and Mosquito could match the range of Japanese fighters. To keep Wavell happy, de Havilland were asked to scale down the Mosquito to produce a 1,500-mile long-range single-seater fighter, which would lead to the Hornet, but Portal doubted it would be a success. Against a strong defence with adequate warning the long-range fighter stood 'little chance', he still insisted. This was true for the twin-engined approach he was suggesting, but it was not true for the single-engined fighters with drop tanks the Japanese were using.

With the Japanese flying regular long-range missions, it was a problem that was not going to go away. The Admiralty was also taking note of what Japanese fighters were achieving. In August 1942, the Admiralty approached Fighter Command about the possibility of escorting their torpedo-bombers in strikes off the south of Norway, about 300 miles from bases in the United Kingdom. Currently twin-engined Coastal Command Beaufighters were escorting the bombers, but there were fears that the arrival of single-seater opposition might force an end to these operations. The Admiralty needed a long-range single-engined fighter and this was precisely the type of operation that Japanese fighters had been excelling in. If a Spitfire could fly over 1,000 miles with a 170-gallon drop tank, surely it ought to be possible to fly escort missions to the Norwegian coast 300 miles away.[77]

The irritated reaction in Fighter Command was that the Admiralty should use their aircraft carriers or get their own long-range fighter, which rather summed up inter-service spirit at the time. In the formal reply the Air Ministry conceded that a 90-gallon drop tank would give a fighter the radius of action the Admiralty wanted. However, there were far too many variables, such as weather and duration of combat, to make the operation practicable. Comparisons could not be made with the Malta ferry flights; navigating along the North African coast was entirely different to flying across open sea.[78] The Japanese, however, seemed to be coping with the variables and nobody was going to argue that there would be navigational problems crossing the Channel.

In the summer of 1942 there was no need for the range of the available fighters to be a factor in the invasion debate. Covering an invasion did not require any great technological advance. It just needed a more open mind about how much fuel existing single-seaters could realistically carry and a willingness to make use of what was available. The quality of the available fighters should not have been a concern either. Although the Spitfire V was inferior to the opposing Luftwaffe fighters, it was nowhere near as inferior as the fighters available in the Western Desert were to the opposition they faced and Allied ground forces had still been expected to go on the offensive. Technical inferiority would also to some extent be offset by numerical superiority. There were only two German fighter wings in northern France with around 200 fighters, whereas Fighter Command could put over a thousand fighters into the air. The situation was far from ideal, but the odds were more favourable on the Channel front than any other front Allied forces were engaged on. The losses on fighter sweeps over France was scarcely encouraging, but, as fighter squadrons in the Middle East had demonstrated, a low-level tactical air battle in support of land operations was very different to an air-only struggle for air superiority at higher altitudes.

Two years should have been long enough to assemble the ground and air forces capable of regaining the ground lost in 1940. It was not long enough because there had never been any serious intention of trying to win the war by this route. The plan was to avoid this route. In terms of air resources the Channel front was at least as ready as any other theatre to go on the offensive, but there was no coming together of minds as to how these air resources might be used to support such offensive action. Even the rather sketchy plans for an invasion in 1942 were not about liberating France and winning the war; their aim was to keep the Soviet Union in the war and ultimately enable the bomber offensive to succeed. Britain still believed it was in a bomber war.

Chapter 6

The Bomber Phenomenon

With hindsight, the resurgence of the bomber strategy in 1942 might seem strange. Pre-war talk of bombers winning wars in weeks or even days now looked absurd. Bombers were killing lots of people, but there was still no evidence they could actually win wars. Following the Butt report, it required a leap of faith to imagine bombers could contribute anything to winning a war.

It had always been faith rather than evidence that had sustained the bomber advocates. It was a faith so strong it was distorting reality and defying common sense. The Air Staff had always seemed prepared to believe anything to keep their strategic bombing dream alive. Inconvenient evidence was brushed aside. Pre-war exercises had demonstrated that bombers could not be expected to hit targets by night with anything like the required accuracy, but when daylight bombing had to be abandoned it was just assumed bombing by night would work. The Blitz did not break the British people, but it was assumed the German people would crack when bombed.

When the bombing campaign was launched against oil plants in May 1940, it was claimed it would soon slow the German advance. Results were promised within weeks. Then it was months. By 1941 it was years. Despite the ever greater resources being pumped into the bomber experiment, success seemed to be receding ever further into the future. The 1941 Butt report seemed to have shattered the last remaining delusions that the bomber strategy was even remotely working. Churchill felt aggrieved that he and the country had been so seriously misled by the supposed experts.

Yet still the policy survived. Indeed, all the setbacks seemed to have surprisingly little long-term effect. The policy had not just gathered sufficient momentum to see it through these difficulties, it was actually gaining in strength. Politicians, the public and even the military were disposed to accept arguments that were at best flimsy. The Air Ministry insisted that bombing should not be judged by what it had achieved so far, but this was simply giving the policy a blank cheque.[1] On this basis, the bomber offensive need never achieve anything and continuing with it would still be justified. Over the years the argument that Britain had no choice has gained currency, but the choice between a method of waging war that was clearly working for the enemy and the bomber strategy always existed.

Everyone had their reasons to keep the bomber offensive going. For the Air Staff, an independent bombing strategy had always helped justify an independent air force. It was not in their interests to believe alternative strategies to bombing would work. The need to preserve RAF independence was dictating policy. Rather than analysing and questioning the general perception that bombers would decide wars, the Air Ministry sought to reinforce the perception. The War Office saw bombing as the only way to compensate for Britain's inferior manpower and industrial resources. Even the Admiralty could have some sympathy for a policy that, like their blockade, took years to bear fruit. Churchill needed the bomber offensive to convince Stalin that Britain was not leaving all the fighting to the Soviets. However, mere political and military expediency or departmental empire-building cannot alone explain the continuing dominance of the bomber philosophy.

It certainly cannot explain why just one apparently successful raid on a small Baltic port should revitalise the bomber project. Lübeck was destroyed, but it did not make any difference to the fighting strength of the German armed forces on any front. It did not bring the end of the war one day nearer. It was a victory because a lot of Germans were killed and a large number of homes destroyed. That this should be seen as a victory, not just by air commanders but by the entire nation, was the culmination of decades of conditioning as to what victories in modern war comprised.

Even before the outbreak of the Great War, mighty Zeppelins ensured bomber paranoia was firmly implanted in the British psyche.[2] In the First World War the British people had endured Zeppelins and Gothas. The raids may not have matched the lurid imagination of pre-1914 theorists but nevertheless men, women and children had been killed. After the First World War, the nation shuddered at the apocalyptic predictions of how much worse it would be in the next war.[3] In a democracy these fears were far more likely to be heeded by politicians and feed into government defence policy. It was a vicious circle. The terrifying talk from politicians stoked even greater fear among the public. The spectre of a country being devastated by bombing haunted politicians and public alike. The public had decades to get used to the idea that future wars would thrust civilians, men, women and children, into the firing line.

The bomber threat permeated every level of thought from grand strategy to popular culture. Wells' 1936 film *Things to Come* had graphically described the horrors of aerial bombardment. Just as with the Zeppelins of the First World War, the Wellsian nightmare proved to be an exaggeration, but the horror of nightly attacks during the Blitz was real enough. The carrying of gas masks (or at least the entreaties to carry them) was a constant reminder of how much worse it might get.

Distinguished experts were on hand to reinforce the message. Bomber theory is often associated with Giulio Douhet and his book *Command in the Air*. This had been published in many countries in the 1930s and did much to reinforce public fears abroad. However, it had never appeared in Britain. It was the most complete exposition of the theory and it is perhaps no coincidence that in 1942 an English translation of Douhet's book finally found its way into British bookshops. The British public now had a chance to read the visionary's teachings. The message was stark. Any country that did not embrace the bomber as the way to win wars was condemned to suffer annihilation from the air and defeat. For Britain's bomber policy to have the backing of such a renowned authority was reassuring. The fact that this backing came from one of the enemy, and indeed an enemy that seemed to be ignoring his teachings, made the theory all the more appealing.

As a way of taking the offensive, it was visually compelling. Unlike the complexities of mechanised warfare, it was easy to understand. Mighty Stirlings and Lancasters heading off into the night sky was a powerful, inspiring image. The bombing war could be shown with a clarity that was more difficult for battles on the ground or at sea. Cinema audiences could see the RAF winning. Newsreels showed the bombs falling on what the narrator would describe as 'industrial cities'. It looked clean and clinical, but with newsreel titles like *Terror from the Skies*, no one was in any real doubt about the consequences for the German civilians below.[4] Every opportunity was taken to underline the idea that it was essentially a bomber war. Every aircraft had to play its part. The humble Lysander was scarcely as awe-inspiring as a Lancaster or Stirling. However, after witnessing its extraordinary short take-off and landing capabilities, cinema-goers were reminded it could also carry bombs. 'The more we take the offensive, the more bombers of all kinds we shall need,' the newsreel presenter stridently proclaimed.[5]

Cinema audiences were not just reminded of the new face of war in the intervals. In the Oscar-winning *Mrs Miniver*, released in 1942, the film concludes with the local vicar reminding the survivors of a recent bombing attack, and indeed the watching audience, that this was 'a war of the people; all the people' being fought in the cities as well as the battlefields. Men, women and children were all combatants and casualties had to be accepted as the price for ultimate victory. In the Second World War there was none of the outrage the 'baby-killing' Zeppelins of the First World War had provoked, just a fatalistic acceptance that this was how wars were now fought. In the latest Sherlock Holmes film, *Sherlock and the Secret Weapon*, Britain's intrepid detective had the task of ensuring a Swiss inventor of an astonishing new war-winning weapon did not fall into German hands, along with his invention. The secret weapon was not some new devilish way to destroy tanks or sink submarines – it was a bomb-aiming device that would turn Bomber Command into an even more fearsome force.

The British public were conditioned to believe the bomber would decide the war, just as a future generation were led to believe wars would be decided by atomic bombs. With an entire nation – military, politicians and public – all consumed by the bomber, it is perhaps not such a great surprise that, despite its problems and the clear evidence the war was being decided by other methods, the bomber strand of Britain's military strategy survived. Even when the strategy was failing, the few who saw the flaws in the bomber policy had to overcome three decades of presumption that this was how future wars would be fought and won. It was not a policy forced on a reluctant country by devious Air Force leaders or ruthless politicians, it was a policy that the nation readily accepted. When Lübeck was destroyed, the nation rejoiced.

The Lübeck raid was followed in April by an attack on Rostock, another easy-to-find coastal town. Over four nights, 531 sorties were flown against the German port. While there really were no worthwhile industrial targets in Lübeck, Rostock could at least claim the Heinkel factory in the southern suburbs. This was the target for some of the bombers, but so was the centre of the historic town. Sixty per cent was flattened. This and the Lübeck raid were quite justifiably described as 'terror raids' by German propaganda and an infuriated Hitler ordered retaliation.

In words strikingly similar to the instructions recently given to Bomber Command, Hitler ordered that priority should go to targets 'where attacks are likely to have the greatest possible effect on civilian life'.[6] In practice, Hitler wanted towns, like Lübeck, of low economic but high cultural or historic value, to be targeted. Baron Gustaf Braun von Stumm at the German Foreign Office is credited with suggesting suitable targets could be plucked from Baedeker tourist guides and this gave the series of raids its name. Like Lübeck, such towns had very little anti-aircraft defence and, with no barrage balloon cables to worry about, bombers could fly as low as they liked.

After a false start on the night of 23/24 April against Exeter, when only one bomber got its bombs within the city boundaries, the Luftwaffe was soon dispensing terror on the Lübeck scale. The following night, the Luftwaffe returned to Exeter. Fifty bombers in two waves killed seventy-three and injured fifty-four. On the following two nights, Bath was the target with 380 killed. Norwich was next on the Baedeker list with over 200 killed in two concentrated attacks in three days. Eighty died in the raid on York on 28/29 April. In a week the death toll had reached 750. In the same period, four Bomber Command raids on Rostock killed 200 German civilians. The Luftwaffe was proving it was better at killing people than Bomber Command.

Through the prism of Air Staff thinking, the Baedeker raids were a German attempt to replicate Bomber Command's war-winning strategy. This was not the case. There was never any expectation that these raids would change the course of the war. The German aim was to demonstrate that targeting German civilians would just bring reprisals, and therefore there was nothing to be gained for either side by continuing the policy. By killing civilians and destroying homes, the Luftwaffe had achieved its aim.

Any hope that Hitler had that this might demonstrate the pointlessness of bombing unimportant, undefended towns never had any chance of success. For the Luftwaffe, the Baedeker raids were a distraction from the more useful roles their aircraft were performing. Aircraft on minelaying duties, units bombing Malta and even training units were thrown into the offensive. It was a very improvised response. For Bomber Command the Lübeck raid was a stepping stone to victory. Bombing cities was not a distraction from more useful applications of airpower; this was what the RAF had been set up to do.

The destruction of the strategically unimportant Lübeck was just a dress rehearsal for what would be visited on more strategically important German cities. These might contain more important industrial objectives, but hitting these was, as far as Harris was concerned, still only a useful bonus. Residential, not industrial, areas were the target. The aim of the area bombing strategy was to break the will of the German people.

British civilian deaths were part of the price the country would have to pay in this 'people's war'. It might seem callous, but even a thousand deaths in a week was just a tiny fraction of the horrendous casualties that had been predicted before the war. The pre-war doom-mongers had made the price being paid seem far more acceptable.

The Baedeker raids could never have deterred an Air Staff so committed to the bomber doctrine, but they should have provided food for thought on how successful it was likely to be. The German raids had inflicted heavy loss of life, but, as the Blitz of the previous winter had already demonstrated, this had not provoked any pressure on the government to seek a peace with Nazi Germany. RAF night-fighters were also notching up an impressive number of victories, reinforcing the message that darkness did not provide as much protection as expected, as so many Bomber Command aircrews had already discovered to their cost.

With both sides resorting to area bombing, there was less need for the accuracy manned bombers can at least attempt. Hitler started taking more interest in weapons that could deliver retaliation more efficiently. The Army was developing von Braun's rocket-powered A-4 missile and the Air Force the pulse-jet-powered Fieseler Fi 103 pilotless aircraft. Previously, these had been considered far too inaccurate to be of much use. However, if revenge was all that was required, these indiscriminate weapons were a much better way of dispensing it than bombers requiring highly trained crews.

The logic was indisputable. In 1941 Britain, using the same reasoning, had briefly considered restarting its pilotless weapons programme. An argument against had been that the country was already too heavily committed to the manned approach. Germany was not so committed. The industrial resources the German pilotless aircraft and missile programme required arguably meant a diversion from more useful weapons' programmes, but it was nothing like the proportion of industrial and scientific resources the British bomber strategy had been absorbing for decades. It was also giving Germany a head start in technologies that would be crucial in future weapon development. The huge effort poured into building heavy bombers based on mid-1930s' technology was accelerating the development in Germany of cutting edge missile and guidance technology.

Harris knew he had to do a lot better than torching medieval towns if the bomber strategy was to justify the resources being poured into it. The Air Ministry and RAF had always had the knack of capturing the imagination of the nation in a way the Navy and, in particular, the Army had found it more difficult to do. Putting one thousand bombers over a major German city was something the newsreels and propaganda machine would be able to exploit to the full. At the time, the front-line strength of Bomber Command was nowhere near 1,000 planes. To achieve the magic number, any plane that could carry a bomb would have to be thrown in, with some flown by instructors and even the more advanced pupils from training units. Even if they just headed in the general direction of Germany and came back without their bombs, that would count. On 30/31 May 1942, 1,103 aircraft set course for Cologne. Once again a high degree of concentration was achieved. Cologne was a more modern city than Rostock or Lübeck; there was no preponderance of easily inflammable wooden buildings so there was no similar conflagration. Nevertheless, nearly 20,000 homes were destroyed or seriously damaged and nearly 500 civilians were killed. Most of all, however, the first 'thousand bomber raid' was a huge media triumph.

Harris enthused the nation in newsreel and radio broadcasts. One thousand bombers would not be possible every night, 'not yet' at least he ominously added, but that was the direction the bomber offensive was going.

> When the storm bursts over Germany they will look back to the days of Lübeck and Rostock and Cologne as a man caught in the blasts of the hurricane will look back to the gentle zephyrs of last summer.[7]

It was stirring rhetoric that the Army and Royal Navy could not match. Biblical references to Germans sowing the wind and reaping the whirlwind were what the British public wanted to hear. Wavell and other army commanders around the world, struggling to contain German and Japanese advances with inadequate air support, were less impressed. While they struggled, Harris was promising victory.

> There are a lot of people who say that bombing can never win a war. Well, my answer to that is that it has never been tried yet, and we shall see.[8]

In fact it had been tried and there had not even been the slightest hint that it could win a war. The Germans had tried in the First World War with Zeppelins and Gothas. The bomb loads dropped may have been smaller but, for a less prepared public, the shock and outrage was far greater.

The government was put under enormous pressure to do something, but no one was suggesting surrender; the call was for retaliation. The pressure on the government was so great that, in the throes of a world war, the Royal Air Force was created to deliver this, but it too failed to intimidate the people it bombed.[9] Fifteen years later the aircraft were more advanced, more bombs could be dropped and more people could be killed. But defences were stronger; countries and people were better organised and prepared. Surrender was not a realistic option. For civilians on both sides it was not so obvious that there was any point in submitting to a foreign power that used such brutal methods.

Harris, however, was convinced he would succeed where others had failed. An overstretched Germany 'will make a most interesting initial experiment', Harris assured the British public. 'Japan will provide the confirmation.'[10] It was bold, ear-catching rhetoric, but there were no plans for Britain to make any effort to play any part in this 'confirmation'. When Japan launched its attack on British possessions in the Far East, the Joint Planning Staff (Captain Charles Lambe, Brigadier Guy Stewart and Air Commodore William Elliot at the time) came up with five methods by which Japan might be defeated. One of these was the 'heavy and sustained bombing of industrial areas in Japan from shore bases'. How this might be even attempted was not clear. It could only be done from bases in the Soviet Union, but that country was not at war with Japan.[11] Britain had never even tried to develop the bombers that might attempt such an offensive from British-held territory. For all their fervour, the British Air Staff had never taken their thinking to its logical conclusion.

The Americans had. They were not put off by the enormous technical challenges of developing inter-continental bombers. They already had a mock-up of their six-engined Consolidated (Convair) B-36 which, it was hoped, would have a 10,000 mile range, putting targets 4,000 miles away within reach. This would enable it to target Berlin from the United States or attack cities in Japan from Hawaii or Alaska. It was technically extremely ambitious and perhaps operationally impossible, but the Americans were determined to apply bomber theory to any potential enemy.

The Air Ministry had no such ambitions. In 1936, any idea of a bombing offensive against Japan was specifically ruled out because of the enormous distance from British bases.[12] In the late 1930s Vickers had put forward some huge six-engined bomber proposals, with ranges of around 5,000 miles with an impressive 10,000lb bomb load, sufficient to reach Moscow from Britain and possibly even Japan from bases in Burma, the closest reasonably secure British possession. Harris for one, believed these were precisely what the RAF needed to meet its European and colonial commitments, but the Air Ministry considered it too futuristic.[13]

In 1941, Vickers had come up with a less ambitious six-engine proposal designed to carry a ten-ton bomb (the future 'Grand Slam' earthquake bomb) to a target 1,800 miles away. With a smaller bomb load, this would have been capable of reaching Japan from Burma. It would have led to something in the same league as the American Boeing B-29. With Japan in the war, such an aircraft might have been the basis for the sort of bomber Harris would need for his 'confirmation', but four weeks after Japan attacked, Vickers was told continuing the project was 'not, in present circumstances, justified'.[14] Harris's ambitious plans for bomber theory were not part of Air Staff thinking. In the current conflict, only substantial advances on land could get RAF bombers within range of Japan even to attempt to provide Harris's 'confirmation'. For the British, in the Far East a bomber offensive against Japan was not an option; the war there would have to be won by other means.

Much to Harris's dismay, there was now growing momentum to win the war by other means in Europe as well. When Churchill showed Harris plans for a possible landing in France, his bomber commander was stirred to write a passionate defence of his alternative strategy.[15] He did not waste time getting to the point. 'Victory, speedy and complete, awaits the side which first employs air power as it should be employed' was his opening line. What followed was a complete rewriting of history.

Harris insisted that the Battle of Britain had been a strategic air offensive against the country. Once again, German air policy was being seen through the prism of Air Ministry bombing theory. Neither cities nor industry had been the primary target in the summer of 1940. The daylight offensive was an attack on Fighter Command as a prelude to an invasion. The object was to gain air superiority over the beaches the German forces would be landing on, not defeat the country. Nevertheless, Harris insisted the Luftwaffe had tried to win the war on its own and had only missed victory by 'a hair's breadth'. Harris would have been on stronger ground claiming the subsequent night offensive was an attempt to defeat Britain but even here, no one would suggest the Blitz had come anywhere near succeeding.

Since then, Harris went on, the Luftwaffe had become 'entangled in the meshes of vast land campaigns' from which Germany now found it impossible to extract her air forces for 'strategically proper application'.

All this, he declared was 'historical fact'. Britain now faced that same choice and mustn't make the same mistake. 'Involvement in land campaigns, especially continental campaigns, serves but to reduce us to the level of the Horde. We are not Horde … our lead … is in brains not brawn.'[16] It was perhaps an unfortunate turn of phrase to defend a policy that relied on indiscriminate brute force.

> It is a fact that the only substantial successes that we have achieved in this war, apart from the destruction of the Von [*sic*] Spee, have been entirely or chiefly due to air power. When the Army has met any but the Italian enemy it has invariably been defeated. Norway, France, Greece, Crete, Malaya and Burma. (*sic*) Even in Libya where a lavish provision of sea and air power has limited the enemy's resources, when he, not we, has been at the disadvantage, we have failed after 18 months to obtain a decisive success.[17]

As Churchill read this he might have recalled the scathing criticism Portal had laid at Brooke's door for overlooking the success of the Crusader offensive. It was by any standard an extraordinary analysis. But Harris was not alone in failing to see that the resources sucked into the bomber offensive, and the mindset that saw the bomber as the only correct use of air power, had been a major factor in the string of defeats he took such pleasure in listing.

Harris insisted that, at best, with the help of Russian and American armies and uprisings throughout Europe, 'in the very long run' victory might be gained with conventional armies but only after the slaughter of Britain's youth in the mud of Flanders and France. That was the best case scenario, Harris warned. At worst, military intervention on the continent would end in another Dunkirk. To win the war, Britain had 'to abandon the disastrous policy of military intervention in the land campaigns of Europe'.

> We are displaying a growing inclination to revert to old and archaic methods of war, wilfully to reduce ourselves to the level of the Horde by engaging in Continental gladiatorial combat. Such a decision history will show to have been grievously wrong. We need now only the wisdom and the courage to make a decision which both swift event and history will show to be right.[18]

For anyone thinking of straying from the bomber path, reminding them of the horror of trench warfare was always a good tactic. Dunkirk was another useful topic to raise.

To win the war his way, Harris needed more bombers and he was not short of ideas about where they should come from. Coastal Command was almost as strong as Bomber Command and equipped mostly with the sort of aircraft he needed, yet, he claimed, it had contributed almost nothing to the war effort. The damage Bomber Command had inflicted on submarine production in the last three months as a 'side line' to its main task of destroying cities was far more than Coastal Command had achieved in the entire war. The bombers he had lent Coastal Command were just being used 'to bolster further the already over-swollen establishments of the purely defensive Coastal Command'. It is difficult to imagine a commander in the Army or Navy being so rabid, not just about the contribution of sister services but also about a branch of their own service. 'Coastal Command is therefore merely an obstacle to victory', he dogmatically concluded.

The return of the bombers he had lent Coastal Command might result in the loss of a few more ships, he conceded, but these ships would not even be needed if Britain stopped sending armies overseas. The Middle East and Far East should also return their bombers. The Americans and Soviets should be asked to send all their bomber crews and bombers to the UK and the United States instructed that in future the RAF only wanted bombers. Such a force 'could during the next year, beyond any shadow of doubt, grind into dust and ashes a sufficiency of the enemy's major cities and resources to make the further prosecution of the war impossible to him'.[19]

The results of recent bombing was the proof 'for all but the wilfully blind to see' that bombing 'is the only course offering either a quick or a certain victory'. Harris feared that if those wanting to invade France got their way, 'our last bomb will have been dropped on Germany' and the RAF would be forced to support the Army. A continental landing 'will deprive us of the obvious, the only, the best and indeed hitherto agreed means to victory'. It was decision time, he told Churchill. 'We are now at the cross roads.'

It was decision time indeed. The reality was that until the RAF became 'entangled in the meshes' of a land campaign, victory was forever going to be a very distant prospect. Indeed, without a military intervention in Europe, Britain would in all probability have to accept as a permanent arrangement either Nazi Germany or a potentially hostile Soviet Union as her immediate neighbour and the dominant European power.

Harris kept up the barrage with a further note to the Prime Minister towards the end of June. In it he listed all the ways in which his Command was helping to win the war. Ironically, he relied heavily on the tactical uses his Command had been forced to carry out, against the wishes of the Air Staff and bomber commanders. In 1940 it had stopped the invasion by bombing the invasion barges. In 1941 it had helped win the Battle of the Atlantic by bombing German battleships in French ports. Bomber Command squadrons flying from Malta had also helped the armies in the Middle East by bombing Axis convoys. In reality, only the last of these could be considered an unqualified success.

Harris listed all the factories inside Germany 'known' to have been destroyed. The bombing of the Heinkel factory at Rostock was having 'the most serious effects on the enemy's air operations on all fronts' and attacks on other factories had deprived ten to eleven motorised divisions of the armoured fighting vehicles they required. He would do even better if he got back the twenty-four bomber squadrons lent to Coastal Command and the Middle East.[20] Never afraid to take the law into his own hands, he had already sent what Tedder described as 'three pages of hysterical verbosity' in which he complained that of the thousand bomber crews despatched by Bomber Command Operational Training Units to the Middle East, hardly any had come back.[21] Harris spoke of Coastal Command being 'an obstacle to victory', but in truth he believed the entire war was getting in his way.

Trenchard weighed in with his own personal note to the Prime Minister. 'The risk is that we shall try to go down two roads,' he ventured. Britain and the United States did not have the industrial resources to create the sort of Army that would be needed to defeat Germany, he continued. It would be foolish to take on the Germans in the one area, their Army, where they were stronger. Attempting to do so would mean that Britain would get 'inextricably entangled in large schemes and protracted operations of two dimensional warfare'. The Germans had won early victories in the war with their 'tank blitz', 'we can smash the German machine by the "bomber blitz"'.[22] The obvious flaw in Trenchard's analysis was that, so far, the 'bomber blitz' had not achieved much and the German 'tank blitz' had.

Trenchard insisted that getting involved in Germany's 'two-dimensional' First World War approach would extend the war and cost millions of lives. War in the third dimension was the way forward. In fact with airpower an essential ingredient of the blitzkrieg, the German method was very three-dimensional. Trenchard's bombers may be flying in three-dimensional space, but the actual strategy was very one-dimensional. As far as Trenchard and Harris were concerned, it was just a question of dropping bombs on cities until the German people had the good sense to surrender.

Churchill felt both Harris and Trenchard were 'spoil[ing] a good case by overstating it'. Significantly, Churchill still believed it was essentially 'a good case'. Although he no longer believed bombing alone could win the war, he had moved some way from his position the previous autumn, when the best he could hope for was that the bomber offensive would become a 'seriously increasing annoyance'.[23] Indeed, Churchill was now rather concerned by others expressing similarly pessimistic views.

It was scarcely true for the United States but Trenchard was right about Britain not having the resources to create the sort of Air Force he and Harris wanted, and at the same time the Army and the tactical air force that would eventually be needed. Yet Harris and Trenchard could scarcely complain about the effort Britain was putting into bomber production. This might not be so obvious from the numbers of aircraft being built, but long-range bombers require far more man hours and resources to build than other types. Output in terms of aircraft weight provided a more accurate picture of where the country's efforts were being focused. At the beginning of 1942, half the aircraft industry's output by weight was already heavy and medium night bombers, and the proportion was increasing. The rest had to meet all the RAF's other requirements (light bombers, fighters, naval aircraft, trainers etc.).[24] Harris and Trenchard were getting the priority they wanted. Harris might not be getting all the bombers being built, but the only way he could get more was by further weakening other branches of the armed forces.

Churchill was sympathetic and was determined to give the bomber offensive every chance of succeeding. He firmly resisted calls to move more of Bomber Command's resources overseas. He badgered the Air Ministry and MAP over the slow progress towards the introduction of the latest navigational aids, especially the radar-mapping H2S which would make navigation so much easier. He urged better training for aircrews, and demanded more and better bombs be delivered. There were no such clarion calls for the training and equipment a tactical air force would require.

Despite Harris's and Trenchard's fears, the bomber bandwagon was in fact gaining ever more momentum. While the War Office, and indeed Churchill, were finding all sorts of problems with the proposed cross-Channel invasion of France, Bomber Command was making light of its problems, taking bold action and achieving eye-catching results. Harris inspired loyalty in all around him. Lieutenant Colonel Charles Carrington, the Army's liaison officer at Bomber Command, was doing his utmost to spread the word for the need for a powerful tactical bomber force, but even he was enthralled by the thousand-bomber raid on Cologne and stoutly defended the area bombing policy. He even hailed the Lancaster as the best bomber any country produced in the Second World War. It was a remarkable accolade from an Army officer for an aircraft that was the very antithesis of what the Army needed.[25] It was a measure of how smitten by the bomber policy even ardent advocates of tactical air support could become.

Harris was well aware he needed to convince those beyond his immediate circle and organised a very slick public relations operation. In his radio and newsreel appearances, he bristled with a confidence that no one in the Army or Navy could match, at least not until Montgomery arrived with his own brand of dogmatic certainty. Harris entertained dignitaries in his country home where they were invited into his 'conversion chamber' where they could view carefully selected stereoscopic images of the damage the bombing was causing. This 'missionary work', as he called it, was an expensive business, which, Harris was not slow to point out to his superiors, was not covered by his £25 a month entertainment allowance.[26] It might be draining him financially but he believed it was money well spent.

Similar displays were on show at open days in Whitehall, organised for all serving personnel but aimed principally at any top brass more reluctant to accept his homely hospitality.[27] The images on display were specially chosen to emphasise damage to industry. Whether this was a cynical ploy to mislead or a genuine act of wishful thinking was probably not clear in Harris's own mind. He was just as ruthless about promoting his policy as he was putting it in to practice. For Harris, the end would always justify the means.

American long-range bombers were beginning to assemble in the United Kingdom to join the offensive against Germany. Like Harris, Americans were also engaged in a slick campaign promoting their daylight-bombing policy.[28] The bombing campaign was attracting all the attention. There was certainly no evidence from the Middle East that the Army was achieving decisive results and plenty of evidence that defeating the German Army was still a very daunting task. Some questioned the ability and even the desire of the Army to achieve anything. Bomber Command had restored its reputation. Now the British Army had to do likewise.

Chapter 7

Crisis in the Desert

Rommel's counter-attack in January 1942 had recovered half the ground gained in the 1941 Crusader offensive. There followed an uneasy pause as both sides built up their resources as quickly as possible in the hope of getting their next blow in first. With the Far East making huge and very justifiable demands on what was available, this would be an uphill struggle for the Commonwealth forces in the Western Desert.

On the Allied side, the lessons of Crusader were absorbed and units reinforced. The Blenheim IV could no longer be considered a front-line day bomber but replacement Boston and Baltimores were slow to arrive. After initial problems with its Cyclone engines in the harsh desert environment, the Boston III was turning into one of the most reliable planes in the command. The Baltimores were an improvement on the Maryland, although Tedder was disappointed by the plane's lower range, a complaint which perhaps gave an indication of where Tedder felt his bombers could be best used. On its first operational mission, four Baltimores set off without a fighter escort; they were intercepted by Bf 109s and three were shot down. There were extenuating circumstances; the rear guns of some of the Baltimores involved had jammed during the action, but future missions would be escorted.[1] Every new design seemed to revive hopes that bombers could defeat the enemy fighters sent up to shoot them down. Each time the lesson that fighter support was required had to be relearned.

The Boston and Baltimore were to become the standard Allied light bombers. Initially, the idea was to use the few remaining Blenheims for night bombing, but the Blenheim IV was not particularly suited to this role. The Far East desperately needed reinforcements, so most of the remaining Blenheim squadrons were transferred there, where it was hoped they could continue to operate by day against the supposedly weaker Japanese opposition. It was perhaps a reasonable decision – there were no easy decisions when such limited resources had to serve two theatres – but it reduced the potential to expand the light-bomber force in the Western Desert. By May 1942 only one squadron had converted to Baltimores and along with two Boston squadrons constituted the entire Desert Air Force light-bomber force.

The Blenheims were not the only aircraft Tedder was sending to the Far East. In all, some 450 aircraft were transferred from the Middle East. Taking his cue from Air Ministry policy towards the Middle East, it was now Tedder's turn to off-load his second-best equipment. The Air Ministry instructed him to send Hurricanes IIs, but Tedder sent Hurricane Is, arguing they would be perfectly adequate against inferior Japanese fighters. Nobody was taking the Japanese fighter force seriously. Portal did not seem to dispute this argument. Indeed, using the same reasoning, he wondered if the forty-six Gladiators in the Middle East might be sent as well, but Tedder decided that those that were still flyable were so old they would probably break down on the way. Pilots would be spared the daunting task of taking on Zeros in worn-out Gladiators.[2]

Bomber Command was not just sucking in the resources overseas commands needed, it was draining away what little Tedder had. Harris's demand that Bomber Command crews be returned left Tedder bemused. He saw no reason why any should be 'returned' and the ones who had been lost in action could clearly not be 'returned'. However, Portal ordered Tedder to send sixty Wellington crews back to the United Kingdom, further reducing his front-line strength.

Everyone in Britain seemed to be convinced that the Middle East was just a bottomless pit of waste. Douglas wanted assurances from Tedder that the pilots Fighter Command was sending each month were not sitting around in the rear doing nothing for lack of aircraft. Douglas was right: there was a shortage of fighters, but it was Douglas's determination to make sure not too many went to the Middle East that was part of the problem. The solution was scarcely to restore equilibrium by matching the shortage of planes with a shortage of pilots.

The arrival of fighter-bombers made up to a large extent for the weak light-bomber force. The Kittyhawk could carry a drop tank or a bomb. In March 1942, No. 112 Squadron successfully carried out trials with a Kittyhawk carrying a single 250lb bomb and this unit became the first official Kittyhawk fighter-bomber squadron.[3] Ventrally mounted bombs were likely to hit the propeller if the plane was dive-bombing so Middle East Command improvised their own bomb racks, carrying one 250lb bomb under each wing. One of the Hurricane II squadrons was also equipped with aircraft adapted to carry 250lb bombs under the wings. Indeed Tedder wanted all fighters to be capable of carrying bombs; only the shortage of bomb racks prevented this from being immediately implemented. In April, the first Hurricane IID tankbusters, armed with two 40mm cannon, arrived in the Middle East and No. 6 Squadron began re-equipping with the plane. Light bombers still had a role to play. They could operate by night and in less than ideal weather and, unlike heavy bombers, could (in the right circumstances) attack at low altitudes. However, as Portal suggested, they had to a large extent been replaced by the fighter-bomber.

Tactically, fighters were now organised in wings of four to six squadrons. Pilots were encouraged to adopt looser four- and six-plane formations, but these were far from universally accepted and it would still be some time before Allied fighter tactics matched those of their German opponents.[4] The quality of the fighters available was still a major problem. Kittyhawks were only coming through in limited numbers and, although superior to the Hurricane II, were no match for the Bf 109F. Coningham was anxious to get something better, but there was little pressure on London from Tedder. The first tropicalised Spitfire was tested in December 1941 and the plan was to deliver seventy tropicalised Spitfire Vs a month. Nos 145 and 92 Squadrons would be the first two Spitfire squadrons to go to the Middle East. The next question was where in the Middle East? Coningham was not the only commander who needed better fighters.

Malta's air defences were creaking. At the beginning of 1942 they consisted of elements from five Hurricane II day squadrons and a night-fighter flight, with around eighty Hurricanes in all. The weight of Axis attack was only moderate compared to some of the previous Axis efforts, but even this had pushed the defences to the limit. In February, Middle East HQ reported that losses had become so heavy that Malta was becoming a liability.[5] By the beginning of March, there were just twenty-one Hurricanes left on the island and most of the Wellingtons, Albacores and Blenheims had also been destroyed.[6]

If Malta was going to be a base for operations against Axis convoys the island had to have priority with Spitfire deliveries. The British Army would have to wait a little longer for the protection Britain's best fighter could offer. On 7 March 1942, fifteen Spitfires, with 90-gallon slipper tanks, were flown off the aircraft carrier HMS *Eagle* and headed for Malta. They landed without incident and, three days later, some two and a half years after the outbreak of war, Spitfire fighters flew their first fighter sorties from a base outside the United Kingdom.

The Spitfires arrived just in time to counter a major escalation in Luftwaffe attacks. The number of day bombing sorties tripled in March and increased a further fivefold in April. It was a rerun of the Battle of Britain, in miniature; a desperate battle for control of the skies with the prospect of an invasion if the British fighters lost their battle. The four radar stations on the island provided the early warning and directed the fighters to the approaching enemy, and the four airfields the fighters were operating from were the main targets. As in the Battle of Britain, combat with fighters was to be avoided if at all possible; pilots were told to focus on the bombers. It was easier said than done. Initially, all the Spitfires could do was to try and protect the vulnerable Hurricanes.

Even against bombers, the Hurricane was beginning to struggle. Dispirited pilots often found they lacked the speed to close in on the Ju 88s. The Hurricanes armed with four cannon had more than enough firepower; indeed two of the cannon were usually removed in order to reduce weight and squeeze a little more performance out of the fighter. However, machine-gun-armed Hurricanes found it difficult to make much impression on the well-protected German bombers. The Spitfires could not always provide the protection they needed and were themselves often struggling against the Macchi C.202 and Bf 109F.

Another nine Spitfires arrived on 21 March, followed by seven more on the 29th. Even these small reinforcements noticeably stiffened the defences of the island and the Germans were determined to nip any further reinforcements in the bud. For the next major convoy on 20 April, the USS *Wasp* flew off forty-seven Spitfires to the island. The Luftwaffe closely monitored the approach of the convoy and launched fierce attacks on the airfields as the reinforcements landed. A dozen or so were immediately destroyed or damaged and those that survived were found to be in poor condition with non-functioning radios and guns incorrectly aligned. Ground crews worked through the night, but by next morning the island could still only muster twenty-one serviceable Spitfires. Air Vice-Marshal Hugh Lloyd, commanding RAF units on Malta, was furious at the condition of the fighters and demanded future deliveries arrive ready to use. He was also none too pleased with the pilots' level of experience. No. 601 Squadron had just converted from Airacobras to Spitfires, and the pilots were scarcely familiar with their new equipment. Seven of its twenty-three pilots had no operational experience whatsoever.

For the next consignment an effort was at least made to get the technical side right. On 9 May, sixty Spitfires made it to the island and this time they would be as ready as they could be for combat. Many of them arrived while a raid was underway, with some being pursued by ground-strafing Messerschmitts as they tried to land. Each Spitfire was taxied to a pen where ground crew stood ready to refuel and re-arm the plane. A pilot stood by to replace the one who had flown the plane in. In less than ten minutes the aircraft was ready to be scrambled. Despite fierce fighting, the defenders still had around fifty serviceable Spitfires at the end of the day.

The fighter force was now predominantly Spitfire, and Luftwaffe losses were rising. By mid-May some 150 Spitfires had reached Malta, providing the island with a reasonable degree of security. The Spitfire V might be inferior to the Bf 109F but it was a huge advance on the Hurricane. Its arrival transformed the fortunes of the defence, and in the process underlined the enormous handicap the RAF had been operating under in so many previous campaigns. Holding on to Malta was proving to be an expensive business, but fighters are built to be used. The way to deal with Spitfire losses was to build more, not restrict their use. Other fronts were in just as much need as Malta, but so few were being allowed to leave the United Kingdom the island was absorbing nearly all of the Middle East Spitfire quota. The first Spitfire unit, No. 145 Squadron, did not reach the Western Desert until 30 April, and only became operational a month later. The Far East was still waiting.

Malta had weathered the storm. In 1940, in the Battle of Britain, it had been the arrival of autumn that had signalled a lessening in the pressure. Over Malta it was the arrival of summer, as German units dispersed to more important fronts. It was a sign of the changing times. Before the invasion of the Soviet Union, the Luftwaffe had been able to focus as much of its air strength as was required on any front it chose. Now, with the failure to inflict a quick defeat on the Soviet Union, the Luftwaffe was being pulled one way then the other. Rommel needed air support, the Luftwaffe was playing a vital role in the Atlantic, night defence of the Reich was a growing need, Hitler was demanding retaliation against British cities and, most significantly of all, the Soviet Air Force on the Eastern Front was growing in effectiveness with each passing month. Even without an active front on the ground in Western Europe, the Luftwaffe was not capable of meeting all the demands being made of it.

Some of the units attacking Malta were transferred to the Western Desert to support Rommel. The Germans realised that suppressing Malta by air attack was not a long-term solution; the island had to be occupied. However, Rommel was expecting the British to strike soon and feared the worst unless he got his blow in first. A spoiling attack would disrupt British plans and indeed Rommel planned no more than that. The air reinforcements he had received were only supposed to be temporary. As soon as the British threat had been neutralised, it was planned to switch forces back to Malta, invade the island (Operation Mercury) and eliminate the threat once and for all. Only then would Rommel push on towards Egypt.

On paper the RAF in the Middle East had expanded; sixty-one squadrons were available in the region compared to fifty at the time of the Crusader offensive the previous November. However, many were in the rear awaiting re-equipment. While for Crusader the total number of aircraft available exceeded the theoretical front-line strength of the squadrons, in May 1942 many of the units at the front were under strength. The single-seater fighter force in the Mediterranean theatre had expanded from twenty-five to thirty squadrons. Eight of these were equipped or re-equipping with the Spitfire, but most of these were in Malta. There were only eight serviceable Spitfires in Egypt and only one squadron, No. 145, was anywhere near ready to begin operations. With the fighting over Malta absorbing most of the tropicalised Spitfires, and forty-eight due to be shipped out to Australia to defend Darwin, there was little prospect of the situation improving.

There were thirteen fighter squadrons in the forward area in the Western Desert in May 1942, one less than for the start of Crusader. This figure included the non-operational Spitfire-equipped No. 145 Squadron. The Baltimore squadron was about to be withdrawn to sort out the problems with its guns, leaving just two Boston day-bomber squadrons. This was seven squadrons fewer than the number available for the Crusader offensive the previous November. The number of Wellington squadrons had increased from five to nine, although actual front-line strength was about the same. Two of the Wellington squadrons were for naval operations, one of them was equipped with air-to-surface radar for maritime reconnaissance and the other was a torpedo-bomber squadron. All in all, the total bomber force was smaller and a smaller proportion was available for daylight operations.

The overall quality of the Desert Air Force had improved. The Blenheim IV and Hurricane I had disappeared from the front line and there was a flight of photo-reconnaissance Spitfires. Even so, the gap in quality between Allied and Axis forces remained. Whereas the RAF had mustered some 700 planes for Crusader, only around 400 were available to oppose Rommel's assault. With the Axis air forces operating around 600 aircraft

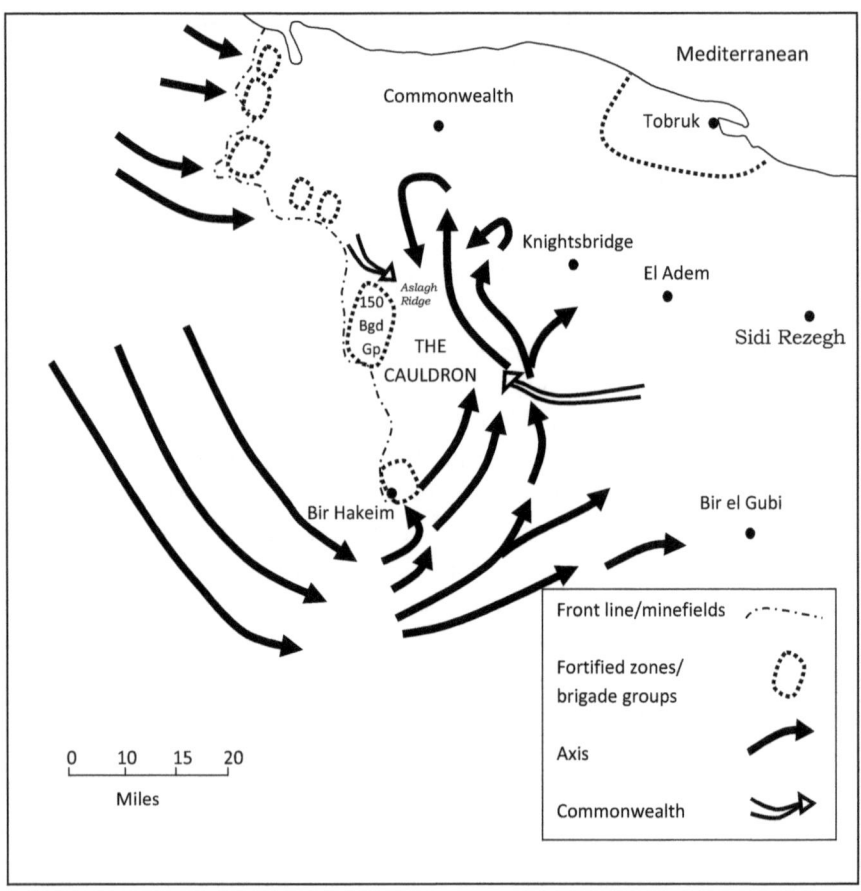

close to the front, the tables were very much turned. Tedder's determination not to upset his masters in London by asking for more was not helping the Desert Air Force's cause.

On 26 May 1942, Rommel launched his attack. The Commonwealth defences consisted of continuous minefields as far south as Bir Hakeim, These were backed up by closely packed brigade group strongpoints on the northern sector of the line, with more spaced-out brigade groups to the south. While Axis forces pinned down the main Allied forces in the north, Rommel tried to outflank the Allied defences by swinging south of the Free French forces at Bir Hakeim. He then began working his way north behind the Commonwealth fortified positions and minefields. Initially, the Luftwaffe managed between 300 and 350 sorties a day, mostly fighter and dive-bomber. The Italian Air Force contributed a little more than

100 sorties daily, nearly all fighter, flown by Macchi C.202s and ground attack missions flown by older Macchi C.200s and Fiat C.R.42s.

On the opening day, Boston squadrons, supported by around one hundred strafing and fighter-bomber attacks, hit concentrations of enemy transport heading for Bir el Gubi, the 90th Light Division suffering particularly heavy losses. These attacks continued on the 27th, mainly on the eastern flank of Rommel's advance northwards, the 15th Panzer division, advancing towards El Adem, being especially hard hit. Meanwhile, Rommel's main force established itself in the Knightsbridge area, to the rear of the main Allied defensive line and behind the 150 Brigade Group. Rommel had not been aware of the existence of this force and it was blocking the crucial supply lines he was trying to establish through the minefields. The main role of the fighters was supposed to be to deal with the Ju 87 dive-bombers, which invariably meant taking on their escorts. However, on the 28th, the Army appealed for more close support to slow Rommel's advance. With Commonwealth fighters performing better at lower altitudes, Cross, commanding the Commonwealth fighter force, had no qualms about obliging.

The main targets were now in Rommel's precarious bridgehead to the rear of the 150 Brigade Group, an area which soon became known as the 'Cauldron'. The Desert Air Force was still relying for the most part on aerial reconnaissance for targets, which tended to pick out the German tanks roaming eastwards, which were not necessarily key in the battle. On the first three days of the German offensive there were twenty-nine reports from aircraft of suitable targets for air strikes, compared to ten requests for support from the Army Air Support Controls attached to forward troops. In all there were thirty-five operations, amounting to around 250 sorties. The response time was reasonable, with requested air strikes arriving on average in around an hour, with some arriving as quickly as 30 to 40 minutes, a vast improvement on the three hours that was common in the Crusader operation. On the 29th, Rommel's forces had pushed as far north as the area known as the 'Commonwealth'. Most missions flown this day were in response to requests from Army Air Support Controls. Even the light bombers were involved in close support, a pre-planned strike by Bostons assisting in the capture of a German position in the 'Commonwealth' area.

Despite Rommel's rapid progress and the threatening positions his forces had taken up in the Allied rear, their position was far from secure. They had already suffered heavy tank losses in skirmishes with British armour and were also desperately short of supplies. The 150 Brigade Group and the French stronghold at Bir Hakeim were both preventing supplies getting to Rommel. Only very tenuous paths had been cleared through the minefields around the 150 Brigade and these became the focus for Allied fighters on the 30th.

Commonwealth losses among the low-flying fighter squadrons were beginning to rise as the German fighters began to make inroads. Twelve were lost on the 30th from around 200 sorties, another sixteen from 170 sorties flown on the 31st, while the Germans lost just three fighters and two dive-bombers. The low-flying fighters were doing some excellent work, but the absence of a high quality fighter to control the skies above them was sorely felt. In the first full five days of operations, fifty Allied fighters failed to return, about one fifth of the number available at the start of the offensive. With reserves, in particular the Kittyhawk, in short supply these were worrying losses for Coningham. It was decided fighter operations should be scaled back on 1 June to give Commonwealth squadrons a chance to recuperate, although as it turned out, sandstorms limited operations anyway.

Rommel also had plenty to worry about. Low on ammunition, fuel and, most importantly of all, water, Rommel was forced to pull his northernmost forces back to the rear of the 150 Brigade position. He was almost completely surrounded. A counter-attack by Commonwealth forces might have finished him off, as German commanders were all too aware. However, General Neil Ritchie, commanding Eighth Army, delayed and 150 Brigade was also now running low on ammunition. On 1 June, in one last desperate fling, Rommel's exhausted forces, supported by a fierce Ju 87 assault, overran the Brigade's defences. Rommel now had secure supply lines running through the minefield, but the situation was still critical. Rommel had avoided a catastrophe, but the battle was still very much in the balance. His forces were still pinned down in a small area with British minefields to their rear and, farther south, Bir Hakeim was still holding out.

The impact the Stukas had on 1 June forced Cross to switch his fighters from low-level support to air cover. The Spitfires of No. 145 Squadron flew their first mission on 1 June, but there were only sufficient machines available to provide one flight. This was used to give some rather scanty top cover to the Hurricanes and Kittyhawks. Axis pilots might at least now be forced to pay more attention to what might be above them, but it would take more than one flight to make this a real threat.

Fresh squadrons were moved up to the front, but these scarcely compensated for units being pulled back to the rear to recuperate. Requests for Beaufighter squadrons to be moved forward to operate in the enemy rear were turned down because they would soon be needed to cover the latest convoy about to set off from Alexandria for Malta. The Kittyhawks of No. 250 Squadron were withdrawn so they could be fitted with long-range tanks to escort this convoy. This, and another Hurricane squadron that had been withdrawn, were replaced by a couple of fresh Hurricane squadrons, one of which only had experience of coastal patrolling in the rear and arrived with instructions that it had to be treated 'gently' because of its lack of experience. The Baltimore squadron returned on the 7th, but the light-bomber force was still too small to make much of a contribution.

Rommel's next priority was to eliminate the stubborn French forces holding Bir Hakeim. Again waves of Ju 87s pounded the French fortress. On 3 June, Tomahawks claimed ten Ju 87s, but the fighters paid a high price as the German escort, led by the redoubtable Hans-Joachim Marseille, intervened to claim nine fighters. Actual Allied fighter losses for the day were at least eight.[7] The next day, Tomahawks claimed another six German dive-bombers in a single engagement. Claims rarely reflect actual losses, but ten Stukas failed to return on these two days and this was a serious blow for the Luftwaffe.[8] These combats took place in full view of the French defenders and were a huge fillip to morale. These interventions, however, were the exception rather than the rule. For the most part, the escorts kept the fighters away from the vulnerable dive-bombers.

The Bir Hakeim garrison was now brought some relief by events further north. On the night of 4/5 June, Ritchie finally launched his counter-attack, from the north and east, against Rommel's forces, still pinned to the back of British minefields. This now became the focus of attention for both the Luftwaffe and the Desert Air Force. Initially, the British tanks advanced relatively unopposed. A pre-arranged strike by Bostons helped capture a German position south of the Aslagh Ridge, again demonstrating that these light bombers could be used in a close support role, but there were far too few of these supporting strikes. The British tanks ran into German anti-tank guns and immediately began suffering heavy losses. Fifteen calls for air support came in from the Army Air Support Controls during the course of the day, but the heavy losses already suffered and the desire to keep something back for a real emergency meant that none of these requests were met.[9]

It was a negative, defensive mindset that mirrored Ritchie's tentative delayed counter-attack on the ground. Instead of boldly using all available air power to help the tanks burst through the German defences, it was being held back in case the attack failed and it was needed to deal with a

German counter-attack. There was an element of self-fulfilling prophecy about the policy. While the RAF fighters and fighter-bombers sat on their airfields, the British tanks were being drawn into the murderous fire of the anti-tank screens. By the evening the Commonwealth forces had been routed and Rommel's tanks were giving chase. The next day, the Commonwealth fighter and fighter-bombers were unleashed, but the opportunity to help push for a victory had passed; all they could do now was help save the day.

When the counter-attack had started the Army was in reasonable control of the situation and was able to nominate targets for the fighter-bombers to strike. Now, in the confusion of retreat, the Army Air Support Control system and communications in general started to break down and close air support became much more difficult to organise. On 6 June, fighters flew 132 fighter, strafing and bombing sorties, but the lack of accurate information meant they again had to be confined to targets on the fringes of the battlefield for fear of hitting friendly forces. Individual attacks were successful but were not taking place where they were most needed.

Rommel had meanwhile turned his attention back to the Bir Hakeim stronghold still defying the Axis forces surrounding it. The Desert Air Force made a huge effort on the 8th, flying a record 357 fighter sorties, but the Macchi and Messerschmitt escorts proved especially effective and Allied pilots could not even claim to have destroyed any bombers. On the 10th, the Luftwaffe launched twenty Ju 88 and forty Ju 87s against the French stronghold. Close escort was provided by fifty Bf 109 and Bf 110s with more fighters at altitude. It was an almost impenetrable shield and the Commonwealth squadrons were only able to claim two of the attackers. Of the twenty-four major raids on Bir Hakeim during the siege, only six were effectively opposed by Allied fighters. The Germans had flown around 1,000 sorties against the stronghold, but Commonwealth pilots had only been able to claim thirty enemy planes. With Commonwealth fighters failing to make any inroads into the German bomber formations, the position of the French troops was fast becoming untenable.

On 10 June, the French were ordered to pull out. On the next day, Rommel's forces in the Cauldron area struck towards El Adem. A huge tank battle developed on the 11th and 12th. With the Commonwealth forces now on the defensive, there was no question of holding Commonwealth squadrons back. Poor weather on the 11th limited aerial activity, but the next day over 150 Boston light bombers, Kittyhawk and Hurricane fighter-bombers as well as the Hurricane IID tank-busters attacked German panzers and their supply columns, provoking complaints from the panzer commanders about the lack of air cover. The 583 fighter sorties flown on the 12th was the highest so far in the battle. However, attempts to deal with the large numbers of Axis aircraft reported in the El Adem and Knightsbridge areas brought little reward. Despite multiple claims, it seems only two German aircraft were lost at a cost of eleven fighters. On the ground, Rommel's experienced tank commanders demolished the remainder of the British tank force. Very little stood between the Germans and the Mediterranean coast south of Tobruk and, on the 14th, Ritchie ordered a general retreat along the entire front.[10]

From the start it had been a disastrous battle for Eighth Army. They had been beaten by a force with fewer men and tanks. Throughout the fighting Rommel had been quick to decide when he could afford to attack and when he needed to go onto the defensive. He had taken risks his opponents had not been willing to take and had reaped the reward. Air power had played its part. Unlike the Commonwealth air forces, the Luftwaffe had been used to help gain victory rather than being held back in case things went wrong. It was a dispirited and broken Commonwealth army that began a general retreat in the direction of Tobruk and the Egyptian frontier.

Despite losses, squadrons were still able to maintain a high level of operations. As the Axis forces advanced eastwards, the Bf 109s, with their limited endurance, were not able to dominate the battlefield to the same extent. Communication with the Army Command had broken down, but with Rommel's forces sweeping east, often unopposed, aerial reconnaissance was able to supply useful targets. With the German forces not in immediate contact with the Allied forces, light bombers could be used from medium altitudes without danger of hitting friendly forces. The fullest use was made of the available fighters. Fighter-bombers that had delivered their bombs took on any enemy aircraft that happened to be around and fighters at the end of offensive patrols would use up any leftover ammunition on targets of opportunity.

On the 16th, Bostons made seven attacks and fighter-bombers another twenty on German forces surrounding El Adem and heading towards Sidi Rezegh. The 21st Panzer Division reported heavy losses from cannon-firing fighters; the Hurricane IID 'tank-busters' of No. 6 Squadron were making their presence felt. The slow-flying Hurricanes, weighed down by their 40mm cannon, were vulnerable but, operating against tanks which had advanced beyond effective air cover, they proved extremely effective. The Hurricanes claimed the destruction of thirty-one tanks and twenty-eight vehicles in ten days of operations. As always, claims rarely match actual losses, but German prisoners testified to the alarm the cannon-armed planes generated and Rommel was sufficiently impressed to take an example of the armour-piercing shells back to Germany to show everyone what his tank crews had to contend with.[11]

Interestingly, Tedder's reaction to the success of the tank-busting Hurricanes was somewhat different. The disastrous way the battle had gone was provoking huge criticism back home and once more the knives were out for an air force that appeared to be unable to match the feats of the opposing Luftwaffe. As Sinclair prepared to defend the performance of the RAF in Parliament, Tedder pleaded with him not to mention the success of the Hurricane tank-busters, as this would give the impression the RAF ought to be engaging enemy tanks.[12] For Rommel the tank-busters were a dangerous threat; for Tedder they were an embarrassment.

Coningham directed his squadrons with admirable skill and coolness. He kept his squadrons at forward bases for as long as he dare, with one even managing on one occasion to deliver a telling blow against enemy units attempting to occupy the airfield from which the aircraft were operating. When squadrons were forced to pull back, it was not the ragged retreat of January 1942. Airfields in the rear were ready and waiting to re-launch the retreating squadrons on the advancing Germans. The Luftwaffe, in contrast, was struggling to keep up with the panzers and the number of sorties dropped as fuel supplies began to run low. With many Axis units grounded, the long columns of retreating Allied forces were spared serious air attack.[13]

As the retreat gathered pace, there was indecision on the Allied side about whether to try and hold Tobruk or not. Tedder appeared to assure the Army that he could continue to provide air cover if the port was surrounded, a judgement that seemed to rely on a very optimistic view on the likely scale of the Commonwealth retreat. Initially, the Army did not believe the port could be held. Then they decided that perhaps it could, even without air support, just as it had been in 1941. There was a last-minute decision not to evacuate the port and 35,000 troops prepared for another siege.

The Germans once again demonstrated the decisiveness the British commanders had not been able to muster and once again tactical air support was the key. Rommel was determined that Tobruk should not foul up his rear communications as it had the year before. The Axis air forces were on their last legs, losses had been building up, fuel and spares were in short supply, but there was no desire to hold back what still remained. Everything would be thrown into the assault on Tobruk.

Tedder and Coningham do not appear to have been 'singing from the same hymn sheet'. On the 18th, Coningham pulled his units back to the Sidi Barrani area, in Egypt, putting all the single-seater fighters, apart from No. 250 Squadron's Kittyhawks with their long-range fuel tanks, out of range of Tobruk. One squadron could not stop the Luftwaffe and the Germans took full advantage. On the 20th, the Axis air forces flew 600 sorties, including some bombers flying from Crete, against the perimeter defences. In response, the RAF could manage one Boston strike escorted by the No. 250 Squadron Kittyhawks. In yet another stunning blow to Allied morale, the defences were overwhelmed and, by the evening of the 21 June, the port had fallen, with the surrender of some 33,000 troops.

The post-war Air Ministry official narrative was quick to criticise the way the Luftwaffe was misused as 'long-range artillery' against the Bir Hakeim and Tobruk strongholds. It was, according to the narrative, 'a measure of Rommel's poor understanding of the role of tactical air forces that the Luftwaffe was employed to such a large extent against what was, in fact, an Army target'.[14] This said as much about Air Ministry understanding of the value of tactical air power in 1942 as it did about their understanding when the narrative was written in 1948. Bir Hakeim did hold out for some time in the face of fierce ground and air attack, but this was more down to French heroism than a misuse of air power. This same so-called misuse of air power at Tobruk had seen Commonwealth defences overwhelmed and the port fall.

Ironically in London the episode was viewed primarily as another inept performance by the Army rather than another clear example of how important battlefield air support was to any army commander, in defence or attack. Churchill did not even try to hide the humiliating scale of the defeat. However, instead of redoubling his efforts to ensure Commonwealth forces got the sort of air support that had proved so decisive at Tobruk, he was increasingly relying on the bomber offensive to bring him the morale-boosting victories the flagging Allied cause needed.

For several days after the fall of Tobruk there was little Axis air activity over the retreating Commonwealth forces. On 22 June, Axis forces reached the Egyptian frontier. Rommel had achieved his objective of securing his eastern flank. The plan now was to switch forces to the rear, launch Operation Mercury to capture Malta and eliminate the troublesome Allied base once and for all. However, Rommel had done much more than just delay the next Allied offensive, he had routed the Allied army. With the Commonwealth forces in disarray, and the huge stockpile of materiel captured at Tobruk, the temptation to finish off a disorganised enemy and push on to Cairo was too great. Rommel decided to continue his advance, even though he knew he could not count on much support from the Luftwaffe.

The Allies sensibly decided not to make a stand on the Egyptian frontier. On 23 June, Ritchie was given permission to pull back to Mersa Matruh. Two days later Auchinleck took over from Ritchie as the commander of Eighth Army and immediately decided that what was left of his force would pull back even further, to El Alamein, some 250 miles inside Egypt and only 60 miles from Alexandria. With the Qattara Depression to the south, it provided Auchinleck with the shortest and easiest line to defend. By trading space for time, Rommel's supply lines would be lengthened. It was a dangerous game to play. Without control of the skies, a prolonged retreat could easily have turned into a rout. The Air Force, however, was up to the challenge. Everything was being done to reinforce air force squadrons. Greater efforts were made to repair the thousand-odd damaged planes in the rear. Aircraft heading for the Far East were either held in the Middle East or diverted to the Middle East. Training units were combed for any combat equipment that might be used. Worn-out Hurricane Is were issued to some squadrons to help out with rear defence.

While Luftwaffe effort was decreasing, Allied aerial activity was increasing. Light-bomber sorties rose from forty-five on 23 June, to seventy-two on the 24th, and ninety-eight on the 25th. On the night of the 25th/26th, the night bombers based in the Delta switched their efforts to the battlefield. Fleet Air Arm Albacores illuminated the targets with flares and low-flying Wellingtons bombed them. Around a hundred sorties were flown in what was to be the start of a continuous round-the-clock bombing offensive. It was an air offensive that gnawed away at enemy morale as it became more obvious with every passing day that the Allies were dominating the skies.

Nevertheless, Rommel's advance continued. On 26 June, Axis fighters were back in strength over the front and the day saw a series of fierce tussles. Rommel attempted to encircle the Allied forces in Mersa Matruh. Engaging Allied ground forces had become the only way Rommel's forces had of evading the constant Allied air attacks. During the course of the day the Kittyhawk squadrons were particularly active. No. 450 squadron flew eight escort missions, No. 3 Squadron RAAF flew ten missions and No. 112 Squadron alone flew sixty-nine sorties. In all, Commonwealth forces flew 128 light-bomber and some 178 fighter-bomber sorties in addition to 310 fighter sorties, with some pilots flying up to five missions.

Rommel attacked on the very day that the Allies had decided not to make a stand at Mersa Matruh, which caused some confusion among the defenders and another 3,000 troops were captured, but the vast majority slipped away. Ju 87 and 88s inflicted losses on retreating New Zealanders but for the most part the desperately vulnerable columns of Commonwealth forces continued their retreat eastwards largely unmolested, while Rommel's forces were constantly battered by the round-the-clock bombing.

Squadrons were now highly flexible mobile units practised in the art of rapid movement, either back or forward. Perhaps Coningham's greatest achievement was that he got his squadrons back to El Alamein in reasonable order. Only forty-odd planes had been left behind in the retreat. By the beginning of July, the Desert Air Force had 470 planes in the Western Desert. These included a second Spitfire squadron, No. 601, transferred from Malta and Halifaxes flown out from Bomber Command squadrons in the United Kingdom.[15]

On 1 July, Rommel attempted to storm the El Alamein line before Auchinleck could organise his defences. However, Auchinleck marshalled his scattered resources with considerable skill and all Rommel's units were now experiencing the full weight of Allied air attack, even in the midst of battle. In a 24-hour period the Allies were flying around 1,000 sorties, four times the effort the Luftwaffe could manage. On 3 July, 624 fighter sorties were flown, more than twice as many as on the first day of the Gazala offensive. The light-bomber squadrons flew 156 sorties and the Wellingtons and Albacores based in the Delta continued their low-level attacks under cover of darkness. On 4 July, 90 tons of bombs were dropped by Bostons, Baltimores and Kittyhawks on the panzer spearheads. With his forces exhausted, short of supplies and demoralised by the constant aerial bombardment, Rommel was forced to call off the attack.[16]

In the first week of the battle the RAF had flown 2,414 sorties; in the sixth week the number rose to 4,245. Serviceability rates for single-seater fighters at the beginning of the battle were 67 per cent; after five weeks of retreat they were 84 per cent. It was a prodigious effort. The Desert Air Force had played a huge part in stabilising the situation in the Western Desert. Not since the German spring offensive of 1918 had a retreating British army benefited in such large measure from the intervention of British air power. A year before in Greece and Crete, the RAF had been rechristened the Royal Absent Force by embittered soldiers. There could be no such talk now. Arguably, Rommel's position was now more precarious than the Allies'. Auchinleck was even tentatively thinking of going on to the offensive. Some telling tactical defeats were imposed on the Axis forces before the fighting petered out.

It was an impressive display of air power, but it was air power used to support a retreating rather than an advancing army. The RAF was still most effective when Allied forces were not closely engaged with the enemy and close co-ordination with ground forces was not so vital. Even in these circumstances, there had been some tragic mistakes. On no less than six occasions between 3 and 5 July, South African forces had been attacked in error. As a result, from the afternoon of the 5th, air strikes had to be directed to less important targets well away from the front line.[17]

The quality of the available fighters was still a major problem. The Hurricane II continued to struggle. On 3 July, three of a formation of more than twelve were shot down by Bf 109s. Two hours later, four out of five were shot down in another clash with Messerschmitts. The higher losses inferior types suffered were bound to make it more difficult to sustain operations. At crucial stages of the Gazala battle, squadrons had to be rested to allow time to recover. In the closing stages of the retreat, with the Luftwaffe struggling to keep up with the advancing Axis forces, air superiority had been achieved but more by weight of numbers than quality. It was not an efficient way of winning the air battle.

The handful of Spitfires available were able to provide a modicum of top cover, but on 1 July there were still only twenty-one serviceable Spitfires in the Western Desert, compared to the 800 Fighter Command had in the UK. Slessor's 1939 comment about the danger of having 600 fighters sitting idly by in the UK while the fate of Britain was decided on the battlefield in France was just as true in 1942. In 1940 Britain had lost her most important ally; in 1942 Britain risked losing Egypt and the vital oilfields beyond.

Tedder was partly responsible for this. He was determined to avoid the 'moan, moan, moan' tag his predecessor, Air Chief Marshal Longmore, had acquired for constantly demanding more and better equipment. A few days into the battle, Portal was genuinely taken aback by Tedder 'suddenly' referring to his 'painfully limited resources', when Portal was under the impression Tedder's position was quite strong.[18] Quality was an even more important concern than quantity. It took a visit by Air Chief Marshal Edgar Ludlow-Hewitt, a former commander of Bomber Command and now an air force inspector, to get the message across. On 28 May, with the Gazala battle at its height, Ludlow-Hewitt signalled the Air Ministry from Tedder's headquarters with a startling assessment of the current state of the fighter force. The Hurricane could no longer be considered a front-line fighter.

Those still based on Malta had been 'roughly handled' by the enemy and had been withdrawn because they were just using up scarce resources. In the Western Desert, the Kittyhawk was totally ineffective above 15,000 feet. Allied fighters were having to operate without any effective top cover and were always having to concede the initiative to the enemy. Ludlow-Hewitt urged the immediate despatch of more Spitfires.[19] It was a message that caused alarm in London. The Air Ministry was still planning to build large numbers of Hurricanes for the Middle East, Far East and the Soviet Union. First the Soviets and now the Middle East were turning their noses up at the Hurricane.

The Air Ministry signalled back, expressing their surprise that more use could not be made of the Hurricanes. This arrived after Ludlow-Hewitt had left for India and was dealt with by Tedder. He reassured London that he wanted as many Hurricanes as possible, although only for long-range intruder missions and as fighter-bombers. Given the desperate situation at the front, Tedder was understandably grateful for any reinforcements. Nevertheless, he was not asking for Spitfires.

Instead of increasing the pressure on the Air Ministry, Tedder turned his fire on the Ministry of Aircraft Production. At the beginning of July he complained that German squadrons got the best German equipment available, whereas Commonwealth squadrons had to make do with 'second best, sometimes scarcely even second best'.[20] The arrival of the FW 190 and B109G would leave the Desert Air Force 'further down the scale of obsolescence' and that even the Spitfire might be outclassed.[21] He claimed too much fuss was made about the need for tropicalisation and, no doubt suspecting this was always a good excuse for not sending the best fighters, he suggested the latest fighters be sent unmodified and they would sort out the desert equipment they needed in the Middle East.

By September, Tedder was also sending Portal the same clear message. Tedder described how the inferiority of the Hurricane and Kittyhawk to the Messerschmitts they faced made it impossible to break through the Stuka escorts. 'Inferiority in performance is an incessant handicap in every way.' 'There is no doubt the real answer is Spitfires.' Yet there was still a rather feeble air to his plea: 'I do hope it will be possible to give us at least a fair proportion of our best first-line types.'[22] Douglas at Fighter Command was being far more assertive.

Tedder's comments were perhaps coming a year too late. Douglas had come to the same conclusion about the Hurricane II in the spring of 1941. Some straight talking from the Middle East sooner about the value of the plane as a fighter might have forced the Air Ministry and Ministry of Aircraft Production to rethink their plans to build so many. It was too late now. Large numbers had been ordered and the Hurricanes were pouring off the production lines.

It was not just the equipment that was causing concern. When No. 601 Squadron arrived in Malta, Lloyd had not been pleased at being sent inexperienced pilots unfamiliar with the planes they were flying. At least in Malta they were flying the interception missions they were familiar with. When the squadron was transferred to the Western Desert, operations in the Western Desert in the battle zone revealed more problems. Tedder felt the pilots were unprepared for the more fluid nature of tactical fighter operations as opposed to the controlled interceptions they had been trained to perform. As an example, Tedder described an operation on 6 July when four Spitfires had engaged three Junkers 88s escorted by three Bf 109s. The Spitfires had claimed one of the bombers but had lost two of their number in the process. Tedder only knew half the story. What actually happened underlined the pilots' lack of tactical guile. There had been two more Bf 109s flying at a higher altitude covering the lower escort and it was these that had surprised and shot down the two Spitfires.[23] The Spitfire pilots had taken no such precautions and seemed unaware that there might be danger lurking above them.

The squadron had to be withdrawn from the front and redeployed in the Delta for the air defence duties it was more familiar with. Indeed, dealing with high-flying reconnaissance planes, the squadron immediately began to have more success. This, however, was not where the Spitfires were needed. As the war approached the end of its third year, RAF training was still dominated by the needs of strategic offence and defence. Pilots had to acquire the skills required for tactical air combat as they went along. Later, after additional training, No. 601 Squadron would perform well in a tactical role but not enough was being done to prepare pilots for the tactical front-line operations that were required in the Middle East, Far East or indeed would be required for an invasion of France.

It was taking the RAF a very long time to adapt to the war it found itself fighting rather than the war it had spent the 1920s and 1930s preparing for.

Chapter 8

Dieppe Disaster

The retreat of Eighth Army in North Africa was the final straw for Operation Sledgehammer. Churchill argued that the loss of the Nile Delta would have implications for the Middle and Far East every bit as decisive as the collapse of the Soviet Union. Churchill persuaded Roosevelt that American forces must now act to save the Allied position in North Africa. Operation Gymnast, an operation designed to take advantage of a victory in the Western Desert, was revived and renamed Torch, with the aim of saving the Commonwealth Army in the Western Desert. Stalin would get his second front in 1942 but in North Africa, not France. Marshall was frustrated by what he saw as an unnecessary diversion but, for the air element of the US Army, there were advantages. The rapid capture of North Africa would provide bases for bombing southern Europe with the added advantage that they would not be affected by the British climate. A full-scale invasion of France, Operation Roundup, would not now take place until the spring of 1943.

However, a major raid was still an option. Mountbatten had been considering such a raid, Operation Rutter, since April. This would at least draw the Luftwaffe into battle and, it was rather optimistically suggested, a decisive victory might transform the balance of air power on all fronts. As far as Leigh-Mallory was concerned, the naval units involved and the troops on the ground were essentially more attractive bait than the Blenheims, and the occasional Stirlings, Bomber Command had been persuaded to risk by day over northern France.

The operation involved the capture of the port of Dieppe and was scheduled to take place in late June or early July. It involved a very brief stay of between eight and seventeen hours on the continent. This, it was hoped, would be long enough to destroy port facilities and, more out of bravado than their military value, barges the Germans had been intending to use to invade Britain would be brought back for a future invasion of France.[1]

135

One of the initial proposals involved landings on either side of Dieppe, where the defences would be less formidable. These would be supported by paratroopers dropped on key artillery positions. Both forces would then swing around to take the port from the rear. This was ambitious and daring but perhaps possible. However, the plan eventually adopted was a frontal assault on the more strongly defended Dieppe seafront. Just before the main assault, landing parties and paratroopers would eliminate the artillery positions covering the seafront. Altogether the operation would involve 6,000, predominantly Canadian, troops and 160 tanks.

The Royal Navy had no intention of committing any ships larger than a destroyer in waters where the Luftwaffe still posed a major threat. The 4-inch guns of the eight accompanying destroyers would be the only naval artillery support the assault troops could count on. Bomber Command was to soften up the defences of the town with a night-long bombing offensive, and Fighter Command army support squadrons would hit beach defences as the troops went ashore. It was a significant event. For the first time, RAF squadrons in north-west Europe would be providing Allied ground forces with close air support.[2]

The airfield north of St Aubin, 4 miles inland would be occupied and installations there destroyed. The Wehrmacht headquarters at Arques, 5 miles inland, would also be captured and, with any luck, a cache of secret documents might fall into Allied hands. Two emergency airstrips would be set up within the bridgehead for any Allied aircraft in trouble. It was certainly audacious. Indeed, if a port could be captured so easily by so few troops and the forces landed could strike 5 miles inland so quickly, one might be tempted to question the wisdom of voluntarily withdrawing and abandoning such a priceless foothold. The very ambition of the project should perhaps have set alarm bells ringing about its practicability with such meagre numbers and firepower.

Slessor warned that too much faith could not be placed in Bomber Command as bombing restrictions on French towns meant that unless crews could be certain of hitting military targets they would have to bring their bombs home. Harris had no intention of participating anyway. It was, as he saw it, yet another misuse of his bombers. In the end Leigh-Mallory and General John Roberts, the Canadian land commander, acquiesced, persuading themselves that a heavy aerial bombardment might have lost the Allies the element of surprise, and the destruction in the town itself would probably have slowed down the advancing Canadian tanks.

Indeed, far from getting Bomber Command support, Mountbatten found himself struggling to ensure Bomber Command did not get its hands on some of the other squadrons taking part in the operation. Harris was scratching around for aircraft to make up the numbers for his 1,000 bomber raids and Army Co-operation Command had a couple of Whitley squadrons it was going to use to drop paratroopers. Even flown by experienced crews, the Whitley was proving particularly vulnerable over Germany, but Harris needed every plane he could get for the first of these raids against Cologne planned on 30 May.

Mountbatten was horrified when he discovered Harris had been lent the squadrons. He told Portal that the loss of any crews on this raid would be impossible to replace in time for the Rutter operation. Portal assured Mountbatten that Barratt had given his full approval. However, it transpired that Barratt had been on leave at the time and the 'Air Staff', presumably Portal, had decided in his absence that the 1,000 bomber raid had priority.[3] When Barratt returned from leave, he got the decision reversed, but it was all rather symptomatic of an Air Ministry determined to give the bomber offensive every chance of succeeding at the expense of all else.

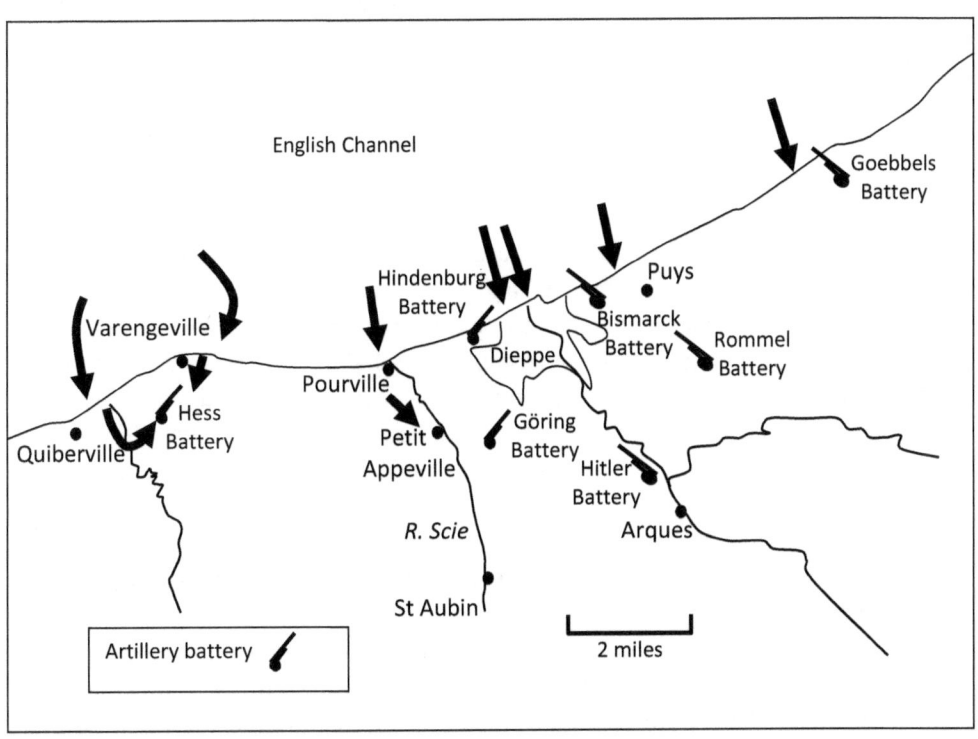

Without Bomber Command 'heavies', support for the Dieppe landings was left in the hands of the two remaining Boston squadrons, six Hurricane squadrons, one Spitfire squadron, two Hurribomber squadrons and the 4-inch guns of the eight destroyers. The Hurricane squadrons were supposed to start engaging the beach defences while the landing craft were still half a mile from the shore and continue until five minutes after the troops had landed. Once the troops were ashore, air support would be directed towards enemy reinforcements moving towards Dieppe. If no suitable targets emerged, at least one squadron was supposed to stay on in the area and be at the disposal of the ground commander. Repeat missions would be flown as soon as the crews could be briefed and planes could be refuelled and re-armed. If required, all the fighter-bomber and ground attack squadrons could be redirected to more suitable targets as they crossed the Channel.[4]

Operation Rutter almost took place. After several postponements because of poor weather, on 7 July, a German bomber hit two of the troop-carrying vessels involved in the operation and the suspicion that the Germans knew all about the plan caused the operation to be cancelled. Almost immediately, however, the operation was revived for the following month as 'Operation Jubilee'. It was essentially the same except the paratrooper drop was abandoned. Commandos would be used instead to eliminate the shore batteries while the RAF dealt with the gun batteries further inland. The main assault on the Dieppe seafront would be supported by sixty Churchill tanks.

Leigh-Mallory was having second thoughts about the lack of Bomber Command participation and tried again to get the heavies of Bomber Command involved. He wanted to use them to attack the buildings along the seafront, all of which were believed to be occupied by German troops. To maximise the devastation, he suggested that they attack at dawn with 4,000lb bombs just as the first troops stepped ashore. Harris, however, could not be persuaded. He insisted that standing orders meant heavy bombers always had to be well clear of any enemy coast by dawn.[5] It was a deliberately pedantic application of existing rules to make sure Bomber Command was not involved in the operation. The order was there to remind returning bomber crews that flying within range of German air defences in daylight was not recommended. It was not meant to rule out supporting a dangerous dawn landing on the enemy coastline with 6,000 Canadian soldiers in the firing line.

Leigh-Mallory pleaded for some flexibility. Surely the Dieppe operation justified an exception being made. The risk of interception was exaggerated, he insisted. There were no night-fighters in the region and the Luftwaffe was not in the habit of flying standing patrols at daybreak. From the moment the alarm was raised it would take the German fighters thirty minutes to get to the Dieppe area, by which time the bombers would be well on their way home. As an extra precaution, Leigh-Mallory was prepared to train some fighter pilots to take off in pairs and fly to Dieppe in darkness to cover the bombers as dawn broke.[6]

Harris, however, remained adamant that he could not risk his bombers on yet another unnecessary diversion from their main task. There was nothing unusual about Harris's stance; he was just doing what previous commanders at Bomber Command had done – giving the bomber offensive absolute priority, even over active land operations. The Dieppe raid was a risky operation and at the very least merited as much effort and commitment as Harris was putting into hitting his thousand-bomber target.

The proposed bombing was probably not the wisest way of supporting the landing. Bomber Command crews were not equipped or trained for missions that required such precision. Bombing as the troops landed would have almost certainly resulted in friendly casualties. Even if a preparatory bombardment had been accurate enough to destroy the buildings along the seafront, it might not have helped that much as bombed buildings often provided good defensive positions. However, the significance was not so much in the wisdom of the proposed bombing, it was the attitudes displayed in the debate. Until attitudes changed, there was going to be no progress on establishing how air power might help the troops establish themselves ashore.

Air cover for the operation looked substantial enough. Twelve fighter squadrons were to move south from other groups which, along with three USAAF squadrons, would bring the total day-fighter force up to forty-eight squadrons, four of which were Spitfire IX, three Typhoon, two Spitfire VI and the rest Spitfire V. The Typhoon's troublesome engines and structural problems meant these could not be risked in the main combat zone and they would be restricted to a decoy sweep off the Belgian coast. Indeed, so suspect was the Typhoon, the pilots were offered the option of not taking part at all, but they were determined to be involved in some way.[7]

Four Mustang squadrons were to provide tactical reconnaissance and Blenheims and Bostons would lay smoke screens along the beaches. Three Douglas Havoc night-fighter intruders would join the initial strikes on artillery positions, a number which rather summed up the operation's small-scale thinking and feeble fire support. The Americans were going to contribute two Flying Fortress heavy-bomber squadrons, symbolic in more ways than one; they were the forerunners of the massive American bomber fleet that would soon be assembling in Britain, but they were also a fair representation of the sort of bombers these reinforcements would largely comprise.

Nearly three-quarters of the aircraft available were fighters assigned the task of covering the landing, but this did not mean they could only be used for air combat. By this time, all fighter squadrons were supposed to be capable of ground attack and most had received some training. Douglas was very aware of how fighters were being used in the Middle East. A memo from Tedder and Auchinleck on their experience, describing how fighters were regularly being used for ground attack, prompted a directive from Douglas, issued in June 1942, in which he stressed that low-flying attacks were one of the many roles fighters might be asked to perform. If circumstances required it, all available fighters might have to be used for army support, which meant attacking ground targets as well as providing cover.[8] Although the report was mainly focusing on how fighters would be used to help defeat a German invasion, it seemed that Fighter Command was prepared to use its squadrons as flexibly as they were being used in the Middle East.

On paper it was an impressive concentration of fighter resources, with some 80 per cent of Fighter Command's strength available for the operation. This was a far higher proportion than had been used to defend the Dunkirk evacuation in 1940. Dowding had never managed to get more than seventeen squadrons, about 30 per cent of available strength, over the beaches on any one day. It was also a much higher percentage than Dowding had managed to concentrate in the south-east of the UK during the Battle of Britain.

The intent was right but the way the squadrons were deployed made achieving the required concentration over Dieppe difficult. Fighter Command was a very static organisation used to operating from its regular airfields. The fighter squadrons assigned the army support role were based on airfields that were as close to Dieppe as possible to minimise time between missions. However, the fighter squadrons responsible for defending the landing were operating from airfields far and wide, including Hornchurch and Northolt north of the Thames and equally distant Manston, all linked into the air defence system run from Leigh-Mallory's Uxbridge headquarters but all some way from the Dieppe beaches. It was to avoid this rigidity that the War Office opposed Portal's plans for a Fighter Command controlled 'Eastern Air Force' concept.

The number of available fighter squadrons available was impressive, but every one of them would be needed to compensate for the short patrol times possible. The aim was to provide an 'aerial umbrella'. The Air Ministry always fiercely objected to using fighters in this way for land operations, but when the Navy was involved the objections always seemed remarkably muted. Between three and six squadrons were to be above the beaches at all times. Squadrons were allocated thirty-minute patrol times over Dieppe, which was comfortably within the capabilities of Spitfires carrying a 30-gallon drop tank. However, it was stretching it a bit for Spitfires not so equipped. The number of fighter squadrons available would only allow maximum strength six-squadron patrols to be maintained for four hours.

There were not enough fighters to patrol at all altitudes. The majority would fly at around 6,000 feet with some degree of top cover provided by fighters flying at 10,000 feet, but there would be nothing above this. It was significant that priority was given to low-level cover, recognition that, as was happening in the Western Desert and the Eastern Front, land and sea battles will inevitable draw the aerial fighting down to lower altitudes.

Jubilee was launched on 19 August. The air, naval and ground aspects of the operation were co-ordinated from the destroyers HMS *Calpe* and *Fernie*, with the Canadian commander General Roberts on board the former. The destroyers could communicate directly with the low-flying fighters and the Army support fighter squadrons and, indirectly, via Portsmouth, with Leigh-Mallory at No. 11 Group headquarters in Uxbridge.[9]

On the right flank, the operation went well. Commandos landed near Quiberville and further east at Varengeville. A lone Spitfire provided a diversion by attacking the lighthouse that overlooked the approach. Once ashore the commandos made their way to the Hess Battery. By 6.30 am they were ready to storm the position. On time, twelve more Spitfires raked the battery with cannon- and machine-gun fire. This was genuine close support, a little too close at times. Under pressure from intercepting FW 190s, some houses that commandos were sniping from were strafed by mistake and one soldier was wounded. As soon as the Spitfires completed their attack the commandos stormed the gun position. It was a spectacularly successful co-ordinated air/ground start to the operation.

A little further east, Canadian forces surprised the German defences, occupied Pourville, established a bridgehead on the west bank of the River Scie and pushed a mile inland to occupy the village of Petit Appeville. This early success suggested landings on either side of the port would perhaps have been a wiser plan. The Canadians attempted to capture a bridge across the River Scie but ran into some stiff resistance. To make any further progress, they needed the support of the main force, especially the tanks that were supposed to drive through Dieppe.

These reinforcements, however, never arrived. The main landings were made at 5.20 a.m. under intense enemy fire. As the troops landed, twelve Havocs and Blenheims along with twenty Hurribombers attempted to eliminate the Hitler and Göring batteries to the south of Dieppe.[10] Bombing from between 3,000 and 7,000 feet, the light bombers had neither the accuracy nor the weight of bombs to have much chance of success. The dive-bombing Hurricanes had more chance of hitting their target, but they too failed to eliminate them. Equally unsuccessful were the commando raids on the remaining coast batteries. Within minutes of the troops setting foot on the beaches, there were desperate pleas to deal with the incessant fire from these batteries.

Forty-seven cannon-armed Hurricanes attempted to suppress enemy fire from the buildings along the seafront while Blenheims and Bostons laid smoke screens along the beach. Some of the Hurricanes made two strafing runs. It was dangerous work: eight Hurricanes were lost and twenty damaged. The cannon fire might force the Germans to stay low for the duration of the attack, but they could not inflict any permanent damage. Within ten minutes all the Hurricanes had exhausted their ammunition and the attack was over. Ten minutes was simply not long enough to enable the infantry to cut through the wire and get off the beaches. As the smoke screen lifted, the Canadians were exposed to intense fire from all quarters. At 5.45 a.m. *Calpe* asked for an extension of the smoke screen. Twenty minutes later the appeal was repeated, but no aircraft could return for two hours.[11]

By 6.20 a.m., an hour after the initial landings, HMS *Calpe* was already signalling that the troops were still stuck on the beaches and in desperate need of more air support. *Calpe* began requesting strikes on the Hitler, Rommel and Bismarck batteries, all still pouring fire on to the beaches. Bostons of No. 88 Squadron were despatched but repeated attempts failed to eliminate the guns. At 7.00 a.m. *Calpe* pushed in close to the shore to get a better picture of what was happening. The main landing was already considered a failure and the Canadians were in serious trouble. They desperately needed to get off the beaches to escape the murderous fire, but the commanders offshore could not get a clear picture of what was happening and there was no clear information coming from the beaches.[12] It was all going horribly wrong.

The Hurricanes were re-armed and refuelled as quickly as possible. An hour after they had landed they were in the air again. Leigh-Mallory believed he could do no more. By the time the Hurricanes had got back to the beaches, two and a half hours had passed during which the exposed troops had received no air support. Twenty-four Hurricanes attacked enemy positions along the seafront at around 8.00 a.m. Again the relief they brought was welcome but brief. Another twenty-four Hurricanes were despatched to intercept E-boats reported to be heading for Dieppe. Fear of E-boat attack was a major concern in the planning stage but perhaps not now the most immediate danger, given the plight of the Canadians. Requests for air support were made throughout the morning with growing frequency and desperation as the tragedy on the beaches unfolded, but it took time for the Hurricanes to return to base, re-arm and fly back to the beaches. Another three hours were to pass before more air strikes were made on German seafront positions.[13] It was a very long three hours for the Canadians on the beach.

Above Dieppe, the Spitfires of Fighter Command were on patrol but, in the early stages of the landing, Luftwaffe reaction was relatively light with just a handful of hit-and-run raids by FW 190 fighter-bombers. At this point it is tempting to speculate that a Middle East air commander, more in tune with the needs of ground forces, would have thrown caution to the wind and switched some of the covering Spitfires to much more needed direct support for the desperate Canadians on the beaches. The Air Ministry had always argued that No. 11 Group was best placed to organise close air support because it had the communication systems to do it. Douglas had ensured Fighter Command pilots were getting some training in ground attack and his June 1942 directive had underlined that in an emergency that was how fighters could be used. The situation on the Dieppe beaches seemed to be that emergency.

Such possibilities might have occurred to Leigh-Mallory had he been on HMS *Calpe* witnessing the massacre at first hand; it did not occur to him in his underground Uxbridge bunker. Nor would he have decided a possible attack by E-boats was the immediate danger if he had been shoulder to shoulder with General Roberts. The forward controller on HMS *Fernie* was in contact with the fighters providing low-level cover and on occasion directed them towards enemy aircraft, but redirecting them to attack ground targets was not within his brief.[14] The instruction had to come from Fighter Command. Leigh-Mallory, however, was fully focused on defending the task force from air attack and the decisive air battle he hoped this would lead to. As the requests for more air support came in, it simply did not occur to Leigh-Mallory to switch some of the fighters from the air defence of ships not under serious attack to ground attack in support of troops that were.

In the half-light of dawn, the fighter pilots patrolling above could see enemy fire pouring on to the beaches. They could not know precisely what was happening, although even from 10,000 feet some of them were soon fearing the worst.[15] Just as Guy Gibson and his squadron had felt at the time of Dunkirk, the pilots involved instinctively believed there was something not quite right about the way they were being used.[16] They felt they ought to be down there supporting the ground forces. Like Gibson in 1940, the fighter pilots over Dieppe had to follow orders.

At around 9.00 a.m., after nearly four hours on the beaches, it was decided to withdraw the survivors as quickly as possible. Leigh-Mallory was asked to provide as much air support as he could as well as another smoke screen. Leigh-Mallory was not impressed with this sudden change of plan. The naval and military commanders were not impressed with the RAF's apparent lack of flexibility. At this point, a couple of Leigh-Mallory's squadrons had already flown their second mission of the day, but nineteen still had to fly their first. With the stay in France being cut short, there was plenty of scope for throwing fighter squadrons being held back for later air defence duties into a more immediate and desperately needed ground attack role.

Even before the first smoke-laying planes arrived, the Navy was doing its best to rescue as many of the Canadian infantry as possible. At 11.00 a.m., twelve Hurribombers with twelve Hurricane escorts on their way to bomb the German batteries in the rear were redirected by HMS *Calpe* to strike instead German forces along the seafront, but there was little else they could do to help the survivors trying to get off the beaches.

At around 10.00 a.m., the Luftwaffe began to appear in strength over Dieppe. This was what Leigh-Mallory had been waiting for. The battle on the ground had already been lost, but Leigh-Mallory's battle could now begin. It would begin without Leigh-Mallory's best fighter – the Spitfire IXs, which were all involved escorting the Flying Fortresses bombing Abbeville airfield. The operation seemed like a good idea; this would probably be when Luftwaffe operations countering the landing would be getting into their stride and the airfield would be busy. The thinking was right but evidence from the Middle East suggested that scattering even the impressive total of 35 tons of high explosive and incendiaries over an airfield from 23,000 feet was unlikely to cause much damage and later reconnaissance confirmed this.[17]

The responsibility for top cover over the beaches would lie in the hands of the less capable Spitfire V squadrons. Like their counterparts in the Desert, the pilots were still trying to match the tactics the opposition was using. Fighter squadrons now operated as wings and the pair was supposed to be the basic tactical unit, with two pilots working as a team. Group Captain Harry Broadhurst, the deputy Senior Air Staff Officer at No. 11 Group, had emphasised the importance of fighters operating in well-spaced pairs and fours, but old habits die hard. Fighter squadrons were often still flying in formations that were far too bunched.

Broadhurst was no desk-bound commander. On the day of the Dieppe raid he was flying over the beaches observing how the air battle was going. He noted how small formations of German planes were diving past any closely bunched formation almost at will.[18] The controller on HMS *Calpe* also noticed how fighters operating in much looser formations were much more likely to be successful.[19] These were the tactics the Luftwaffe had been using against the RAF since the outbreak of war. Once again, it seemed that, at every level, adapting to the war that was raging all around them was a painfully long journey for the RAF.

Broadhurst realised there was a need for some higher cover to take on the small groups of FW 190 fighter-bombers before they started their diving attacks. He suggested to Leigh-Mallory that Spitfire IXs be instructed to patrol at altitude in pairs.[20] Spitfire IXs returning with the Fortresses were redirected to Dieppe to provide this additional cover. Redeploying the fighters in this way was a straightforward matter and an example of the flexibility Fighter Command was capable of, but it was a flexibility reserved for the aerial battle, not the battle on the beaches.

The air battle the RAF so wanted did not go well. At the end of the day Leigh-Mallory was convinced his Fighter Command had secured a resounding victory. The RAF had lost 108 aircraft, but by adding his pilots' confirmed victories to their probables, he was able to come up with a figure of 141 Luftwaffe planes destroyed, with another 140 German planes damaged. Nothing like this had occurred. Twenty-five of the 147 bombers despatched by the Luftwaffe had been lost, which were by no means trivial losses. However, the Germans had lost only twenty-three fighters, compared to Fighter Command's sixty-nine Spitfires and four Typhoons. German bombers sank the destroyer HMS *Berkeley*, but Leigh-Mallory could claim his squadrons had prevented further loss to the naval units. In the aerial battle, however, Fighter Command had suffered a resounding tactical defeat.

In numerical terms the air operation was impressive enough. Some 2,500 sorties had been flown during the course of the day. However, around 2,000 of these were pure fighter, compared to just 242 strafing and fighter-bomber missions and 56 medium-bomber sorties. The lack of balance would not have been so significant if the fighters had been used more flexibly. In the Middle East there was no clear distinction between pure fighter and fighter ground attack missions. Douglas was doing his best to turn Fighter Command into a much more flexible force but, when it mattered, Leigh-Malory's instincts were to focus on air defence. For the RAF the aim was not to ensure the raid was a success, the aim was to defeat the Luftwaffe. The air battle was seen as an end in itself. In the UK, air force success was measured by how many enemy planes were shot down, not whether the overall operation was a success.

Dieppe was a thumping defeat in every way. German troops had comfortably beaten off a full-scale attack with just the light forces in place along the seafront without having to deploy any reserves. Of the 6,000 troops landed, 1,000 died on the beaches and another 2,000 were taken prisoner. The Canadians fought the battle, but it was a very British operation. Unlike previous defeats, this time there was no foreign, incompetent ally to blame as there had been in France. Long lines of communication could not be used as an excuse, as they had been in the Middle East. There was no enemy surprise as there had been in the Far East. British and Canadian air and ground commanders had been able to make their plans, assemble the forces required and choose the time and place. Yet it had all gone horribly wrong.

The Germans were amazed that an attempt should be made to take a well-defended port with such meagre and poorly supported forces. Stalin had constantly criticised his western allies for not opening a second front in France. If he had known the attempt would be made to breach defences where they could be expected to be at their strongest with such feeble firepower, he perhaps would have understood better Churchill's reluctance to try. No Soviet or German commander would be expected to succeed in such circumstances. The Dieppe operation did not demonstrate it was impossible to invade France in 1942; it merely demonstrated it was impossible to seize a strongly defended port with such inadequate means.

The Dieppe operation was a measure of how little progress had been made in the two years since Dunkirk towards integrating the different elements of Britain's armed services into a force capable of threatening Germany's western front. Even worse, this was now all too clear to the Germans. Far from diverting resources from the Eastern Front, the raid merely reassured the German High Command that they had nothing to fear in the west. In strategic terms the Dieppe raid was therefore worse than useless. It should at least have been an opportunity to learn lessons, but on the air side it was not an opportunity that was taken. To RAF commanders, there seemed no lessons to learn.

After the operation, Leigh-Mallory claimed the RAF had won 'the greatest air fight the world has ever known' and German positions at Dieppe were 'drenched' with cannon, machine-gun fire and bombs'.[21] Mountbatten replied, describing how the troops were 'equally enthusiastic about the air support which they received throughout the Battle of Dieppe'.[22] Mountbatten thanked Portal for the 'faultless air support' during the operation. 'Dieppe sets a new standard in air co-operation with the Army and Navy which the Germans might have equalled but could hardly have surpassed.'[23]

Such statements, intended for wider, more public distribution, are always necessary to demonstrate appreciation for the brave efforts of those who had risked their lives. Even so, they were so at odds with reality the comments carried an air of irony. The Army's private verdict on the air support provided made more sobering reading. The attempts by Bostons to hit individual gun positions from several thousand feet were futile. Pre-arranged attacks on beachhead defences were helpful but insufficient. Low-level cannon-armed fighters were accurate, but 20mm shells were not enough against fortified positions. Requested close air support had been a 'fiasco', for which, the War Office freely conceded, both the Army and Air Force were to blame.[24] The Mustang tactical reconnaissance squadrons had not been able to contribute much, mainly because there had not been much to spot in the way of reinforcements heading for Dieppe. More critical in this particular battle was the lack of any short-range observation of the beaches to see what was happening and where to direct fire.[25]

From the Army's point of view, there seemed no real Air Force desire for co-operation. During the operation they felt that their input had been unwanted at every stage and at every level of command.[26] General Roberts, the Canadian commander, made it clear that all future seaborne landings had to have far more substantial fire support by both naval and air forces. This, he insisted, must include heavy daylight bombing of any defended coastlines.[27] Mountbatten, too, regretted allowing the aerial pre-bombardment to be dropped.

What amounted to tactical area bombing from altitude was attracting all the attention, partly because that was what Bomber Command could do, but it was very much a First World War solution to the problem. Carpet bombing can be useful although, as Mountbatten and Roberts were aware, it can also obstruct the advance. More precise support is more useful, which naval guns from distance and bombing from altitude cannot always provide. This was where low-level air support came into its own. In operations as dangerous as the Dieppe amphibious landing, the air support had to be as continuous as possible, if only to keep the heads of the defenders down. Occasional large-scale attacks were less useful than more frequent smaller scale attacks.

Leigh-Mallory, in his report on the operation, emphasised the futility of expecting brief strafing attacks to make much difference against fixed defences. Continuous attacks, he cautioned, would simply require too many fighters, leaving insufficient for air defence. It was an argument against using fighters for Army support rather than looking for ways of making close air support more effective. Leigh-Mallory was right; against fortified positions something more than cannon was required and the Hurribombers provided it. At Dieppe, these had been the most effective way of delivering close support, but there were only two squadrons equipped with bomb-carrying fighters.[28]

It was easier to develop a joint-service, combined-arms approach in the Western Desert where there was no English Channel to contend with, but in Britain the gulf between Army and Air Force aims and expectations was a far bigger barrier than the English Channel. Nor should the English Channel have been such a huge obstacle. While the Japanese were supporting their ground forces from airfields hundreds of miles away, at Dieppe the RAF had been unable to do as well from less than 100 miles. The problem was not distance or equipment; the problem was attitude. The Air Force did not see supporting the Army as their primary role.

Most worrying for the War Office was Leigh-Mallory's conviction that the Dieppe operation demonstrated the wisdom of organising the operation from No. 11 Group control centre at Uxbridge. The War Office believed the operation had clearly highlighted the flaws in Portal's 'Eastern Air Force' concept. Mountbatten was also not convinced by Portal's approach. He questioned whether the Uxbridge headquarters could expect to exert any influence on the battle over Dieppe from such a distance and suggested the forward air controllers should have had more power. Leigh-Mallory strongly rejected the idea. The ship-bound forward control could not have the same 'extensive and essential picture' available in the No. 11 Group plotting room. The existing Fighter Command communication systems 'was bound to be superior to any alternative forward control scheme'.[29] It would be 'undesirable if not dangerous' to vest more control in forward command units.[30] In reality, the view of what was happening on the beaches from the destroyers was far more informative than the information on the plotting table at Uxbridge.

Leigh-Mallory insisted the problem was that the forward air controllers on *Calpe* and *Fernie* had been unable to state the nature of the targets they wanted attacked with sufficient definition for the purposes of his Uxbridge HQ. What was required would have been far more obvious to Leigh-Mallory if he had been in the firing line. The air controllers on the spot had no difficulty redirecting the Hurribombers to targets along the seafront. Leigh-Mallory's sophisticated systems were just lengthening the lines of communication, reducing both clarity and response time. All that was required were instructions from the destroyers below to the planes flying above. Centralised control from a distance did not work. More responsibility had to be delegated to lower levels of command.

Instead of hastening the development of an effective army support capability, Dieppe was ammunition for those who believed trying to defeat the German Army was a futile task that it was best not to attempt. Once again a military setback seemed to strengthen the argument that the bomber offensive was the only way of bringing pressure to bear on Germany. For the War Office it was more frustration. They could begin to tackle the problems of landing tanks on to and getting them off the beaches, dealing with strongpoints and the host of other problems the Dieppe operation had thrown up. But getting the air side of such operations right was not within their control.

There were signs that the RAF was moving in the direction the Army wanted it to go. It was perhaps a force wrestling with itself, one that was struggling to break free from Trenchardian dogma. Its preoccupation with maintaining its independence was undoubtedly slowing progress. Trenchard's influence was still overpowering, especially among some more extreme elements of the RAF leadership. Nevertheless, Dieppe had seen the use of close air support. The Air Force was attacking targets in the front line. The scale may have been inadequate but then the scale of everything in the Dieppe operation was inadequate. Portal, Slessor and Douglas all wanted to develop some sort of army air support capability. The failure at Dieppe was perhaps a measure of how far Trenchardian ideas had dragged the Air Force back. Progress had been made but it was from the lowest of starting points.

Douglas had perhaps been the most consistent supporter of an air force army support role. It had been Douglas who, as invasion threatened in summer 1940, had wanted to get the Douglas Bostons and Martin Marylands out of their packing cases and into the squadrons. Now, in 1942 at home and overseas, in defence or attack, he believed that 'in the fourth year of this war it is abundantly clear that no land operations against the enemy can hope to succeed unless arrangements for air support are of the highest order of efficiency'.[31] Churchill might consider such comments a statement of the obvious, but it was revealing that such a statement even needed to be made with the war entering its fourth year. The problem was agreeing how to achieve this desirable state of affairs. For all Douglas and Portal's enthusiasm for promoting the Army support fighter-bomber, achieving this 'highest order of efficiency' was going to be difficult as long as the Air Ministry jealously guarded the air support weapon as its to develop and control. Air power was still seen as a self-contained element of warfare. Even in the tactical domain, the air commanders wanted to fight their own, separate air war.

After the Dieppe operation, Douglas re-issued his June directive on using fighters for ground attack, with more emphasis on using them to support an invasion of France rather than defeat an invasion of Britain. By September 1942, all fighter squadrons had received some training in ground attack and forty squadrons had trained with Army Air Support Controls.[32] The emphasis the Middle East was putting on fighters carrying bombs was also influencing Fighter Command. Initially, only the two Hurribomber squadrons of the fifteen set aside for ground attack could carry bombs but this was now changing.

In July 1942, Douglas asked if the Westland Whirlwind could carry bombs. The conversion to enable it to carry a couple of 500lb bombs was straightforward enough for it to be done at the bases the fighters operated from.[33] The first bomber sorties were flown by Whirlwinds in September. In August the first Typhoons were fitted with bomb racks.[34] To begin with, 500lb bombs would be carried, but eventually this would be increased to a couple of 1,000lb bombs. Initially, the Spitfire was to be exempt from carrying bombs but, in November 1942, a report from Malta described how an improvised bomb rack carrying a single 250lb bomb had been fitted

Arthur Harris with his staff at Bomber Command HQ. (Crown)

The remains of Lübeck cathedral poke through the smoke still rising from the smouldering city.

Heavy "Stirling" bombers raid the Nazi Baltic port of Lübeck and leave the docks ablaze

BACK THEM UP!

Left: A propaganda poster suggesting Lübeck's industries were the target. (Crown)

Below: The *Daily Mirror* celebrates the destruction of Lübeck.

WHAT WE DID TO LUBECK

Mercy trip by

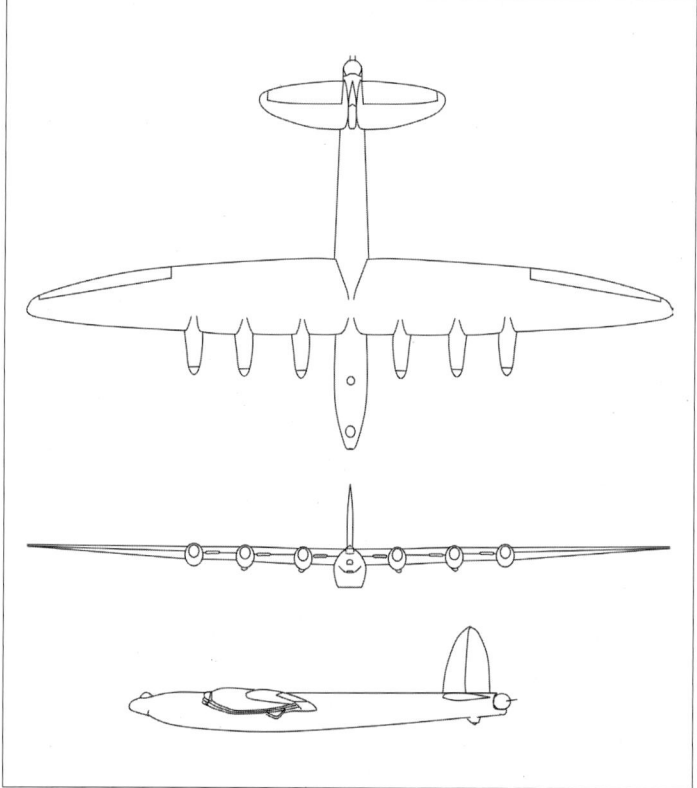

Above: The Americans were already planning to take bomber theory to its logical conclusion with bombers like the inter-continental Consolidated B-36.

Right: The proposed Vickers high-altitude bomber. British attempts to develop an ultra-long-range bomber never got off the drawing board.

Left: Arthur Coningham, the commander of the desert tactical air force. (Crown)

Below: The Curtiss Kittyhawk with the Flying Tiger nose of No. 112 Squadron. (Crown)

PHOTO © JOHN DIBBS COLLECTION

Above and below: RAF light/medium squadrons relied heavily on American imports. Above: the Douglas Boston; below: the Martin Baltimore. (Crown)

Above and below: The requirement for a compact, manoeuvrable ground attack plane led to some imaginative tandem-wing designs. Above: the Boulton Paul P.100. Below: the scaled-down Miles M.39B used to test the Libellula configuration their M.42 ground attack plane was to use. (Crown/Les Whitehouse)

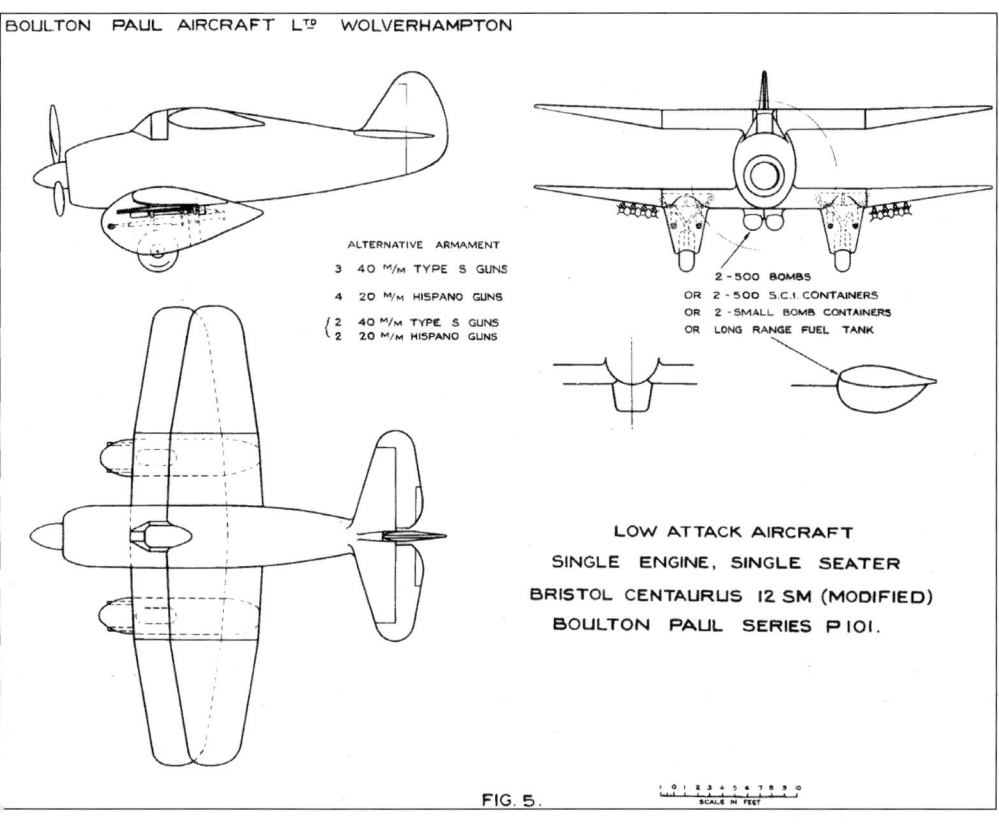

ALTERNATIVE ARMAMENT

3   40 $^{M}/_{M}$ TYPE S GUNS

4   20 $^{M}/_{M}$ HISPANO GUNS

{ 2   40 $^{M}/_{M}$ TYPE S GUNS
{ 2   20 $^{M}/_{M}$ HISPANO GUNS

2 - 500 BOMBS

OR 2 - 500 S.C.I. CONTAINERS

OR 2 - SMALL BOMB CONTAINERS

OR LONG RANGE FUEL TANK

LOW ATTACK AIRCRAFT

SINGLE ENGINE, SINGLE SEATER

BRISTOL CENTAURUS 12 SM (MODIFIED)

BOULTON PAUL SERIES P 101.

FIG. 5.

SCALE IN FEET

The Boulton Paul P.101 biplane was the simplest way of meeting the ground attack requirement. (Les Whitehouse)

The helicopter would prove to be the ideal way of providing low-speed air support. The first practicable helicopter, the Sikorski R-4, was just entering production. (Crown)

The FW 190 that fell into British hands in June 1942. (Crown)

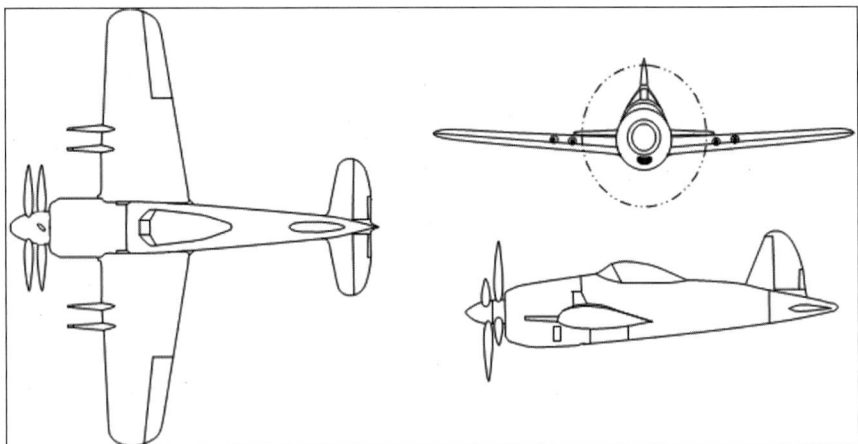

The Air Ministry hoped Folland's Fo.117 would mark the beginning of a new chapter in British fighter design.

The Allison-powered North American Mustang came out of the trials with the FW 190 with more credit than most. (Crown)

The 2,200 hp Centaurus-powered Tornado. The Tornado and early versions of the Typhoon still had the streamlined cockpits which restricted pilot view. (Crown)

The 2,500 hp Centaurus V-powered Tempest II with an all-round vision cockpit canopy. (Crown)

Above and below: The controversial American dive-bombers. Above: the Vultee Vengeance; below: the Brewster Bermuda. (Crown)

The Lockheed Ventura was developed from the Lockheed Lodestar civil transport. (Crown)

The de Havilland Mosquito in its light-bomber guise with a glazed bomb-aiming position in the nose. (Crown)

Above and below: The Spitfire Vb with a 90-gallon slipper drop tank. (Crown via Phil Butler)

Spitfire with 170-gallon slipper tank used for ferrying. (Crown via Phil Butler)

Hurricane IVs of No. 170 Wing in Burma. The Hurricane remained a versatile short-range Army support plane, capable of carrying bombs, 40mm cannon or rockets. (Crown)

In the UK the higher performance Typhoon was the preferred aircraft for army support. (BAe Systems)

The breached Eder Dam after the attack by the Lancasters of No. 617 Squadron. (Crown)

Canterbury following German retaliation for the 1,000 bomber raid on Cologne.

A Turbinlite Boston with searchlight in the nose with four of the Alan Muntz engineers that helped develop it. From left to right: Richard Becker, Dennis Roberts, Leslie Baynes and Bruce Benson. (Crown)

A Lancaster scattering Window over Germany. (Crown)

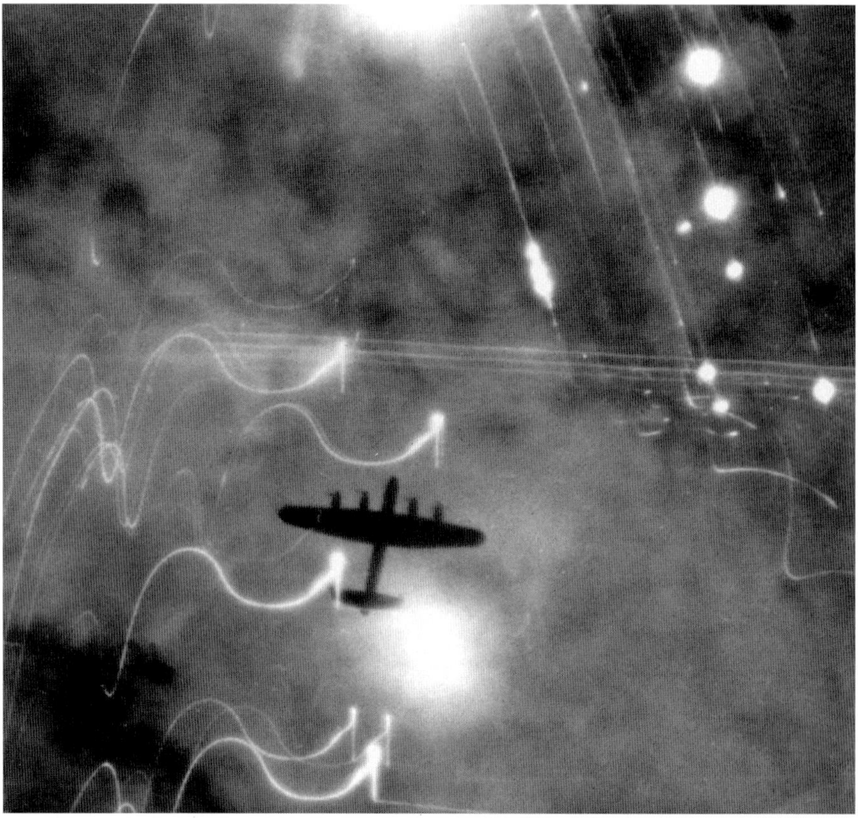

A Lancaster stands out against clouds lit up by the fires and searchlights below. (Crown)

The city of Hamburg after the July 1943 bombing

to Spitfires for 75-degree dive-bombing attacks on airfields in Sicily.[35] Douglas, in one of his last acts as the commander of Fighter Command, now wanted Spitfires to carry bombs as well. The Spitfire did not have the lifting capacity of the Typhoon or Hurricane, but by December it was official policy to make all Spitfires capable of carrying one or two 250lb bombs.

Douglas was leaving behind him a much more flexible fighter force than he had inherited in 1940. To the very end, Douglas's absolute priority was the air defence of the United Kingdom, which, as head of Fighter Command, was to be expected. Nevertheless, he had done a lot to advance the army air support cause, and his departure to Cairo to head Middle East Command in what would soon become a backwater of the war, was perhaps unfortunate.

There was still much debate about which of the available fighters made the best fighter-bomber. Although the Typhoon, in its various guises, was being touted as the natural successor to the Hurricane in the ground attack role, this was not the view of the Air Fighting Development Unit. In comparative trials with all the available options, the Typhoon was praised for providing a very steady gun platform and its high speed would be useful for evading interception but, the unit concluded, it lacked the manoeuvrability of the Spitfire and Hurricane to jink past anti-aircraft fire. In the final assessment the Typhoon ended up in joint fourth place with the Spitfire, behind the Mustang (first), Hurricane (second) and Whirlwind (third).[36] The Mustangs were earmarked for the tactical reconnaissance squadrons and the Whirlwind was no longer in production, which left the Hurricane as the favoured ground attack fighter.

It might seem a surprising result. In the assessment there was perhaps a failure to distinguish between the high-performance fighter-bomber and the specialist ground attack plane. The Hurricane could not claim to be the former but it had many of the attributes of the latter. It could carry a wide variety of weapons and was one of the few aircraft that had the low-speed manoeuvrability to use the 40mm anti-tank gun effectively. This particular combination was very much Portal's pet project. Such was Portal's pleasure over the achievements of the Hurricane IID tank busters in the Western Desert, he thought it worth sending the Prime Minister a note devoted entirely to how successful it had been.[37] Portal saw a huge role for the plane and in the summer of 1942 there were plans for up to nine squadrons in the Mediterranean and Europe by the spring of 1943. Ironically, one of the problems Portal faced in creating his ground attack force was that, on so many fronts, the Hurricane was still expected to operate as a fighter. Portal was sternly warned that every Hurricane squadron created for ground attack was one less fighter squadron for air defence in North Africa or India.[38]

The plan was to carry on building the Hurribomber until the end of 1942, at which point all Hurricane production would switch to the Mark IID 40mm cannon version. By this time it was hoped that a new universal wing would enable the Hurricane to carry 40mm cannon, bombs or rockets as required. The Merlin XX, optimised for performance at altitude, was scarcely ideal for the low-level ground attack role, and plans were soon afoot for a Mark IV with the Merlin 24/27 engine, boosted to give 1,600hp low down. This version would have 350lb of armour and would continue in production at a rate of sixty a month. With armour and 40mm cannon its top speed was now just 280 mph.

The decision to give the Hurricane a healthy quantity of armour removed the last vestiges of its fighter capability. It was, however, nowhere near as heavily armoured as the Soviet Sturmovik. The ground attack Hurricane fell between two stools; it was neither a heavily armoured assault plane nor a high performance fighter-bomber. It was justifiable to use up existing Hurricanes in the close support role, the traditional fate of aircraft that were no longer good enough for air-to-air combat. More powerful, armoured versions were justified as an interim, but the Hurricane could be no more than this. It was just an adapted fighter. Something far more effective might emerge if designers started with a blank sheet of paper. This was what the specialist ground attack aircraft Sorley had proposed earlier in 1942 was supposed to deliver.

Several companies had been asked to see what might be possible. The plane was supposed to be simple, small and manoeuvrable, be able to operate from small, primitive forward airfields, have a range of 750 miles and a top speed of 280 mph. It was a stiff requirement that inspired some imaginative proposals. To keep the design compact and still provide plenty of lift, designers turned to various tandem-wing combinations including canard designs like the Boulton Paul P.100, the Phillips & Powis (later Miles) M.42 with its Libellula configuration or just a straightforward cantilever biplane with the Boulton Paul P.101.

The idea of a biplane might seem bizarre but made perfect sense if high speed was not the aim. The configuration also had the advantage that it was not an unknown quantity like some of the more exotic configurations on offer. Unbeknown to the Air Ministry, there was support for the biplane approach from the Eastern Front. The German 200 mph Henschel

HS 123 was proving so useful in the ground attack role that, in January 1943, it was suggested the ancient biplane should be put back into production.

At the other end of the technological spectrum, Boulton Paul suggested jet engines could be used as they had no vulnerable protruding propellers and were easy to armour. For firepower, various combinations of machine guns, 20mm and 40mm cannon, bombs and rockets were proposed. Cunliffe Owen suggested a design that could carry a battery of no less than thirty machine guns or nine 40mm cannon.[39] Only the Boulton Paul biplane was anything like the unsophisticated plane Sorley wanted and the only offering that might be available by 1944. However, with its conventional tractor engine blocking forward view, it really offered no advantage over the Hurricane and was quickly eliminated.

Designers were showing enormous ingenuity but the requirement they were trying to meet was essentially flawed. The original 90 mph attacking speed had been abandoned, although the plane still had to fly slowly enough to use the 40mm cannon. Landing and take-off requirements were relaxed, but no one questioned the need for 750-mile range. The War Office had only ever wanted a plane that could operate over forward troops, but inevitably the Air Ministry required something that could fly much further. More range meant larger, more powerful aircraft that would have to operate from larger airfields in the rear. Operating against targets deep in the enemy rear increased the chances of interception which increased the need for higher performance.

Although Sorley's specification only required a top speed of 280 mph. all the proposals promised speeds in excess of 300 mph.[40] Designers knew how the Air Ministry mind worked and all tried to achieve the fastest possible speed compatible with the other requirements. Everything was taking the idea in the direction of a large, powerful, high-performance combat plane. The MAP considered one of the better proposals to be the massive 62-foot-span Cunliffe Owen Twin with a wing area greater than the Blenheim.[41] Even when the aim was to create a specialist close support plane, with no strategic bombing capability, it seemed it was always destined to end up being large.

With the benefit of hindsight it is easy to see the helicopter was the slow-flying aircraft the Army was feeling its way towards. Britain had abandoned development of helicopters in 1940 and handed over all they had learned to the Americans. The first practical helicopters were now just entering production in the United States and both the Royal Navy and War Office were following the progress of the latest Vought-Sikorski

R-4 helicopter (the future Hoverfly in British service). The prototype flew in January 1942 and the design was already capable of flying for two and a half hours and lifting 440lb. Sikorski was hoping to increase this to 1,100lb by the end of 1942.[42] The Admiralty was already looking into the possibility of using this helicopter for anti-submarine duties. At this stage, the War Office was only interested in the helicopter as a liaison aircraft; the army combat helicopter was still a decade away. However, designers had shown no reluctance to consider other highly novel and experimental configurations. It is possible that, without the maximum speed and range requirements, helicopters might have been considered as a way of meeting Sorley's ground attack requirement.

Sorley's requirement proved to be a very short-lived foray into the specialist ground attack field. None of the proposals put forward seemed to offer enough advantage over the Hurricane to warrant developing an entirely new aircraft. The MAP did not feel anything beyond the Hurricane would be needed until at least 1945 and in April 1943 the development programme was abandoned. From the perspective of the Ministry of Aircraft Production it was a sensible decision. Its job was to maximise production and win the war. That meant introducing as few new types as possible. The Air Ministry had a wider responsibility. Even after victory, Britain would still need an effective air force. As the prospect of defeat receded, a longer term view was required to ensure the RAF was ready for whatever challenges the post-war era might bring. The specialist ground attack aircraft had been a gap that needed filling ever since the Salamander had been abandoned in 1918. 1943 was as good a time as any to begin the process of filling that gap. Indeed, to find the replacement for the Hurricane in 1945 that the MAP conceded would be required, development had to begin in 1943.

The specialist close support aircraft was not the only gap in the RAF armoury that required a fresh start. The air superiority fighter was another specialist type that, in 1918, had been an important part of existing RAF front-line strength and future development programmes. This had been another victim of the bomber strategy and the Air Ministry's focus on long-range bombers and short-range bomber interceptors.

Chapter 9

Fighter Revolution

For some time it had been apparent there were fundamental problems with the RAF fighter force. Fighter Command was finding it difficult to shake off its air defence origins. Its squadrons were tied to airfields that were linked to the air defence system. Equipment had been designed and the pilots trained to intercept unescorted bombers. Some tinkering had overcome some of the disadvantages the fighters suffered from when they had to take on enemy fighters, but they were still essentially modified bomber interceptors.

The key requirements had always been the highest possible speed, the ability to reach whatever altitude the bombers were flying and the firepower to shoot them down, however mighty they might be. Four 20mm cannon was a standard requirement and there was talk of increasing this to six or even eight cannon. Other possibilities included 40mm cannon and air-to-air rockets. Even after the fighting in France and the Battle of Britain had demonstrated fighters had to do much more than just bring down bombers, firepower, speed, and the highest possible ceiling were still the primary Air Ministry requirements. Nobody thought there was any need for a fundamental rethink about what else a fighter should be capable of.

The only new fighter to be ordered into production since the outbreak of war was the jet-powered Gloster Meteor, mainly in the hope that its jet engines would enable it to deal with the high-altitude bomber threat. It was a measure of how great this fear was that in 1941 scarce production capacity was being put to one side for a fighter that had not even flown, just to deal with a threat that had not yet emerged. To speed up development, no fewer than twelve prototypes had been ordered. Gloster were expecting extraordinarily high speeds but, after raising such high hopes in 1940 and 1941, and with 300 already on order, the project was in serious trouble. The only 'flight' was a brief hop into the air that only demonstrated the engines were not powerful enough to sustain flight. By the end of 1942, far from rolling off the production lines, the prototype had still not flown and interest

155

in the whole project was on the wane. The production contract for 300 was cut back to fifty and the number of prototypes on order reduced to six.

While engineers struggled with this bomber interceptor of the future, it was not high-altitude bombers that were proving to be Fighter Command's biggest challenge. The problem was the German fighter. In their sweeps over France, RAF pilots were having enormous problems grappling with the latest Bf 109s and, in particular, the phenomenal FW 190. As always, it was assumed more power and higher speeds would solve the problem. There was a general belief that the latest Merlin, Griffon, Centaurus and Sabre engines would close the performance gap. As late as July 1942, Douglas believed the predicted 450 mph of the Sabre IV-powered Tempest I ought to give the RAF a fighter faster than any fighter the Germans could put into the air, at least until their first jets arrived.[1] In Douglas's eyes faster meant superior. While Fighter Command awaited fighters powered by these new powerful engines, the shortcomings of existing equipment continued to be underlined by some one-sided engagements over France. On 1 June 1942, No. 65 Squadron lost four Spitfire Vs in a tussle with FW 190s. The next day, No. 403 Squadron lost no fewer than seven Spitfire Vs in a single engagement.

On 23 June, three Spitfire squadrons escorting Boston bombers were caught up in another one-sided battle with the FW 190. This time seven Spitfires were lost. One of the victims was shot down by Oberleutnant Armin Faber in a furious dogfight that ended over Cornwall. Unfortunately for Faber, during the battle he had become disorientated. Having completed the kill, he set off in what he thought was a southerly direction, but he was in fact flying north. He mistook the Bristol Channel for the English Channel and, short of fuel, landed at the first airfield he came across – Pembry in south Wales. It was an enormous stroke of luck. Britain had been gifted Germany's latest fighter. RAF pilots would now have the chance to find out what made the FW 190 so good. What they discovered set alarm bells ringing.

Often the capture of the latest enemy fighter tends to ease concerns rather than intensify them. In the First World War, when the British got their hands on the dreaded Fokker E1 Eindecker, RFC pilots had been relieved to discover they had far less to fear than they had imagined. The same had happened with the Albatros. The alarm the arrival of a new enemy design can provoke can lead to its qualities being exaggerated. It was very different with the FW 190. As soon as British pilots took the fighter into the air, it became clear that Allied pilots had not been overestimating the opposition. The FW 190 was a remarkable warplane. Its high horizontal, climb and diving speeds were impressive, but it was the exceptional flying characteristics of the plane that most impressed the pilots who tested it. Unlike the Spitfire, and indeed the Bf 109, there was no problem controlling the plane at high speed. The superbly harmonised controls enabled all manoeuvres to be carried out throughout the speed range with the minimum of difficulty. The Focke-Wulf was a joy to fly. Pilots noted how little time it took to become fully comfortable on the type, a huge advantage in wartime when pilot training had to be as brief as possible.

The Spitfire IX retained the traditional British advantage in turning circle, thanks to its large wing area and low wing loading. However, the disadvantages of large wings now came to the fore; high-span wings tend to act as brakes when the pilot tries to change direction. Like most continental fighters, the FW 190 had a much shorter wingspan than most British fighters, which helped give the FW 190 a far better rate of roll.

However, it was much more than a question of wingspan. The FW 190 was just much easier to control. Pilots could change direction astonishingly quickly at all speeds. In comparative trials, the only Allied fighter that came close to matching the FW 190 in this respect was the Allison-powered Mustang. The Typhoon was especially embarrassed by the superb manoeuvrability of the Focke-Wulf. The Typhoon could not even match the turning circle of the German fighter. It climbed more slowly and even lost ground in the early stages of a dive, until the greater weight and power of the Typhoon began to take effect. It was small compensation for the fighter's deficiencies in all other respects.

The climb and acceleration of the FW 190 was also impressive; in this respect it outperformed all Allied planes, apart from the Spitfire IX, which was broadly similar. The light weight of the Bf 109 had always been one of its notable features. The FW 190 was far more robust and heavier than the Bf 109, and indeed it was heavier than the Spitfire, but its empty weight was around 1,000lb lighter than the contemporary Typhoon. The FW 190 was also smaller and more compact. The size and weight of British fighters was something the Air Ministry would have to start looking at.

Other advantages of the FW 190 included the superb all-round view. Although some efforts had been made to tackle this problem, RAF pilots were still huddled in their semi-streamlined cockpits which added a few mph to top speed but made it very difficult to see behind. Four of the Focke-Wulf's six guns (two machine guns in the fuselage and two cannon in the wing roots) were synchronised to fire through the propeller, providing a high concentration of fire at all ranges, as opposed to the single point of concentration possible with the wing-mounted guns on RAF fighters. Perhaps most significantly of all, the FW 190's supercharger was geared to give optimum power at 18,000 feet as opposed to 27,000 feet on the Spitfire's Merlin. After years of straining for the highest possible speed at the highest possible altitude, RAF fighters were being seriously embarrassed by a fighter that gave its best performance at low and medium altitudes. There was little to criticise about the German machine. Even the high degree of workmanship was noted. There was none of the uneven finish that was a characteristic of mass-produced British fighters.

Pilots are often very good at persuading themselves that their own more familiar aircraft are superior. A degree of wishful thinking and patriotic loyalty tends to creep into the judgement. British pilots had managed to persuade themselves that the Hurricane, indeed even the Defiant, could hold its own against the Bf 109E. German test pilots had not been over-impressed by the Spitfire. What some might see as an advantage, others can re-interpret as a disadvantage. To British pilots, the American Thunderbolt dived like a brick; to American pilots the Spitfire dived like a leaf. There is usually a tendency, amongst all test pilots, to view more unfamiliar foreign designs less favourably than they sometimes deserve. These prejudices make the praise lavished on the FW 190 all the more striking.

On reading the report, Douglas was forced to concede the FW 190 was without doubt 'the best all round fighter in the world'. Yet it was a fighter whose performance dropped off dramatically above 25,000 feet, a characteristic which had damned so many American fighters. To lavish such praise on such a fighter was, by previous standards, an act of heresy. In its own way, the report on the FW 190 was as startling as the Butt report of 1941 on the failure of bomber offensive. In both cases evidence had been accumulating for some time and everyone accepted that there was a problem. Steps were already being taken to put things right. However, it took the Butt report and the FW 190 trials for the true scale of these two very different problems to be fully appreciated.

For the pilots in the front line, the trials merely confirmed what they already knew. Leigh-Mallory's belief that the Typhoon and Spitfire IX would restore British technical superiority was just wishful thinking. The RAF did not have anything to match the FW 190. In July, Portal and Douglas were horrified when Parliament was told that the latest British fighter designs, a reference to the Spitfire IX, were superior to the latest German designs. Portal pointed out that a fighter that had been in service with the Luftwaffe for nearly a year was being compared with a British fighter that had not yet reached the squadrons in any numbers and, in any case, the claim of technical superiority 'hangs by a slender thread'.[2] Such claims would immediately be recognised as untrue by front-line pilots who had to deal with the FW 190 and such a blatant misrepresentation of the facts would, Portal believed, be bound to have a damaging effect on morale within the service.

For the Typhoon, the trials with the FW 190 were the final straw. In a report compiled by squadron commanders, they quite correctly argued the fighter was fine as long as it was used in its intended role as an interceptor. The Typhoon's speed and firepower were ideal for intercepting Luftwaffe hit-and-run fighter-bomber attacks. However, as infuriating as these might be, they were not going to determine the course of the war. The Typhoon's fundamental problem was its interceptor origins. In the words of the squadron commanders' report, 'The Typhoon was not designed primarily for fighting fighters, whereas the FW190 clearly was.'[3] For more offensive operations, the RAF also needed something 'designed primarily for fighting fighters'.

Douglas feared things could only get worse. The FW 190 was at the very beginning of its development life whereas the Spitfire was probably approaching the end of its. The FW 190 had already been in service for nearly a year and improvements to the design were almost certainly on the way. There were already reports of turbo-supercharged and inline-engined variants in the pipeline. Douglas feared that, by the spring of 1943, more advanced versions of the FW 190 would totally outclass even the Spitfire IX. Everything suddenly seemed to look a lot gloomier. Douglas rated the Griffon 61-powered Spitfire XXI as no more than the British equivalent of the Bf 109G, which was already in service with the Luftwaffe. Unless development of the Spitfire XXI could be speeded up considerably, he feared this, too, might be obsolete on entering service. Douglas was a very worried man. He did not believe the MAP appreciated how serious the situation was.[4]

The Air Ministry shared Douglas's despair. The Spitfire XII was now considered a complete waste of time. It lacked speed and climb and would be obsolete before it even reached the squadrons. The Merlin-powered Mustang seemed the only ray of hope. American designers had always tended to attach more importance to control, which was why the Tomahawk and Kittyhawk had proven to be more successful than the Hurricane. The Allison-powered Mustang had come out of the comparative trials with the

FW 190 with more credit than most, reinforcing the view that the Merlin-powered Mustang might well be the best fighter the Allies were likely to get in the immediate future. The Air Ministry was in no doubt that the Mustang/Merlin 61 was the only American fighter that would be good enough to compete in European skies in the summer of 1943.[5]

However, even the Merlin/Mustang did not look quite as attractive as it had done before the FW 190 fell into British hands. Although American fighters had always impressed with their finely harmonised controls, they also tended to be rather heavy, and the P-51 Mustang was no exception. Compared to the FW 190, the American fighter was poor in terms of climb and acceleration. Ironically, while the FW 190 had forced the Air Ministry to rethink the importance of keeping weight down, American designers were in awe of the 'light-weight' Spitfire. Teams arrived from the United States to study ways in which the British approach to structural design and policies on safety margins might be applied to American designs and this would lead to a whole range of lightweight versions of their own fighters.[6]

The need for quick solutions led to another round of tweaking. Even a small reduction in wingspan could produce a significant increase in rate of roll. The Duxford Air Fighting Development Unit conducted trials with a Spitfire V with its wing tips removed. This not only improved rate of roll, it also slightly increased acceleration and diving performance at all altitudes, which also helped close the gap a little. The lower wing area reduced the fighter's turning circle, but the modified Spitfire could still turn comfortably inside the FW 190. So clear were the advantages of the clipped wings that the modification was immediately ordered for the Spitfire IX as well. Clipped wings might help the Spitfire roll quicker, but more fundamental changes were required. Part of the Spitfire's problem was the way the wing distorted at high speed. A new stiffer wing was required, which would involve a complete redesign. Thoughts were turning to a much revised fourth generation of Spitfire fighters. Rolls-Royce was asked to see what it could do about improving engine output at lower altitudes. This resulted in the Merlin 66, which gave the Spitfire its maximum speed at 21,000 feet instead of 28,000 feet.[7] It was a strange twist of fate that an engine designed for high-altitude operations should end up being optimised for medium altitudes. The Merlin 66 would begin arriving early in 1943.

The Spitfire's Merlin 45 could also be modified to improve performance at low altitudes. The Merlin 45M enabled the Spitfire V to achieve a maximum speed at 6,000 feet rather than 20,000 feet of the standard version, which gave the Spitfire about the same speed as the FW 190 at the lower altitude, albeit at the price of an even greater inferiority at higher altitudes. However, in tactical operations, fighters needed to operate at these low levels, as the air fighting in the Middle East was demonstrating, and the Spitfire IX could provide cover at higher altitudes. The modifications were easy enough to be applied in the field; it just required three-quarters of an inch to be shaved off the engine impellor. This became the Spitfire LF (Low Fighter) Mark V or the 'clipped, cropped and clapped' version as it was known by the pilots: 'clipped' because of the wings, 'cropped' because of the engine impellor and 'clapped', because most of the Spitfires modified were clapped out. From 1943 most Spitfire Vs built were of the low-level LF variety.

These were all useful interim measures but there was only so far tinkering could go. For the first time, the Air Ministry felt obliged to rethink its entire approach to fighter design. It was not that British designers did not know how to produce a fighter with the fine handling qualities the FW 190 possessed, it was just that this was not what they had been asked to do. Bomber interceptors did not need a high rate of roll, finely harmonised controls or excellent manoeuvrability throughout the speed range. This did not deter some designers from producing fighters with these qualities; Henry Folland in particular, with fighters like the Gloster Gauntlet, had produced some outstandingly agile fighters.

The warning signs had been there for some time; indeed they were there even before Fighter Command pilots found themselves dog fighting with Messerschmitts. In 1939, the French had tested a Spitfire and were not the least impressed because control at high speed was so poor and far worse than the fighters the French Air Force was using. A perplexed Air Ministry borrowed a fighter the French were very happy with, an American Curtiss P-36, for trials and discovered it was indeed far easier to manoeuvre at high speeds. The trials with the FW 190 stirred memories of these 1939 trials.[8]

Another fighter that had taken part in these trials was Folland's Gloster F.5/34 prototype. At the time, pilots noted that Folland's fighter had many of the fine handling characteristics the Curtiss fighter possessed. Following the FW 190 trials, the full significance of these 1939 trials was now sinking in. Since designing his F.5/34 fighter, Folland had left Gloster and set up his own small company, building components for aircraft like the Blenheim and Spitfire and the odd specialist one-off designs, like his 'Folland Frightful', an aircraft designed as an engine test-bed. Effectively he had retired from combat aircraft design. Nevertheless, suddenly, Folland was the name on everyone's lips.

On 30 July 1942, representatives from the Ministry of Aircraft Production and Air Ministry, including Portal, Freeman and Sorley, together with Douglas from Fighter Command, met to discuss the crisis in British fighter design. It was agreed by all present that the Spitfire V was, to all intents and purposes, obsolete. It was hoped that improved superchargers might keep the Spitfire IX reasonably competitive in 1943. With low and medium altitude performance now seen as key, even the Spitfire XII might have a useful role to play at altitudes up to 12,000 feet. However, the comments on the Typhoon and Tempest were damning. Both Hawker fighters might be useful in a defensive role as interceptors and would make good 'low-level strafers'. They might even prove effective in the night-fighter role but, because of their poor manoeuvrability, neither would make a good 'rough and tumble' day fighter.[9]

The MAP immediately agreed to phase out the Typhoon I at Hawker as quickly as possible. In order to speed up development of the Sabre IV-powered Tempest I, the two Griffon versions were dropped. The Centaurus Tempest II order was reduced to just 200 machines and the Tempest I was reinstated, with production expected to begin in October 1942. This would become the principal variant with production rising to 200 machines a month by 1944, although monthly production would not get into double figures until June 1943. As the Sabre IV was unlikely to be available before mid-1943 at the earliest, it was also agreed that the first fifty Tempests would have the Sabre II, this version becoming the Tempest V. Quite what miracle would enable the Sabre IV to be available by the middle of 1943 was not clear to anyone.[10]

The Air Ministry was not the least bit impressed by these proposals. Even if the Sabre IV overcame its problems, they believed even the Tempest I would not be good enough to take on future versions of the Bf 109 and FW 190. The MAP was growing equally doubtful about the entire Tempest project. To guard against further delays, the MAP was already considering alternative production plans. The country could not go on building Hurricanes and Typhoons until the Tempest was ready. The Griffon 61-powered Spitfire XXI was effectively another new design and was considered as great a risk as the Tempest. The only safe alternative was the Spitfire VIII. The MAP now started preparing contingency plans for the production of this version of the Spitfire in the Hawker/Gloster group.[11] Camm might yet see his Typhoons and Hurricanes replaced by his rival's fighter. The other immediate alternative was the Merlin 61/Mustang – if they could persuade the Americans to build them.

As far as the Air Ministry was concerned, all these fighters were only short-term interim solutions that were not really tackling the fundamental problem. Tinkering with essentially flawed designs was not the answer. A fresh start was needed. In a strange way, history was repeating itself. Just after the end of the First World War, the Air Ministry, convinced that bombers would decide future wars, had summoned Air Commodore Thomas Higgins, the commander of the home defence fighter force, to come up with the ideal bomber interceptor. His conclusion was that it would look nothing like the agile dogfighters that had fought over the Western Front. The Air Ministry now had to do the reverse. It needed a fighter designed to take on other fighters, not simply shoot down bombers. It needed to define what such an ideal air superiority fighter should be capable of and then see what designers came up with. It might take more than two years to bear fruit but it would be worth it. The captured FW 190 would provide an excellent template.

The MAP was extremely sceptical about embarking on such a project. Two years was a long time and introducing an entirely new plane would inevitably result in a loss of production. Jet-powered aircraft were already a reality, despite the problems the Meteor was experiencing. Two years into the future, the required performance might well be defined by entirely new criteria that jet propulsion would establish. The Ministry of Aircraft Production was therefore very much against developing an entirely new piston-engined design at this late stage. Neither side was willing to budge. Indeed, the question generated so much discord that it reached the prime minister's office. Lindemann, Churchill's influential scientific advisor, came down on the side of the MAP, insisting the Tempest/Sabre combination remained the solution.[12] Portal made it clear to Churchill that this was not the case; the Tempest might have the necessary speed but that was about all it had. British designers had to make a fresh start.[13]

Ignoring MAP objections, the Air Ministry went ahead and formulated an entirely new fighter specification: F.6/42. It would revolutionise the thinking behind British fighter design. No longer would it be the likely performance of the opposing bombers that would determine what was required; now it was the likely performance of the opposing fighters that would set the criteria. The aim of the new specification was simply to produce a fighter that was superior in horizontal speed, climbing speed and manoeuvrability to any enemy fighter. Far more attention would have to be paid to harmonising controls to ensure maximum manoeuvrability throughout the speed range. Particular attention was to be paid to manoeuvrability in the rolling plane, one aspect of performance the specification emphasised that had been neglected in previous interceptor designs. Excellent acceleration was also expected, which meant keeping weight as low as possible.

The Air Ministry believed the fighter had to be capable of at least 450 mph, but designers were not to compromise the other performance characteristics in the quest for speed. The aim was to achieve the highest possible horizontal speed, consistent with other requirements, not at the expense of other requirements. In particular, the Air Ministry emphasised that climbing performance was to take precedence over horizontal speed.[14] The fighter was expected to carry four 20mm cannon, still a hefty punch, but at least there would be no more talk of six or eight cannon. To keep weight down, equipment would be kept to an absolute minimum. This included internal fuel, which was perhaps a hangover from interceptor requirements, but the ability to carry drop tanks would be standard, as would carrying bombs. Finally a good all-round view for the pilot was essential.

Two versions of the specification emerged, one optimising performance at medium and low level, the other optimising performance at high level. The former demanded a top speed of 450 mph at 20,000 feet and the latter the same speed at 32,000 feet.[15] The two versions mirrored the high and low altitude fighters of 1917–1918. No mention was made of First World War fighters in the discussions and indeed it would probably not have occurred to anyone that there was anything from that conflict relevant to the debate that was worth remembering. However, in effect, the Air Ministry wanted to get back to the dog-fighters of the First World War.

For such a fighter to arrive in time for the current conflict, design and development had to be completed as quickly as possible. The Air Ministry wanted the plane to be operational by 1945. To achieve this, the Air Ministry suggested that the best designers from different aircraft companies should be brought together. With the qualities of the Gloster F.5/34 very much in mind, the Air Ministry suggested this team should be led by none other than Henry Folland. Not surprisingly, the suggestion of a joint effort, never mind one led by a semi-retired designer, was unanimously rejected by all the major aircraft companies and they all put forward their own proposals.[16] The MAP backed them by insisting that only proposals from companies with the production capacity to mass produce the end result would be considered, effectively ruling out Folland. The Air Ministry, however, made sure Folland was kept fully informed about what it wanted.

There were three engines available to designers, the Sabre IV, the Griffon 61 and the radial Centaurus 12. Napier was predicting its Sabre would eventually be capable of 2,500hp but the company's track record was hardly encouraging. The Griffon already existed and it was hoped by the time the new fighter entered production it would be producing close to 2,000hp. This engine was the lightest but had the least attractive power/weight ratio. The Centaurus was an improved version of the model already proposed for the Tempest which, interestingly, got round some of the overheating problems the earlier version had suffered by adopting the internal engine-driven fan the Germans used with the FW 190's BMW engine. The Centaurus promised 2,500hp. Whatever engine was chosen, the prototype would have to be flying by May 1943 with production beginning in June 1944.[17]

Hawker, Supermarine, Armstrong Whitworth and Boulton Paul were asked to put forward proposals. The need for rapid development tended to discourage too much innovation. The Vickers/Supermarine proposal was no more than a modified version of the Griffon 61-powered Spitfire XXI, which was already earmarked for production. Hawker put forward a slightly improved version of its existing Centaurus-powered Tempest. This was precisely the tinkering with existing designs the Air Ministry did not want and they made sure Folland also got to enter a proposal, despite the MAP stipulation that the winning design had to come from a company capable of mass producing the fighter. In its analysis of the entries, the Air Ministry, heavily influenced by the FW 190, made clear its preference for a radial-powered fighter. With no vulnerable cooling system, such a fighter would be far more resistant to battle damage and the radial engine ought to result in a more compact and therefore a more manoeuvrable plane. Only Hawker and Folland put forward proposals with the Centaurus radial.[18]

Folland's Fo. 117, which had traces of his previous Gloster F.5/34, offered outstanding pilot view, an aspect which was considered particularly poor on the Hawker design. Folland's entry did not have the highest speed, but it did have the highest climb rate and the Air Ministry was confident Folland would be able to reproduce the outstanding handling characteristics of his previous designs. The Air Ministry declared Folland the winner and the other contenders were instructed to abandon their proposals, much to the consternation of the Supermarine team who found themselves having to check if the Air Ministry was referring to just their F.6/42 entry or their entire Spitfire XXI programme![19]

This was definitely not what the MAP wanted. The introduction of a new design by a company that clearly lacked the means to organise production was, from its point of view, the worst possible outcome and it desperately sought to convince Portal that modifications to existing types could satisfy F.6/42. With some prompting from the MAP, Hawker and Supermarine came up with new proposals. To improve pilot view, Hawker offered a raised cockpit similar to the one in the Folland proposal. It also removed the inner wing sections, reducing wingspan, thereby reducing weight and improving the rate of roll.

Hawker and the MAP estimated that this lightweight version of the Tempest (the future Hawker Fury) would have virtually the same performance as the Fo.117 and would be available from January 1944 whereas Folland's proposal, they suggested, could not possibly be available until mid-1945. In reality the Hawker redesign was just more tinkering. The lightweight Tempest was still going to be larger and heavier than Folland's proposal.

The revised Supermarine proposal relied on recent developments at Rolls-Royce. Up to this point, the 27-litre capacity of the Merlin seemed to place an upper limit on the power the engine could generate. The Merlin 61 had already taken the engine far further than anybody had imagined possible. However, defying all expectations, Rolls-Royce engineers were working on yet another major upgrade. Their tried and trusted method of running an engine at higher power until it failed, and strengthening or modifying the component that failed, again produced remarkable results.

The upshot was the R.M. 14S.N. and R.M. 15S.N., the forerunners of the Merlin 100 series. The former would give maximum power at medium altitude, the latter maximum power at higher altitude. Both could be fitted to the standard Spitfire VIII airframe and should be available in late 1943 or early 1944. With direct fuel injection, an improved supercharger and using 150 octane fuel, Rolls-Royce was pushing the output of the Merlin towards 2,000hp. The smaller, lighter Merlin would be offering around the same power as the Griffon 61, a remarkable achievement.[20] With the high altitude version, the Spitfire VIII ought to achieve 450 mph at 35,000 feet.[21] This was faster than the predicted performance for the Griffon 61-powered Spitfire XXI and with Griffon deliveries slipping back to late 1943, doubts were growing about the need for the larger Griffon.[22]

The Air Ministry welcomed Supermarine and Hawker's efforts to incorporate as many improvements as possible into existing types. It was especially impressed with the Supermarine proposal and was delighted that the new lightweight Tempest would be available so soon. However, the whole point of the specification had been to make a fresh start. In particular, the Air Ministry made it clear that it wanted to end the Hawker/Supermarine monopoly on fighter design. Folland would provide the fresh blood British fighter development required.

As much as the Air Ministry welcomed the extension to the life of the Spitfire VIII which the Merlin 100 provided, it still did not offer everything it wanted. In terms of offensive armament (still two cannon and four machine guns), defensive armour, rolling performance, climbing ability and pilot view it did not meet the F.6/42 requirements. The Air Ministry were even more scathing about the proposed lightweight Tempest. This was simply a 're-hashed Tempest', which, in turn, was an attempt to rescue the failed Typhoon.[23]

Portal found it difficult to believe that a design that in its initial form had proven so unattractive that it had to be completely redesigned (and even in its redesigned form was 700lb heavier than the Folland Fo. 117), could, with the same engine, possibly have the same performance. The fact that Hawker had already been compelled to incorporate some aspects of the Folland design into its own proposal demonstrated the advantages of a little competition. Why go for a poor imitation when one could have the real thing, Portal argued. In response, Portal received a 'technical statement' from the MAP. It was a statement that scarcely attempted to blind the Chief of Air Staff with science. It simply said the Tempest was better because it had an aerodynamically cleaner wing and fuselage and, if Portal was not convinced by these unsubstantiated claims, the clinching argument, as far as the MAP was concerned, was that they did not believe Folland's performance figures.[24]

By the time these ideas had been exchanged, it was nearly 1943. Time was on the side of the MAP. Each delay in getting design work started put back the date the fighter was likely to enter service. No new design started now could possibly be ready until the summer of 1945, the MAP insisted, whereas what was referred to as the 'Tempest II' would be available from early 1944.[25] By this time, the early 1944 date could only possibly refer to the original unmodified Tempest rather than the F.6/42 lightweight (Hawker Fury) version, but it seems Portal was supposed to take it as a reference to the latter.

To make the Spitfire a more attractive proposition for the Air Ministry, the MAP instructed Supermarine to do everything possible to bring the fighter in line with F.6/42. Armament would be increased to four cannon and extra armour would be fitted. Supermarine was also to go ahead with a new stiffer wing it had been working on to help improve rolling performance.[26] This, it was hoped, could be grafted on to the Spitfire VIII,

IX and XXI and was expected to be available around August 1943.[27] Looking further ahead, Supermarine was working on an entirely new laminar-flow wing and a new all-round vision cockpit.

The MAP estimated the high-altitude version of the upgraded Spitfire VIII would now have a top speed of 468 mph at 32,000 and the MAP simply did not believe it was possible to do any better with an entirely new design.[28] The MAP dug its heels in and refused to proceed with any new fighter projects. In January 1943, Portal seemed to concede defeat but put on record his 'very serious and considered protest' about not proceeding with the Folland design.[29] In fact, Portal had still not completely given up. In April 1943, the Chief of Staff made an unofficial approach to Sinclair, the Secretary of State for Air, pleading with him to support the Folland fighter and not accept the MAP view that the 'Tempest II is the last word in fighters'.[30] Portal, in true cloak and dagger style, asked that his memo should be destroyed upon reading, although exactly why is not clear.

Portal did not get his way but his stand was not entirely in vain; it inspired considerably refined versions of the Tempest and Spitfire. So radical were the changes to these designs, they were eventually given new names, the Supermarine Spiteful (F.1/43) and Hawker Fury (F.2/43) However, they were still adaptations of planes designed as bomber interceptors and much more might have been achieved by starting from scratch. Even these adaptations would take some time to develop. The Spiteful was supposed to take to the air in August 1943 but did not fly until June 1944.[31] Even this was only a Spitfire VIII fuselage with the laminar wings grafted on. An entirely new deeper fuselage, offering the required improved view, was still being designed. The Hawker F.2/43 Fury prototype was supposed to fly in December 1943 and the company thought production might begin in mid-1944. The MAP thought December 1944 was a more realistic date.[32] As it turned out the Fury prototype did not fly until September 1944.

The MAP might claim that events would prove it took the correct decision. As it turned out, not even the Spiteful and Fury appeared in time to play any part in the Second World War. There was no reason to believe Folland could have done any better with his F.6/42 offering. However, as with the specialist close support plane, there was a clash of departmental aims. The MAP and Air Ministry were both trying to win the war, but the Air Ministry was also trying to develop an air force. The RAF would still need fighters once the war was over and fighter development would continue. F.6/42 was not just about trying to improve on what was already available; it was an entirely new approach to fighter design. At some stage a decision had to be made about exactly what sort of fighter should follow the Tempest/Spitfire generation and this was the right time to be doing this.

The emerging jet-powered fighter was a major complication. From the very beginning, the MAP had argued that developing a brand new piston-engined fighter was not sensible when it seemed jet fighters were on the way. Indeed, during the course of the debate, there were ominous indications that, in Germany, jet development was already very advanced. Since 1940, intelligence had been picking up indications that the Germans were working on the He 280 jet fighter. By 1942 it seemed that it had flown and in September 1942 the Air Ministry was crediting it with a speed of between 495 and 530 mph, a service ceiling of 49,300 feet and a climb rate of 5,900 feet per minute.[33] This was not only well in excess of any conventional Allied fighter, it was also far in advance of anything expected from its British equivalent, the Gloster Meteor. Indeed Britain's first jet fighter was still rather ignominiously restricted to taxying trials. It seemed very likely that the latest Bf 109 and FW 190 might represent the peak of piston-engined fighter development. Their successors were likely to be jets and these might indeed revolutionise aerial warfare in ways it was difficult to predict.[34]

Attitudes towards the need for a new piston-powered fighter reflected the assessments of the two ministries on the prospects for the new jets. With the Meteor not even able to get off the ground, there were, in Air Ministry circles, growing doubts about jet fighters appearing in the near future. The MAP, on the other hand, remained enthusiastic. In 1941, de Havilland was working with Frank Halford on the Goblin jet engine, a simplified version of Whittle's engine, which was expected to produce twice the power. Both the Meteor and He 280 needed two engines to get into the air, which meant a larger and less manoeuvrable plane. This was not ideal for a fighter, especially the sort of agile fighter the Air Ministry now wanted. With the 3,000lb thrust Halford was predicting, a single-engined design seemed possible. With jet engines, the air intake has to be fairly close to the thrust output so de Havilland planned a twin-boom design around the Goblin engine mounted in a truncated central fuselage. The twin booms took weight away from the centre of gravity, which would not help manoeuvrability, but it would still be much more compact and therefore more manoeuvrable than the twin-engined Meteor.

With no interest within the Air Ministry for taking the jet fighter concept any further than the Gloster Meteor, it was left to the MAP to take the initiative and draw up a specification around the de Havilland proposal.

As it was not an official Air Ministry requirement, the specification had to carry the experimental 'E' classification (E.6/41), but the de Havilland fighter was required to carry four 20mm cannon from the outset. The MAP wanted a fully operational combat plane, not just an experimental demonstrator. De Havilland began work on its DH 100, which would become the Vampire.

With their Meteor struggling, Gloster, too, was interested in Halford's more powerful Goblin engine and was beginning to look to a second generation single-engined jet fighter, the Gloster Ace, with the engine mounted in the fuselage with wing-root air intakes but, unlike the de Havilland jet, a conventional fuselage and tail plane.[35] Again the MAP was leading the way, writing specification E.5/42 around the Gloster project. Estimates in September 1942 predicted a top speed of 520 mph at 30,000 feet with a service ceiling of 48,000 feet.[36] Again the experimental plane would be armed with four 20mm cannon. The MAP saw it as a prudent insurance against the unknown quantities of the unconventional twin-boom de Havilland E.6/41 and the heavy twin-engined Meteor. The MAP was often criticised, with some justification it has to be said, by the Air Ministry for focusing on output rather than quality, but with jet-powered combat planes, the MAP was bolder and more farsighted than the Air Ministry.

MAP enthusiasm for the jet helps explain its lack of enthusiasm in starting a new piston-engined fighter project. Conversely, the Air Ministry's doubts help explain Portal's enthusiasm for developing the piston-powered F.6/42. With both Gloster and de Havilland considering single-engined jet fighters, there was scope for a fighter that was a lot more manoeuvrable than the Meteor. The ideal long-term solution would perhaps have been to invite designers to consider using jet power for the F.6/42 fighter project. This would have ensured Air Ministry ideas on what it wanted from future fighters fed into the jet fighter development programmes.

However, it would have required a leap of faith to embark on an agile jet. Although with hindsight it is clear that manoeuvrability would be as important in the jet age as the FW 190 had proved it was in the piston engine era, this was not obvious at the time. It might not be possible to transfer the thinking behind FW 190 and F.6/42 to jet-powered fighters. The leap forward in aircraft speeds might well be just as great as had occurred when fighter designers belatedly switched from biplanes to monoplanes. Just as many had thought then that the emergence of high-speed monoplanes meant the end of dog fighting, so might the arrival of the jet.

F.6/42 provided an opportunity to break free from the stranglehold the bomber-interceptor approach had on British fighter design and begin the jet era with a different frame of mind. When German designers started thinking about single-engined jets like the Focke-Wulf TA183, they took with them some of the thinking behind their piston fighter designs. The designs were light and compact. The much higher speeds jet power could generate combined with excellent control and manoeuvrability would be a deadly combination. By not persevering with the thinking behind F.6/42, Britain would carry the bomber-interceptor approach to fighter design into the jet age. A war stretching into 1946 might have seen Meteors struggling to deal with jet-powered Focke-Wulfs just as Spitfires had struggled against piston-engined Focke-Wulfs.

Folland's F.6/42 proposal was the nearest Britain got to developing a specialist air superiority fighter. Never since the First World War had the need for such a fighter been so clearly seen, nor what was required so clearly defined. Unfortunately, the emerging jet, coupled with the MAP's priority to win the war in hand rather than some future hypothetical conflict, tended to muddy the waters. It would be the 1970s and the beginnings of the Eurofighter/Typhoon project before Britain was once more involved in an air superiority fighter project.

The 1941 Butt report on the failing bomber offensive and the F.6/42 debate on future fighter design were not unrelated matters. Britain had abandoned the First World War Sopwith Camel type air superiority fighter precisely because it was believed future wars would be decided by bombing and the priority became specialist interceptors. Within the space of twelve months, the failure of the bomber offensive and the disadvantages of interceptors designed to deal with such an offensive had become clear for all to see. Like the Butt report, the FW 190 trials shook the Air Ministry establishment to its very foundations. However, again like the Butt report, the long-term impact on policy turned out to be relatively minor. Instead of taking a fresh look at the way air power was applied and the aircraft it required, Britain remained stuck in a strategic bomber/bomber interceptor mindset.

The air superiority fighter suffered the same fate as the specialist ground support aircraft. Both types were key elements in 1918 plans for the future RAF. Both were abandoned and forgotten in the inter-war bomber mania. Both concepts briefly resurfaced in 1942, but it proved to be a false dawn. Britain would fight the rest of the Second World War and prepare for future conflicts without making any attempt to develop specialist planes for either role.

While the future of British fighter development was being decided, the problems with the current crop were not abating. The Typhoon's Sabre engine was still a problem. Merlins could run for as long as 1,000 hours before failing whereas the Sabres were on average only lasting less than seventy hours.[37] Nearly all the problems were connected with the sleeve valves the engine used. The fighter was already more expensive to build than the Spitfire, but the cost of equipping squadrons was even greater because statutory strength of Typhoon squadrons had to be two higher than other squadrons to ensure enough were available for operations. Even then, only constant servicing allowed the Typhoon squadrons to maintain a reasonable number of serviceable planes, which placed extra pressure on ground crews. It took twice as long to inspect an engine because each sleeve valve had to be regularly checked. Typhoon squadrons had to have twice as many fitters to keep up with the extra work. The fighter was not just a failure, it was an expensive and resource-sapping failure. Napier was no nearer working out why the sleeve valves wore out so quickly and seemed more interested in disputing Fighter Command's engine failure rate figures than solving the problem.[38]

It was also a dangerous failure. Aircraft designers were only just beginning to get to grips with the problems posed by airflow approaching the speed of sound and the stress this put on aircraft structures. The Typhoon, with its thick wings, was proving particularly susceptible. At the time, the structural problems with the Typhoon seemed to defy rational explanation. In October 1942 there was another spate of fatal accidents.[39] All that MAP could suggest was that the risk to pilots be minimised by telling them not to exceed 400 mph, unless chasing the enemy. This was hardly likely to inspire much confidence amongst pilots and the advice was not passed on. Douglas felt he had no option but to carry on and hope for the best.[40] A whole series of modifications were introduced, but, as with Napier and the sleeve valves, Camm and the MAP was just guessing.[41] While the Typhoon struggled, the Hurricanes continued to roll off the production lines, making up about a third of all single-seater fighter output.

Spitfires comprised about half of deliveries but in late 1942 most of these were Spitfire Vs. This version might be considered obsolescent, but it was still very much in demand. The latest client to demand more was the Fleet Air Arm. They were already getting Seafires as an interim single-seater carrier fighter while the Blackburn Firebrand was being developed. However, by the autumn of 1942 it had become clear that the Firebrand was a failure and what had been a temporary commitment had become a permanent requirement.[42] Indeed, with Royal Navy aircraft carriers expected to cover the landings in North Africa, it had become an urgent requirement.

The USAAF squadrons in the UK also needed Spitfires. The Americans were confident their P-38 Lightning and P-47 Thunderbolt would meet their air force needs, but these were just entering production. There was little point in wasting shipping space by transferring their current equipment to the UK, so American fighter units transferring to Britain left their fighters in the United States and converted to Spitfires on arrival in the UK.

In September the Russians announced they had had enough of the Hurricane, and in future they wanted Spitfires instead.[43] The Air Ministry did briefly toy with the idea of using Typhoon output to meet the promises made to the Russians, with a plan to send 90 Typhoon and 110 Hurricanes a month from January 1943.[44] However, not even the Air Ministry dared send Sabre-powered fighters to experience the rigours of the Eastern Front. (The possibility of waiting until the worst of the Russian winter was over before sending them was briefly considered![45]) Instead a first batch of 150 Spitfires Vs, all reconditioned machines that had seen service, was to be sent instead of Hurricanes. By this time the first three Spitfire squadrons were preparing to transfer to Australia to defend Darwin from Japanese air raids. It was also hoped to have the first of four Spitfire squadrons in the Far East operational by January 1943.[46] By the end of 1942 Spitfire requirements overseas had risen to nearly 300 a month.

The MAP, and Tizard in particular, had always believed that Britain should be building more fighters, and it was becoming increasingly clear they needed to be Spitfires. It was not the role of the MAP to make policy decisions about the balance between fighter and bomber production, but it could highlight potential production difficulties and use this as a justification for a change in priorities. In June 1942, the MAP suggested that, with the United States having to focus on its own air force, Britain could no longer rely so heavily on American fighter imports. It seemed rather late in the day to be mentioning this problem, but it provided a reasonably plausible reason for increasing fighter production.

To guard against any shortfall in American deliveries, the MAP proposed reducing Wellington production at the Vickers Blackpool plant from 100 to 60 a month and building Spitfires instead. At a time when the Wellington was suffering increasingly heavy losses in raids over Germany, it seemed like a bomber the RAF could safely do without. Up to October 1943 an extra 1,000 Spitfires could be built at a cost of 400 to 500 Wellingtons.[47] The Air Ministry, however, were not interested. They saw no reason to go beyond the current target of 900 single-seater fighters a month. Indeed, they wanted Spitfire production cut so that more spares could be built.[48] This was by no means a trivial matter. Now that Spitfires were flying increasingly intensive operations in the Mediterranean, the demand for spares had rocketed.

Undeterred, a couple of months later, the MAP came back with a different argument and an even more radical solution. As well as the uncertainty of American deliveries, about two-thirds of British fighters were being built at just three locations (Castle Bromwich, Langley and Gloster). It seemed sensible to have another major source in case one of these was bombed, so the MAP suggested replacing the Wellington entirely at the Vickers Blackpool plant and building 240 single-seater fighters a month. Again the Air Ministry objected; it would put bomber production even further behind schedule.[49]

The alternative to more Spitfires was to get Mustangs from the United States. With this project, the Air Ministry and MAP could join forces. The Americans were still reluctant to take the Merlin 61/Mustang combination seriously. It did not help that the quality of American designs had become a very sensitive subject. The USAAF was facing a lot of criticism at home about the inferiority of American fighters when compared to foreign equivalents. It was not the best time to be suggesting that the Americans build a plane that had been designed to British requirements and was now going to be powered by a British engine, in preference to the fighters their own experts had chosen.

The Air Ministry used all their contacts to put pressure on the Americans to adopt the Merlin 61/Mustang. Spaatz, as well as John Winnant, the American ambassador in London and his staff, were all kept informed about the progress of the project and they both sent on favourable appraisals to Washington. The deputy Air Attaché in London, Thomas Hitchcock, proved a particularly useful ally. In October he told Washington that the Mustang 'is one of the best if not the best fighter airframe that has been developed in the war to date'. Even with its Allison engine, he went on, it was already recognised as an outstanding fighter by those who had flown it. However, it had not got the attention it deserved because it had been 'sired by the English out of an American mother' and had no 'parent' in the US Army Air Corps to highlight its qualities.[50]

These appraisals helped pave the way for crucial discussions in late autumn. A delegation from the MAP, including Tizard, arrived in the United States to look at various areas of joint interest to the two countries and Mustang production was one of the items on the agenda. A small order for 400 had been placed in August, which at least averted the danger of the plane going out of production altogether, but it still had a lower priority than the P-38 Lightning and P-47 Thunderbolt. Indeed even the P-39 Airacobra and Curtiss P-40 had a higher priority.

The Americans dismissed out of hand the idea of the P-51 becoming the principal Allied fighter in place of their P-47 and P-38. They even refused to consider reducing P-39 and P-40 production in favour of the P-51. More advanced versions of these two fighters were now in production and the Americans insisted that they were adequate for most of the fronts the United States was fighting on. Switching to a new plane would result in a massive drop in output. Again it might have crossed the minds of the British team that similar arguments had been used and similar decisions made over whether the Spitfire should replace the Hurricane.

Licence production in the UK was considered, and the Americans did not object, but there would inevitably be problems 'anglicising' the Mustang for British manufacturers. As an alternative, Britain offered to assemble complete fighters, up to 400 a month, from parts built in the United States. However, the Americans would also have to provide the Merlin 61 engines.[51] It seemed whichever approach was adopted, finding the engines would always be the problem. Packard were now building Merlin 61s under licence but it was feared none would be available until late 1944.

At least the obvious British enthusiasm for the Merlin 61/Mustang and the reports arriving from their own sources got the Americans thinking. They agreed to switch to the Merlin 61 version and increase production from 150 to 380 a month. Even so, it was still more to keep the British happy than any recognition that the Merlin 61/Mustang might be the best fighter available to the Allies. The first Merlin-powered Mustang was flown in Britain in October 1942 with a Merlin 65 engine and eventually managed a top speed of 427 mph. A month later the more fully developed American version achieved the originally predicted 441 mph.[52]

The Americans had no intention of letting a Merlin 61 shortage get in their way. Rolls-Royce tended to rely on the skill of their workforce to overcome problems created by inaccurate individual components. Packard simply made sure the components were accurate enough for semi-skilled labour to assemble the engines. The first American-produced Merlin 61 rolled off the production lines in December 1942 and was soon being built in vast numbers. Despite the extensive modifications to the airframe, production of the Mustang got going quite rapidly, the first production P-51B flying in June 1943. Even so, the P-51B was not going to play much part in any fighting until late 1943.

Meanwhile, in Britain, the shortage of Merlin 61s was as acute as ever, which meant the RAF was going to have to rely heavily on the Spitfire V for some time to come. This was slower than the Typhoon, and therefore less effective as a pure interceptor, but arguably it was still a better offensive dog-fighter. There was certainly no chance of the Typhoon, with its temperamental Sabre engine, being used overseas. Nor was it possible to continue denying overseas theatres Spitfires. The Spitfire shortage was becoming more acute with each passing month.

To overseas commands it might still seem that Fighter Command still possessed a more than healthy number of the fighter but, with more Spitfires being sent abroad, current output could not maintain the Command's existing squadrons.[53] Typhoons were replacing Spitfire Vs mainly because there was nothing else available. As one MAP assessment put it, 'The wheels of Typhoon production appear to be turning faster than our opinion of this aircraft warrants'.[54] Leigh-Mallory was certainly not impressed. On taking over from Douglas at Fighter Command in November 1942, he discovered he could expect to have fifty Spitfire squadrons, thirty-eight Typhoon and, rather optimistically, two Tempest squadrons by September 1943. Leigh-Mallory was alarmed that his command would have to rely so heavily on fighters powered by the troublesome Sabre.[55]

Leigh-Mallory joined those wondering why it was necessary to bother with the Typhoon/Tempest at all. At high altitude the Merlin 61 Spitfire was indisputably the better fighter; at low/medium altitudes with the Merlin 66 it still had the edge over the Typhoon. With the decision that all Spitfires should be capable of carrying bombs, Leigh-Mallory felt there was nothing the Typhoon could do that the Spitfire could not. There certainly appeared to be little reason to take a chance with the Tempest in any of its guises. In Leigh-Mallory's opinion, any fighter that was powered by the Merlin rather than the Sabre had to be better. He admitted to knowing very little about the capabilities of the Merlin 61/Mustang, but he made it quite clear that he preferred this unknown quantity to the all too well-known problems of the Typhoon and the potential problems of Sabre-powered successors.

The entire Tempest programme continued to run hopelessly behind schedule. The Sabre IV required by the Tempest I was still nowhere near ready. The prototype Tempest II flew in June 1943, but no one was expecting production of its Centaurus engine to get going until late 1944.[56] None of this was encouraging but, with the shortage of Merlin 61 engines, the MAP had to persevere with the Tempest I and II, and fall back on the Sabre II-powered Tempest V as the first production version. The original idea was that this would go into production with the new wing-embedded radiators required by the Sabre IV, so this engine could be slotted in as soon as it became available. However, the new radiator was still giving problems and the Tempest had already been delayed enough. It would have to go into full-scale production with the original Typhoon chin radiator. The Tempest V was no longer a short-term expedient while awaiting the Sabre IV, it was becoming the principal production version of the fighter.

Yet again there were suggestions that the entire Tempest project should be dropped and all efforts switched to what was still being referred to as the 'lightweight Tempest II' (the future Hawker Fury) inspired by the F.6/42 specification. However, this was still up to two years away.[57] In the meantime perhaps Hawker could build Spitfire VIIIs, it was suggested, but the problem as always was engines. These could only be found at the expense of the Merlins required for bomber production.

Meanwhile the MAP was having to admit it was going to miss their fighter targets. The new lower targets provoked indignant outrage in the Air Ministry. They claimed it meant the loss of over one thousand fighters in the period up to the end of 1943, half of which were Spitfires, with another 600 Spitfire reduction in 1944. This they described as 'nothing less than a landslide in fighter production' and the proposed fighter expansion programme 'threatened with shipwreck'.[58] An equally indignant MAP insisted this was a gross exaggeration. Both sides should at least have been able to agree that more factory space had to be found for fighter production.

In October 1942 the MAP repeated its offer to build Spitfires at the Vickers Blackpool plant instead of Wellingtons, which by now everyone agreed were obsolete and needed to be phased out anyway. Still the Air Ministry insisted that the need to maintain the bomber offensive was paramount.[59] When the choice was between a bomber of questionable value and one of the best fighters in the world, the Air Ministry preference would always be for the former. Indeed, the Air Ministry wanted the Vickers plant to carry on producing Wellingtons until the high-altitude Vickers Windsor could replace it on the production lines in the summer of 1945. This heavy bomber was going to be powered by four of the precious Merlin 61s. To free the resources to build more of these engines, the Air Ministry wanted the cabinet to approve switching more of the country's production capacity from Army needs to Air Force expansion.[60] When engines were needed for bomber production the Air Ministry was determined that nothing should stand in their way. The cabinet was not convinced such a diversion was justified. Indeed, they were rather alarmed that the Air Ministry seemed to be working on the assumption that the bomber offensive against Germany would have to continue into 1946.

In the struggle for air superiority the fighter was proving the key weapon, not the bomber, but in the struggle for production priority the fighter was constantly losing out to the bomber. The Air Ministry attempts to have the bombers it wanted and the fighters the active fronts needed was proving beyond the country's capabilities, even with the Americans supplying most of the RAF's tactical needs. When Sir Stafford Cripps took over from Llewellin at the MAP in November 1942, his staff sternly warned him to resist firmly any pressure from the Air Ministry to reduce fighter production in order to increase bomber production as they were invariably soon back demanding more fighters.[61]

On every front, Allied armies continued to pay the price for the Air Ministry's failure to provide the quality fighters they needed. In the Western Desert, Allied forces holding the line at El Alamein had their backs to the wall. Axis forces were just 60 miles from Alexandria. The battle was on a knife edge; one final push from Rommel might see the Commonwealth forces defeated and Egypt fall.

For the raid on Dieppe, forty-five squadrons of Spitfires were on hand. For the defence of the Nile Delta there would be three.

Chapter 10

The Tide Turns

Auchinleck's defensive victory in the first Battle of El Alamein was not enough to save him from being the latest general to lose Churchill's confidence. Lieutenant General William Gott was to replace him as commander of the Eighth Army, but he was killed when the Bombay transport plane he was flying in was shot down. Lieutenant General Montgomery was drafted in as a replacement.

Montgomery and Coningham made an odd couple. Montgomery kept his headquarters as austere as possible, Coningham liked his surroundings to be as pleasant as war would allow.[1] Both possessed huge self-belief bordering on arrogance, which perhaps initially encouraged a mutual respect but laid the seeds of future problems. Montgomery was not a risk taker: in future, no Commonwealth soldiers would die as the result of ill-prepared offensives or rash counter-attacks. Any advance would only be attempted when everything was in place and maximum fire support was available. That fire support included air support. The retreat to El Alamein had seen the intrinsically repulsive Army and Air Force commands spring apart yet again. Montgomery insisted Army and Air Force staff work together with Montgomery and Coningham in adjacent command posts.

Following Rommel's failed attempt to storm Auchinleck's defences at the beginning of July, both sides set about building up their forces. This was much easier for the Allies than it was for the Axis with their now much extended lines of communications. German difficulties were increased by an aerial offensive from bases in Egypt and Malta against Axis ports and convoys. Rommel knew the long-term advantage lay with the Allies and he could not afford to wait too long if he was to stand any chance of breaking through to the Nile.

The Axis forces were still outnumbered in terms of tanks and aircraft, but at the end of August Rommel decided he was as ready as he would ever be. In terms of quality the Axis had the clear edge with 100 Bf 109s, nearly all the 'F' version and 80 Macchi C.202s. Half of the Commonwealth fighters were still Hurricanes (nine squadrons) and even the rest (three Spitfire V, five Kittyhawk and one Tomahawk) were, in varying degrees, inferior to the Bf 109F. The Spitfire V was clearly the best available Allied fighter and Ludlow-Hewitt, whose report had highlighted the Spitfire shortage in the Mediterranean, reported back to London following another tour of inspection, that even the few that had arrived had 'made a difference ... out of all proportion to their numbers'.[2] Once again, that a fighter now rated as obsolescent by the Air Ministry should make so much difference rather underscored the enormous and unnecessary handicap Commonwealth and RAF fighter pilots had been forced to fight under in so many previous campaigns. It was also an indication of how much easier it might have been had all eighteen fighter squadrons, rather than just three, been equipped with Spitfires. More than six years after the fighter had been ordered into production, four years after it entered service and three years into a war, this was not an entirely unreasonable expectation.

In all, 450 Axis fighter, fighter-bombers and Stukas were faced by 467 Commonwealth fighters and fighter-bombers and 178 light bombers. However, with petrol in short supply, the German and Italian forces would never be able to make full use of the aircraft that were available. The USAAF was beginning to make a contribution, although at this stage their P-40 Warhawk fighter (the USAAF's Kittyhawk) and B-25 Mitchell bomber squadrons in the theatre were only flying a handful of sorties.[3] As in 1918, however, just their presence was an ominous omen for the Axis forces. Even in the build-up to the offensive, Rommel's forces were hounded by Allied air power. From 22 to 30 August, 500 bomber sorties, by day and night, were flown against the assembling German forces. Low-level fighter-bomber attacks picked out individual targets by day while the light bombers focused on lines of communication leading to the front from higher altitudes, mostly by night.

Tactical reconnaissance Hurricane and Tomahawks kept an eye on the German build up, albeit at heavy cost. In August, No. 208 Squadron lost twenty-one aircraft destroyed or badly damaged, with seven pilots killed or missing, providing this vital information. Fourteen of these losses were Hurricanes. At dusk on the 30th, No. 208 Squadron flew its last reconnaissance mission of the day. It was an impressive display of strength with the single reconnaissance machine protected by nineteen Spitfires and twelve Hurricanes. The aircraft spotted a substantial concentration of German mechanised forces poised to advance through the British minefields.

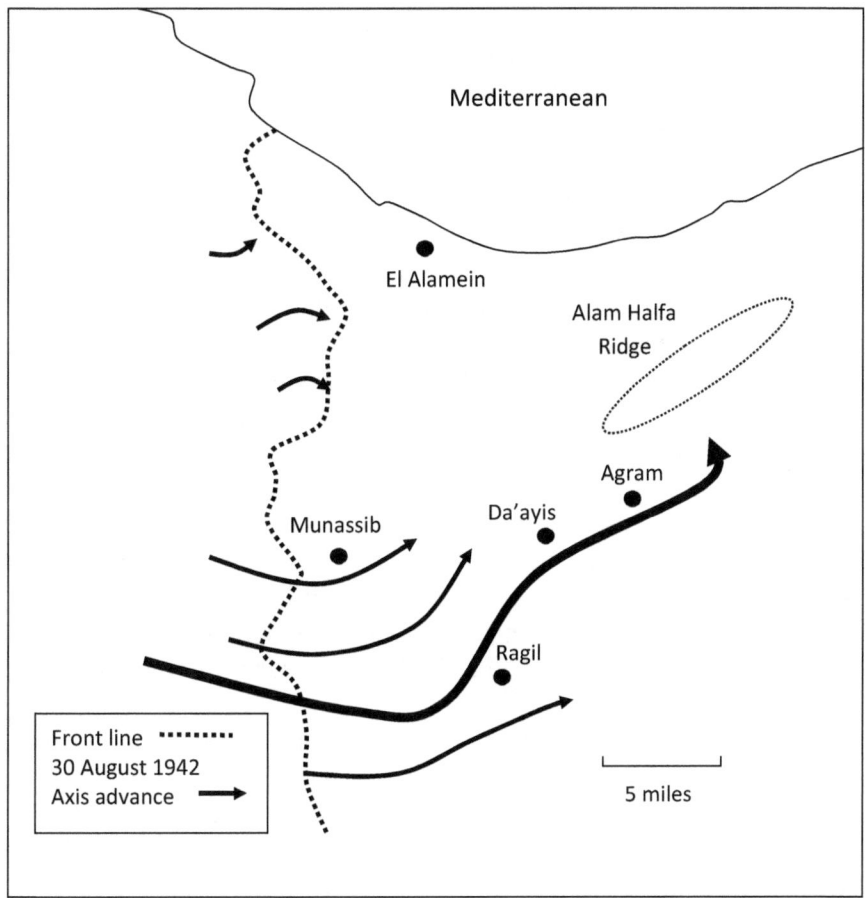

It was too late to call in the day bombers, but No. 205 Group was alerted. Fleet Air Arm Albacores were despatched to drop flares on the German concentration and Wellingtons followed. For the Axis forces it was unnerving at such an early stage of their offensive to be literally under the Allied spotlight. Not least of the successes gained was the strike on the Africa Korps headquarters, which killed several staff officers and wounded the corps commander, General Walther Nehring.

By dawn, far from being deep in the Allied rear as planned, the German forces had only just managed to get through the minefield. It was mid-morning before the bulk of the German forces could start moving eastwards. Sandstorms at Allied bomber airfields on the morning of the 31st gave Rommel some respite. However, he was already well behind schedule and with the element of surprise lost, and dwindling fuel reserves, he opted to wheel north sooner than originally planned. Rather than bypass the Allied forces along the Alam el Halfa Ridge he would now try to eliminate them.

Once the sandstorms subsided, Allied bombers were in action, but only fifty-five light-bomber sorties could be flown, a third of the planned effort for the day. Even so, these imposed further delays and Rommel was not able to engage the Allied forces on the Alam el Halfa Ridge until late afternoon. Montgomery made no attempt to outmanoeuvre the German panzers. Instead, his tanks, hull-down in the sand, and with supporting artillery, stood their ground and beat off the German frontal attacks. Dusk brought a respite for the defenders but not for the attackers as the Wellingtons and Albacores returned, flying as low as 200 feet, low enough for the gunners to strafe targets of opportunity as well as drop bombs. Within forty-five minutes of landing some Wellingtons were back in the air to sow more disorder amongst the Axis ranks. Only sixty-nine sorties were flown, but they had an effect out of all proportion to their number. With little anti-aircraft fire to worry about, they were able to operate at far lower altitudes than their compatriots in Bomber Command over Germany. The Wellingtons picked off their targets with a precision and effectiveness that Bomber Command could only dream about.

On 1 September, the light-bomber squadrons were out in force, flying 125 sorties, all but fourteen of these against targets in the Munassib-Da'ayis-Ragil area. The Afrika Korps reported considerable losses, especially in vehicles. Now it was clear that a major offensive was under way, all No. 205 Group effort was switched to tactical targets. Over 100 Wellington and Albacore sorties were flown in the battle area. The effect was magnified by individual bombers making several attacks on separate targets, often dropping their bombs one at a time. It was a fine example of Churchill's dictum that once ground forces were engaged, all air effort should be focused on winning the battle, regardless of how attractive more distant targets might be.[4] The Wellingtons and Albacores kept up the pressure by night, with some of the Wellingtons carrying 4,000lb bombs for the first time. Once again these nocturnal efforts made a big impression on the enemy; although only around one hundred sorties were flown, to the Germans it seemed twice that number.

Rommel realised that the attack had failed and his forces began pulling back. An attempt was made to cut off the German line of retreat, but this was beaten off comfortably. It was left to the Air Force to pursue the German armour. On 2 September, the light bombers flew a record

176 sorties, including nine by USAAF Mitchells, all in the Agram and Ragil area. During the battle, when weather permitted, the Allies were able to fly between 500 and 600 fighter sorties a day, about half escort and half fighter sweeps. Fuel shortages severely restricted the Luftwaffe response. In two days, the Ju 87s launched six major raids on British positions, each with a heavy escort, but they could not prevent Allied fighters getting through and disrupting the attacks. Conversely, German fighters were not able to make any impression on the Allied bombers. From 31 August to 6 September only five light bombers were lost, all to anti-aircraft fire. In three days the RAF flew 2,500 bomber, fighter-bomber and fighter sorties.[5]

The battle demonstrated that even in the age of the fighter-bomber there was still a role for the traditional light bomber. During the first four days of the offensive very little use was made of fighter-bombers. The German forces tended to be fairly concentrated as they pushed through the narrow mine-swept corridors and formed up for attack, making them a reasonably easy target for flak to defend. Low-level fighter-bomber missions were considered too risky, whereas the light bombers operating from safer, higher altitudes had a very good chance of causing some damage amongst the relatively tightly packed enemy forces. As the German units began to retreat and disperse, and the anti-aircraft defences became more diluted, so they became more attractive targets for low-level fighter-bombers.

The German commanders were in no doubt that Allied bombers and fighter-bombers had been a major factor in the German defeat. For Rommel the implications were clear. 'The possibilities of ground action, operational and tactical, become very limited if one's adversary commands the air with a powerful air force', he concluded.[6] It was almost as if the value of air superiority was only fully appreciated by German generals now that the Luftwaffe could no longer guarantee it.

The quality of the Axis fighters and the superior tactics of German fighter pilots still meant that the Allies could only maintain superiority at a price. On 1 September, twenty Allied fighters were lost, compared to just seven Axis planes. The next day another ten were lost, while Allied pilots were only able to claim the destruction of three enemy fighters. The Allies had air superiority but, once again, it was only being achieved by weight of numbers – a method that was costly in the lives of pilots. With losses continually weakening the force, it was also more difficult to exploit fully or even maintain air superiority for any length of time. By the 5th, there were so few serviceable Kittyhawks that there were not enough to fly offensive sweeps and escort the day bombers, forcing a reduction in the number of bombing missions. The problems with the Hurricane were highlighted on the 6th when eight Bf 109s surprised twelve Hurricane fighter-bombers being escorted by another nineteen Hurricanes. Only one of the fighter-bombers was lost but, in the space of fifteen minutes, no fewer than seven of the escort were shot down.

The German offensive had been defeated by overwhelming firepower, both land-based and aerial. It would perhaps be an exaggeration to say the Allied forces at Alam el Halfa had turned the panzers back with as much ease as the Canadians had been repelled at Dieppe just a few days before, but the victory had been comfortable enough. Perhaps most ironic of all was that Montgomery, who had been involved in the early planning stages for the Dieppe raid, should be responsible for orchestrating the impressive display of defensive firepower which had cost the Germans so dear. The Canadians on the beaches of Dieppe had paid an even higher price for being outgunned.

The Air Force had played its part in supplying friendly fire support. Just as had occurred at Dieppe, the fighter forces had provided effective defence for the forces deployed below, but a far higher proportion of available strength was used to exploit this superiority by attacking ground targets. The German materiel and personnel losses were mainly the result of air attack rather than ground fire.[7] Once again, the use of night bombers on the battlefield had proven very effective, so much so that Field Marshal Albert Kesselring, the German theatre commander, ordered the Luftwaffe to copy these tactics.

In the Western Desert at least, the RAF had become a very efficient tactical weapon. Indeed so efficient that there was already an Army tendency to let the Air Force finish the job. Once Montgomery's rather half-hearted attempts to cut off the retreating Germans had failed, he was more than happy to leave the Air Force to pursue the retreating enemy. Coningham was equally happy to have his Air Force fighting the battle on its own without the complication of ground forces. However, such air action can rarely be decisive. Air strikes can inflict casualties, spread confusion and cause delay, but they cannot defeat an army.

Rommel pulled his force out successfully but found himself in a tricky position. His army was precariously positioned at the end of very long and vulnerable lines of communication and was dangerously outnumbered by a well-supplied enemy. Rommel had gone very quickly from the brink of outright victory to staring disaster in the face. The very best he could hope for was to hold on to his existing position and unless more supplies could get through he would be very hard pressed to achieve even this.

The resources siphoned off for Rommel's drive into Egypt, and the supplies he needed to hold what he had gained, meant an invasion of Malta was off the agenda. The air offensive against the island was resumed, but the defences now possessed no fewer than five Spitfire squadrons, the most formidable Allied fighter concentration in the west outside the United Kingdom. From 11 October, heavily escorted raids were carried out on the island by the German and Italian air forces, but losses proved so heavy that, within a week, operations by day had to be abandoned. Wellingtons, Beaufighters, Beauforts, Swordfish and Albacores were able to continue their punishing attacks on Axis convoys.

Tedder was by this time applying more pressure to his superiors in London for better equipment. He gently suggested that 'the poor old Hurricane is becoming more and more out of date, especially as the Bf 109G is now on the map' and described how the tactical reconnaissance squadrons, still equipped with Hurricanes and Tomahawks, faced a 'grim task'.[8] As a fighter, there were fears the Hurricane simply lacked the speed to catch the latest Ju 87D and Ju 88, perhaps an exaggeration in the case of the former but an indication of how demoralising reliance on the Hurricane was becoming. With so few Spitfires, Kittyhawk squadrons still had the task of watching over their less fortunate comrades flying Hurricanes, but it was a responsibility they could do without, given the Kittyhawk was itself significantly inferior to the Bf 109F and Macchi C.202.[9]

The Wellington was another plane in short supply. This was proving surprisingly successful in the tactical battle. Tedder felt that tactical night bombing had perhaps been even more useful than day bombing, and asked for his allocation of Wellingtons to be increased. Harris, however, was as determined to keep as many Wellingtons for Bomber Command as his counterpart in Fighter Command was to hang on to his Spitfires. Indeed, the Middle East was losing ground. In July there had been 130 Wellingtons in the Middle East theatre, but by the end of October this had dropped to seventy. Even more alarming for Tedder was the Navy's sudden decision to transfer the two Fleet Air Arm Albacore squadrons. The biplane Albacore was scarcely a front-line day torpedo-bomber but its slow-flying capabilities had proved ideal in the nocturnal target-marking role and the experience gained by the crews could not be easily replaced. Tedder managed to get the Navy to delay the transfer until after the El Alamein offensive, but the RAF could not go on relying on naval squadrons to meet its army support commitments.

By October 1942 Montgomery was ready to launch his counter-offensive. The Allied forces comprised an impressive 200,000 troops compared to the 100,000 Axis troops that faced them. Montgomery's infantry would be supported by slightly more than 1,000 tanks, while the Axis forces possessed barely more than 500. While Rommel could count on few reserves, there were over 1,000 more tanks in Eighth Army repair depots and workshops. Montgomery also had nearly twice the artillery Rommel possessed. The RAF had around 1,000 aircraft in the Mediterranean with around 600 in the battle area. The large number of aircraft under repair in the rear provided a potential reserve and there was no shortage of fuel. There were also three, albeit under strength, USAAF P-40 Warhawk squadrons, with thirty-seven fighters and three B-25 Mitchell squadrons with a similar number of bombers operating alongside the Commonwealth squadrons. The Italians and Germans each had around 1,300 aircraft in the Mediterranean theatre. They were also able to station some 600 in the battle zone. However, spares were in short supply and less than half of the available aircraft were serviceable. The shortage of fuel would prevent these from operating all out for long.

Montgomery's plan was a simple single-thrust advance. Montgomery knew his Eighth Army could absorb far heavier losses than the Axis forces and that he would inevitably win a battle of attrition. On the evening of the 23rd, covered by a massive artillery bombardment supplemented by sixty-six Wellington and twelve Albacore sorties, the infantry started picking their way through the enemy minefields. It was a slow process and, throughout the 24th, the Allied forces remained held up within the minefields. Despite poor weather, over 1,000 sorties were flown by the Desert Air Force during the day, including 274 by light bombers. Flak proved particularly troublesome, shooting down eight bombers and damaging another twenty-seven. However, German fighter sorties were few and no attempt was made to penetrate Allied fighter patrols to attack Allied forces on the ground. Again fighters were used flexibly. Such was the degree of air superiority on the first day, on the next day, many of the fighters on escort duty carried bombs, so they could attack targets on the ground if no enemy fighters appeared.

When Montgomery's forces finally emerged from the minefields, they found themselves contained by seemingly impenetrable German defences. From the 25th, German Ju 87s and Italian Fiat C.R.42s attempted to support German counter-attacks but found it difficult to break through Allied fighter defences. On the Commonwealth side, air support was arriving within half an hour of the request being made. Nevertheless, the German lines held. Losses were heavy on both sides but proportionally were more serious to the Axis forces. Even so, by the 26th, Montgomery was forced to accept his initial thrust had failed.

In the pause that followed, both Montgomery and Rommel, who had just returned from sick leave, ordered reinforcements north from the quiet southern sector of the front. For the British this was a straightforward matter, but the German 21st Panzer Division was delayed by Wellingtons on the night of the 26th/27th. The next day, some 200 light bombers struck the formation as it attempted to slice into the Allied salient. The German counter-attack was supported by Ju 87s and C.R.42s escorted by Bf 109s and Macchi C.202s. However, these were spotted and engaged by USAAF P-40 Warhawks on a fighter-bomber mission and also by Spitfires of No. 601 Squadron escorting Kittyhawk fighter-bombers. Hurricanes of Nos 33 and 213 Squadrons were scrambled to join the P-40s and Spitfires. The flexible use of the available resources, with fighters switching roles mid-mission when required, again ensured the Allied aerial umbrella remained solid while maximising the support for troops on the ground.

That evening, Montgomery attempted to push north from the salient his limited advance had created. The attack was supposed to take place under cover of darkness, but the defensive minefields took longer than anticipated to penetrate and the Allied tanks found themselves exposed to massed anti-tank defences in broad daylight. The 15th and 21st Panzer divisions counter-attacked, the Allied forces suffering heavy losses, but Allied fighters prevented the Stukas from adding to their problems. A lull in the fighting now set in. With no clear concentration of enemy forces to attack, fighter-bomber sorties became the main way of harassing the enemy.

Both sides set about re-organising their battered forces. On 1 November, the Germans launched another counter-attack in an attempt to relieve the growing pressure. Again Ju 87 support was called in, but American P-40 Warhawks and Kittyhawks of No. 112 Squadron returning from a fighter-bomber mission broke up the attack, shooting down five of the dive-bombers. The RAF's own specialist 40mm cannon-armed Hurricane was not getting much chance to prove its worth. A second squadron, No. 7 SAAF, had been re-equipped with the tank-busting Hurricane IID, but as far as Tedder was concerned, it was a slow, one-mission plane that was vulnerable to enemy fighters and ground fire. It was indeed a rather specialised one-mission plane but in the era of mechanised warfare it was a pretty important single mission. During the course of the battle, the Hurricane tank-busters achieved a fair amount of success but were used mainly against fringe targets to the south of the main battle.

In the early hours of 2 November, Montgomery returned to the attack. During that night the Wellingtons and Albacores, again many of them flying two missions, managed in excess of 100 sorties. The next day another 900 Allied sorties were flown. These included nearly 250 Hurricane sorties above the spearhead to ensure no Axis aircraft interfered. Two attempts were made by Stukas to break through this aerial umbrella but neither succeeded. Over 200 day-bomber sorties were flown immediately in front of the advancing tanks and infantry. Still the outnumbered Axis hung on. The next day, Allied air activity increased with another 100 nocturnal bombing sorties and over 1,000 in daylight, nearly 300 of which were by light bombers.

To Rommel the resources of the Allies seemed limitless. Although his forces were still holding on, he feared total collapse at any time and possibly the loss of his entire Army. On the 3rd he decided to pull back and, by the afternoon, this retreat had become clear to the Allies. The German front was still holding, but the coast road was packed with vehicles moving west and these immediately became the targets for 250 low-level strafing attacks and 200 bomber and fighter-bomber sorties. The damage inflicted seemed like a fair return on the fifteen fighters lost. Once again the tank-busting Hurricanes were side-lined. No. 6 Squadron asked for permission to join in these attacks but this was refused and the squadron continued to be confined to targets well to the south of the main action.[10] On the morning of 4 November, Eighth Army finally broke through what was now just an Axis rearguard. A counter order from Hitler on the 4th briefly halted the German retreat, the indecision placing Rommel's army in even greater jeopardy of being cut off and destroyed.[11]

There was an opportunity for a decisive victory but there was no consensus between the air and ground commanders about how this should be achieved. Tedder was scathing of Montgomery's cautious pursuit of the enemy and frustrated by his demands that his advancing forces have maximum fighter cover, thereby reducing the air forces available to harass the retreating Axis forces. On 5 November there were huge traffic jams of Axis transport reported in the town of Fuka, but they attracted only occasional attacks. On the 6th and 7th there was more congestion in the Matruh area, with many more attractive targets. On 8 November, the narrow Halfaya Pass provided still more targets, but only fifty-odd fighter-bomber sorties were flown in the region. For Tedder, a huge opportunity to wreak havoc among the retreating German columns was being missed. For their part, when Montgomery and his chief of staff, Major General

Francis de Guingand, were able to see how much destruction air power had inflicted on the retreating Axis forces, they were not impressed by the apparent Air Force failure to complete the rout.[12]

It is easy with hindsight to see that there was going to be no immediate revival of Axis air power and all aircraft could have been thrown into an all-out assault on the Axis columns. There is no doubt much more damage could have been inflicted on the retreating German columns, but an air force cannot wipe out an army truck by truck. Tedder was right; there was an opportunity to inflict a major defeat on Rommel. Montgomery was also right in believing his troops deserved air cover. But the two were not mutually exclusive. The fighters should have been protecting Montgomery's forces as they advanced to block Rommel's retreat and complete the rout. There was an ideal opportunity to inflict a blitzkrieg-style defeat on the German Army.

It was what Rommel feared most. The Desert Air Force had the equipment and the mobility to support a more audacious approach and with the Sherman and Grant tanks this was probably the only time in the war when Allied armour was not outclassed by the German opposition. Montgomery was blessed with far greater resources than Lieutenant General Richard O'Connor possessed in 1940 when he cut off and destroyed an Italian army. However, neither Montgomery nor Tedder had the air/ground policy that might reproduce the dramatic victories achieved by the Wehrmacht or indeed O'Connor. The constant carping from the Air Force 'armchair generals' and counter-carping by the Army was scarcely the atmosphere in which the greater inter-service understanding required for such operations was likely to develop. Unless Allied commanders could reproduce O'Connor's success in enveloping the enemy, not just pushing him back, final victory was going to be a very long haul.

The number of squadrons that could be moved forward to keep up with the advance was limited and it was natural that Spitfire and Kittyhawk squadrons should get priority. The Hurricane squadrons stayed behind and would in future only be used for rear air defence duties. These included the two Hurricane tank-buster squadrons, which might have found many attractive targets among the rapidly withdrawing German forces. Indeed, not only were these squadrons denied the opportunity to disrupt the German retreat, both were re-equipped with the fighter version of the Hurricane and would subsequently be used for shipping protection duties, much to the dismay of the pilots. Any interest the Middle East had in these highly specialised Army support planes was fading fast.

The Wellingtons did their best to keep up the pressure on the retreating forces. From the night of 4/5 November these attacks were reinforced by the first use of the four-engined Halifax heavy bomber. However, the weight of bombs they could carry gradually dwindled as the distance to the retreating columns increased. It became impossible to fly more than one sortie a night and the German forces soon passed beyond the effective range of the flare-carrying Albacores, making it far more difficult to identify targets. Nevertheless, the Germans reported significant losses in the Sollum region. As the Axis continued their retreat though Libya, units became more dispersed and the navigational problems for the Wellingtons became greater. On the night of 12/13 November very few targets were spotted and the night offensive was called off.[13]

Rommel was liable to dramatic mood swings and a deeply depressed Rommel seemed as anxious to retreat as Montgomery was reluctant to advance. Even when Montgomery was beginning to feel the inconvenience of stretched lines of communication, Rommel kept retreating, much to the dismay of his superiors. Rommel thought it was a hopeless battle. He likened fighting an opponent with control of the skies to savages taking on a modern European army. 'In future the battle on the ground will be preceded by the battle in the air,' he lamented. It was the sort of quote the official post-war Air Ministry narratives liked to pounce on as supporting evidence for British Air Staff conviction that air superiority was a pre-requisite for any successful operations on land.[14] In fact, air superiority had never been a pre-condition for any of Rommel's previous offensives; he had often advanced without it. Nor would it be a pre-condition for his future efforts. However, he was right that winning control of the skies was an enormous advantage.

Rommel did not stop retreating until he reached the Tunisian frontier where his forces took over the Mareth Line, originally built by the French to guard against Italian aggression. Montgomery would have to start again, this time with Rommel having the advantage of short lines of communication.

Chapter 11

Torch – The Second Front

Meanwhile, at the other end of the Mediterranean, Operation Torch was underway. This had originally been seen as a way of taking the pressure off Eighth Army. With Montgomery's success at El Alamein, the objective reverted to the original idea of a landing to help the Eighth Army clear the African continent of Axis forces. The operation essentially made use of the forces that would have been available for a 1942 invasion of France. The main objective was to capture Algiers and advance into Tunisia and take the port of Tunis. However, to secure lines of communication and guard against any Spanish response, or German action through Spain against Gibraltar, landings would also take place at Oran and Casablanca.

The capture of Algiers and Oran were to be accomplished by British and American troops arriving from the United Kingdom. The Americans were solely responsible for the capture of Casablanca with forces that would come directly from the United States. The whole operation was to be commanded by General Dwight Eisenhower. The First British Army under General Kenneth Anderson would land in Algiers, while the American Major General Lloyd Fredendall and General George Patton would lead the forces heading for Oran and Casablanca respectively.

Unprepared and unsuspecting French defences might not pose the same danger as German divisions in France but it was far from a risk-free venture. The reaction of the French was difficult to predict. The British were not popular with the Vichy regime or indeed many French people. Many Frenchmen believed they had been left in the lurch in 1940 by the British retreat to Dunkirk and dismay turned to outrage when the British turned on their former ally, attacking the French fleet and killing over 1,000 French sailors. These events had left deep scars and Vichy forces had put up some stiff resistance when Allied forces occupied Syria in 1941. In an attempt to avoid anti-British feeling leading to stiffer resistance, an effort was made to make the operation look as American as possible with some British planes having their RAF roundels replaced by the American star.

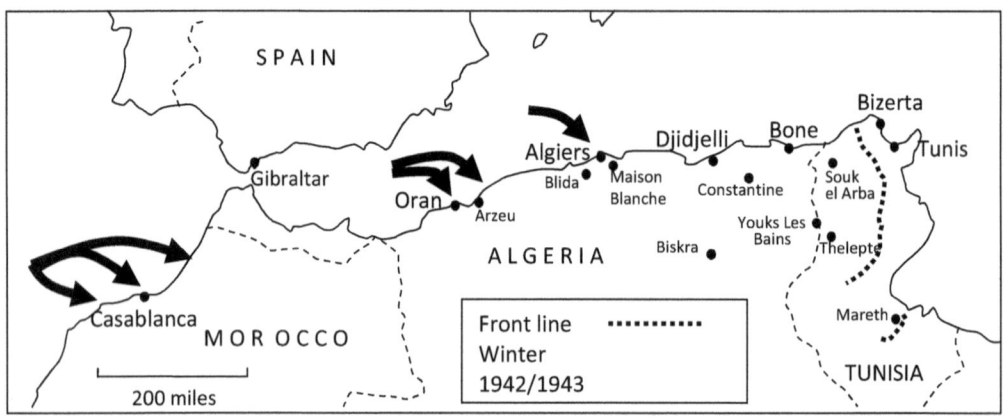

The initial landings could only be supported by carrier-based aircraft and, even if substantial bridgeheads were established, lines of communication with the United Kingdom and the United States were long and vulnerable. Instead of the 100 miles a cross-Channel invasion involved, some 110,000 troops would have to be transported over 1,500 miles across waters patrolled by German U-boats. If the Germans persuaded the Spanish to take the opportunity to occupy Gibraltar, it could easily turn into a disaster. These were huge risks simply to ensure that when the British and American forces landed they were not faced by German defenders. Much to the dismay of Marshall, and no doubt the frustration of Stalin, even the landings in Algiers would be twice as far from Berlin as a landing in northern France.

The plan was to start flying in RAF squadrons from Gibraltar on the second day. Comparing the air forces supporting Montgomery's Eighth Army and those earmarked to support Anderson's First Army, it was difficult to believe they were part of the same organisation. The RAF component supporting Anderson, Eastern Air Command commanded by Air Marshal William Welsh, was an off-shoot of the United Kingdom-based RAF and its organisation, equipment and thinking reflected this.

Hailing from the United Kingdom had its advantages. There was no question of air cover being provided by anything other than Spitfires. The Fleet Air Arm squadrons covering the initial landing included five Seafire squadrons. Five RAF Spitfire squadrons would arrive with the first wave, with four more soon following. There would also be six American fighter squadrons equipped with Spitfires.[1] The deployment of fifteen Spitfire squadrons at a stroke in North-West Africa did not go unnoticed

192

in the Western Desert. Suddenly it seemed there were plenty of Spitfires available for the African theatre. There would be no Spitfire IX squadrons; they would all be Spitfire Vs. Nevertheless, in the Western Desert these were undreamt of riches.

The troops landing in North Africa would have better protection than their Western Desert counterparts, but they would not be so fortunate with battlefield air support. There was surprisingly little effort by those planning Operation Torch to draw on the experiences of the Desert Air Force. The original plans for air support were based on the force that had operated at Dieppe and looked reasonably adequate on paper. First Army was to have six cannon-armed Hurricane II squadrons, five of which had operated over Dieppe, and also the two Hurribomber squadrons. Welsh, however, had the more traditional downbeat Air Ministry view of the value of close air support and, as plans for the landing progressed, the ground attack fighter support element of his force was gradually whittled down.

Two of the Hurricane II squadrons were withdrawn and the two Hurribomber squadrons were replaced by two 'army co-operation' squadrons, which would be responsible for tactical reconnaissance and ground attack. To enable the squadron to perform both roles, machine-gun-armed Mustangs were replaced with cannon-armed Hurricane IIs. This increased the offensive capabilities of the squadrons, but the lower performance Hurricanes would be less effective in the reconnaissance role. The two army co-operation Blenheim squadrons used for smoke-laying at Dieppe had converted to the Bisley, the specialist ground attack version of the Blenheim the Air Ministry had been promising the War Office since 1940. Two similarly equipped squadrons from No. 2 Group Bomber Command would provide the specialist bomber support.[2] More than two years after the Bisley/Blenheim V had been ordered as an interim lash-up, it would finally get the chance to show what it was capable of.

The name Bisley and Blenheim V had always been used interchangeably, and even in the Torch order of battle the No. 2 Group squadrons were described as Blenheim V and the army co-operation squadrons had the Bisley label.[3] The Army had never wanted a large twin-engined close support plane and the Middle East had already given it the thumbs down. Indeed, when it arrived in the Middle East this latest product of the British aircraft industry aroused bemusement. The Blenheim IV had been phased out as a day bomber and it was difficult to see how the Blenheim V/ Bisley represented any improvement. The Middle East Command was not quite sure what to do with its Bisleys. They either stayed in storage or were shunted off to squadrons engaged in coastal anti-submarine patrols. This was the plane the Eastern Air Command was expected to use as its front-line tactical day bomber.

While the Bisley was a step backwards, the introduction of the Austers of No. 651 Squadron was a genuine innovation. The plane provided the priceless ability to fly a few hundred feet into the air from small forward airstrips and not just direct artillery but provide army commanders with a view of the battlefield without calling in distant high-performance reconnaissance planes. It was the sort of capability army commanders had felt the need for in the Dieppe operation. The Air Ministry had never believed a slow unarmed plane could survive over the battlefield and there was a real nervousness about using these squadrons. Every possible precaution would be taken to avoid losses. Strict time restrictions on the length of a sortie would, it was hoped, reduce the risks of interception. If enemy fighters were known to be operating in the area, the pilots would be warned. Anti-aircraft guns would be on hand to defend the plane if required. At the other end of the performance spectrum, the strategic reconnaissance unit, No. 4 PRU, was equipped with Spitfires.

Torch would see the first major deployment of the United States Army Air Forces in the western hemisphere. The Twelfth Air Force, commanded by Major General Jimmy Doolittle, was just an offshoot of the UK-based Eighth Air Force and had the same dual purpose tactical/strategic role. It would be divided into a strategic XII Bomber Command and a tactical XII Air Support Command (ASC), although it would soon became clear the former was the dominant element. Initial plans for the Torch operation required four fighter, three medium-bomber, two heavy-bomber and one light-bomber groups, which would amount to a formidable force of 300 fighters and 300 bombers.[4]

The four American fighter groups could be covered by forces in the UK (two Spitfire and two with the as yet untried Lockheed P-38 Lightning). They were joined by a fifth Curtiss P-40 Warhawk group that arrived from the United States. The fighter groups were only supposed to be used for air combat; the USAAF at this time did not want any of their fighters to have their fighting qualities impaired by flying with bombs or associated bomb-dropping equipment. Fighter pilots were trained solely for air combat.

The promised American contribution did not fully materialise. The burden of tactical air support would initially fall on RAF shoulders but it was not a responsibility that would weigh heavily on the air contingent commander. Welsh was of the old school, who saw fighters as fighters and nothing else, and certainly did not want his air force used as a substitute for Army artillery.[5] The American and British air commanders shared very similar views on air warfare.

The Algiers and Oran landings were covered by three Royal Navy fleet carriers and four escort carriers with fifty-four Seafires, thirty-nine Sea Hurricanes, forty-two Martlets (the British name for the American Wildcat), six Fulmars and thirty-six Albacores. The landings at Casablanca would be covered by one US Navy fleet carrier and three escort carriers with 109 Wildcats, 36 Dauntless dive-bombers and 19 Avenger bombers.[6] The Fleet Air Arm was still struggling to become a force that could take on land-based opponents. By comparison with the American Avenger, or even the much older Dauntless, the biplane Albacore seemed to hail from a different era of warfare.

The Americans were equally far ahead in the design of carrier fighters but, rather ironically, the development of British carrier fighters was such a shambles that the Fleet Air Arm had been forced to adapt what turned out to be the best fighter available to either navy. The Spitfire was scarcely ideally suited for operations from aircraft carriers but, if its undercarriage could take the strain, it was the best naval fighter available and arguably the only fighter superior to the opposing French Dewoitine D.520s. The French Air Force was reasonably well equipped. Aircraft like the Dewoitine D.520, Bloch 174 and American Douglas DB7 (Boston I) and Martin 167 (Maryland) had arrived too late to affect the outcome in France in 1940 but were still useful planes in 1942. The French light bombers were all far superior to the Bisley. Ironically, the invading American forces now found themselves confronted by the bombers, and Curtiss H-75 (P-36) fighters, they had been supplying to the French in 1939–1940.

At Oran, unopposed landings were made on the beaches and the small port of Arzeu was soon captured, but an attempt to storm the port of Oran itself was defeated with heavy casualties. The fighting in the air was fierce too. Dewoitine D.520s intercepted eight Albacores attacking the airfield at La Senia, south of Oran, shooting down three and damaging another three. A fourth was shot down by ground fire. Escorting Seafires and Sea Hurricanes shot down four of the French fighters and the French suffered further heavy losses on the airfield itself.

Tafraoui airfield, 20 miles south of Oran, was quickly captured, but strafing attacks by Dewoitine D.520s and French artillery fire made it difficult to use. The USAAF 31st Group arrived at Tafraoui with its Spitfires in the evening and, like RAF fighter squadrons before them, soon found that in the heat of a tactical battle they were required to do more than just engage enemy aircraft. The fighters were soon being used for tactical reconnaissance, reporting the approach of French forces backed by light tanks. Having spotted the danger, they were then used to help turn back the Vichy forces, the Spitfire's 20mm Hispano-Suiza cannon, ironically designed by the French, proving very effective against the lightly armoured French tanks. La Senia airfield was eventually taken but this, too, remained within range of French artillery.[7]

At Casablanca even stiffer resistance was encountered. French LeO 451s, Martin 167s and Douglas DB7s, escorted by Curtiss H-75s, bombed American shipping. French fighters strafed the American forces as they landed while others shot down several US Navy Dauntless dive-bombers. The next day carrier-based aircraft were required to strafe French counter-attacks. In three days fighting, the US Navy lost forty-four planes.

At Algiers heavy mist prevented French aircraft taking off. An attempt to storm the harbour was defeated, but local French commanders along the coast ordered French forces to offer no resistance. Allied forces pushed inland and captured the airfield at Maison Blanche where two groups of Dewoitine D.520 fighters were grounded by the mist. By the end of the day the port and airfield were in Allied hands and RAF fighter squadrons began flying in to Maison Blanche. At dusk on the 8th the first German bombers, fifteen Ju 88s, appeared over the Allied fleet.[8]

On 9 November, Admiral Darlan ordered all French forces to lay down their arms. There followed a few days of confusion as the opposing French factions battled for control, but on 11 November the matter was put beyond all doubt by the German decision to move into unoccupied France and Tunisia. French Air Force units now became available to the Allied cause. In November the first unit, GC II/5, began conversion to P-40 Warhawks. In the desperate days of 1940 or even 1941 these French reinforcements would have been priceless, but now they were dwarfed by the flood of American materiel pouring into the area.

Allied forces pushed eastwards towards Bizerte and Tunis as rapidly as possible, but Kesselring, the German theatre commander, was soon flying German troops and equipment into Tunisia. Luftwaffe reinforcements included the first FW 190s to operate in the Mediterranean. It was a spectacular display of the value of the sort of air transport fleet the War Office was so keen to acquire. Both sides were using airborne troops to capture airfields as far forward as possible, in the case of the airfield at Bone, the opposing paratroopers reaching it almost simultaneously, the British just beating the Germans to it. On 16 November, British forces, still 50 miles short of Bizerte, ran into German reconnaissance parties.

On the same day, American Flying Fortresses flying from Maison Blanche flew their first mission against Sidi Ahmed airfield near Bizerte. The next day, after a few operations by night, the Bisleys of No. 18 Squadron flew their first daylight mission, attacking the same airfield at low level, but four out of eleven were shot down. It was not an auspicious start. Luftwaffe units were also busy against targets in the Allied rear, with units operating from Sardinia delivering some punishing blows on the ports and airfields the Allies had captured.

While both sides were striking targets in the rear, only the Luftwaffe was providing air support on the battlefield. As the Allied forces advanced on Tunisia, they soon came within range of the FW 190 fighter-bomber and Stuka dive-bomber units. The Americans were the latest to be surprised by the effectiveness of the underrated and much maligned German dive-bomber. Being much lighter than twin or four-engined bombers, they could operate from more primitive airstrips closer to the front line and their relative proximity to their targets meant they could fly multiple missions.[9] They were sometimes operating from airfields so close to the front that their prospective targets, trying to battle their way out of the mountains, could see them taking off in the plain below. With both sides thin on the ground in numbers and materiel, the intervention of the Stukas often made the difference.

The Luftwaffe had far better airfields to operate from and the plain west of Tunis meant it was easy to set up temporary airstrips. In the mountains the Allies were trying to break out of it was much more difficult to improvise airfields. However, it was also true that neither the British nor the Americans had anything with the Stuka's ability to operate from small, forward, primitive airstrips. The one exception was the artillery observation Auster, which could operate from the smallest of temporary airstrips. By 21 November, seven aircraft had joined the advancing British forces and these were operating from very close to the front line, indeed so close that in the fighting around Tebourba, just 15 miles short of Tunis, a section of No. 651 Squadron ground personnel joined the infantry defending their landing ground from a German counter-attack.[10]

In two weeks, the handful of Austers flew thirty-five sorties, not just spotting for artillery but also liaising and reporting on the position of friendly and enemy forces. Despite the local air superiority the Luftwaffe had established, and on occasion contrary to orders from nervous commanders in the rear, these sorties continued and only one plane was lost.[11] Low performance planes could operate in a hostile environment as long as they did not stray too far into enemy air space and stayed fairly low. The Austers provided vital information for local commanders. On occasion they sent startled German infantry scurrying for cover from the unarmed planes, perhaps suggesting what armed, slow-flying aircraft might achieve.

Like all army commanders confronted by the Ju 87 menace for the first time, Anderson and the American commanders were struck by the huge psychological impact the plane had on front-line troops, especially the inexperienced, and Allied commanders were soon demanding something similar.[12] The USAAF was still part of the Army, so getting something was not quite the uphill struggle it had been for the War Office. The standard attack category planes like the Douglas A-20 were considered too big for the low-level role. Single-engined dive-bombers were what the Army wanted, so the Americans began experimenting with air brakes fitted to Allison-powered Mustangs. Bombing was not what American fighters did, so it was given an attack designation, becoming the A-36 Apache. These, however, would not reach the front until the summer of 1943.

The RAF had the Hurricane for close air support, but supply difficulties limited the number of squadrons that could be maintained close to the front and priority went to Spitfire squadrons. This denied the Army its only specialist close support element, but it would seem this was not considered a great loss by Welsh. He saw no great need for ground attack aircraft and viewed the Hurricanes more as fighters anyway. He believed they could contribute more in the rear by escorting convoys. Denied the opportunity to operate over the front and with few successes in the convoy escort role, morale in the Hurricane squadrons slumped.

For any bomber support, Anderson had to rely rather heavily on the USAAF. With little sign that Spain intended to join the Axis cause, the substantial American forces in North-West Africa guarding against this possibility could be moved east. The P-38s of the 14th Fighter Group and the recently arrived Douglas A-20s of the 15th Light Bomber squadron moved to Youks-les-Bain late in November, but this was all Anderson could call on. The Lightning was more useful for low-level attack than the Boston. Both were a considerable improvement on the Bisley.

On 4 December, nine Bisleys set off to bomb another enemy airfield and all nine were shot down. There was no close escort; three Spitfire squadrons operating in the general area were supposed to provide protection. It seemed that the lessons of previous campaigns were having to be re-learned. Trenchardian First World War ideas of using a handful of fighters offensively to clear huge volumes of enemy airspace and the dogged belief that any bomber worthy of the name ought to be capable of defending itself were once more emerging and RAF aircrews were paying the price. Day operations with Bisleys were immediately abandoned and the decision taken to re-equip the squadrons, although with what was not immediately clear. Britain had nothing suitable and the RAF could no longer necessarily rely on the Americans filling the gap. The Bisley squadrons withdrew to the rear to await news of what they might get.

With Luftwaffe strikes on his front-line troops hammering home the value of close air support, Anderson was becoming increasingly frustrated at Welsh's reluctance to use his aircraft as 'long-range guns'. Welsh, however, would not be moved; only in an emergency would they be used to support ground forces. Any support was provided grudgingly in a manner Anderson described as 'farcical'. The Air Force insisted that, because of its other commitments, five hours' notice was required for any army air support mission and when it arrived it only consisted of a few strafing Spitfires.[13] In truth there was little to call on. The Bisleys had been withdrawn, the Hurricanes of No. 225 Squadron were too occupied in the tactical reconnaissance role and the cannon-armed Hurricanes were stuck in the rear. It was a very different story in Libya where the value of tactical air support was more appreciated and more effort was devoted to making sure it was available.

By the beginning of December, German forces were launching powerful counter-attacks and the Allies were struggling to hold on to the ground gained. The Hurricanes of No. 225 Squadron needed such extensive escorts that tactical reconnaissance virtually ceased. At the end of the year the squadron was withdrawn to recuperate and was replaced by the second Army Co-operation squadron, No. 241, also equipped with Hurricanes. With demand for more air support growing, more effort was made to use these as fighter-bombers. However, the dual reconnaissance/ground attack role was an unreasonable expectation from a handful of aircraft that dare not penetrate too far into enemy airspace without fighter protection. The means to direct them, however, was functioning well. The Army Air Support Control operating with the British Army was exceeding all expectations, being used to direct fighters as well as ground attack missions. The problem was there were only a handful of ground attack Hurricanes to direct.[14]

At the beginning of December there were still only a small number of Allied fighters within range of the front line. Two squadrons of Lightnings with a total of thirty-seven planes were operating from Youks-les-Bains, 150 miles from the front and a further forty-five Spitfire Vs from various squadrons operating from Souk-el-Arba, 70 miles from the front.[15] This was about the same distance as the sea crossing to Dieppe. The extra range the Spitfire needed to operate over France was just as necessary in the fighting in North Africa. With Spitfires only capable of operating over the front for short periods, the main responsibility for tactical air defence fell on the shoulders of the higher endurance P-38 Lightning squadrons.

This was an excellent opportunity for the much vaunted American fighter to demonstrate its capabilities. Unfortunately, the one real asset of the fighter, its high speed at altitude, proved of little value as they were forced to engage far more manoeuvrable single-engined German and Italian fighters at low and medium altitudes. Even in the escort role, where the American Fortresses forced the Axis fighter pilots to operate at altitudes more favourable to the P-38, the American fighter was not a great success. A P-38 escort was better than no escort at all and the Lightnings did achieve the first objective of any escort by drawing away some of the intercepting fighters from the bombers. However, losses were heavy. On 3 December, sixteen P-38s escorting a formation of B-17 bombers were bounced by Bf 109s, losing six of their number. A total of nine P-38s were lost on this day alone and the regular losses were affecting morale.

British doubts about the Lockheed fighter seemed fully justified. It was all rather ironic. The British had spent the previous two years telling the Americans how performance at altitude was all-important for a fighter and how this was one aspect of American fighter performance that had to be improved. These criticisms reinforced the American belief that the future lay with turbo-supercharged fighters. Having seen what the FW 190 could do, the Air Ministry had changed its tune and was trying to focus on improving fighter performance at medium and low altitude. Meanwhile, the Americans found themselves committed to two fighters (the P-47 Thunderbolt and P-38 Lightning), with bulky turbo-supercharger systems, which lacked the agility to deal with the fighters that opposed them.

It was a major setback for Arnold at a time when the performance of American combat planes was coming under some close scrutiny in the American press. It cannot have helped that on a tour of the Tunisian front the commander of the P-38 equipped 14th Fighter Group told Arnold that he had flown the Mustang, presumably the Allison-powered version being used for tactical reconnaissance and preferred it to the fighter his group had to fly.[16] Even in an improvised dug-out at a North African front-line airfield the message for Arnold was the same – the Americans were not making use of their best fighter.

In the low/medium altitude role the Curtiss P-40 had its advantages, as the RAF in the Western Desert had discovered. The latest P-40F version was powered by a Packard-built Merlin XX series engine, which enabled the fighter to fly higher and achieve maximum speed at 20,000 feet rather than 15,000 feet, but it was the fighter's manoeuvrability at medium and low altitudes that was its big advantage. Where possible, P-40F Warhawk squadrons were moved up to the front to support the twin-engined Lightnings.

By the end of the year, there were 300 Commonwealth planes in thirteen fighter and six bomber squadrons in North-West Africa. Leaving aside squadrons in western Algeria and Morocco, the Americans had eight fighter, and twenty-five bomber squadrons with around 400 aircraft. With 700 British and American planes in the Western Desert the Allied numerical superiority was becoming overwhelming. From this point on in the war, it was the types of aircraft available and how they were used that would be the key topic for debate, not numbers.

The RAF force in North-West Africa was essentially a tactical force, although this was more out of a desire to keep the four-engined heavies in Britain rather than any great conviction in the value of a specialist tactical force. The American contingent, however, was becoming ever more strategically orientated. By the beginning of 1943, the USAAF strategic XII Bomber Command had twenty-one bomber groups, of which nine were equipped with the Flying Fortress, along with three fighter groups for escort duties. The tactical XII Air Support Command had just four bomber squadrons and five fighter. The emphasis was on striking targets in the rear rather than in and around the battlefield. This, according to American air force commanders, was why air forces existed. Spaatz, now in command of all USAAF units in the European theatre, which included North-West Africa, claimed that just thirty-six B-17 sorties a day would cut off Axis supply lines to North Africa.[17] It was reminiscent of Churchill's ideas back in 1940 of a handful of Wellington squadrons dispensing destruction on such a scale that they could transform the balance of power in the eastern Mediterranean.[18] The destructive power of the bomber was still being overestimated.

The emphasis on attacking targets in the rear coupled with the Luftwaffe's activity over the front was bound to provoke the suspicion among the troops on the ground, and their commanders, of an air force not pulling its weight where it counted most. The obvious logistical difficulties the Air Force was experiencing were cutting little ice in Army circles. The problems were real enough but did not explain why so many large resource-hungry strategic bomber squadrons and so few specialist close support units were being deployed. From the Army's standpoint, each Luftwaffe air strike was a reminder of their own air force's apparent desire to be somewhere else. American air commanders now joined their British counterparts in insisting the German dive-bomber was hopelessly vulnerable and would be blown out of the skies as soon as their fighters got to them. This was little consolation to the front-line troops waiting for the fighters to get to them.

For the British Army it was all very déjà vu. It was Norway, France, Greece, Crete and Malaya all over again. There were all the familiar arguments that had been around since the First World War. The Army wanted more control because the Air Force was not operating where it was needed. The Air Force counter argument was that the Army did not understand how to use air power. The Army wanted more focused air cover over the front and the Air Force commanders wanted to go for the enemy jugular in the rear. To both sides the other looked intransigent and ill-informed about what was required in modern war. The problem for those favouring indirect support was that they were attacking the jugular with a far blunter instrument than they imagined.

Poor liaison between British air and ground was not helped by the fact that Anderson insisted on establishing his Army headquarters well to the rear at Constantine, where air force commanders felt he was out of touch with the RAF tactical headquarters and even his own corps commanders. Welsh saw no point in moving his headquarters so far back. The army and air commanders were as divided geographically as they were philosophically.[19]

Meanwhile, Eisenhower was not happy with some of the aircraft he had been assigned and, unlike Tedder, he would not be shy about demanding what he felt he needed. He had been gifted the largest force of Spitfires to operate in any theatre outside the United Kingdom, but it soon became clear the Spitfire V was outclassed by the Bf 109G and FW 190. He needed and expected Merlin 61-powered Spitfires. The Spitfire VIII was earmarked for the Middle East and was being tropicalised but none were yet available. However, in Tunisia, especially in winter, the need for tropicalisation was borderline[20] and Eisenhower was told untropicalised Spitfire IXs might be risked. These were in very short supply but perhaps one squadron could be re-equipped with Spitfire IXs. To Eisenhower, one squadron scarcely seemed worth it. At least two or three squadrons were needed to make any difference.[21]

In January, the first of two RAF squadrons began re-equipping with the Spitfire IX. The Spitfire IX flew its first mission in Tunisia on 31 January 1943, No. 81 Squadron immediately claiming a couple of Bf 109s. The next day, No. 72 Squadron withdrew from the front to re-equip with the Mark IX.[22] It might all seem rather small-scale to Eisenhower but he was doing a lot better than the Desert Air Force. Air support and tactical reconnaissance was a far greater problem for the British contingent than fighter cover. No. 225 Squadron returned to the front on 19 January to join No. 241 Squadron, now equipped with a few Spitfire Vs for tactical reconnaissance missions, but these two squadrons were all that was available for reconnaissance and close support.

With the weather fast deteriorating, Eisenhower had declared no further attempt to advance on Tunis would be made until the following spring. This would also allow time for the huge supply problems all branches of the armed services were facing to be overcome. It was still hoped to clear all Axis forces from North Africa by 1 June. What should happen after that was one of the questions decided at the Casablanca conference in January 1943.

Marshall was still pushing for an invasion of France in 1943 but was getting little support. Brooke wanted German military might shattered by bombing before considering invasion, a precondition the bomber protagonists were more than happy to comply with. Churchill had promised Stalin an invasion would come in the spring of 1943, but he too was not enthusiastic about the operation. Both believed the Mediterranean should remain the Allied focus. Even Eisenhower now accepted an invasion of France would not happen until 1944.[23] It was agreed that, after North Africa was cleared, the main effort should continue in the Mediterranean, with Sardinia or Sicily the main candidates for the next move. Sardinia would offer air bases from which southern Europe could be bombed, while capturing Sicily would open the lines of communication through the Mediterranean to the Far East. Sicily won the day. The invasion of France that Stalin had been promised could still take place in August or September, which, Stalin might have noted, was very late in the invasion 'season'.[24]

There were plenty of excellent reasons for invading Sicily, but the Mediterranean was where Hitler was hoping the Allies would continue to focus their efforts. It would mean there would be no major distractions on his western front as the German Wehrmacht on the eastern front geared itself up for one more decisive battle, Operation Citadel, which planned to envelop Soviet forces in the Kursk region. The war was in its fourth year and Hitler was still on the offensive. This was scarcely how the war was supposed to pan out. The argument had always been that Germany was not capable of fighting a long drawn-out war. It was supposed to be a nation forced to adopt a quick victory or bust strategy. Indeed, a protracted war on two fronts should have spelt disaster for Hitler's regime but, with the western Allies continuing to focus their efforts in the Mediterranean, Hitler would have a third summer to force a decisive victory in the east.

Before Sicily could be threatened, North Africa had to be cleared. The American II and French XIX Corps would now be brought up to the south of the British First Army, forming a continuous front as far as the impassable Chott el Djerid depression. XII Air Support Command (ASC), under Brigadier General Paul Williams, would provide air support for Fredendall's II Corps. Effectively, the British and American armies each had their own air support.

Late in November 1942, Tedder visited Algiers to discuss the co-ordination of the North-West African and Western Desert air forces as the net slowly closed around the Axis armies in Tunisia. Eisenhower was impressed by Tedder's comments on the lack of co-ordination between the British and American camps and he asked Tedder to spend a couple of weeks in Algiers to advise on how things could be improved.[25] Tedder had no intention of becoming a mere adviser, but he was interested in commanding a new expanded Mediterranean air force. He proposed a North African air force which would combine all American, French and British Commonwealth units, both tactical and strategic. Within this air force there would be three commands, one containing heavy and medium bombers and long-range fighters for strategic operations. A second would have fighter and bomber units required for coastal and naval operations. Finally there would be a command for units that co-operated directly with ground forces. It was essentially the organisation already operating in the Western Desert and put the tactical air forces on a par with the strategic air forces, something the Air Ministry had resisted for so long in the United Kingdom. The Desert Air Force would retain its identity but, along with the British No. 242 Group, and the American XII ASC would form a single tactical force. The new organisation would effectively transfer Eastern Air Command from United Kingdom influence and jurisdiction to Middle East control and practice.

Tedder's combined command made sense militarily but was not what the Americans wanted from the grand strategy point of view. Eisenhower wanted to keep North-West Africa and the United Kingdom as a single theatre. The Torch operation was supposed to be a temporary diversion of the forces earmarked for an invasion of northern France, which Roosevelt and Marshall still saw as the quickest way to win the war. Tying these forces into a Mediterranean command would make it more difficult to extract them for the invasion of France. Nevertheless, the new organisation was so logical it was difficult to object to it. Spaatz became the commander of the North-West African Air Force, with Tedder the overall commander of all air units in the Mediterranean, and as such worked alongside Eisenhower. Doolittle commanded the strategic element and Group Captain Barrett, soon to be replaced by Air Vice-Marshal Hugh Lloyd, the maritime air units. All the tactical forces would be under Coningham and the American USAAF Brigadier General Laurence Kuter was transferred from the UK to be his deputy.

Under the guidance of Coningham, it was the principles and organisation of the Desert Air Force that would in future be applied to all tactical air units in North Africa. The Air Ministry in London was forced to concede that the Desert Air Force was now the model on which tactical air forces should be based. The name of the new command provoked much thought and discussion. Anything involving the word 'co-operation' was seen by the Air Force as far too ancillary and subservient. As Coningham put it, 'Co-operation often means the other fellow co-operating with you,' and the Air Force did not want to be the 'other fellow'.[26] Even 'Army Command' seemed to draw attention to the rather obvious gap that had always existed in the UK-based RAF Fighter/Bomber/Coastal Command set-up. Tedder avoided any controversy by choosing the functional and eminently appropriate title of 'Tactical Air Force'. Nevertheless, it was scarcely encouraging that the word 'Co-operation' had to be expunged.

The USAAF were very happy with the arrangement. The creation of a 'Strategic Air Force' gave the USAAF full licence to pursue its independent strategy. The tactical air arm became more than just an offshoot of the strategic bomber fleet, it was a parallel and equally important component. Crucially, USAAF commanders believed they had broken free of army control in both the strategic and tactical domains. The new organisation was seen as a useful step on their road to independence. The growing divide between American ground and air forces would ensure there was plenty of scope for dispute over how the tactical air force should support the army. Before this new organisation was implemented there would be more opportunities to highlight the weakness of the available tactical forces and the problems with the existing command arrangements.

With Eisenhower's forces on the defensive, it was the Germans who were able to take the initiative. From 17 January, General Hans-Jürgen von Arnim, the commander of the Axis forces in Tunisia, continued his small-scale counter-attacks aided by limited but effective Luftwaffe support. The Germans were helped by a total lack of co-operation between the British and American air components with requests from one being refused by the other. Coningham was on leave at the time, but his deputy, Kuter, stepped in and took over command of both No. 242 Group and XII ASC, in an attempt to get the British and American air forces acting as one.[27]

Meanwhile, Rommel's forces had settled into the Mareth Line. With Montgomery struggling to keep up with the rapid Axis retreat, Rommel's southern front was temporarily secure and he was able to turn his attentions to the French and American forces threatening his lines of communication to the north-west. Von Arnim was also in an aggressive mood. There was an opportunity not just to embarrass the Allies but to achieve a strategic breakthrough which might even open up a path to the sea at Bone, cutting off the American and British forces in Tunisia.

On 30 January 1943, the 21st Panzer Division surprised and overwhelmed French forces holding the Faid Pass. The USAAF XII ASC managed fewer than fifty fighter and attack sorties against the advancing Germans. The next day a more substantial intervention by the Luftwaffe ensured American reinforcement arrived too late to intervene effectively. On 14 February, the panzers started pushing forward again towards Sbeilta, supported by over 300 aircraft. The one bomber and three fighter groups of the American XII ASC could at best muster around 150 planes. Further north the RAF had five Spitfire squadrons and two Hurribomber squadrons, but these were not called upon.

Further to the rear there were substantial numbers of B-25 and B-26 medium and B-17 heavy bombers, along with P-38 escort fighters, all earmarked for strategic operations. Amidst plenty, the Allies had managed to allow a situation to develop where they were outnumbered where it mattered. Too little of what was available was suitable for supporting ground forces. Bell P-39 Airacobra-equipped squadrons had now been moved up to the front and these were available for ground strafing but only because the fighter was not considered good enough to operate as a fighter.

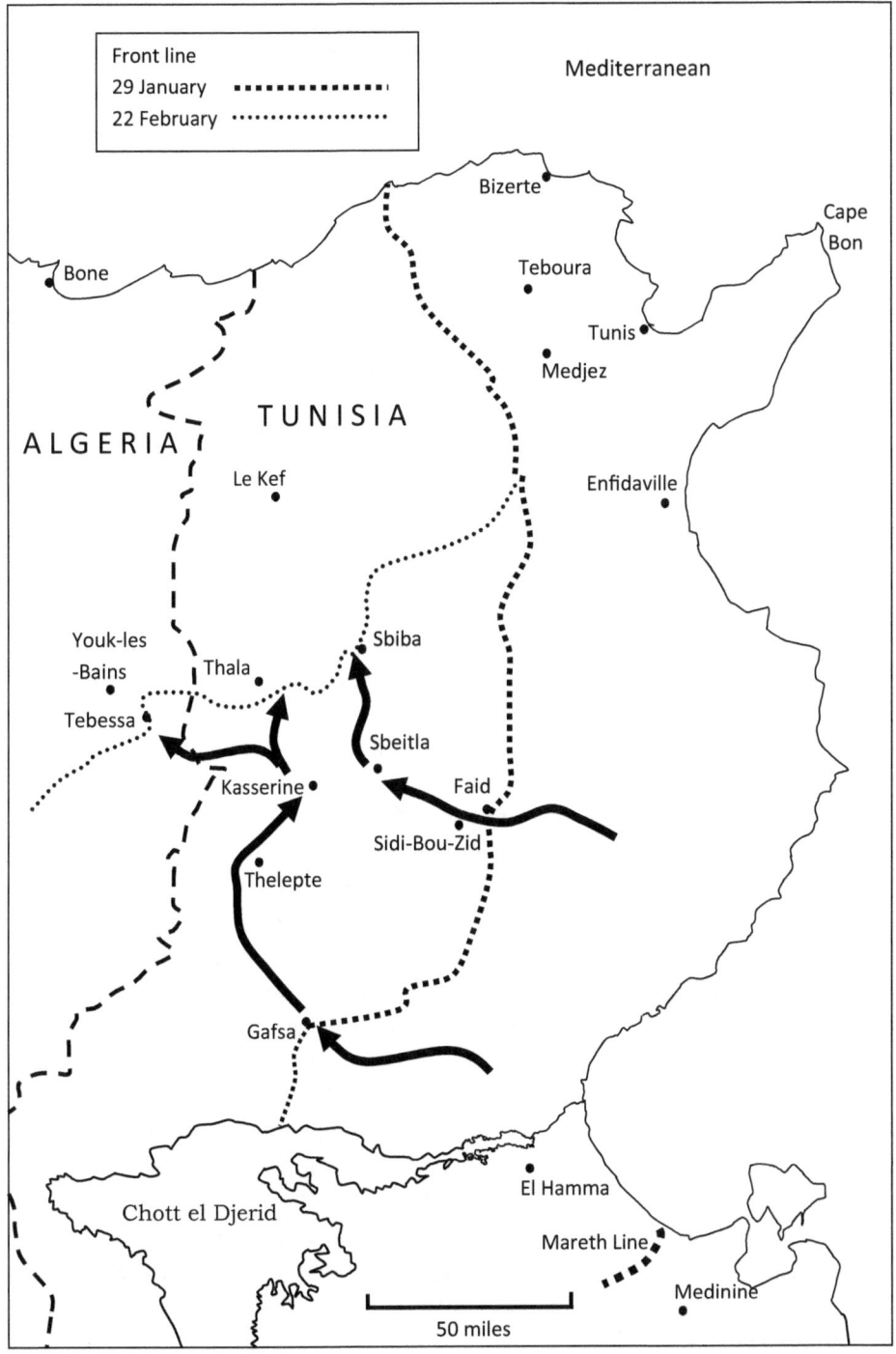

The French P-40s of GC II/5 also seem to have been relegated to this role. Close air support was just a way of using aircraft not suitable for more important roles.

On 14 February, 10th and 21st Panzer Divisions launched a pincer movement from the Faid Pass, surrounding American forces and capturing Sidi Bou Zid. Spitfires escorted A-20s, while P-39s and P-40s strafed enemy columns, but the advancing Germans were getting more substantial support from Ju 87 dive-bombers as well as Bf 109 and FW 190 fighter-bombers. On the first day the Luftwaffe flew more than 350 sorties, maintaining 250 on the second and third days. Once again the Stukas seemed to have the freedom of the skies over the battlefield. On the second day the American armoured forces attempted to strike back but suffered heavy losses at the hands of German 88mm guns. The road to Sbeitla was open and indeed the American retreat did not stop until they reached the Sbiba Pass.

Further south, on the 15th, Rommel launched an attack on Gafsa. The American forces were overrun and fell back on the Kasserine Pass. P-38 squadrons from the rear were now being thrown into the ground attack role, but these reinforcements barely compensated for the aircraft already lost. The Luftwaffe still dominated the skies. Rommel's advance forced the Americans to abandon Thelpte airfield on the 17th, destroying twenty-five unserviceable planes before they left. It was the first of five forward airfields that had to be evacuated.

There was no shortage of American air power, but it was the wrong type and was being used against the wrong targets. On the 17th, as American forces retreated in southern Tunisia, the biggest Allied effort was against airfields in Sardinia, with eighty B-17, B-25 and B-26 bombers escorted by over fifty P-38 Lightnings taking part.[28] Helping the struggling American Army was not the US Army Air Forces' immediate priority. On 19 February Rommel drove American forces out of the Kasserine Pass. Poor weather restricted air operations on both sides which, remarkably given the overall balance of power in the region, favoured the Allied forces.

The Allies were fortunate that disagreements within the German camp over the scope and aims of the offensive prevented them taking full advantage of the confusion on the Allied side. Rommel was quite happy just to push on through the Kasserine Pass and take Tebessa, and possibly the nearby Youk-les-Bains airfield. However, the Italians, encouraged by the rapid American retreat, wanted to advance on the Sbiba Pass as well, then on to Thala and eventually Le Kef.

On 17 February, Coningham took over command of the tactical air forces and immediately criticised No. 242 Group for staying on the defensive and leaving all the fighting to the Americans. The RAF units in the north were now ordered to intervene, although weather delayed this until 23 February. On the 20th, Spaatz put most of his strategic bombers at the disposal of Coningham and these began flying in support of the ground forces from 21 February.[29] The situation had become so serious that the Bisley squadrons were thrown back into the daylight bombing role on the 20th with a dawn strike on German columns near the Kasserine Pass. Only one Bisley failed to return, once again demonstrating that low performance need not be a disadvantage if aircraft are used on hit-and-run raids against forward troops rather than attempting to strike targets deep in the rear.[30]

On the ground, Allied reinforcements were rushed to the threatened area and the German advance was held at Tebessa and Thala. By the 22nd, resistance had become so severe that Rommel feared a counter-attack might catch his forces seriously overstretched and ordered a gradual withdrawal. The Allied commanders felt they were in far more trouble than Rommel imagined. Far from organising a counter-attack, they feared a major further retreat might be required and airfields in the path of Rommel's forces were still being evacuated as Rommel retreated. The 22nd saw the Luftwaffe Stukas and fighter-bombers out in strength, but all Allied air effort was now focused on the retreating German forces. This included B-17 heavy bombers, which were far from ideal for attacking enemy columns, but they were available and had to do.

The poor showing of the Allied air forces was causing bemusement and irritation amongst Allied leaders. Churchill raged at Portal for the inability of the overwhelming numerical superiority in the air the Allies now possessed to bring any reward on the battlefield. German lines of communication did not seem to be inconvenienced and, when Allied armies were attacked, 'You could give no support to our troops worth speaking of,' the Prime Minister complained, adding with more than a tinge of sarcasm, 'Of course there was always the weather, which, as everyone knows does not affect the enemy.'[31]

As Portal was quick to point out, the weather really did not affect the enemy as much as the Allies. The Axis were operating from much better airfields that were not so affected by poor weather. Nevertheless, Churchill's frustration is understandable. In the past he had often exaggerated Allied air strength in the Middle East, but now he was right – the Allies had overwhelming air strength, but they did not appear to have air superiority where it mattered. Portal blamed the poor results on the low serviceability rates in USAAF squadrons and the inexperience of American pilots and indeed the American Army, which, like every defeated army, he claimed, was blaming all its setbacks on the lack of air support.

Portal seemed to be hoping to pass off a fundamental flaw in air policy as mere American inefficiency. It was all very well for Portal to complain that armies were using the same old excuse, but the same old excuse was as valid as it had ever been. Making the same mistake repeatedly did not invalidate the error. The lack of air support was by no means the only reason for this and previous setbacks, but it had been a significant factor in every Allied defeat since Norway in 1940. Now the situation was even more frustrating as the Allies had a clear numerical advantage in the region, but the Luftwaffe was still dominating the skies above the battlefield.

Numerical superiority meant nothing if the available planes were not designed, the aircrews not trained and the air commanders unwilling to support forces on land. The Allies had a lopsided air force with too many heavy- and medium-bomber squadrons that might help the Army indirectly but not enough planes to help the Army win on the battlefield. It was also frustrating because the Desert Air Force had seemed to be showing the way forward. Even in Britain, ideas seemed to be changing. Just twelve months earlier, Portal had had visions of a fleet of Hurricane tank-busters descending on European and African battlefields. Such ideas seemed to have evaporated.

A War Office review of army/air co-operation used the Air Ministry's own figures to underline the growing divide on how air power should be used. According to the Air Ministry, the Luftwaffe in North-West Africa had 350 serviceable aircraft of which seventy were specialist ground attack or dive-bombers. The equivalent figures for the Allied air forces was 1,200 planes of which none were specialist ground attack or dive-bombers.[32] In fact the figure was not quite zero, but it was significant that it was the Air Ministry that was claiming it was. They seemed to want to emphasise that, unlike the Germans, they did not waste their air resources on specialist ground attack aircraft. Neither the figures nor the attitude were encouraging. In North-West Africa, everything was going wrong that the War Office feared would go wrong in an invasion of France.

General Anderson was learning about the importance of tactical air support the hard way. As the resistance on the ground stiffened and Axis air intervention grew more effective, so his demands for better air support became more strident. He might have entered the battle thinking four light-bomber squadrons was enough but, given the way the fighting had evolved, he was making it known that he no longer thought this was the case. Even the four squadrons he had been allocated were not available as they waited in the rear for Bostons to arrive to replace their Bisleys. Portal, anxious to avoid diverting resources from Bomber Command, wanted to know from Tedder if it was really true that four light-bomber squadrons, along with the two night-bombing Wellington squadrons that had just joined them, were inadequate as a tactical bomber force.[33]

The answer should perhaps have been obvious but Tedder was still rather over anxious not to displease his masters in the Air Ministry. Tedder explained that it was 'difficult to give a precise answer to general criticism of this character'.[34] Tedder suggested the constant demands from the Army to strike 'petty' targets was a more significant factor in the failure of the RAF to have more impact, although, in reality, there were scarcely any RAF strikes against any targets, petty or otherwise. However, even Tedder realised that there was only so far his anti-Army rhetoric could go. He had to concede that there were not enough tactical bombers.

The problem for the RAF was that American light bombers were now in short supply and there were few home-grown alternatives to American imports. The Bristol Buckingham was supposed to be the long-term replacement for the Bisley, but it had never had high priority and the prototype only flew in February 1943. Trials were not going well and there was nothing else in the pipeline.

Rather than accepting that the Air Ministry was getting its priorities wrong, Portal blamed the Americans for the shortfall in tactical air support. The United States had promised that a force of 550 Douglas A-20, B-25 Mitchell, B-26 Marauder bombers and A-31/35 Vultee Vengeance dive-bombers would be assigned to the XII ASC but only 161 machines were actually available, he protested. Portal told Tedder to have words with Eisenhower about this failure, but blaming the Americans for a shortage of aircraft to support a British army was hardly likely to go down well with an ally that had been so generous in gifting the British the very sort of combat plane the Americans were being accused of holding back. It was not likely to impress the War Office either, after years of trying to persuade the Air Ministry it had to take tactical air support more seriously. In truth, more fighter-bombers like the Kittyhawks the Desert Air Force was using would have been more useful to Anderson than light bombers, but these, too, were American.

Tedder chose to see the whole problem purely as a question of control rather than the type of aircraft available or the role they should play. The Army had to get used to not having its own private air forces. As soon as Coningham could exert control, and do things the Air Force way rather than the way the Army wanted to do things, everything would be fine. This was precisely what Coningham was trying to do. He made a memorable first impression on his new American air force colleagues. One of his first decisions on breezing into the Air Force HQ to take over command from Kuter, was to cancel a proposed visit by an air force officer to co-ordinate airfield construction with ground operations planned by First Army. 'To Hell with that, we'll set up the airfields and First Army will conform to our plan,' Coningham barked.[35] This was the sort of Army/Air co-operation many in the US Army Air Forces could get to like very quickly.

Many of the changes Coningham introduced were much-needed steps towards a more effective tactical force. The fighters on the north-western front would become as flexible as those of the Desert Air Force. All fighters were now to be capable of carrying bombs. This included Spitfire squadrons, No. 152 Squadron being the first to switch to the fighter-bomber role.[36] This meant reversing previous USAAF policy and American fighters would now fly fighter-bomber missions when required.

The idea of 'air umbrellas' was to be abandoned. The term always inspired apoplexy in air force circles, although it seemed to be the term rather than the practice they objected to most. This opposition would continue until the naval 'combat air patrol' term was adopted, which allowed the diehards to retreat with grace. There was indeed nothing strange about flying fighter patrols to defend important and well-defined targets and the RAF often provided continuous fighter cover for limited periods of time. It was, however, clearly impossible everywhere, all the time. Coningham demanded a more aggressive fighter policy, with fighters operating in strength rather than being widely dispersed in an effort to cover all targets. The cover could not be permanent and the Army had to get used to dealing with air attack with their own anti-aircraft guns. This was all very reasonable and sensible, as long as these stronger patrols were where they could best benefit the Army and not so distant from the action they became irrelevant. Coningham's approach, with air commanders dictating terms, was precisely what American air commanders wanted to hear. Coningham was seen as a messiah who would free the US air forces from the bondage of their Army. A bond between RAF and USAAF commanders was growing, but so was mistrust between ground and air forces.

At a higher level Tedder was also spreading the word. However, the interchange of ideas was more subtle and not as one-way as the Americans and indeed Tedder and Coningham believed. Many of the beliefs American air commanders held so dear struck a chord with the natural instincts of Tedder and Coningham. Ideas which Tedder had suppressed because of the need to come to a working arrangement with the Army on battlefield intervention began to re-emerge. In truth, Tedder had never been a dedicated supporter of tactical battlefield air support. Tedder was a pragmatist, he followed the least line of resistance. He had been under pressure from the Army, for practical reasons, and from the Air Ministry in London, for political reasons, to create an effective army/air co-operation force capable of intervening effectively on the battlefield as well as in the rear. This he had done. In the process he and his service had won the respect of Auchinleck and Montgomery. Tedder was quite rightly proud of this achievement.

However, in Tedder's eyes, his service had always been more than just an equal and was capable of much more than just supporting the Army. Tedder was not the most dogmatic product of the Trenchard era, he was far too acquiescent for that, but he was still a bomber man at heart. He believed the bomber was a war-winning weapon and was puzzled that there were still those who did not think this was the case. Even if it did not win the war outright, it would make a decisive contribution.[37] While Marshall fretted at the delay the decision to invade Sicily imposed on his plans for invading France, Tedder welcomed the delay for it would give plenty of time for air power to prepare the way for the invasion and 'cause in the coming months the maximum devastation of German productive capacity'.[38]

Like Trenchard, Tedder believed the other armed services existed to serve the Air Force. Since the 1941 Greek campaign Tedder had been talking about the war being essentially a battle for airfields, and it was the Army's task to win them. Tedder's views were not quite as extreme as Slessor's, who looked forward to the day when 'what is left of a field army will be a component to the RAF', but Tedder was tending in that direction.[39] While the Army seemed to serve some purpose by winning airfields, Tedder saw little reason at all for having a navy. Tedder almost felt sorry for Admiral Andrew Cunningham, the commander of the British fleet in the Mediterranean, with his outmoded ideas on naval power. For Tedder, the air now dominated the Mediterranean. 'The victory at Matapan was the last dying flicker of naval supremacy in the Mediterranean,' he told Portal. 'Reasonable security for ships, whether naval or merchant, can only be attained by coast crawling under fighter cover.'[40] The Navy could not do anything without Air Force support. The Air Force, on the other hand, did not need the Navy; sea power was in terminal decline, or so it seemed to Tedder.

Tedder was right that traditional naval encounters dominated by battleships were a thing of the past and the Royal Navy was waking up to the fact that, to survive, it needed fighters operating from aircraft carriers that were as effective as land-based fighters. However, Tedder's dismissive suggestion that navies were becoming irrelevant had a very Trenchardian ring about it. Aircraft were playing a crucial part in naval warfare but this did not reduce the importance of the Navy; it just increased the importance of the Navy having the air resources it needed to do its job.

Tedder might not think so but the RAF needed the Navy. It was the Navy that protected the convoys that provided the RAF in the Mediterranean with the supplies that kept Tedder's air force in the air. Nor did the current war provide any basis for Tedder's assertion that naval power was of decreasing importance. It was the Navy that turned back the seaborne invasion of Crete, not the Air Force. As successful as the anti-shipping air strikes were, it was Royal Navy submarines that were inflicting most damage on the convoys supplying the Axis forces in North Africa. The Navy would never be reduced to humiliatingly hugging coastlines to crawl under the air cover land-based fighters could provide. The three services needed each other to function successfully as a whole. This, however, was far too 'auxiliary' an approach for Tedder.

Tedder was as convinced as Trenchard that air power would be the increasingly dominant factor in future wars. For Tedder, taking the post-war RAF into the atomic age as Chief of Air Staff, would not involve any fundamental change of heart. The transition from the commander of a tactical air force to the driving force behind the creation of the V-bomber force would be quite seamless. In this respect Tedder's career closely mirrored Trenchard's.

Tedder always liked to give the impression that Navy and Army air co-operation had been developed on Air Force terms, the successful conclusion to his 'education' of Army generals and Navy admirals. In fact, the Navy had got the specialist Naval Co-operation Group it wanted and the Eighth Army had got its specialist air support on the battlefield. It was Tedder who was shifting position and, in the process, he was acquiring a rather exaggerated reputation as the architect of Allied tactical air power. Montgomery was Tedder's latest convert and now there were a lot of Americans who needed educating.[41] Perhaps, more accurately,

Tedder himself was on a refresher course being given by his American colleagues as he started reverting to his core belief that air power should support Armies much more indirectly.

Like Tedder, Coningham found the attention he was getting in American circles as the air power guru rather intoxicating. He was more a true advocate of tactical air power than Tedder; having previously commanded the Whitleys of No. 4 Group Bomber Command he knew all too well the difficulties strategic bombing involved. In the desert he had forged an impressive weapon that was capable of striking powerful blows in the rear of the enemy as well as on the battlefield, but it had always been the former that he had seen as more important. The ability and willingness to hit the targets the Army wanted eliminated was central to the new air of trust that had grown up between Army and Air Force in the Western Desert. However, Coningham had never been entirely comfortable playing a mere supporting role. He was certainly enjoying his new role as Allied tactical supremo. The attention he was now getting seemed to demand a more distinctive, independent approach to Army/Air co-operation.

Tedder and Coningham were not the only experts in demand in Algeria for their hard-earned battle experience; Montgomery was also holding court. In February 1943 a collection of British and American generals and senior officers were assembled to hear the 'gospel according to Montgomery' as Tedder put it. Fearful that Montgomery might get it wrong, Tedder made sure that Coningham was there too. Even if Montgomery got it right, Tedder suspected Coningham would have a hard time persuading other army officers to abandon their 'fantastic ideas of soldiers controlling aircraft'.[42]

Montgomery's talk was on a range of issues related to army command. It formed the basis for a leaflet that was later widely circulated. A small section of Montgomery's talk was devoted to the role of airpower in the tactical domain. It was a typically crisp description of the advantages of air intervention on the battlefield. The concentrated use of air power was a battle-winning factor of the 'first importance', Montgomery proclaimed. The flexibility of airpower meant it could be switched from one objective to another within the theatre of operations and all its resources focused where they were required. However, for this to happen control had to be centralised. The soldier should neither expect nor wish to control it. Parcel out air units to individual army commanders and air power lost its advantage. Within the Eighth Army the system already existed for the Army to obtain 'the fullest support whenever and wherever necessary. All that is required is that the two staffs, army and air, should work together at the same HQ in complete harmony, and with complete mutual understanding and confidence.'[43] It all sounded remarkably straightforward.

Coningham added his thoughts on the question of air support. He emphasised that while the soldier commands the land forces and the airman the air forces, the whole operation was directed by the army commander, which was no doubt reassuring to the Army element of his audience. However, 'co-operation' no longer adequately described the process. He spoke of the negative connotations associated with the word 'co-operation', it usually meant the Air Force co-operating with the Army and Navy but not the other way round. Now there was as much army co-operation for the air as there was air co-operation from the Army. Indeed, the Army and Air Force had gone beyond the stage of 'co-operation', now the Army and Air Force were one.[44] It was a very rosy picture of blissful integration.

Coningham went on to explain what this meant in practice. 'I think it is generally accepted that with adequate fighter superiority and bomber forces the air has a governing influence on what happens within reach on the ground or on the sea,' he boldly proclaimed.[45] He described how crucial the Air Force had been in the battle of El Alamein. Bombers had sunk ships and attacked ports 'many thousands of miles' from the battle area. UK-based Bomber Command had even bombed Genoa to prevent the port being used to send reinforcements to El Alamein. It was an interesting extension of the operational zone. It is doubtful if Montgomery included Genoa in his theatre of operations.

The benefits of this bombing, Coningham went on, became clear to the Army as they advanced westwards and passed countless trucks abandoned with no petrol. Coningham warned that air power had to be used judiciously. An army commander might be confronted by a 200-strong enemy mechanised force but 15 or 20 miles away a force of 2,000 might pose a more serious longer-term threat. In these circumstances the immediate need of the commander at the front would have to be sacrificed so that the strategic threat could be dealt with.

It was at first sight a persuasive argument but perhaps not quite as clear cut as Coningham was claiming. If overcoming the immediate obstacle led to a breakthrough it might have consequences that made the larger forces in the rear an irrelevance. The way the French armoured divisions in the rear had been swept aside in the May 1940 Sedan debacle was an example of this. Indeed, RAF commanders had too often spent too much time worrying about future threats and not enough about winning the current battle. The failure to respond to army calls for air support during the Allied counter-attack in the 'Cauldron' during the Gazala battle was an example. In its own way, the Air Force's bold determination to see the bigger, strategic picture was just as cautious and negative as Montgomery's reluctance to use his forces more boldly.

It was perhaps significant that the only example in his speech of battlefield air support, the 200-strong mechanised force holding up the advance, was one that he stressed should be turned down. Many in the Air Ministry would have approved. It also went down well with American air force commanders. Brigadier General Williams, at XII ASC, praised Coningham for overcoming 'the concept of using the air force as artillery'.[46] Unsurprisingly, American Army generals were not quite so enthusiastic. It was clear Coningham believed less in 'close support' than in 'strategic' air strikes deep at the enemy's rear bases and airfields.[47] Coningham was indeed rapidly distancing himself from close air support.

In his talk, Coningham went on to describe how the Army had only one task, the defeat of the opposing Army, but the Air Force had two battles, the enemy air force and their land forces. 'It has first of all to beat the enemy air so that it may go into the land battle against the enemy land forces with the maximum possible hitting power.' Coningham claimed that in North Africa the Luftwaffe was almost defeated. 'To all intents and purposes we have won our war', which meant 80/90 per cent of hitting power could be used to strike enemy land forces.[48] However, in Coningham's mind, 'our war' was a distinct parallel war to the one being fought on the ground. Americans recorded how in private Coningham made it clear that he saw the first task as getting the German Air Force 'off our backs'. When this was done 'we will do all the air support and anything else that the Army wants'.[49] On 2 March, Coningham issued instructions stating air supremacy had to be achieved before land forces could expect maximum air support and commanders were to operate with this in mind. Heavily escorted attacks on enemy airfields would either destroy the enemy fighters on the ground or draw them into an unequal battle above their bases.[50]

In such a policy were the echoes of Trenchard's offensive fighter policy in the First World War over the Somme and, more disastrously, during the 'Bloody April' of 1917.[51] Fighter forces cannot fight their own private war regardless of what is happening on the ground. Fighter effort has to be focused where the enemy is likely to be found. Enemy airfields are one obvious place but the battle zone is another and there are times when it is far more useful to provide direct protection rather than attempt to provide more indirect protection by attacking airfields. Foch had it right in

1918 when he insisted that the first role of the Air Force was to support the forces on the ground.[52] The battle zone is a very profitable hunting ground for fighters.

The staged, systematic approach Coningham was now tending towards appealed to Montgomery's ordered mind, 'You must first win your air battle before you fight your sea and land battle,' Montgomery proclaimed.[53] However, reality was not so neat; air and land warfare cannot be compartmentalised so easily. Montgomery later wrote: 'You will find I have never fought a land battle until the air battle has been won. We never had to bother about the enemy air because we won the air battle first.'[54] However, previous commanders did have to bother about the enemy air. Montgomery was just fortunate that, when he took over, the Allies already had a fair measure of air superiority and this eventually became air supremacy. Previous commanders did not have the luxury of being able to wait until they had had won control of the skies before fighting their battles. Enemies are not so accommodating. Retreating armies in need of air support cannot wait for the air force to win its air battle. The British Army had spent most of the war waiting. As the Luftwaffe was demonstrating, outnumbered air forces can still be very effective if used judiciously.

Nor should air superiority be a precondition for going on the offensive. Indeed such a policy carries great risks. However advantageous it might be, you cannot delay for ever while air superiority is sought. Other military and political factors have to be taken into account. Delay might mean opportunities being missed or the enemy taking advantage of the delay to reinforce its defences or take the initiative. Nor is establishing air superiority in advance of action on land an easy process. Bombing factories and engaging in independent offensive fighter operations rarely brings quick results. As the Luftwaffe had so often demonstrated, forcing the enemy air force to engage in combat over the battlefield is often the quickest way of achieving air superiority.

Nor should the need for air superiority override all other issues during the course of the battle. This had not been the policy in the Western Desert. The RAF had been used much more flexibly. As desirable as air superiority might be, Coningham had not been afraid to abandon the air battle so that his air force could come to the aid of a struggling army. Conversely, if army units were being hammered by the Luftwaffe, he had switched fighters from ground attack to air defence. Coningham had used his resources flexibly according to the needs of the moment, not a pre-determined list of priorities.

The Kasserine setback was a chastening experience for the American Army. Heads rolled, troop training was reviewed and tactics revised on the ground as well as in the air. The dynamic, flamboyant Patton took over from Fredendall as commander of the American Corps. However, none of this could stop the divide between the air and ground forces growing wider. The USAAF was part of the American Army but, like the Royal Flying Corps in the First World War, it was drifting ever further from its parent body. For those wanting an independent air arm, this was progress. For the US Army it was not so welcome. The same was true of the Desert Air Force. Like the Royal Flying Corps, it, too, was beginning to go its own separate way.

With Patton in charge the growing divide was always likely to be highlighted more colourfully. A strafing attack on Patton's headquarters caused the American general to demand round-the-clock fighter protection. It was scarcely an inspiring reaction to a very light raid and encouraged a mindset in which it was possible for a strange order to be issued instructing the crews of light anti-aircraft guns to abandon their weapons if attacked by Stukas.[55] It seemed that from the highest general to the lowliest infantryman the expectation was total immunity from air attack.

It was an unreasonable expectation and, in Patton's case, an apparently bizarre one. Patton might be criticised on many grounds but no one would suggest he feared the dangers that came with war. Patton's and indeed the reaction of so many of his American and British predecessors was more to do with trust than fear of air attack. Within any armed service not everything will always go according to plan. An artillery barrage might not be as effective as the infantry were hoping, a submarine might slip past destroyer escorts. But there is an assumption that everyone involved was doing their best. Troops on the ground would have accepted Luftwaffe bombers getting through if they believed everything was being done to try and stop them, but they were not convinced.

The air force tendency and indeed undisguised intention to fight its own war with the enemy, not just with strategic operations but also at the tactical level, was bound to encourage mistrust. The Air Force seemed more interested in taking on the Luftwaffe over its own airfields rather than over the front line. When the US Army was in trouble at Kasserine, the USAAF was making its maximum effort over Sardinia. It may only have been army commanders who were aware of the competing ideas on how closely related the land and air battle should be but the distrust seeped down to the lowliest infantryman. It was easy to misinterpret the absence of friendly aviation as a service not pulling its weight rather than one that was being misdirected.

Tensions soon came to an explosive head. On 1 April, Patton complained that 'Forward troops have been continuously bombed all morning' and the 'Total lack of air cover for our units had allowed the German Air Forces to operate almost at will.' When Coningham discovered that this signal was the result of fewer than twenty German bombers operating over the entire American front and casualties had been just four soldiers, he told Patton the American soldiers concerned could not be 'battle worthy'. An infuriated Patton leaked Coningham's comments to the press, the incident became public and Coningham was forced to apologise. Tedder was furious with Coningham for the damage done to Anglo-American relations, although privately he fully agreed with what Coningham had said, and felt some good would come of the incident if it stopped the Americans from 'bellyaching'.[56]

American Army generals, however, felt they had plenty to bellyache about. Independent RAF attitudes seemed to be spreading to their Army Air Forces commanders and the US Army was not happy. The USAAF set about rewriting its tactical air policy. FM 31-35 was declared obsolete and replaced with FM 100-20. In US Army circles this rewrite was seen as no less than the USAAF declaration of independence. In many ways it was a step backwards. A key element of the earlier FM 31-35 was the need to focus effort on winning the struggle on the battlefield. However, encouraged by the work and words of Tedder and Coningham, the new doctrine released in July 1943 had very different priorities. The first priority and 'primary role' was to establish control of the skies. Second priority was to isolate the battlefield, which 'may decide the battle'. The third priority was to provide direct support for land forces on the battlefield. These were 'priorities' rather than phases, and the document emphasised that in practice air supremacy could never be achieved and would always require some effort. Nevertheless, it is easy for priorities to become phases. The desire to guarantee air superiority and over-insure against air attack inevitably limits the resources available for close air support. This was what happened at Dieppe. Interdicting the battlefield can be an endless struggle. It becomes a wasted struggle if you do not use air resources to exploit the advantage gained and help win the land battle.

The laboured progression from one stage to the next was to become a characteristic of future Allied air operations. It was not the way the German Army and Air Force had achieved their success. The new approach had none of the dynamic interaction between air and ground forces that characterised the German blitzkrieg. Winning control of the skies helped German forces advance, but simultaneously advancing German forces disrupted enemy air operations and helped the Luftwaffe tighten its grip. In the German approach, success on land contributed as much to winning the air battle as success in the air contributed to the land battle. The two were intimately linked; the effectiveness of the combination was greater than the sum of the parts. This was what combined arms warfare was all about and this approach was behind the success of the Desert Air Force.

The only time the Wehrmacht had adopted a more methodical staged approach was in the Battle of Britain, when the Germans decided to win air superiority first and then begin the land battle. The air-only assault gave Britain's defences the chance to focus on dealing with the aerial threat in isolation, rather than having to deal with multiple threats to their land, sea and its own air forces. The Germans did not achieve air superiority in the summer of 1940. As a result invasion plans were abandoned and the opportunity to defeat a makeshift British Army was missed. It was the Luftwaffe's first defeat and the Wehrmacht's first setback. A failed German strategy had become the Allied blueprint for success.

Yet the new Allied approach was rather brashly portrayed as an advance on German thinking. Kuter, in a press conference to explain how Allied air strategy was evolving, described how the Allies were moving away from the idea of using aircraft as artillery. 'Although it is the method by which the Germans advanced through France, where air opposition was very scant indeed,' Kuter explained, 'it is surely the method which was found to be totally obsolete and leading more toward defeat than victory in operations against a well-trained Army and a well-trained Air Force in Africa.'[57] It perhaps rather underestimated the achievements of a method that had defeated most of continental Europe and pushed the mighty Soviet Union to the brink of defeat, not to mention throwing a numerically superior American force into headlong retreat in North Africa.

If the German method of using mechanised forces in conjunction with tactical air support was going to be dismissed as obsolete so readily, it was likely to take a very long time before the western Allies would be able to incorporate German thinking into Allied strategy. Instead of learning from German methods, the message was that the Americans and British would now show the Germans how it should be done. It was fortunate for the Allied cause that the Soviet Army was in their camp. They had a firmer grasp of how air and ground forces needed to combine to deliver decisive results.

Ironically, so did Coningham's Desert Air Force.

Chapter 12

Tactical High Water

By March 1943 the new command structure for Allied air forces in the Mediterranean had come into effect. All tactical light- and medium-bomber groups in North-West Africa were placed within a single formation. These were the four Bisley squadrons, the American 47th Bomber Group with Douglas A-20s, a couple of American Mitchell squadrons transferred from the Western Desert, and the French *Groupement de Bombardment 6* with LeO 451s.

It was a very mixed bag. There was a certain irony about the French contribution. The LeO 451 was a long-range bomber the French had designed to bomb Berlin, Budapest and Naples. In the French production plans of 1939 it had a higher production priority than fighters. It was difficult to build; mass producing it had absorbed a huge chunk of the French aircraft industry, denying production space to more useful tactical aircraft. When it came to the Battle of France, the French discovered it was not what they needed to halt the panzers. The same might be said of British and indeed American production plans in 1943. Germany's enemies in the west were still bedevilled by the same long-range bomber syndrome that had so damaged the Allied cause in 1940. The crucial difference in 1943 was that the bulk of the German Army was tied up in the Soviet Union.

The French LeO 451 could only be used by night and the Bisley squadrons were in the rear awaiting re-equipment and could not be used at all. This just left the American A-20s and B-25 Mitchells as the tactical day bomber force.[1] The gap in fighter quality continued to narrow. The handful of Spitfire IXs came as a surprise to Axis pilots used to using their superior horizontal speed to pull away from the slower but superficially identical Spitfire V. Spitfire Vs began to take over the fighter-bomber role from the Hurribombers. The Hurricanes of No. 225 Squadron concentrated on tactical reconnaissance, gradually converting to a mixture of Spitfires and Mustangs, but No. 241 Squadron would soldier on with the Hurricane for some time to come.

Late in February 1943, the Desert Air Force was finally ready to restart large-scale offensive operations in preparation for Montgomery's forthcoming offensive against the Mareth Line. Coningham's replacement as commander of the Desert Air Force was Air Vice-Marshal Harry Broadhurst. He was a new generation of air force commander, too young to fight in the First World War and unusual in that he transferred from the Army to the Air Force, against the wishes of his retired Army officer father. He had seen service in India where he was engaged in low-level bombing and strafing of rebel forces in support of the Army during the 1930s' uprisings on the North-West Frontier. He had commanded No. 60 Wing of the Air Component in 1940 in the closing days of its operations in France when his squadrons had been used for both air combat and ground attack.

He had briefly been deputy Senior Air Staff Officer at No. 11 Group Fighter Command and had been involved in the fighter operations during the Dieppe raid. In November 1942 he had taken over as Senior Air Staff Officer in the Desert Air Force and was therefore Coningham's natural successor. Transfer to the Middle East had allowed a natural inclination to support the troops on the ground to flourish, no doubt in part encouraged by his family background and perhaps a lack of exposure to the Trenchard doctrine. His enthusiasm for using fighter-bombers for low-level strikes on battlefield targets had already caused some conflict with Coningham but, with the Eighth Army now pushing up close to the German Mareth Line, it was exactly the sort of support Montgomery wanted and needed.

With the Hurricane squadrons of the Desert Air Force now confined to air defence duties in the rear, the fighter force had a more up-to-date feel about it. Nevertheless, with only four Spitfire squadrons, all equipped with the Mark V, the fighter element was still going to struggle. The Spitfires had to provide top cover for eight Commonwealth Kittyhawk and eight USAAF P-40 Warhawk squadrons. On the first day of the Desert Air Force's pre-Mareth offensive, bomb-carrying Kittyhawks, covered by Spitfires when available, but sometimes non-bomb-carrying Kittyhawks, attacked Axis airfields. Fourteen Kittyhawks were lost during the course of the day in clashes with Messerschmitts, underlining the continuing inferiority of Commonwealth equipment.

With much shorter lines of supply, Rommel had recovered some of his former confidence and was anxious to take the initiative by delivering a spoiling attack on Montgomery's forces. Rommel's plan involved a frontal pincer movement with the aim of recapturing Medenine. General Giovanni Messe, his Italian superior and commander of all German and Italian units, preferred a wide sweeping flank attack around the Matmata Hills to take

Medenine from the south. Rommel doubted Messe's much bolder plan would work as it gave the Allied air forces too many opportunities to strike the Axis forces as they moved into position. Allied air power was cramping Rommel's style. Rommel lost the argument and it was Messe's plan that was adopted.

On 3 March 1943, Axis forces began their three-day approach march around the southern Allied flank. The next day, Allied reconnaissance planes spotted the move and fighter-bombers switched their attentions to the advancing columns. On the 6th the German forces were finally in position to deliver their attack. The weather that day was not ideal for operations, but the Luftwaffe was very active, flying close support missions with FW 190, Me 210 and Ju 87s, covered by Italian and German fighters. However, Montgomery had plenty of time to organise an anti-tank screen and allowed the German tanks to dash themselves against this barrier. It was a typical Rommel tactic. The attack was comfortably held. At no point was it felt necessary to commit reserves to support the defensive positions or switch the light bombers from their preparatory bombing offensive to support the efforts of the fighter-bombers. Fifty-two tanks, more than a quarter of the attacking force, were lost. These were losses the panzer divisions could ill afford. The Axis forces withdrew to their start positions, hounded by fighter-bombers.[2]

The Allies were now ready to go on to the offensive on all fronts. Following the reverses they had suffered in February, Patton's II Corps was given the limited role of recapturing the airfields in the Thelepte area lost in February, and in the process hopefully draw Axis forces away from the Mareth Line. Montgomery would follow with his offensive on the night of 19/20 March. The Mareth Line was a formidable obstacle, built along the Wadi Zigzaou, a watercourse with steep sides and soft sand that made a natural anti-tank trap. Montgomery's plan was to launch a diversionary flank attack through the Tebaga Pass, which involved moving substantial forces in a wide detour, round the Matmata Hills. It was hoped that this would draw German reserves away and make it easier for the main blow in the south.

The American attacks in the north were supported by the USAAF XII ASC, but the northern and southern fronts were now so close that many of the sorties flown were against targets affecting the Mareth Line. This allowed Broadhurst's Desert Air Force to concentrate all its efforts on targets in and around the battlefield. American fighter units withdrawn earlier in the year were now returning refreshed and, more significantly, with a much better idea of how to get the best out of their equipment. The Spitfire IX was also

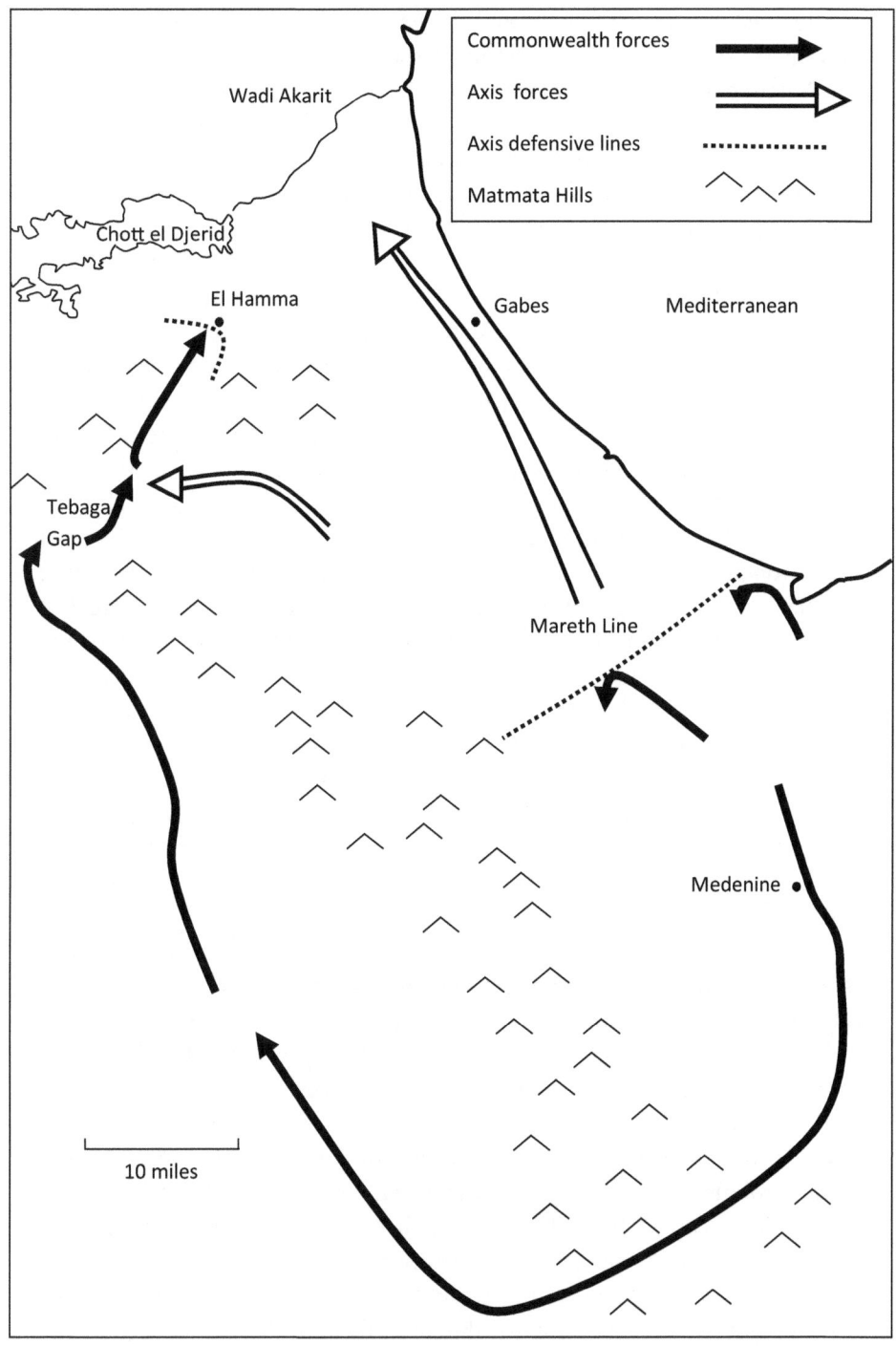

Commonwealth forces

Axis forces

Axis defensive lines

Matmata Hills

Wadi Akarit

Chott el Djerid

El Hamma

Gabes

Mediterranean

Tebaga Gap

Mareth Line

Medenine

10 miles

beginning to make an impression. With an ever-increasing Allied numerical advantage, Axis units were beginning to suffer heavy losses.

Air support for Montgomery's attempts to establish a bridgehead across the Wadi Zigzaou included the Hurricane IId tank-busters of No. 6 Squadron. The return to the front line of this squadron was largely due to the efforts of their new commander, Squadron Leader Donald Weston-Burt. Early in 1943, frustrated with the coast defence duties in the rear that his squadron had been relegated to, he set about getting his unit back on tank-busting operations. Tedder was not keen, but the unit was re-equipped with the 40mm cannon-armed Hurricane IId and returned to the front.

Despite the massive air support the Desert Air Force was able to provide, Montgomery's frontal assault made very little progress; indeed by the evening of the 22nd it was being thrown back. Montgomery therefore decided to switch his main effort to what had been the diversionary attack through the Tebaga Pass. The New Zealanders would push on to El Hamma and then to the coast, cutting off the Axis forces in the Mareth Line. The fact that Montgomery's new line of attack had already succeeded in attracting substantial enemy forces was a major disadvantage of the new plan. The New Zealanders were hurriedly reinforced by an armoured division, but it was not so easy to move more artillery into position. To compensate, Broadhurst proposed a massive and continuous aerial 'blitz' on Axis positions in the front line.[3] Montgomery agreed but Coningham was apparently not so impressed with the idea and, according to Montgomery, he sent emissaries to his headquarters to get it stopped.[4] When this failed he tried to get at least a proportion of the available forces diverted to targets in the rear. Broadhurst, however, stuck to his plan. All effort would be focused on achieving a breakthrough.[5]

The attack was launched on the afternoon of 26 March. Initially, dust storms caused the first strikes by fighter-bombers to be replaced by light bombers, but the weather had the advantage of concealing the movement of Allied tanks. Once the storms had cleared, Allied fighter-bombers were ever present over the front. Two and a half squadrons were kept permanently over the battlefield, with each wave being relieved at 15-minute intervals. Units involved included the Hurricane tank-busters of No. 6 Squadron and Hurribombers operating from the recently recaptured Thelepte airfields in the American sector, 100 miles north of the Tebaga Pass. Above the fighter-bombers, Spitfires provided protection.

Twenty-six squadrons were involved in a two and a half hour period. The operation saw the use of the first forward Visual Control Post.

An RAF officer, with radio equipment enabling him to communicate directly with the fighter-bomber pilots above, observed the battle from a forward position, directing pilots to their targets and indicating the positions of Allied troops. It was indeed very close support as the fighter-bombers picked off the anti-tank guns holding up the advance. In little more than two hours, 412 sorties were flown. By early evening the British tanks had burst through the German defences. Eleven fighter pilots and one light bomber crew were missing, which were not light losses, but the Allies had the breakthrough.[6]

It was the first time the Allies had relied so heavily on air power to overcome a defensive line. It was in effect the Battle for Medenine in reverse, the difference being that the Allies had the air power to swamp the defences. It was a classic example of the ability of air power to switch the centre of gravity of an offensive from one sector of the front to another, just as Montgomery had described in his Algiers address. It was also a striking example of using all available means, ground and air, at the decisive point. It was remarkably similar to the way the Luftwaffe had swamped French defences at Sedan in 1940. It was the type of air assault that might have enabled the Canadians to get off the beaches at Dieppe. Interestingly, the airfields in the Medenine area from which the fighter-bombers were operating were roughly the same distance from the Tebaga Pass as the distance across the Channel to Dieppe. Unlike Dieppe, at Tebaga the aim was to win the battle, not defeat the Luftwaffe. At Sedan, Dieppe and Tebaga circumstances had meant that the artillery that normally accompanies an army was not available in sufficient quantities and air support was needed as an alternative. At Sedan and Tebaga the required level of air support was duly provided.

Even at Tebaga the breakthrough did not lead to a decisive victory. The Axis forces were in a difficult position. The decision had already been taken to pull out of the Mareth Line and move back to the shorter, easier to defend Waka Akarit Line but, with the New Zealanders just 15 miles from the coast, the decision might have come too late. However, stiff resistance in the outskirts of El Hamma held up the Allied advance. Whereas at Sedan the Luftwaffe had disrupted the immediate efforts by the French to restore the line, at El Hamma the follow-up air support was too distant. Instead of keeping the forward momentum of the advance going, the fighter-bombers were switched to targets further in the rear on the El Hamma-Gabes road.

Some fifty-three sorties were flown by Kittyhawks against these targets early on the 27th, but the Germans flak defences in the rear were stronger and better organised than over the front. Six planes were lost, a heavier loss rate than had been suffered the previous day for far less reward.[7] Repeating the effort of the previous day and focusing on the German forces holding up the advance might have been more productive and less costly. There were echoes of the August 1918 Amiens offensive where air effort was switched from the battlefield to the bridges over the Somme. These achieved little and aircraft losses were heavy, while the advance at the front ground to a halt.[8]

The losses suffered by the Kittyhawks resulted in a ban on low-level missions that was not lifted until the 29th, by which time it was too late.[9] The forces blocking the Allied advance at El Hamma were able to hang on for long enough for the immobile forces in Mareth Line to withdraw in good order. Montgomery was delighted with the overall result and thanked Broadhurst for the 'superb support to the land battle' the Desert Air Force had provided, but yet again a decisive victory had slipped from the Allies' grasp.[10]

The events of the 26th totally vindicated Broadhurst's decision to concentrate his resources on the battlefield. On 30 March, Churchill described to the House of Commons how the breakthrough at Tebaga had been 'aided to an extraordinary degree by the novel forms of intense air attack, in which many hundreds of Allied aircraft were simultaneously employed'.[11] Broadhurst, however, did not feel there was anything novel about the operation; it 'merely used normal forms of attack closely linked to a normal Army problem'.[12]

Despite his objections, once the operation was proclaimed a victory, Coningham was quick to attach his own name to the success and publicly praised the operation to the hilt as an 'example of the proper use of air power in accordance with the principle of concentration'.[13] His force had achieved a degree of efficiency never matched by the Luftwaffe. It was a model for all theatres and there was no reason why these results could not be improved on, he ventured. Privately, Coningham and Tedder were rather concerned about this becoming a 'normal' operation with the Air Force playing a supporting and what they would see as a subservient role in land operations.[14]

The Tebaga breakthrough was the last major operation the Desert Air Force was involved in as a separate entity. It would continue to retain its Desert Air Force name long after it left the desert, but in future it would be a component of the Allied air forces in the Mediterranean. The force had rediscovered the importance of close air support and developed the fighter-bomber as the method of delivery. The breakthrough at Tebaga was a fitting climax of and justification for the effort that had gone into developing this aspect of air warfare. However, rather than marking the beginning of a new era in close support, the breakthrough to El Hamma was very much the highwater mark. The movement away from the closely integrated ground/air tactics developed in the Western Desert was gathering pace as Coningham and Tedder increasingly promoted a more independent approach to army support.

The Hurricane tank-buster was one of the victims of this approach. This was one tactical innovation that Portal and the Air Ministry deserve full credit for, but the Middle East Command had never been as enthusiastic. No. 6 Squadron had experienced mixed fortunes. On 24 March ten tanks and nine other vehicles were claimed in two operations. However, four of the nineteen planes involved were lost and on 25 March six out of ten failed to return. On 7 April another six were lost and only one tank and two other vehicles were claimed. Since returning to combat the unit had lost twenty-four aircraft during the course of 117 sorties. The mission on 7 April proved to be the last of note in this theatre.

The losses had been heavy, but the missions were very short range. Many of the planes crash-landed in friendly territory and many of the pilots made it back unharmed. Only four pilots were lost. Broadhurst saw more armour as the solution and this would undoubtedly have made the proposition more practicable. The Hurricane was scarcely ideal; something along the lines of the slow-flying more specialised ground attack planes the War Office and Sorley had wanted might have been the long-term answer. However, even Broadhurst had his doubts about the tank-buster. He feared there would be problems finding targets in a non-desert environment and, while he believed a small specialist anti-tank force would always be useful, he did not feel it justified the large-scale production of a specialist plane.[15]

There was no doubt that the cannon was an effective anti-tank weapon and it was used extensively and successfully by both Soviet and German air forces. However, tank armour was getting thicker and the Vickers 40mm cannon could not penetrate the armour of the latest Tiger tanks, which were just beginning to appear in Tunisia. The British had the 57mm Molins cannon lined up to replace the Vickers. It was believed this could pierce the side armour of a Tiger, but it needed a plane like the Mosquito to lift it into the air. With its slow rate of fire, a high-speed plane like the Mosquito would only have time in its approach to aim three rounds at best at the target.[16] In the end it was decided that the launch of eight destructive, albeit highly inaccurate, rockets in rapid succession was a better option.

For Tedder and Coningham the Hurricane's problems were a vindication of their views. They did not want to get involved with short-range tactical aircraft that eliminated one tank at a time. It was not part of their vision of how air power should be used. Cutting supply lines deep in the enemy rear, so that the tanks never even reached the battlefield seemed a far more productive route to take. This was all well and good, but tanks that reach the front also have to be dealt with.

In Tunisia, from the south and west, the Allies were relentlessly closing in on Tunis. Hitler felt that a bridgehead in North Africa had to be held to keep Italy in the war, but the Axis forces found themselves in a hopeless position. Supplying the bridgehead was becoming impossible. It may have taken more than the thirty-six B-17s Spaatz had originally predicted, but the combined effort of submarines and bombers was taking its toll. The contribution by RAF and Fleet Air Arm squadrons had always been significant but, by the end of 1942, sinkings by air attack were drawing level with losses inflicted by submarines and in the first five months of 1943, aircraft were actually doing better than submarines.[17] By March, one half of all shipping was being lost and the supplies that did arrive constituted less than a sixth of what was required.

In desperation the Germans assembled a huge fleet of transport planes to make the 100-mile hop from Sicily to Tunisia. In March one quarter of all supplies arriving in Tunisia were being flown in. The slow vulnerable transports would stand no chance if intercepted, but flying at low level they might reasonably have expected to survive the short crossing. In the circumstances it seemed a risk worth taking. The Germans, however, had no idea how loaded the dice were against them. Ultra intercepts revealed the full details of the airlift and in April on half a dozen occasions the transports were savaged by Allied fighters. During the course of the month 150 transports were lost. By May supplies reaching North Africa by any source had been reduced to a trickle. It was a triumph for the advocates of interdiction. It made the final battle easier to win, but that final battle would still be fierce and hard fought.

Italian and German air force sortie rates had not in any sense collapsed. The Luftwaffe flew around 400 sorties per day throughout March and April, the Italians maintaining their effort at little more than a hundred. This was fairly typical of Axis sortie rates throughout the campaign in North Africa. The difference in early 1943 was the huge number of sorties the Allies were now flying. Axis air forces were forced on to the defensive by sheer weight of numbers. Forty per cent of all Luftwaffe fighter sorties were in defence of the shipping lanes between Sicily and Tunisia. Much of the remaining effort was required to defend ports in Tunisia, Sicily and mainland Italy, not to mention the lumbering transports flying in supplies. Those that remained were hard pressed to defend the airfields they operated from.

The quality of the Allied fighter force continued to improve as more Spitfire IXs entered the fray. During April American Spitfire squadrons began to receive the Merlin 61-powered version. The Air Ministry fears that the Bf 109G would represent a leap forward in German fighter design proved exaggerated. Early versions of the latest Bf 109 were marginally rather than substantially superior to the Bf 109F. Arguably a more dangerous opponent for the Allied fighters was the Italian Macchi C.205, a version of the MC 202 with the same engine as the Bf 109G, which was beginning to appear in small numbers.

The technical gap was also being closed in an unanticipated way. The appearance in Tunisia of the rugged B-25 and B-26 medium bombers and the even more daunting B-17 Fortress forced Axis fighters to increase their firepower. German and Italian fighters began operating with a couple of extra 20mm cannon slung under the wing, which inevitably reduced their dog-fighting capabilities. The heavy bombers the Americans were using were not achieving air superiority by shooting down droves of enemy fighters but, by forcing Axis fighters to adopt heavier armament they were reducing their effectiveness in a fighter-versus-fighter role. It was scarcely planned but, by a rather roundabout route, the American bombers were helping to win air superiority.

On 19 April the final assault began. Against a determined enemy compressed into a small area, it was always going to be a bitter struggle. The Allied air forces were capable of maintaining a daily sortie rate in excess of 2,500. With no room for manoeuvre, there is often little subtlety about the form the final assault on a beleaguered stronghold takes. With such a high proportion of available strength being heavy or medium bombers, there was even less likelihood of much finesse. On 6 May, for the final assault, over 2,000 bomber sorties laid a carpet of bombs 4 miles by 1,000 yards on the approach to Tunis. The result was always inevitable but it was 13 May before the last Germans surrendered.

It was quite a remarkable turnaround. Six months before German and Italian forces had been at the gates of Alexandria; now Axis troops had been swept from the continent of Africa. It was as rapid an advance as any German offensive had managed, but it was only when German forces were trapped against the Mediterranean and Hitler forbade retreat that it turned into a catastrophic defeat for the Axis forces.

For some time Luftwaffe strength in the west had been a façade but it was now a fast fading façade. For the Allies, the Tebaga breakthrough seemed to show the way forward with mobile air support providing the means to eliminate battlefield targets and giving land commanders more options for achieving surprise. These were capabilities army commanders were beginning to get used to having. This should have been taken by RAF commanders as a compliment; instead it was seen as a problem. From the Air Force perspective, the Army seemed to be acquiring an unhealthy reliance on air support. In fact it was no more unhealthy than their reliance on artillery, tanks or any other form of support. Air force commanders seemed to resent just being another cog in the wheel, however important everyone agreed that cog was.

In one sense, Tedder and Coningham were right; the Army reliance on air power was becoming unhealthy, although not in the way they imagined. There was a growing belief within the Army that the airmen could not just help achieve a breakthrough but could also finish the job the troops on the ground had started. Once enemy defences had been broken, there was no need to risk more casualties pursuing a beaten enemy. Air power could complete the rout. It was what the more extreme air power enthusiasts had always claimed was possible and was a perfect fit for the quasi-independent tactical role the Air Force felt happy with. The ability of air power to be decisive on its own had always been at the heart of pre-war Air Ministry thinking. The Trenchard vision had been that air forces would make it impossible for armies and navies to function. Completing a rout started by the Army was a step in this direction. There would soon be some persuasive evidence that Trenchard had been right with his more extreme position. Perhaps air forces could win outright victories without requiring any help from the army.

The next step after the clearance of North Africa would be the invasion of Sicily. Halfway between Sicily and North Africa was the tiny island of Pantelleria. It was garrisoned by 10,000 troops and its cliff coastline was riddled with caves from which submarines and torpedo boats could operate. Lying right on the invasion path, it was a threat that needed to be eliminated. It also possessed a large modern airfield, which would get at least some fighter squadrons closer to the invasion beaches. Its steep cliffs meant the only practical site for a landing was the very well-defended port, attacking which was a rather unpromising prospect following the Dieppe disaster. Indeed, there were serious doubts the island could be captured. Eisenhower ordered the entire might of the Allied air forces be turned on the island in a prolonged aerial offensive, which would culminate in an invasion. For Coningham this smacked too much of the Air Force once again being subordinated to Army operations. Tedder, however, saw it as an interesting laboratory experiment which might provide a better idea of what an intensive aerial bombardment could achieve.[18]

From 1 to 10 June 1943, nearly 5,000 tons of bombs were dropped on the island. One-third of these were dropped on the day before Allied troops went ashore, more than the weight of bombs dropped on the first thousand-bomber raid on Cologne. On 11 June, Allied landings were accompanied by a heavy air and naval bombardment. It all proved too much for the garrison, who surrendered with scarcely a shot being fired. Like Tebaga it was another stunning demonstration of the effectiveness of air power. However, whereas Tebaga had relied on precision low-level attacks on pin-point targets, this was largely high-level tactical carpet bombing. Nevertheless, it appeared to have been even more successful. There was no resistance. Tedder recorded how the Pantelleria defences had been wiped out and 'most of the artillery had been crippled or obliterated'.[19]

A closer examination of the results was not so conclusive. Solly Zuckerman, the Air Ministry's top scientific adviser, happened to be in the Mediterranean at the time. He had studied the effects of bombing in Britain and was in the Middle East conducting similar studies. With the island occupied, Zuckerman set to work analysing the effects of the bombing. Even though the weather had been ideal and the fighter and anti-aircraft defences limited, only 3.3 per cent of bombs dropped by four-engined bombers fell within 100 yards of their target. Fighter-bombers rather surprisingly did not even do as well as this.[20] The bombing had caused widespread devastation, the town of Pantelleria had been flattened, but only 200 of the 11,000 garrison were casualties and although many of the guns needed to be extracted from debris most still functioned.

What was indisputable was that the aerial offensive had had a decisive effect on the morale of the defenders. For those in the USAAF and RAF this was clear proof air power could win battles singlehandedly. In the end the task of the Army had been merely to move in and occupy territory. It was a small-scale example of what the Air Staff had always envisaged happening on a much larger scale on mainland Europe. It was what Trenchard had always predicted. Eisenhower was impressed. Total air superiority appeared to be paying some real dividends. He saw no reason why this formula could not be repeated again and again, starting with Sicily.

Tedder had mixed feelings about the results. As pleased as he was with the surrender the bombing had provoked, he saw the result as a 'curse', as there would now be more calls for air power to intervene on the battlefield rather than provide indirect support. It was in some ways a surprising reaction. It was a glorious vindication for all those who claimed the bomber was all conquering. If the Air Force could really repeat this sort of performance and hammer the Axis forces into the ground every time they made a stand, it would demonstrate that armies were only needed to occupy territory. Yet for Tedder this was still just reducing air power to the status of mere army artillery.

The surrender of Pantelleria was remarkable but there were perhaps extenuating circumstances. The troops on the island had no battle experience and they could expect no assistance from outside. There was no escape. They had been abandoned and left to their fate. It was not the first time bombing had achieved such dramatic results. The destruction of Rotterdam in May 1940 had induced the Dutch surrender, although here too the Dutch troops had been very much left to their fate by their Allies. Nevertheless, in both cases victory had been achieved without a defensive shot being fired. It was tempting to conclude that if you dropped enough explosives on the enemy, surrender would follow. For the Allies, air power seemed to be breaking new ground and nobody could be sure of the implications for warfare. The much larger island of Sicily would provide a stiffer test for the air power theorists.

The air offensive that would pave the way for the invasion of Sicily lasted nine days with targets as far away as Rome. Airfields in Sicily and southern Italy were high priority targets for Allied bombers, but most Axis bomber units had withdrawn to bases in central Italy or even southern France to escape the onslaught. In the seven days before the invasion, 1,500 tons were dropped on Gerbini airfield and its twelve satellites alone.[21] In the six weeks up to the invasion, the Luftwaffe lost 122 planes on Italian airfields.[22] It was not a brilliant return on the investment made. Apart from a couple of airfields, most were back in some sort of working order the same or the next day.[23]

In truth, whatever the losses suffered before the invasion, the Axis air forces were so weak numerically they were always going to struggle to make an impression on the invading forces. The Allied air superiority was as overwhelming as it had been in Tunisia. As anxious as Hitler was to prevent Italy surrendering, it was still militarily a sideshow compared to the titanic struggle on the Eastern Front, especially with the key battle for Kursk underway. The Allies had some 4,000 aircraft available for the invasion of Sicily. The Luftwaffe had fewer than 200 planes in Sicily with around 450 in Italy. The Italians could offer surprisingly little support in defence of their homeland. There was nothing wrong with the quality of their aircraft, but there was a lot wrong with their ability to build them in large numbers. There were only a handful of the latest 'Serie 5' fighters (Macchi C.205, Fiat G.55 and Reggiane Re.2005) and ageing Fiat C.R 42 biplanes were still in service with some ground attack units. The Italians were so short of modern fighters, some squadrons were using French Dewoitine D.520s acquired by the Germans in the occupation of Vichy France.[24] In all, the Italians had 150 planes in Sicily with 320 they could call on in Italy.

Unlike the Dieppe operation, the troops landing on the beaches would have the firepower battleships could provide. It was with some trepidation that the US and British naval commanders committed major capital ships just off an enemy coastline. The American Navy was still haunted by the memory of the ease with which Japanese bombers had sent battleships to the bottom at Pearl Harbor, and the Royal Navy had bitter memories of heavy losses in the Mediterranean and Far East. Exaggerated ideas of Axis air strength led to estimates that some 1,500 combat planes were in the immediate vicinity or near enough to intervene.[25] The worst-case scenarios put Allied losses at 300 vessels. The concerns of the Allied naval commanders would ensure air defence had top priority. The navies expected fighter cover to be substantial and permanent. No one on the air side questioned the need for what was undeniably a request for an aerial umbrella.

Complete air cover, however, would not be possible. Cape Bon on the North African mainland, was about 100 miles from the Sicilian coast, about the same as the distance from the south of England to the Normandy coast. However, there was not much space on the narrow mainland peninsula. Malta and Pantelleria were about 60 to 70 miles away, but there were only a few airfields on the two islands. The short-range fighters these airfields could hold would not be enough to provide permanent cover. Only two landing beaches could be guaranteed fighter cover throughout the day; the others could only be covered at certain times.[26] The gaps would leave naval commanders nervous. However, the warships were not totally reliant on fighter protection; they had their own very effective anti-aircraft defences, as they would subsequently demonstrate against both friend and foe.

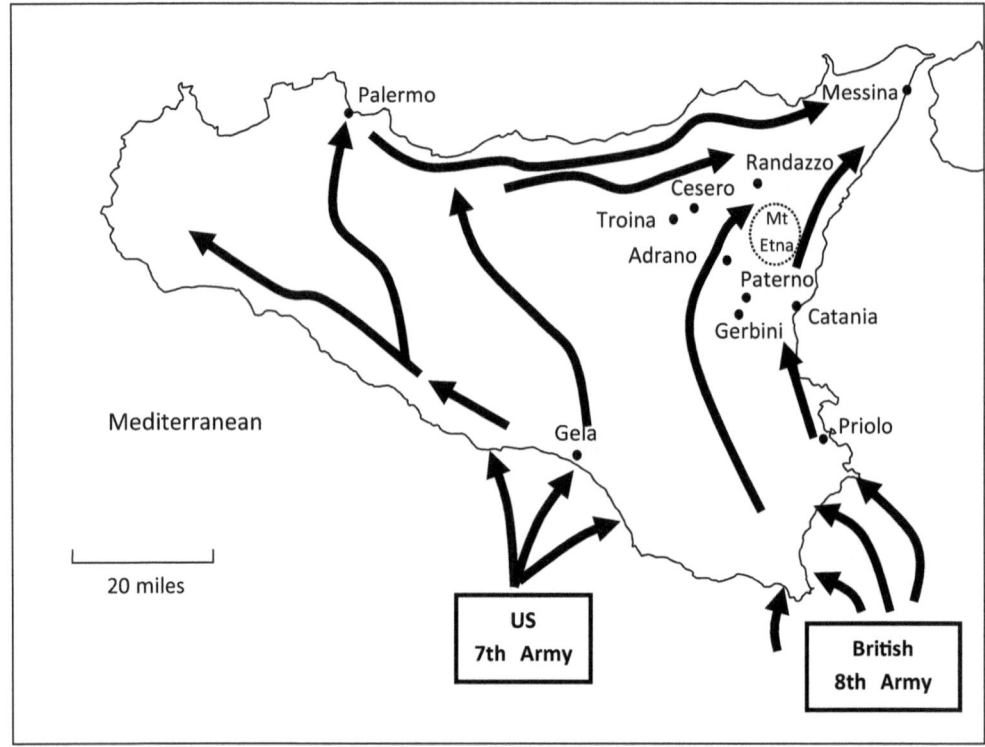

The priority for air defence meant there were no airfields far enough forward for the shorter-range fighter-bombers. This did not rule out close air support in the opening stages of the invasion. The Army Air Support Controls would go in with the first wave and longer-range Boston and Baltimore light bombers, and even medium bombers like the Mitchell, could be used for low-level strikes. The Sicilian campaign would also see the operational debut of the North American A-36, the dive-bomber version of the P-51 Mustang hastily developed to provide the US Army with a Stuka-like capability and this also had the range to operate over Sicily from more distant airfields. Two groups of long-range P-38 fighter-bombers were also available. Despite the shortage of airfields, there were plenty of options for close air support. However, with the new emphasis on indirect support, even after the troops had gone ashore, the targets would remain lines of communication leading to the front. Instead of the light/medium bombers substituting for the short-range fighter-bombers in the close air support role, the Mustangs and Lightnings would supplement the efforts of the interdicting light and medium bombers.

The invasion of Sicily was launched on 10 July. The Allies assembled an impressive armada of over 100 warships, 1,200 transports and 2,000 landing craft. Over 150,000 troops would be landed by sea and from the air, as many as were involved in the D-Day landings a year later. For the Axis defenders it was a daunting prospect but, with the crucial Battle of Kursk in progress on the Eastern Front, it was an armada Hitler far preferred to see off the island of Sicily than the northern coast of France.

The invasion would see the first large-scale use by the Allies of paratroopers. It was an element of the invasion that would turn out to be an unmitigated disaster. Many of the transport planes were shot down by twitchy naval gunners and few paratroopers were dropped in the correct zones. Many perished when they were dropped into the sea. The nuisance value of the scattered groups of airborne troops that survived was a poor return from what was the elite of the Allied fighting forces.

As it turned out the airborne troops were scarcely needed. There was no serious effort to defeat the invasion on the beaches and the lack of close air support for the landing troops was not noticed. The German and Italian air forces managed around 500 sorties on each of the first two days and were especially active over the American beaches, delivering several punishing attacks when no fighter cover was available. However, the 1,000 fighter sorties flown on the first day were by and large effective in protecting the landings. If the enemy bombers got past the fighters there were still the formidable, if somewhat indiscriminate anti-aircraft defences of the fleet. By night, Beaufighter and Mosquito night-fighters, directed by ground radar units operating from Sicily from the very first day, extended the protection.

For four days the fighting in the air was fierce, but the Axis air forces suffered especially heavy losses on the 13th. Many more aircraft had to be destroyed as airfields were abandoned. On the 15th the Axis managed little more than 150 sorties. It was a classic reminder of how the Luftwaffe had operated in its heyday, drawing the enemy into battle over the battlefield and defeating it. Now it was the Luftwaffe that was on the receiving end. Within six days the German and Italian air forces ceased to be a serious factor. Neutralising an air force in combat was a far more efficient way of establishing air superiority than attempting to destroy it on the ground.

The sea and land commanders were not quite so impressed by the achievements of the Allied fighters. Commanders from both services fumed at the lack of air cover. The 1st American Infantry Division around Gela claimed that on the first day of the invasion it had been under continuous dive-bomber attack for two hours and demanded better fighter protection. When Eisenhower arrived on the scene he was besieged with demands for better air cover.[27]

The complaints of the army and navy commanders scarcely seemed justified. Again the root cause of the discontent was the nagging suspicion that the air forces were not doing as much as they could. In fact, in terms of air defence, the Allied air forces could not have done more. Despite the range the fighters were operating over, Allied air and ground defences proved more than sufficient to stop the Axis air forces delivering a fatal, or even a serious blow against the naval armada. Instead of the predicted 300, just twelve vessels had been lost. HMS *Nelson* was damaged by Italian Re. 2002 fighter-bombers, but this was the only Axis success against a major vessel. Admiral Cunningham found it 'almost magical' that the Allies could get away with placing so many inviting targets so close to an enemy coast.[28] In fact, it was not that 'magical'. As long as the Luftwaffe remained heavily engaged on the Eastern Front it could never be the threat it had been before the invasion of the Soviet Union. The Luftwaffe had only remained such an impressive foe for so long because the Allies had not been as good at focusing their air resources where it mattered most.

While Axis air effort dropped from around 500 to less than 200 sorties a day, Allied daily effort remained at a steady 2,000. On the first day there was no need for close air support as American forces pushed several miles inland against weak Italian opposition. However, on the 11th, the Hermann Göring Division launched a powerful counter-attack, supported by Tiger tanks, which broke through American defences and almost reached the beaches. With few tanks and little artillery ashore the Americans were in some trouble. It was the sort of situation where close air support would have been extremely useful, but the fighter-bomber and bomber effort continued to concentrate on communication targets to the rear.

The counter-attack was within range of naval guns and a furious bombardment, of the sort so obviously lacking in the Dieppe operation, helped defeat the German attack. Nevertheless, naval fire from a distance has its limitations; there was a strong case for the more precise support aircraft can provide. Aircraft heading for more distant targets could have been diverted to support the troops on the ground but this sort of flexibility was beginning to disappear from Allied thinking. While the Allied air forces were concentrating on the 'bigger picture' of establishing air superiority and interdicting the battlefield, the Germans, focusing on the more immediate task in hand, had nearly delivered a fatal blow to an American bridgehead, unhindered by Allied air forces.

By the second day, the British bridgehead had been expanded sufficiently to allow planes short of fuel to land to refuel, and by the 13th three airfields were in use on the island. With the Spitfire squadrons moving to Sicily, the Kittyhawk squadrons were able to take their place on Malta and these flew the first mission in support of Commonwealth forces in the east of the island on the 11th. The next day, three Kittyhawk squadrons responded for the first time to an army request, attacking gun positions near Priolo that were holding up the advance of the Eighth Army. However, overall, fighter-bomber support on the battlefield remained on a relatively low scale.[29]

The Axis forces offered little resistance in the advance to Palermo, but Montgomery's advance on Catania was held up by stiff resistance in terrain that favoured the defence. Catania finally fell on 5 August but only after five days of intensive aerial bombardment with a thousand bomber sorties flown against the town and surrounding areas. The relentless bombardment impressed the Allied troops on the ground and was an ordeal for the defending forces. However, German commanders did not believe bombing built-up areas from high altitude achieved much. Destruction of towns did not cause serious delays; it merely imposed the inconvenience of having teams permanently on hand to clear a path through the rubble. No more than four hours' delay had ever been caused by the aerial assault on Catania. German commanders were not particularly impressed by Allied air support on the battlefield; it was not considered as effective as the battlefield support the Soviet Air Force provided its land forces. Low-flying Allied planes had proven to be 'exceedingly sensitive' to ground fire and there was surprise by how little there was of this sort of support.[30] It was a telling judgement.

There may not have been much of it but the close air support provided by Broadhurst's Desert Air Force was becoming extremely sophisticated. In the rugged Sicilian terrain, identifying targets was not always easy and the forward air controllers became even more important for directing air strikes. Requests were usually met within half an hour, on occasion in as little as ten minutes.[31] Eisenhower wanted his forces to get all the air support available but, as the campaign progressed, this increasingly meant Pantelleria-style medium-altitude carpet bombing rather than accurate close air support.

From 18 July to 6 August the American assault on Troina benefited from 265 fighter-bomber, 97 light-bomber and 12 medium-bomber sorties. The latter involved B-25 Mitchells using 20 tons of bombs to knock out three 88mm guns 100 yards in front of advancing troops. The troops were apparently very appreciative. Presumably, the Mitchells were flying at very low level. As well as attacks on the town itself, A-36 dive-bombers engaged enemy artillery positions and troop concentrations in the surrounding hills. Even this level of fairly discriminate attack resulted in so much damage to the town that it apparently took US Army engineers a day and a half to clear a path through the rubble, although why it should take the Americans so much longer than their German counterparts to clear rubble away is not clear.[32]

Further south, Montgomery's drive to the west of Mount Etna was halted by the Axis forces holding Adrano. Between 10 July and 7 August the town was targeted by 187 medium-, 367 light- and 140 fighter-bomber sorties. The American and British forces now converged on Randazzo. From 1 August to 13 August the town was hit by 425 medium-, 248 light- and 72 fighter-bomber sorties. The trend was towards Pantelleria-style mass bombing, with a growing reliance on twin-engined bombers operating from higher altitudes.

The Luftwaffe was not averse to carpet bombing a tactical target as they had demonstrated at Rotterdam in 1940. The Allied air forces in North Africa had also used similar tactics to overwhelm surrounded enemy strongholds. Pantelleria was a prime example. Against a last stand, where no further advance is required, carpet bombing can reduce friendly casualties, although the rubble can also provide excellent defensive positions. Where a further advance is required, there are even more serious disadvantages. Providing friendly forces with a supporting aerial bombardment to ensure the enemy kept their heads down was one thing: flattening towns and destroying lines of communication that would be required to continue the advance was quite another. With the tonnage being dropped, Allied bombing policy was becoming counter-productive.

So effective was the German resistance, Allied commanders were slow to realise that the Axis forces were already preparing to evacuate the island. Just 6 miles separated Messina from the mainland. Shore batteries dominated the straits, so naval intervention was impossible. The Germans gathered together extremely powerful anti-aircraft defences to cover the evacuation and Coningham decided they were far too powerful to allow his fighter-bombers to operate at low level. Bombers operating from higher altitudes would not be so vulnerable, but they would not be accurate enough. As a result, the Germans and Italians were able to evacuate all their troops and most of their heavy equipment.

The continent of Africa had been cleared and the occupation of Sicily had opened lines of communication to the Far East through the Mediterranean. The question for the Allies was where to strike next.

Chapter 13

Invasion of France 1943

With Sicily occupied, the military objectives laid down at Casablanca had been met. This was the point at which the Americans had wanted to switch the naval, air and ground forces in the Mediterranean to the Channel front and launch the invasion of France that Stalin was still expecting. Three years had now passed since the British Army had been flung out of France and it was becoming increasingly difficult to justify keeping the forces holed up in the UK inactive while a titanic and bitter struggle was playing out on the Russian steppes.

Marshall still wanted to attack through northern France as soon as possible, but there was little support for such a venture from his British allies. The 100-mile wide English Channel seemed to conjure up all sorts of problems a similar sea crossing to Sicily did not. Churchill worried that the Battle of the Atlantic was still far too precariously balanced for a 1943 invasion.[1] Brooke believed an invasion of France would only be possible if an invasion of Italy had first tied down German forces.

Eisenhower was not as keen as he had been. The reverses suffered by American forces at Kasserine had shaken American confidence. When Eisenhower discovered there might be more than two German divisions on the island of Sicily he believed the invasion had become an operation fraught with danger. This left a despairing Churchill wondering how the far larger German forces in northern France could ever be dealt with if just a handful of divisions caused so much alarm. Eisenhower seemed to be in no hurry to find out.

Arguably the January 1943 Casablanca conference had already effectively ruled out a 1943 invasion of France. Brooke had insisted that Germany's industrial base must first be wrecked before an invasion was attempted and the British and American bomber forces had scarcely made a start in meeting this aim. There was no shortage of good reasons for continuing the advance in the Mediterranean. The land and naval forces for an invasion of Italy were in place. During the Sicilian campaign, Mussolini had been deposed and, although Italy remained a German ally, there was every chance that, with a little additional pressure, the country might switch allegiance and join the Allied cause. For the American and British air chiefs, the Mediterranean strategy had its advantages. The more time they got to prove bombing worked, the better.[2] For the Americans, the complex of airfields around Foggia as a base for attacks on southern Europe was a major advantage of invading Italy. The Mediterranean was where Churchill and Brooke wanted the focus to stay. However, it was scarcely the quickest route to victory.

No one doubted there would have to be an invasion of France at some point. One of the decisions made at the Casablanca conference was that detailed planning should begin and Lieutenant General Frederick Morgan was appointed Chief of Staff to an as yet unnamed Supreme Allied Commander (COSSAC) to start planning. However, there was so little enthusiasm for the operation that Morgan began to suspect he was the unwitting participant in some massive hoax to hoodwink the enemy into believing an invasion was coming.[3] The fact that there was no hurry about naming his Supreme Commander tended to support this theory.

As the summer of 1943 wore on, many of the arguments for not invading were disappearing. The Allies were winning the Battle of the Atlantic. The German U-boat fleet had been one of the key Casablanca targets for the strategic bomber offensive, but this particular element of the bomber plan had been overtaken by events. Before the offensive could make any inroads into submarine production, the U-boats had been defeated. Long-range Liberators and the growing number of escorting aircraft carriers were now ensuring the entire Atlantic could be covered by patrolling aircraft. There was no hiding place for the German submarines. In May 1943, German U-boat losses rose sharply and Allied shipping losses fell equally dramatically. Harris had mocked the efforts of naval and air forces to defeat the U-boat menace, when compared to what his bombers had achieved as a mere 'sideshow' to their city-busting activities. However it was air and naval forces working together that helped deliver victory in the Atlantic, not strategic bombing. The war was beginning to pass the bomber offensive by.

Was an invasion of France possible in 1943? There was no doubt that the land and naval resources existed. If 150,000 troops could be landed on Sicily they could also be landed in France. Would the Allied air forces in the west have been able to support an invasion? Numerically there was no problem. Germany had thrown away its numerical advantage in the air the day it invaded the Soviet Union. In terms of quality, the Merlin 61-powered Spitfires (Mark VIII, IX) should have been sufficient. It may not have been the ideal dog-fighter but it was still very competitive, especially with the tinkering to engine and airframe the FW 190 had inspired. The problem was that plans laid in 1942 were not even trying to get this version into service in large numbers for 1943. Merlin engines were the bottleneck. With the Merlin XX required by the bombers having priority, Merlin 61 production targets were never particularly ambitious, but Rolls-Royce was failing to meet even these.[4] Even Spitfire Vs were in short supply. In the summer of 1942 a reserve of 500 had caused concern, but estimates in the autumn of 1942 suggested that, at current production rates, the best that could be hoped for in the spring of 1943 was a reserve of just 300.[5]

Even the 300 figure was assuming that the Hurricane would continue to be used as a front-line fighter overseas. This was becoming an increasingly untenable policy, not just because the Hurricane was obsolete as a fighter but because production could not keep up with losses. It was not so long ago that everyone was wondering what could be done with all the Hurricanes being built. The enemy was solving the problem by shooting them down. It was feared that by March 1943 there would be a deficit of 1,000 Hurricanes. Rather remarkably, as late as October 1942 there were suggestions that Hurricane production should be increased, with perhaps more being built in Canada.[6] Spitfires might have to be sent abroad, not because they were clearly superior to the Hurricane but because there were not enough Hurricanes to replace losses.

It was around this time that Tedder began making more of the inadequacy of the Hurricane. For Portal it was the final straw. He felt he had no choice 'but to get the Hurricanes out of the Middle East as early as possible and to substitute Spitfires'.[7] More Spitfires going to the Middle East would cut even further into the Spitfire reserves. Even so, it still seemed the bar for an invasion of France was being set unreasonably high. No one in the Middle East was expecting a reserve of 300 Spitfires before contemplating an advance across the desert or a landing in Sicily.

With 800 Spitfires in front-line squadrons, air commanders on other fronts might find it difficult to comprehend the air of deep gloom that hung over Fighter Command in the autumn of 1942. Before his departure from Fighter Command in November 1942, an exasperated Douglas told Portal that he did not think he was even getting the resources needed to defend the United Kingdom, never mind cover an invasion.[8] His command was well below the minimum seventy-five day squadrons he was supposed to have for air defence. To make matters worse, he had been told to find twelve more squadrons for Thorold's 'Army Air Support Group'. The three American volunteer squadrons within Fighter Command were being integrated into the USAAF for escort duties with the Eighth Air Force. Even his French pilots, frustrated with the lack of activity in the UK, were off to the Soviet Union to fly with the Soviet Air Force as the Normandie-Niemen squadron. He then discovered he was going to lose nineteen of his squadrons for the Torch landings in North-West Africa. He was also not happy that the fully developed Spitfire VIII, with its greater fuel capacity and range, was earmarked for North Africa while Fighter Command would have to make do with the interim Spitfire IX. His mood worsened when he discovered his Spitfire IXs might have to be used for Torch as the Mark VIII would not be ready in time.[9] Even so, with sixty single-seater fighter squadrons, forty-nine of which were equipped with Spitfires, commanders on other fronts would find it difficult to muster much sympathy for Douglas.

Freeman rather sharply reminded Douglas that other commands were carrying the burden of the fighting and that Fighter Command could not always expect the best aircraft while it was not engaged in major operations.[10] The suggestion that his pilots were not fully engaged did not go down well with Douglas. He claimed that only his pilots had to deal with the FW 190 in difficult operations over enemy territory (still true in the early autumn of 1942). Douglas insisted he was not demanding sole rights, just first option, which can scarcely have seemed any more justifiable or reasonable to Freeman. As a very minimum, Douglas wanted sufficient Merlin 61-powered Spitfires to equip the twenty-five squadrons of No. 11 Group and the adjacent Middle Wallop sector in No. 10 Group, the squadrons that would be in the front line of any invasion.[11] Initially, Douglas got his way; only Spitfire V squadrons supported the initial Torch landings, but when Eisenhower insisted he needed Spitfire IXs he got them.

When Leigh-Mallory took over from Douglas at Fighter Command, he found himself in the unenviable position of having to consider converting Spitfire IX squadrons back to Spitfire Vs.[12] In January 1943, Fighter Command was still a force dominated by the Spitfire V, with thirty-seven Spitfire V, two Spitfire VI (the high-altitude version of the Spitfire V), ten Spitfire IX and eleven Typhoon squadrons. Early in 1943 it was decided that to maintain a flow of 290 Spitfires a month overseas, Fighter Command would have to be rationed to 200 a month, of which only fifty would be brand new Spitfire IXs. The rest would be recycled, reconditioned Spitfires, mostly Mark Vs. For the time being, the number of Spitfire IX squadrons would have to remain pegged at just ten.[13]

Leigh-Mallory was no happier than his predecessor about future reliance on the Typhoon and Tempest. By September 1943 nearly half the fighter force would be equipped with these fighters. In the spring of 1943 the engine was attracting as much criticism as it had in 1942. The average engine life was still only a mere sixty hours and over 10 per cent of front-line Typhoon aircraft were without an engine at any given time.[14] However, a solution was on the way. In December 1942, English Electric took over Napier and the new owners prioritised getting the basic Sabre II right rather than putting effort into fancy superchargers and fuel-injection systems. This was the final nail in the Sabre IV-powered Tempest I coffin. A whole series of modifications were incorporated into a new production version, the Sabre IIa, which was supposed to be four times more efficient than previous versions. All production of the Sabre was halted while these modifications were incorporated into the assembly lines.

This was good news in the long term, but all Typhoon squadrons were grounded until they had the modified engines, a move which immediately cut Fighter Command strength by 15 per cent. It was hoped to have a dozen squadrons back on operations by the end of June but deliveries of new Typhoons would be delayed and plans to re-equip three Spitfire V squadrons with the Typhoon had to be put on hold.[15] By late summer of 1943 there were still some 300 Typhoon airframes in storage awaiting engines.

Some sort of solution was also found for the structural problems with the fighter's tail. Various ways of reinforcing the airframe had been tried without curing the problem but aircraft involved in some recent crashes had not had one particular recently introduced modification (twenty fishplates riveted across a rear fuselage joint) and this was hurriedly fitted to all service machines.[16] This seemed to resolve the problem but, even if the engine worked and the tail did not drop off, it was still only a high-speed interceptor; it was not the air superiority fighter the RAF needed for an invasion of France. The Middle East might complain that they were not getting enough Spitfires but Fighter Command might reasonably counter claim that at least the Middle East did not have to cope with the Typhoon. The only good news for Fighter Command in the spring of 1943 was that there was no sign of the turbo-supercharged Focke-Wulf (the FW 190B and C) or the inline engined (FW 190D) versions the Air Ministry feared would result in dramatically higher performance. Nor was there any sign of the Me 209 upgrade of the Bf 109 Air Ministry Intelligence was expecting to appear.

The Air Ministry hoped that the Spitfire V, with the tinkering that improved low-level performance, would not prove too inadequate. Comfortingly, a study of operations in the spring of 1943 concluded that while above 19,000 feet the Spitfire IX was far and away the more successful fighter, up to that altitude the Spitfire V was only slightly less successful. The Spitfire IX was still a better fighter at lower levels, and indeed Spitfire IXs with the Merlin 66 optimised to give higher performance at lower altitudes were considerably superior. Nevertheless, provided the Spitfire IX could offer protection from above, it was felt that the Spitfire V was still capable of making a useful contribution at low and medium altitudes.[17] It was perhaps a more favourable judgement than might have been made if Fighter Command did not have to rely on it so heavily. To the pilots who had to fly the fighter, it was still 'clipped, cropped and clapped'.

In the first months of 1943 there were some signs that the Luftwaffe dominance on the Channel coast was not quite so marked. Patrols over northern France were not proving as excessively costly as they had in 1942. February was a bad month with thirty-seven pilots lost for twenty-one German fighters destroyed, but in March and April it was level pegging.[18] April saw American Thunderbolts joining in these missions. American pilots swapping the Spitfire V for the faster but less manoeuvrable Thunderbolt were not initially over-impressed with their rather large new mount. It proved particularly vulnerable to the FW 190 at low and medium altitudes. On 26 June, the inexperienced 56th Fighter Group lost five planes with four more seriously damaged in a clash with Focke-Wulfs.

However, the Thunderbolt was a rugged fighter. Many badly damaged machines still got their pilots home. American fighter groups were not haemorrhaging planes at the rate Fighter Command had in similar sweeps in 1941 and 1942. Once they got used to their new fighter, American pilots came to appreciate the power it offered. There was little doubt that the P-47 was more useful than the Spitfire V, although the best Allied fighter in service was still the Merlin 61-powered Spitfire. In the summer of 1943, Fighter Command was not ideally equipped to take on the Luftwaffe but on balance it was better prepared than it had been the year before and American support was rising rapidly. Allied armies on other fronts were having to take the offensive with far less effective fighter forces.

The question that was still attracting most concern, however, was not the quality of the available fighters, it was their range. This need not have been a problem in 1942. The 90-gallon drop tank had been available the previous year and this provided sufficient endurance. Portal had told Churchill there was no problem using this in combat. However, this was not the message Morgan was getting. Morgan had settled on Normandy for the landing but confessed to spending much time staring at maps of the Channel and northern France 'superscribed with circles of distressingly small radius centred upon the fighter fields in the South of England'.[19] Morgan was well aware that the 90-gallon drop tank existed and was used for ferrying but Fighter Command continued to insist that the 30-gallon tank was 'ideal'. With this, the maximum patrol time over a Normandy beachhead would be just thirty minutes.[20]

Morgan's attempts to find out why the 90-gallon tank could not be used resulted in a lengthy explanation. This included the stark warning, in bold capital letters lest it be missed, that 'it is unlikely that any of the foreseeable improvements in the near future will enable long range fighters to compete with enemy short range fighters'.[21] This could only change if there was 'some radical change in engine and aircraft design'. This claim was clearly at odds with the performance of Japanese fighters in the Far East. The Japanese had used single-seater fighters based in Taiwan to cover their landings in the Philippines, which was like covering a landing in Normandy with fighter squadrons based around Manchester.

The report used some intriguing reasoning. It clearly stated it was focusing on the question of standing patrols, not long-range escort, yet it claimed that the fuel carried in drop tanks had to be less than internal fuel. This was obviously true for long-range escort, but it was equally obviously not true for patrolling closer to home, where less internal fuel was needed to get home. Fighters could patrol for as long as the fuel in the drop tank lasted. The report insisted the only solution was more internal fuel, which would mean larger, heavier engines, and the overall result would be reduced performance.

It was not just a question of fuel. The report explained to Morgan that huge numbers of fighters would be required to fight an enemy on equal terms because so much flying time would be needed getting to and from the patrol zone. Furthermore, fighters carried limited ammunition and would soon become defenceless and even more fighters would have to be found to shepherd them home. The report, however, helpfully offered possible solutions that might be worth investigating. Aircraft carriers could be used or perhaps enormous artificial floating 'seadromes' might be constructed and these could be moored offshore. It was not surprising Morgan found the problem depressing. The Air Ministry seemed to be determined to make providing fighter cover from airfields 100 miles away seem as difficult as possible.

By the summer of 1943 it was not just the 90-gallon drop tank that was available. The Americans were beginning to tackle the endurance problem, although not with an invasion of France in mind. The USAAF was still convinced that once its bombers could attack in formations of 200 they would defeat any fighters sent up to stop them. However, until they could do this, American bombers were using Thunderbolt escorts in Europe and Lightning escorts in North Africa and there was already a desire to get these escorts to fly further. In July 1943, as a short-term expedient, the Thunderbolts in Britain began flying with a rather clumsy 200-gallon jettisonable ferry tank, which enabled the fighters to fly as far as the German frontier. This did not help the bombers that much as the defending German fighters simply withdrew into German territory. However, the ferry tank gave the Thunderbolt the ability to operate beyond Paris or, more relevantly, a substantial patrol time over the French coast. If France had been invaded instead of Italy, the longer-range Lightnings in the Mediterranean would also have been available.

Even Fighter Command was finally beginning to concede that something more than the 30-gallon drop tank was required. The Fleet Air Arm needed more range and were insisting on a 45-gallon drop tank for their carrier-based aircraft. In January 1943, Leigh-Mallory had agreed to use a 45-gallon slipper tank on the Spitfire, not because he saw the need for it but simply to enable a degree of standardisation. However, a need soon emerged. In August 1943, as the Thunderbolts began to push German fighters back into Germany, Leigh-Mallory found his fighters could not even make contact with the German air defences. Suddenly he decided he needed the 45-gallon tank after all.[22] Unfortunately for Leigh-Mallory, it was the Fleet Air Arm that had requested it and they therefore had priority. Leigh-Mallory found himself appealing for an acceleration in deliveries of a drop tank that originally he had not even particularly wanted.

For both the RAF and the USAAF, it was the desire to take the air war into Germany that was driving the introduction of drop tanks, not the need to cover landings in France. Indeed, so pre-occupied were air commanders with their air offensive, it did not seem to occur to anyone to tell Morgan about these developments. Meanwhile, the war in the Mediterranean seemed to be taking place in a parallel universe. For the proposed landings on the Italian mainland at Salerno, fighter cover would have to be provided over twice the range Morgan would require for his Normandy landing.

As Morgan was digesting the news that any substantial increase in fighter range was out of the question, the Air Ministry was preparing to send 1,800 90-gallon drop tanks to the Mediterranean so that the USAAF and RAF Spitfires could cover the landings.[23] The drop tanks that could have been used for an invasion of France were on their way to the Mediterranean for an invasion of Italy.

In the summer of 1943, the range of Allied fighters should not have been a problem and, in terms of quality, squadrons in the UK were better equipped than their counterparts overseas. Even without reinforcement from the Mediterranean, the Channel front was still where the Allied fighter force was strongest and best equipped to take on the Luftwaffe. Stiffer resistance in the air might be expected with a landing in France but it is difficult to escape the conclusion that the risks and problems with quality, reserves and the range of existing fighters were being maximised to make the option of a landing in France seem as unattractive as possible.

What could an invading Allied army expect in terms of bomber support in 1943? The Anglo-American alliance had no shortage of aircraft that could unload substantial bomb loads on an enemy below. RAF bombers by night and American Fortresses and Liberators by day were capable of flattening built-up areas as Allied bombers had done in Sicily. How useful this would be was another matter. Medium and light bombers were capable of bombing with greater accuracy from lower altitudes by day, but these were not available in such great numbers.

Four USAAF Martin B-26 Marauder groups arrived in the summer of 1943 to join the Eighth Air Force. Trained for low-level missions, these relatively short-range bombers were very much considered cuckoos in the nest by the strategically orientated Eighth Air Force. With its high wing loading and landing speeds, it was not the most popular of planes with aircrews, nor were the low-level tactics a success. On one of its first missions in May 1943 all ten aircraft taking part were lost. The low-level approach was soon abandoned, the bomber having more success from medium altitude. The 250 aircraft of the four groups in Britain represented a useful striking force.

The RAF medium/light bomber contribution was not so impressive. Like the American B-26 groups, No. 2 Group was very much the cuckoo in the Bomber Command nest. For all Portal's promises to the War Office that it would be expanded, it was still a force struggling for survival. At the end of 1942 it lost another two squadrons to support the Allied forces in North-West Africa, leaving just ten in the UK at the beginning of 1943.

It was also a bomber force with no clear purpose. One of its roles had been to supplement 'army co-operation' squadrons in the close air support role, but the Group had never been equipped with aircraft that could do this. Instead of a clear role in helping win the war, the Group had the task of carrying out dangerous attacks on well-defended targets merely to allow the escorts the opportunity to engage the enemy. It was a rather dispiriting and pointless assignment.

It was therefore a rather demoralised force that Air Vice-Marshal Basil Embry took over in June 1943. Embry did, however, now have a clear role for the Group. No longer was it to be bait for Fighter Command; it was there to support the forthcoming invasion of France. It was a task that took Embry full circle. As a No. 2 Group squadron leader he had flown in action over France during the 1940 campaign. His Blenheim had been shot down near Dunkirk, he was captured by the Germans but made his escape and eventually reached Gibraltar after ten weeks on the run. Now, as No. 2 Group commander, he would be in the vanguard of the attempt to regain the ground lost in 1940.

Close air support on the battlefield, however, was not to be part of the Group's role. Its targets would generally be beyond the battlefield: communication centres, ammunition dumps, bridges, radar stations, enemy headquarters and larger batteries in the rear. To attack these targets, Embry wanted two types of bomber, one that could operate from medium altitudes with fighter escort and a low-level attack bomber that would not need an escort.[24]

The Mosquito VI fighter-bomber provided an excellent way of filling the low-level role. This combined the four forward-firing cannon of the fighter version with the bomb load of the bomber version. Two squadrons were already equipped with the unarmed Mosquito IV bomber version. As a day bomber the Mosquito was by no means the invulnerable plane its designers had hoped for. In the first year of operations, Mosquito squadrons had lost forty-eight aircraft during the course of 726 sorties, a loss rate of nearly 7 per cent. This was higher than the 5 per cent loss rate of the armed and escorted bombers of other No. 2 Group squadrons. Admittedly, the Mosquitoes often flew more dangerous missions, much deeper inside enemy territory, even raiding as far as the German capital. Nevertheless, daylight bombing was an expensive business, even with a plane that could carry the same bomb load as the Blenheim V but 140 mph faster.

The Mosquito was not being produced in the numbers its value deserved and everyone wanted the few that were being built. Far from increasing the number of No. 2 Group Mosquito squadrons, the existing squadrons were already on the move. Almost as soon as Embry took over, his two Mosquito squadrons left to join No. 8 Pathfinder Group to support the strategic-bombing offensive. The altitude the Mosquito could fly meant it could use the Oboe marking system deeper inside Germany so it made the ideal pathfinder. Embry was promised replacements would soon be arriving and all his squadrons would be re-equipped with either B-25 Mitchells or Mosquitoes. In the meantime, Embry was left with two Mitchell, three Douglas Boston and three Lockheed Ventura squadrons.[25]

Embry was happy with the Boston and Mitchell but not the Ventura. The American bomber had just suffered heavily in a particularly disastrous mission. On 3 May 1943, German fighters overwhelmed a Spitfire V escort, and ten out of eleven Venturas attacking a power station in Amsterdam were shot down. When Embry tried out the plane he declared it to be slow, heavy, un-manoeuvrable and lacking in defensive armament, although in truth in all these respects it was not much different from the Mitchell. The Ventura was not one of the outstanding designs of its time. It did not exactly look the part; it rather looked like the converted airliner it was. Nevertheless, it was not perhaps as hopeless as Embry was suggesting. The losses it suffered on 3 May were by no means typical, but they were fresh in everyone's minds at the time. A replacement was needed anyway as production was coming to an end. More than anything else, however, it was necessary to turn a new leaf, with better planned and directed missions. The Ventura was a symbol of an unsuccessful past that needed to be erased.

In August, Ventura squadrons began re-equipping with the Mosquito VI. More squadrons were being formed with foreign personnel. No. 320 (Dutch) Squadron on Mitchells and No. 342 (French) Squadron on Bostons brought the Group back up to ten squadrons by August 1943, but this was still six squadrons fewer than No. 2 Group had to support the BEF in France in 1940. Nevertheless, along with the 250 American Marauders, there were around 400 medium/light day bombers to support a 1943 invasion.

For close air support on the battlefield, the single-engined fighter-bomber had become the preferred option. This was capable of low-level attack or shallow dive-bombing. The War Office was happy enough with this, although it still believed there was a place for a more specialised close support plane as well and also still believed a steep dive-bombing capability would be useful. Outside military circles there was more vociferous support for the dive-bomber. No other air issue aroused emotions like this particular category of warplane. The Army wanted them because the Germans had them, the politicians wanted them because the press and public were demanding them and the Air Ministry did not want them because they could not contribute to a strategic air offensive. None of these were particularly good reasons.

The dive-bomber was the bête noire of the Air Ministry, another example of German foolishness, to add to a very long list the Air Ministry was compiling of Teutonic blunders. It was lampooned in a way that was scarcely justified by the fearsome reputation the plane had acquired in so many campaigns. It did not look like a failure to the soldier on the receiving end nor, from afar, to the general public. Over the years, the Air Ministry had repeatedly insisted the dive-bomber was easy meat for fighters but did their cause no good by repeatedly failing to provide sufficient fighters over the front line to put their claim to the test.

The Air Ministry made no distinction between whether they were against dive-bombing or just the Ju 87 Stuka in particular as a means of dive-bombing. The very vehemence of the blanket Air Ministry criticism in the face of its obvious success was bound to make it a topic of national debate and controversy. The Air Ministry argument that Luftwaffe dive-bombers had only been successful when the Germans had air superiority rather rebounded on the Ministry now that the Allies were gaining an ever greater degree of air superiority. Perhaps it was the turn of the German Army to be terrorised by the dive-bomber, many quite reasonably argued.

On the face of it, there did not seem much to disagree on. No one disputed bombing was more accurate if the plane was diving towards the target, and the steeper the dive the greater the accuracy. Kittyhawk pilots were trained to dive at 60 degrees.[26] The first time the Spitfire was used as a dive-bomber, the pilots reported they had dived at 75 degrees. In September 1942, Deputy Chief of Air Staff Norman Bottomley was telling Sinclair that the Typhoon had been successfully dived at 80 degrees, although, with its dodgy tail, there were probably not too many pilots who would volunteer to check this out. The Stuka could dive at 90 degrees, although closer to 80 degrees was perhaps more usual. The Americans had fitted their A-36 Apache dive-bomber version of the Mustang with air brakes, and these aircraft were successfully used both in near-vertical dives using the airbrakes and shallower 70-degree dives without using them.

Essentially the argument was about the best diving angle, taking everything into account. The extra 20 degrees increased bombing accuracy but put more strain on the plane and pilot and air brakes were needed to slow the dive. It was really just a question of whether the extra 20 degrees was worth the complication of fitting air brakes. It scarcely seemed to merit the heat the debate generated. By 1943 it was not even a huge bone of contention between the War Office and the Air Ministry. The Army had always preferred a steep dive-bombing capability, but it was happy with the slightly shallower attacks and low-level strikes fighter-bombers were already delivering.

It remained a highly controversial topic because the argument was about much more than just whether steep dive-bombing was a good idea or not. For many, the dive-bomber had become a proxy term for army air support. The Air Ministry attitude to the dive-bomber was seen as a litmus test of how committed the RAF was to supporting the Army. It was indeed a fair indicator. For the Air Ministry, the dive-bombing tactic was inextricably linked with the German blitzkrieg method they were so anxious to discredit.

In Air Ministry eyes the dive-bomber had always been a particularly dangerous manifestation of the tactical air support doctrine. Although the Air Staff had traditionally believed any form of bomber support on the battlefield, whether it be delivered by dive-bombers or low-level attack planes, was a misuse of air power, it was the former that had always attracted the severest criticism because there was no way such a plane could be used for long-range bombing. Large planes that can carry lots of fuel cannot be safely dived steeply. Although tactically scarcely sound, there were no technical reasons why a low-flying plane could not be large, which was the thinking behind the Bisley. The Air Ministry could claim it was meeting army requirements with an aircraft that could also be used for long-range bombing. The fighter-bomber had never triggered the same concern because this came out of the agreed fighter allocation and therefore did not affect the resources available for bomber production. A specialist army support bomber would come out of the bomber allocation.

The arrival of the long-awaited American dive-bombers kept the debate very much alive. Some 2,000 Vultee Vengeance and Brewster Bermudas had been ordered way back in the dark days of 1940. The first Vengeances did not reach Britain until the summer of 1942, followed by the first Bermudas towards the end of the year. The delays were due to a combination of factors. There were the over-optimistic production schedules in the summer of 1940 by companies determined to cash in on the United Kingdom's desperate plight. When the United States entered the war they took over some of the contracts. In the case of the Brewster Bermuda, the delays were, according to the Air Ministry, just a case of the sheer incompetence of the company.[27]

The original plan was to use the Bermuda to equip army co-operation and No. 2 Group squadrons in the UK and use the Vultee Vengeance overseas. However, when the first Bermudas arrived, they were found to be riddled with technical faults and the remaining contracts were cancelled. The Vengeance was a much better aircraft and this was now earmarked for use by home-based and overseas squadrons. They would go to Burma first where the jungle terrain made it particularly difficult to spot and hit targets, but technical problems were delaying the operational debut of the plane.[28]

In the meantime, Sinclair found himself facing awkward questions on the dive-bomber issue in Parliament. He had a tricky position to defend. His Ministry was fiercely opposed to the dive-bombing concept but was planning to equip RAF squadrons with the type. This resulted in some rather mixed messages. Sinclair listed all the disadvantages of the dive-bomber but then told his colleagues that, with growing Allied air superiority, he hoped 'to find good use for' the American dive-bombers that would soon be arriving.[29]

Every time a report arrived of German dive-bombers in action there were renewed demands to know exactly when the RAF would get some. When reports were published describing German dive-bombing attacks on Allied troops in Tunisia, Sinclair insisted that the reports were mistaken; the enemy had just been using fighter-bombers. When he was quizzed about a newspaper report that Spitfires had been used for dive-bombing, Sinclair denied the report, claiming the term 'dive-bombing' was being used loosely and that these, too, were just fighter-bomber operations.[30] There seemed to be a perverse determination to deepen the controversy by not admitting to any dive-bombing taking place on either side.

When the Air Ministry was finally forced to concede RAF fighter-bombers did dive-bomb, critics argued that by not having dive-brakes the RAF was putting at risk the lives of its pilots simply because 'some air-marshals are bigoted opponents' of them.[31] A desperate Sinclair wondered if the Air Ministry could dig out some past quote from Montgomery, or some other senior Army figure, which could be interpreted as a confirmation that the German dive-bomber was not that successful.[32] It would have seemed easier to ask someone to say something along these lines but no one seemed too keen on doing this. With the Air Minister constantly being pressed for information on when the American dive-bombers would enter service, a harassed Sinclair appealed to the MAP to get at least one squadron operational as soon as possible, just to silence his critics.[33]

That squadron was not going to be in Britain. Embry was horrified when he discovered squadrons in his Command were to fly the Vengeance.

He immediately tried out the plane himself and concluded it was a 'poor [Fairey] Battle', with inferior speed (just 235 mph he claimed) and inadequate range (a radius of action of just 220 miles). Both these figures were far lower than the 310 mph and 1,400-mile range the plane was officially credited with. Manoeuvrability was also poor and defensive armament totally inadequate. This 'relic from the past', as Embry described it, was impossible to escort and could only be successful if there was no effective anti-aircraft opposition. Embry was reliably informed that in the Far East the plane was considered 'absolutely useless'. He did not want dive-bombers and certainly not the Vengeance, the adoption of which, he warned, would be tantamount to signing the death warrants of the crews who flew it.[34]

These were strong words. Comparing the Vengeance to the Fairey Battle was bound to evoke memories of the May 1940 massacres. Embry was right. If the Vengeance was misused in the same way the Battle had been and was sent off unescorted to attack targets deep in the enemy rear its fate would be the same as the Battle. The reference to the plane being 'absolutely useless' referred to the initial teething problems the aircraft sent to the Far East were experiencing. These were overcome and when it began flying missions in May 1943 it was, according to Peirse, the RAF commander in the Far East, a great success. Bombing was far more accurate than conventional level bombing and, in the Arakan campaign in western Burma, the plane was used for three months without suffering any losses.

Official trials in Britain, however, confirmed Embry's opinion. Again the plane was compared to the Fairey Battle and declared inferior in every respect, although this was scarcely borne out by some of the test results. According to the report it was 'difficult to attain a speed of more than 300 mph', a speed the Battle could come nowhere near achieving. The plane lacked sufficient defensive firepower to operate without fighter cover, but it was too slow to be escorted efficiently. Range was limited and its 1,500lb bomb load was 'moderate'.[35]

With No. 2 Group focusing on more distant indirect support, Embry had more reason than most to reject the Vengeance. However, Air Vice-Marshal John D'Albiac, the commander of the recently formed Second Tactical Air Force, considered it unsuitable for any role and the War Office would have to accept this. Such was the delicacy of the situation, it was felt wise to get Paget, the Commander of Home Forces, to inform the War Office. Paget duly complied with a carefully worded letter that suggested he was not entirely convinced. Although the Army had long striven for the accuracy of the dive-bomber, he had been persuaded that the fighter-bomber equipped with rockets and anti-tank cannon was at least as accurate.[36] In fact rockets were far from accurate and there were grave doubts about future fighter-bombers being able to carry cannon that could be effective against tanks.

The War Office might have been persuaded but the public and the politicians were not so easily satisfied. When the British press reported in July 1943 that the USAAF was using North American A-36 Mustang dive-bombers in Sicily there was yet another outcry. With their own allies openly using dive-bombers and plans for RAF and Indian Air Force squadrons in the Far East to use the Vengeance, Sinclair could scarcely undermine the aircrews of these squadrons by openly criticising the dive-bomber concept. Nor indeed did the performance of the Vengeance in Burma justify such criticism.

Indeed the success of the Vengeance in the Far East had become an embarrassment. The Air Ministry tried to get Peirse to play down its success. In any public statements it should be referred to, they suggested, as a 'light bomber' and its versatility when compared to the Stuka should be underlined by emphasising that it was used for level and shallow dive-bombing as well as steep dive-bombing. Peirse found himself in a difficult situation. His crews had perfected the steep dive-bombing technique and were doing very well. Reports from Britain that the dive-bomber was 'dead' were scarcely what his Vengeance aircrews wanted to hear. Indeed they would be baffled. Peirse wanted to give the success of these squadrons more publicity; press stories full of praise for their dive-bombing exploits were ready to go. Peirse was none too pleased that their success might have to be watered down just to fit in with the Air Ministry's official line.[37] The Air Ministry's fanatical opposition to dive-bombing was creating quite unnecessary problems.

The rabid trashing of the Vengeance highlighted the almost irrational Air Ministry odium for the dive-bomber. The Vengeance was no slower than most Allied bombers and, like all bombers, it was vulnerable without fighter support. The concerns about range and bomb load were especially revealing. The Air Ministry still judged a bomber by how far it could fly and how many bombs it could carry. Long range was not needed for close air support. The type of army support provided at the Tebaga Pass was not what anyone in the Air Ministry had in mind. The assessment of the Vengeance makes an interesting comparison with the official verdict on the Hurricane. Both were intended for close air support. In its armoured Mark IV form, the Hurricane carried fewer bombs to less distant targets at about the same speed as the Vengeance, but this was considered to be good enough to serve until 1945. It would seem that the Vengeance was judged by different criteria.

In practice, both were treated in a fairly similar way. The ground attack version of the Hurricane was rugged, manoeuvrable and versatile, but it could not fly deep into enemy air space and hope to survive. Like the Vengeance, the Hurricane IV was shunted off to more distant battlefields, principally in Burma, where its capabilities were more appreciated. Indeed, in the Far East the Hurricane, like the Vengeance, did invaluable work providing genuine battlefield support, knocking out tanks, bunkers, gun positions and strongpoints with bombs, rockets and 40mm cannon right up until the end of the war.[38] From the Army's point of view, the Hurricane and Vengeance had one rather fortuitous advantage; it was not sensible to use them deep in the enemy rear. As far as the Air Ministry was concerned, this was the Typhoon's big advantage; its much higher speed meant less time in enemy airspace on longer range missions and it could therefore be used against more distant targets.

Relying on the fighter-bomber as the means for providing close support in the European theatre was not an unreasonable decision, especially at a time when there were rather exaggerated ideas of what the Luftwaffe was still capable of. On balance, the extra accuracy was probably not worth the problems that came with a plane that could dive 20-30 degrees more steeply. Even so, the preference for aircraft that could operate further in the rear was rather ominous from the Army's point of view. In the summer of 1943 there was little desire to provide an expeditionary force in France with the sort of close support the Hurricane and Vengeance could provide. The Air Ministry and UK-based RAF were losing interest in the very close support provided at Dieppe.

Close air support was not the only element of tactical air warfare that was not getting the attention it needed. In the summer of 1943 the tactical reconnaissance squadrons were still very much the Cinderella of the service. It was only in June 1943 that these squadrons formally lost their 'Army co-operation' tag, and were divided into specialist tactical reconnaissance and strategic reconnaissance squadrons. The transition from the 'Jack of all trades' army co-operation force to one with specialist reconnaissance, observation and ground attack squadrons was complete. The strategic reconnaissance squadrons were supposed to use photo-reconnaissance Spitfires and Mosquitoes, although both types were hard to come by. The seven tactical reconnaissance squadrons had the excellent

Allison-powered Mustang I. By the summer of 1943 some 400 had arrived in the UK but there were still relatively few with the squadrons. As in 1942 there was no urgency about getting these squadrons ready for a possible invasion.

If a decision had been made to cross the Channel in 1943, the deficiencies that plagued many of the available squadrons might well have been attacked with more vigour, although this is by no means certain. In the past, battles raging in Europe or the threat of imminent invasion had not provoked much Air Ministry interest in preparing the RAF to support the Army. Nevertheless, despite Air Ministry priorities lying elsewhere, a reasonable air element for an invasion existed. Fighter Command had around 750 Spitfires (160 Spitfire IX) and 200 Typhoons. The US Eighth Air Force could add 150 Thunderbolts. The Allies had some 400 medium bombers. There were also 400 heavy day bombers of the USAAF and around a thousand Bomber Command night bombers. They faced 300 German fighters in Western Europe, mostly orientated to meet American daylight raids on Germany, with another 400 fighters elsewhere in the Reich, along with 200 bombers and fighter-bombers. Both sides could have called upon reserves from abroad. Logistically, this would have been far easier for the Germans. Strategically, however, the boot was on the other foot. The Allies had nothing to fear in the Mediterranean, whereas the German forces were already fully extended in Russia where, with the Battle of Kursk, the struggle was reaching a climax.

The problem was not so much with the numbers or even the quality of the available aircraft. Arguably, the RAF throughout the war had the aircraft to support the Army; the problem had always been actually using them to support the Army. Achieving the joint-service approach that had made the Wehrmacht so successful was always going to be difficult with the compartmentalised structure of the British armed forces and its proudly separate land, sea and air elements. The War Office was least guilty in this respect; it had always been more open to the greater integration required for armed services to operate successfully, but the Air Ministry always interpreted such notions as a threat to RAF independence. From the Army point of view the RAF still considered itself 'too much a separate entity'.[39] From an Air Ministry point of view this was not a failing; it was policy. The Air Force would support the Army, but they would do it in their own way.

In the autumn of 1942, it was this thorny question of organisation and control rather than the resources available that remained the biggest obstacle to providing the air support an invading army would need.

Portal was still trying to force the command and control system required for army air support into the existing air defence organisation. Brooke wanted army support organised through Barratt's Army Co-operation Command. Thorold's attempted compromise of attaching just twelve of the promised thirty-five bomber/fighter-bomber squadrons to Army Co-operation Command had not got anywhere as Portal had just incorporated these into his Eastern Air Force. The thirty-five squadrons of this force now comprised thirteen ground attack fighter, ten light-bomber and Thorold's twelve squadrons. Portal had extracted ten bomber squadrons from his original commitment, freeing more resources for the bomber offensive. The War Office would have no objections to the new breakdown; more of the squadrons would be of the more useful fighter variety. However, they would not have the control they needed. The Typhoon squadrons Portal planned to create for army support were really just more squadrons for Fighter Command.

Portal's latest plans did not go down well in the War Office. Portal informed Brooke that he intended to create six Typhoon, two Typhoon bomber and four Hurricane IID tank-buster army support squadrons for his 'Eastern Air Force'. The resources diverted to the Torch landing were delaying their creation, he explained, but he was doing his best and pushing ahead with the first two Typhoon squadrons. Brooke was not impressed. He took exception to the Air Ministry deciding what these squadrons should be equipped with and he 'thought [he] had made it clear' that he did not accept the Eastern Air Force concept. In an equally sharp response, Portal made it just as clear that he had no intention of letting the Army decide what should equip these squadrons nor was there any intention of him changing his mind about his Eastern Air Force. Portal insisted the Army had no immediate need for these squadrons now that Torch had indefinitely delayed any invasion of France, and they were needed to replace the fighter squadrons assigned to Torch. They would have to stay in Fighter Command at least until it had reached its seventy-five day fighter squadron target.[40]

Air Ministry U-turns now increased the ill-feeling and frustration on both sides. Perhaps sensing he was on weak ground by hanging on to the twelve army support squadrons, Portal rather surprisingly let Brooke choose if they should reside in Army Co-operation Command or Fighter Command. However, he suggested he discuss it with Douglas before deciding, apparently in the belief that Douglas would persuade him to allow them to stay in Fighter Command. Brooke saw no need to discuss it with anyone and gratefully accepted the offer.[41] Portal was rather peeved that Brooke had chosen not to consult Douglas and no doubt had a hand in ensuring Sinclair overruled the decision and withdrew the offer. The twelve army support squadrons stayed in Fighter Command.[42]

As the war entered its fourth year, relations between the Army and Air Force were not getting any better. There was a growing feeling within the War Office that the personal animosity that existed between Portal and Brooke was the single biggest problem standing in the way of any progress. Paget feared War Office demands were merely antagonising the Air Ministry and slowing progress. An unimpressed Brooke was beginning to see the dark hand of the Air Ministry everywhere and was convinced Paget had been 'got at' by Douglas.[43]

James Grigg, the Secretary of State for War, thought it would be worth giving Portal's approach a go. The Air Ministry would be far more likely to make its own scheme work than an Army Co-operation Command that had been imposed on it. 'I don't believe the Air Staff will play until it is made a matter of their (underlined in the original document) professional reputation that Army co-operation shall succeed.'[44] An Army Co-operation Command the Air Ministry objected to just gave the air marshals the excuse to sideline the whole issue. The aim should have been to get the air support the Army needed, not to pick a fight with the Air Ministry.

Many in the War Office convinced themselves that there were advantages basing the squadrons within Fighter Command. The War Office was genuinely impressed by Fighter Command's sophisticated radar-controlled air defence system and was anxious to make full use of it, even though organising air defence through No. 11 Group Headquarters at Uxbridge had been at the heart of many of the problems in the Dieppe operation. The War Office was perhaps too easily persuaded by the advantages of No. 11 Group running army support and was again adopting a rather submissive stance. On the other hand, given the way the strategic bombing offensive was once again dominating war strategy, it was perhaps necessary to be realistic about how much the War Office could expect to get out of the Air Ministry.

In September, Churchill was dragged back into the debate. In recent months the Prime Minister had been entirely preoccupied by other matters, not least of which was a new heightened urgency about expanding Bomber Command and speeding up the delivery of the new navigational aids the Command needed. Early in September, Churchill was rather taken aback by an unsigned note prepared by Grigg complaining about the lack of progress in resolving the tactical air support question. Rather deviously,

Grigg wanted Churchill to sign it and send it to him and Sinclair to shake things up. The Prime Minister seemed entirely unaware of the dispute raging between the War Office and Air Ministry. With a debate on army/air co-operation due to take place in Parliament, a perplexed Churchill asked his Senior Assistant Secretary, Leslie Hollis, to find out what was going on.[45]

Hollis's report showed much sympathy for the War Office position. He could see why Brooke was so suspicious of Air Ministry intentions, especially with Harris making it clear to all and sundry that he thought bombing could win the war and that investing in army air support was just a waste of time and money. Like Grigg, he thought the Air Ministry might be quite happy to see the unwanted Army Co-operation Command fall by the wayside, but it would not want to see its own counter proposal fail.[46]

Both Grigg and Hollis were perhaps underestimating the determination of the Air Staff to see their bomber strategy through. It was much more than a case of departmental egotism or professional pride. The Air Ministry understood the fundamental problem. Creating a powerful tactical air force would suck resources away from Bomber Command. No amount of diplomatic talk was going to get round the fact that the Air Ministry saw an expanding tactical force outside its full control as a threat to its strategic ambitions and indeed the integrity of the RAF.

Hollis thought things were moving in the right direction and it was best to leave the Air Ministry and War Office to work things out. As he saw it, there was a growing volume of feeling which deplored the recriminations of the past and, with a little pressure from the respective secretaries of state, he felt something positive would surely eventually emerge. It was a remarkably relaxed attitude after three years of trying to come up with any arrangement which might give Britain's armed forces in the UK some chance of taking on the Wehrmacht with reasonably adequate air support.

In October 1942, Churchill attempted to settle the matter by instructing both parties that, in the case of land operations on the continent, he wanted army air support to be based on the Desert Air Force model. This still left open the possibility of an alternative organisation for the actual landings. Reiterating the principles introduced in the Western Desert, he stressed that all forces should be used to support the Army whenever active operations were in progress.[47] The problem was that neither the War Office nor Air Ministry proposals matched the organisation of the Desert Air Force. There was nothing like the colossus of Fighter Command in the Middle East to dominate the debate, nor a Bomber Command to suck resources away. The Army was very happy to make use of Fighter

Command's command and control system but wanted to graft this on to its tactical air force. Coming at the problem from the opposite direction, the Air Ministry wanted to graft the tactical air forces on to the existing Fighter Command set-up.[48]

Not for the first time, Portal used future planned exercises to put off any major decisions. The 'Spartan' exercises were supposed to help determine the organisation that would give an army fighting on the continent the best air support and Portal argued it would be sensible to await the outcome of these before submitting a definitive plan. Since these exercises were not due to take place until March 1943, nothing was likely to be in place in time for a summer 1943 invasion.[49] It was hoped to have the full force of twelve army support squadrons (eight Typhoon and four Hurricane) available by June 1943. Everything was moving very slowly. It was November 1942 before the Air Ministry requested that the problems of armouring the Typhoon for its new low-level attack role be investigated, but there seemed little urgency about getting this work underway.

The War Office hoped some progress could be made by setting up an inter-service committee under its scientific adviser, Charles Darwin, to investigate how best air power should be used to support army operations. On the committee there were representatives from the Air Ministry, War Office, Ministry of Home Security and Zuckerman from the Combined Operations Executive. They gathered information from the various ministries and commands and sought the evidence of officers who had served at the front. It was the first serious cross-ministry attempt to analyse in a more systematic way what effective army air support involved.

Almost inevitably it started with a slanging match between the two sides. The War Office insisted the RAF was failing to adhere to the age-old military principle of focusing effort where it mattered. As an Army report from the Middle East put it:

> Our aircraft are all over the place engaged in a 1,000 activities, while the enemy is concentrated on you, that is, where the battle is.[50]

Interdiction was all well and good but it could never be as decisive as the Air Ministry claimed, especially if targets were too far in the rear to be relevant. The War Office gave examples dating as far back as the unsuccessful August 1918 attempt to interdict the battlefield by bombing the bridges over the Somme in the Battle of Amiens.[51] The further to the rear the attacks were, the more alternative routes there were and the more dangerous the missions would be. It was a case of higher losses for smaller reward.

The Air Ministry countered by pointing to the success in interdicting Rommel's lines of communications in North Africa. However, the Army list of failed interdiction was longer than RAF successes. The Air Ministry accepted that, while the battle was in progress, the RAF would to some extent have to 'be chained to the battle area', a choice of words that scarcely suggested much enthusiasm, but it was anxious to ensure this was not necessarily the main focus. It was pointed out that the RAF consisted largely of heavy bombers that could only be used against targets in the rear. This argument might have carried more weight if, over the years, efforts by the War Office to get a specialist plane to attack targets on the battlefield had not been met with the claim that large, heavy bombers could do the job just as well.

On the practical side of how army support should be delivered there was surprise among the civilian scientists on the committee at the lack of any data on any of the tactics or weapons used, a measure of how little thought either service had invested in the practicalities of air support. It seemed strange that the 250lb general-purpose bomb was still the standard offensive weapon. Although effective against some targets, it was scarcely the best way of attacking all targets. In the open it just buried itself in the ground before exploding. They suggested that, against dispersed targets, a larger number of smaller bombs were better than fewer large bombs. The RAF objection had always been that it took too long to load large numbers of smaller bombs. The committee suggested weapons pods would simplify the task of loading. It also suggested that there should be more specialised weapons with anti-personnel, armour-piercing, incendiary bombs as well as standard high explosive. Fusing needed to be investigated so that bombs exploded at or above ground level. The value of dive-bombers and 40mm anti-tank guns needed more thorough investigation.

While Britain was listing the problem areas for further investigation, the Luftwaffe and Soviet Air Force were already using cluster bombs that released anti-personnel and armour-piercing weapons. The Soviet Union was about to introduce the PTAB hollow-charge, anti-tank bomb, which weighed just 2.5kg, was effective against the heaviest German tanks and could be carried in large numbers by ground attack planes. Britain's bomb expertise tended to go into developing much larger, specialist bombs for more distant strategic targets – the dam-buster bouncing bombs, the 12,000lb

Tallboy and 22,000lb Grand Slam 'earthquake' bombs. It was only by chance that Britain had developed any innovative tactical air-to-ground weapons. Both the 3-inch rocket projectile and the 40mm cannon had been designed to shoot down bombers.

Darwin's report was seen by the War Office Directorate of Research as a useful basis for further planning and research. It was, however, much easier to deal with the technical aspects raised than the more fundamental problem of Air Ministry attitudes.

> The R.A.F., unlike the G.A.F. was never designed primarily for supporting the Army: it designed itself, in fact, to get away from the Army ... . RAF doctrine, *esprit de corps*, functional design, and development are all inherently almost opposed to Operational Co-operation other than the strictly limited form of it undertaken by Army Co-operation Command.[52]

On the face of it, this might seem like yet another scathing Army criticism of the Air Ministry, but the writer emphasised that it was not meant in that way; it was more a statement of a problem that needed to be addressed by both War Office and Air Ministry. The note went on to explain that the Air Ministry and RAF had been created specifically to develop the bomber method of waging war, so it was unreasonable to expect it to be anything other than a strategically orientated force. It was no good the War Office complaining about ineffective air support when the RAF lacked the tools and training. A firm but understanding hand was required if the Air Force was to be guided in the right direction. It was up to the War Office to explain clearly what it wanted and what it expected from the RAF in order to win the war on land, 'for the war must be won on land and the only certain method of winning it is by the destruction of the enemies' land forces by the Allied Armies on the ground'. This meant enveloping and destroying the enemy rather than just pushing them back and to do this the Army needed the Air Force to work closely with ground forces, not just give chase to a retreating enemy. Clearly there were questions here both the Army and Air Force needed to address.

The War Office studies that followed the Darwin report demonstrated that in many areas there was surprisingly little disagreement in the thinking of the two services. In the preparatory phase before a battle, gaining air superiority was the top priority. The offensive against German industry was crucial; attacking lines of communication to the front line was very useful. Nevertheless, the War Office emphasised, however successful these operations were, they could never prevent large, well-equipped enemy forces entering the battle. This was, as Darwin's report emphasised, when 'air and ground forces must be concentrated at the decisive point to achieve success'. Indeed, the War Office believed this contribution would always have more effect on the final outcome than all the air operations that preceded the battle. 'Surely it would be illogical if, after all the preparatory work, the Royal Air Force were not to complete it by a culminating contribution of all their resources on the battlefield.'[53] It was this crowning contribution that the Air Ministry was reluctant to involve the Air Force in.

The War Office also emphasised the need for flexibility. Air superiority could not be an absolute prerequisite for action on land. The struggle for air superiority might still be raging after the battle on the ground had begun. Again, the prime objective of winning the struggle on land had to be kept in mind. If the land battle was at a critical phase, switching fighters from the air superiority role to supporting the Army directly might well prove decisive. This was what the Desert Air Force had become so good at, but it was the sort of flexibility air force commanders increasingly seemed to want to distance themselves from.

The apparent spirit of collaboration between Montgomery and Coningham expressed in Algiers was the cause of much optimism within the War Office. Taking to heart Montgomery's and Coningham's words, there was talk of the need to go further than co-operation. Total integration was required at every level; the two forces should be 'perpetually uniting as one', always an uncomfortable concept for an Air Ministry anxious to maintain its independence.[54]

The Spartan exercise held in March 1943 was an attempt to create this unity. It was the first large-scale attempt to replicate a future land battle on the continent. It involved a 'Southland' force representing the Allies attempting to regain territory captured by the German 'Eastland' force. The 'Southland' force had a composite 'Z Group' with all the fighter, fighter-bomber, light-bomber and reconnaissance squadrons. It was seen as a very temporary arrangement, as its name suggested, and the Air Ministry planned to disband the group as soon as the exercise was over. However, the trials demonstrated this was precisely what was required. It was scarcely a revelation; it was no more than a mini-Desert Air Force. The performance of the Group reinforced the message that the tactical air elements supporting a cross-Channel invasion had to be under a single command and the final organisation of the force that would accompany the Army, once established on the continent, had to be the same as the organisation for the initial Channel crossing. The success of the trials persuaded Portal to keep 'Z Group', the formation acquiring the more permanent title of No. 83 Group. It would contain all the tactical elements apart from the light bombers which continued to be in No. 2 Group. Initially, Portal was able to ensure No. 83 Group was part of Fighter Command, rather than Army Co-operation Command, but the creation of a separate tactical entity within the RAF was now just a matter of time.

The Air Ministry still felt the struggle with the War Office was going its way. Tedder noted joyously how Montgomery's pronouncements in Algiers that an Army commander should not seek to command the Air Force had whipped the carpet from under Brooke's feet. The sense of triumph stemmed from a paranoid Air Force belief that the struggle was all about defeating a War Office plot to take over the RAF. Such a plot only existed in the fanciful minds of the Air Staff. There are plenty of instances where Brooke mentions the possibility of an Army Air Arm, but this was more out of despair than any furtive, devious scheming.

The only control the Army wanted was to make sure squadrons were not whipped away for some other purpose in the middle of a battle. The War Office had never had any objections to Army Co-operation Command being commanded by an RAF officer. Clearly the squadrons in the Command had to be permanently available to the Army and do what the Army wanted, otherwise there was no point in having the Command. This was precisely why the Air Ministry did not want the Command and they most certainly did not want Barratt running it. He was far too willing to give the Army what it wanted.

The creation of No. 83 Group gave the War Office essentially what it was asking for in terms of organisation, with all the tactical elements (ground attack, fighter and reconnaissance) in a single formation. Fighter Command would be a very temporary home for this and No. 2 Group, but it would not be moving to the much despised, in Air Ministry circles at least, Army Co-operation Command. Much to the joy of the Air Ministry, it finally succeeded in getting this Command abolished and its commander Barratt banished. In its place there would be a new Tactical Air Force under Air Marshal John d'Albiac, formerly the commander of No. 2 Group. Barratt's Senior Air Staff Officer, Colonel Woodal, would also soon get his marching orders. He returned to the War Office and an air force officer took his place.

It was essentially a restructuring whose main purpose was to satisfy the Air Ministry's desire to see Army Co-operation Command abolished and its incorrigible commander removed. Having given the tactical formation a new name, it took up residence in the same offices at Bracknell that had been used by Army Co-operation Command with the same support staff.[55] Initially, it would just have the tactical and strategic photo-reconnaissance aircraft, together with the Auster artillery observation planes, but as soon as the commanders for the Allied Expeditionary Force were appointed, the tactical squadrons would detach themselves from No. 11 Group. Although the force would be commanded by an air force officer, it would be under the supreme commander of the Allied invasion force. It was essentially the Desert Air Force model.

In North Africa, the units supporting the Army had been combined into Tedder's 'Tactical Air Force' and this now became the First Tactical Air Force. Tactical air units in the United Kingdom would become the Second Tactical Air Force with similar squadrons in Burma forming the Third Tactical Air Force. In fact, in the Far East and North Africa, this was just a new name for organisations that were already up and running. The terms First and Third Tactical Air Forces were scarcely needed or used. In the United Kingdom bubble it was a revolution – a tactical command dedicated to the task of supporting the UK-based army with fighter, bomber and reconnaissance aircraft. In Britain the name was much needed and used, to emphasise its role and distinguish it from the strategic elements of the RAF.

It had been a long time coming. It was the force Britain had always needed: defensively to deal with a German invasion, offensively to support an Allied invasion. Finally, in June 1943, three years after the essentially similar BAFF (British Air Forces in France) had been disbanded, it was agreed that the army in Britain needed a specialised tactical air force to support it. It was far from a complete victory for the War Office. It had lost their trusted ally Barratt. The Air Ministry had installed its preferred commanders whom it expected to adhere more closely to Air Staff principles. There was still no guarantee the Army would get the sort of support it needed.

No. 83 Group would support the British forces involved in the invasion. It would be commanded by Air Vice-Marshal William Dickson who, in early 1942, had been involved in some of the early planning for a cross-Channel invasion. No. 84 Group would be formed to support the Canadian element of the invasion force. The new group would be commanded by Air Vice-Marshal Leslie Brown, who had commanded tactical air units in the Western Desert and Commonwealth units in the invasion of Syria. Each of these groups was to build up to a strength of eighteen fighter and eight fighter-bomber squadrons. However, this tactical air force continued to evolve at a sedate pace. It would be November 1943 before the Second Tactical Air Force parted company with No. 11 Group and became an independent formation.

Once the organisation was up and running, there would still be much work to do to turn these squadrons into an effective tactical force. The Spartan exercise had demonstrated how unprepared the Air Force was for its new role. With RAF squadrons used to operating from permanent airfields with all the associated facilities and home comforts, it was scarcely a force ready for fast-moving tactical operations. The RAF had to get back to the mobility it possessed in the First World War or even the mobility possessed by the BAFF in the 1940 French campaign. The RAF in the United Kingdom had to start learning what the RAF overseas was already doing. If squadrons were to become truly mobile, air and ground crews had to get used to living under canvas if necessary. The summer of 1943 was lamentably late in the day to be starting this process.

Despite the clear priority the strategic bomber forces were getting, in terms of materiel the Allied air forces in the UK were not too badly placed to support an invasion in the summer of 1943. Many of the available aircraft were not ideal, but the Soviets, and indeed Allied commanders overseas, would argue that things rarely are ideal in war. The skies would have been far more fiercely defended than they would be a year later, but there is no reason to believe that the Allied air forces lacked the air strength to be as successful in defending an invasion of France as they had been in protecting the Allied landings in Sicily.

What was lacking was the organisation and, more importantly, the mindset to use what was available to provide the support the Army would require. There is little to suggest the UK-based commanders were any closer to being ready to use air resources any more flexibly than they had at Dieppe in 1942. Indeed, in 1943 there was less interest in close air support than there had been the previous year. The RAF still wanted to remain a separate entity rather than become an integral element of the British armed forces.

In the end, invading France in 1943 was never seriously considered. Indeed the idea had received more serious consideration in 1942. All three services were in agreement. Brooke did not want an invasion until the German armed forces had been seriously weakened by bombing. He was not even sure it could succeed in 1944. Portal still hoped bombing could win the war outright. The Admiralty was nervous about taking its capital ships close to enemy coastlines. No one on the British side wanted an invasion of France in 1943.

With hindsight we know that there were no catastrophic consequences as a result of the delay, but it was a dangerous game to play. The German defeat at Stalingrad had been followed by a remarkable German recovery with the Soviet Army suffering a resounding defeat around Kharkov in the spring of 1943. In the summer of 1943, the German forces gathering for the Kursk offensive were still formidable and a German victory was still possible. If Germany had succeeded in knocking the Soviet Union out of the war in 1943, the failure to strike while Germany was still occupied on her Eastern Front could have proven to be a very costly mistake. Even in 1943, with the Eastern Front secure, delaying the invasion could still have had fatal consequences. German coastal fortifications were still largely focused on defending the major ports. In the autumn of 1943, War Office intelligence noted a sharp increase in the effort going into defences along the entire coastline. In November Rommel was put in charge. By 1944 there would be considerably more substance to the Atlantic Wall.

For the Air Staff, however, everything was falling neatly into place. The strategic air offensive would get the extra time it needed to see if the bomber really could win the war outright. The Air Ministry was still nailing its colours to the bomber mast. Enormous risks had been taken to keep the policy afloat. Harris had rescued the bomber strategy when the policy seemed doomed. He now had to prove it was worth rescuing and that it could win the war.

Chapter 14

The Bomber War

For the hard-line bomber advocates all the talk of an invasion of France had always been a frustrating distraction from the task of winning the bomber war. As far as they were concerned it had always been a bomber war and bombers would win it, not armies on the battlefield. The 1940–1941 Blitz was what modern wars were all about. By comparison, the crushing defeat of the Allied forces in France that preceded it and the bitter fighting in the Mediterranean, not to mention the titanic struggle on the Eastern Front that followed it, were sideshows whose principal relevance was their effect on the bomber war. For the bomber advocates, an invasion of France in 1944 was as irrelevant to the outcome of the bomber war as the defeat of France had been in 1940.

The realities of the war raging on four continents had forced Portal to take a less extreme view, but he was still a bomber man at heart and the Air Ministry he ran still had fighting the bomber war as its priority. The only task that came close to matching the importance of expanding the bomber fleet was preparing a defence against the German bomber fleet. Through the Air Ministry prism, the bombing of Guernica, Warsaw, Rotterdam, London and Coventry were all consistent with an enemy set on winning the war by bombing, and this was how Germany would attempt to defeat Britain once it had dealt with the distraction of the Eastern Front. The Air Ministry was not going to be lulled into any sense of false security by Luftwaffe inactivity on the western front. Britain was engaged in a life-or-death race with Germany to see who would be first to build the war-winning bomber fleet. An ever-increasing proportion of Britain's industrial capacity was being used to build the aircraft and ancillary equipment required. The country's leading scientists were hard at work developing the technology the bomber offensive and defence against the bomber needed. A massive Commonwealth training programme was providing the aircrews. Air Ministry minds were entirely focused on how the bomber war was to be won.

The decisive German attack might come by day or night. By day the fear was that enemy bombers, operating at altitudes the defending interceptors would not be able to reach, would pick off their targets at leisure. The excellent high-altitude performance of the jet engine seemed to provide the solution to this threat and Gloster was developing the Meteor.

Alternatively, the assault might come by night. Britain had already beaten off one assault, but the country had to be ready for the next attempt. Extraordinary effort was going into the technology that would make night-fighters more effective. The remarkable and highly secret cavity magnetron had reduced radar wavelength from several metres to just 10 centimetres. A 30-cm dish was now all that was required to focus these emissions and this could easily be mounted in the nose of an aircraft. Instead of the emitted rays flying in all directions from aerials, as happened with metric radar (where the wavelength was measured in metres rather than centimetres), all the energy could be directed in a beam, offering better range and precision. Also, with none of the stray reflections from the ground that plagued the earlier metric airborne radar systems, it worked well at low altitudes. Interim hand-built centimetric AI Mark VII sets were rushed to the squadrons, while factories tooled up for the production Mark VIII version. The TRE scientists, led by Bernard Lovell, were already working on the even more advanced AI Mark IX. This would allow the focused beam to detect and then lock on to the enemy plane, providing continuous and more precise information on speed and direction. There was already talk of feeding this information directly into an autopilot, allowing the fighter to close in on the enemy bomber entirely automatically.

AI Mark IX was at a very early stage of development, but Air Commodore William Helmore had come up with what was effectively a low-tech version of the same method, using a light beam instead of a radar beam. Metric AI radar in an unarmed Havoc would be good enough to find the approximate position of the bomber and a searchlight in the nose would then be used to illuminate the target. Two accompanying Hurricanes would then move in for the kill. There was enormous excitement about this so-called Turbinlite system. It was being hailed as a breakthrough in night-interception technique as big as radar itself and the project had an even higher priority than the introduction of centimetric radar. Attempts by General Arnold to acquire some examples of the Turbinlite system in 1941 were refused by Portal on the grounds that, as the United States was not in the war yet, American security would be bound to be lax. 'The loss of the Turbinlite secret would have a disastrous effect on our prospects of winning the war,' Portal melodramatically explained.[1]

In fact, there was no such danger. The entire Air Staff premise was wrong. Germany had its strategic bombing advocates who believed bombing could help win wars either by breaking enemy morale or wrecking their industries. However, mainstream pre-war German thinking had not seen bombing as the principal means of waging war. While Britain was developing the four-engined Stirling and Halifax, the Germans were cancelling their equivalent four-engined bomber programme (the Dornier Do 19 and Junkers Ju 89). The reasons were purely economic; the country could not afford to build these and the mechanised and tactical air forces it needed. The Blitz had given the German bomber advocates a chance to prove their case but, on the basis of what this had achieved, Hitler had concluded that 'you cannot defeat a country by just bombing its people'.[2]

Harris used Warsaw and Rotterdam as examples of Germany applying bomber theory, but both were tactical targets in the front line at the time they were devastated. They were not bombed instead of action on land, they were bombed to hasten the military defeat of the Polish and Dutch forces still holding out in these cities. Guernica, another much quoted example of the application of bomber theory, had also been a key communications centre just behind the front line. The town fell into Nationalist hands just days after the bombing. The land battles in France and the Soviet Union were how mainstream German thinking saw wars being decided. No serious attempt had been made to bomb either of these countries into defeat.

For all the Air Ministry concerns, when the German daylight high-altitude bombing offensive eventually materialised it amounted to no more than a handful of nuisance raids by Ju 86Rs. Bombs dropped from 40,000 feet rarely found their target. On 28 August 1942, one lucky hit killed forty-eight in Bristol but, tragic as this incident was, the high-altitude bombing attacks were not the war-deciding offensive the Air Ministry feared.

Still the Air Ministry was convinced that Britain was in a desperate bomber race with the enemy. The Baedeker raids were a reminder of what the Luftwaffe was capable of. In July 1942, a worried Sinclair informed Churchill that Bomber Command expansion plans were well behind schedule and the force was still lagging behind the German long-range bomber fleet in terms of numbers, although it was edging ahead in the tonnage it could deliver.[3] However, even this advantage might soon be lost, with fears the Germans were about to introduce a new generation of heavy bombers. To keep ahead of the Luftwaffe, the Air Ministry was willing to take a chance and order the four-engined, high-altitude Vickers Windsor off the drawing board.[4]

However, there was no race. As an act of deterrence, revenge or expediency, Hitler would not hesitate to bomb civilian targets. Nor was there any lack of ambition in German bomber development. The German Amerika-bomber programme, which led to the Me 264 and Junkers 390, was far more ambitious than any Air Ministry long-range bomber programmes. However, at this stage of the war there were no plans to build a large fleet of strategic bombers. Hitler, like his generals, believed the war would be decided on the battlefield.

So did General Marshall. However, he also believed the selective bombing of key industrial targets would improve the chances of winning battles on the ground and, unlike Britain and Germany, the United States did not have to make a choice; the United States had the resources to build navies, armies, tactical air forces and strategic bomber fleets. For Marshall, bombing was a useful additional tool: for his air force colleagues it was a lot more. The bomber offensive was an opportunity to demonstrate that air power could, on its own, trigger an enemy collapse. American bomber advocates liberally distributed Trenchard's thoughts on the subject to back their cause, although they were quick to distance themselves from the indiscriminate approach he favoured.[5] They may have had different ideas about how much could be gained from bombing but US Army and air force commanders could agree that the selective bombing of key elements of German industry had a vital role to play in winning the war.

Bomber Command had long since abandoned any such fancy notions. Harris saw no point in chasing well-defined, economically sensitive targets, the destruction of which, the economists claimed, would bring about the immediate collapse of Germany. These 'panacea' targets were, Harris believed, no more than the products of deluded minds and he made no attempt to hide his contempt for such thinking. When, late in 1942, the rather critical American assessments of Harris's indiscriminate approach found their way into British hands, the Americans were rather embarrassed.[6] They need not have worried. Harris would not have been in the least perturbed. He took pride in his approach. His aim was pure and simply the destruction of Germany, house by house, street by street and city by city until the will of the nation was broken. Morale was the target; any industrial targets destroyed in the process were just a bonus. Harris never took the argument beyond this point, or explained what process precisely would take Germany from destruction to surrender. Harris just believed it was self-evident that once every city was destroyed the war would be over.

Portal might not be as certain as Harris, but if Allied bombers ruled German skies, Germany cities and industry had been smashed and the German Army fatally weakened, the German leadership might well consider surrender was the only option left. If they did not, the eventual invasion of France might well just be the formal occupation of territory held by an already beaten enemy. Harris still believed, and Portal still hoped, that this was what would happen.

Despite the extra urgency the arrival of Harris injected into the British bombing campaign there was still very little evidence to suggest that the bomber could win the war. The thousand-bomber raid on Cologne had been a major triumph in terms of destruction dispensed, but two more attempts to reproduce this result did not meet with the same success. Essen was the target of the second effort on the night of 1/2 June 1942. Despite the use of instructors and partially trained crews the attacking force failed to reach the magic one-thousand mark. So disorientated did the attacking force become that the Germans were unaware a major raid had been launched. Scattered bombing was reported throughout the Ruhr; in Essen itself eleven houses were destroyed and fifteen people killed. Elsewhere, stray bombs killed around 200 civilians, but it was a remarkably poor return for close on 1,000 sorties, with the loss of thirty-one bombers and 200 aircrew.

In the third one-thousand bomber raid against Bremen on the night of 25/26 June, a more determined attempt was made to achieve the thousand figure. Blenheims, Bostons and Mosquitoes from No. 2 Group were drafted in. Churchill persuaded Coastal Command to make a contribution, with aircraft like the Hudson taking part. With its negligible bomb load, it was there just to make up the numbers. Even Army Co-operation Command supplied a handful of planes. The magic 1,000 figure was reached, 1,067 eventually setting off. The raid was not the success the Cologne operation had been, but the Germans were at least aware that Bremen had been the target.

If the results of the bombing were not always up to expectations, Harris could always fall back on the argument that the growing offensive was diverting German resources from the Eastern Front. The problem was that the effort going into creating this diversion was considerably greater than the diversion. In the final analysis, four-engined heavy bombers are far more expensive to build and man than the anti-aircraft guns and interceptors that shoot them down. Creating the equipment Bomber Command needed required more than half of the 1.5 million working in the aircraft industry.

Bomber Command employed 140,000 and required a massive training programme to keep up the flow of aircrews.[7]

Germany was having to devote ever more resources to defence. During the course of 1942, Reich anti-aircraft defences increased to some 7,300 guns, with the numbers employed in air defence rising by 100,000 to some 440,000.[8] Even so, the UK Anti-Aircraft Command had nearly 5,000 anti-aircraft guns, manned by 240,000 personnel.[9] Many involved in German air defence were over-age or under-age for front-line duties or, increasingly, women. It was not a human resource that could immediately reinforce the Eastern Front. In terms of fighter defence, Douglas was demanding 1,200 day fighters and 400 night-fighters to defend the United Kingdom and was getting most of what he wanted. By the end of 1942, German fighter defences in the west had risen to around 800 day and night-fighters and over 900 by May 1943, to deal with a much more serious threat.[10] It is debatable which of the opposing bomber threats was provoking the greater defensive effort.

In Britain the effort poured into air defence was caused by a primarily tactical Luftwaffe; Bomber Command on the other hand was a specialist strategic force. Factoring in the industrial and manpower effort involved in creating and maintaining Bomber Command, the Air Ministry's bomber offensive was diverting far more resources away from Allied forces fighting at sea and on land, in the Atlantic, Mediterranean and Far East than the German counter-measures were diverting from the Eastern Front. The British diversion tends to get ignored because it was chosen policy rather than forced on the country by the actions of an enemy. However, the fact that the diversion was self-inflicted did not make it any less significant. It was a contributing factor in the string of military defeats Britain had suffered. None of this was clear to the bomber advocates. They refused to see any connection between the problems British land and sea forces were having and the air resources the bomber war was sucking away from the land and sea battles they were fighting. Indeed, the hard-line bomber advocates saw it the other way round; the battles armies and navies were fighting were sucking resources away from their bomber offensive.

Many, however, found the diversion argument persuasive and it bought Harris more time. It was time Harris needed as it was not getting any easier for Bomber Command to deliver on the promises he had made. The introduction of GEE had resulted in a huge improvement in navigation, but the problem with any electronic aid was that the enemy would eventually jam it. The operational life of GEE was only expected to be six months and, sure enough, in August the jamming began. GEE was still useful for approaching and leaving German air space but over Germany itself it had very little value.

The next navigational system 'off the rank' was H2S which gave bomber crews a crude radar map of the ground below them. Technical problems with the system were delaying its entry into service and this gave those opposed to using the device, with its top secret cavity magnetron, over enemy territory time to marshal their arguments. Fighter Command night-fighters used centimetric radar and Royal Navy vessels were also already using it to spot U-boats. Coastal Command was about to get the naval version of H2S, ASV Mark III. If the cavity magnetron fell into enemy hands, the enemy would be able to develop counter-measures. Increasingly desperate self-destruct mechanisms were investigated, but the magnetron was bored out of solid copper and was very difficult to destroy. In any case, even if it worked, just the existence of a self-destruct system was bound to draw German attention to what it was trying to destroy and any self-destruct mechanism was bound to fail eventually. The controversy rumbled on into the autumn of 1942, but those opposing its introduction could make no progress. Indeed the development of H2S was given priority over the parallel naval ASV Mark III.

Meanwhile, the German defences continued to grow in effectiveness. In May, June and July 1942, the loss rate rose above the 4 per cent mark, hovering just below the 4.8 per cent of the previous November, which had been enough to suspend the offensive. It was only kept below the November 1941 level by the number of attacks against less well-defended targets in occupied Europe. Targets in Germany were attracting unsustainable heavier loss rates. On the night of 24/25 August, 7.1 per cent of the force attacking Frankfurt was lost. Three nights later, 10.1 per cent was lost in an attack on Kassel. On the next night, 14.5 per cent of the force attacking Nuremburg did not return. The average loss rate in August 1942 was 5.8 per cent, the highest monthly loss rate of the war so far. In six months from April to September, over 900 bombers failed to return from operations, more than twice the average front-line strength of the force. It was a loss rate that made it impossible for the force to expand as fast as Portal and Harris needed it to.

The heavy losses and lower than planned bomber production was fraying tempers. In October, Harris made another desperate appeal for the Middle East to return the bomber crews which his Operational Training Units had been turning out. Harris always considered these crews belonged to him rather than the RAF. He was merely lending them to other Commands and, in his view, the Middle East did not need them. It came at a time when Douglas was complaining about the fighter squadrons he was having to part with for the invasion of North-West Africa. In Egypt, Eighth Army needed air support to halt any further advance on Alexandria and drive Rommel back. For Britain, the impossibility of fighting a war on land and sea as well as building a strategic bomber force was becoming more apparent with each passing month.

The growing frustration was all too clear in Portal's stinging response to Harris. 'I do not regard your letter as either a credit to your intelligence or a contribution to the winning of the war,' he scolded. He suggested Harris take 'a rather broader view of the problems and difficulties confronting the Air Ministry and the other Commands.'[11] It was quite a ticking off, coming from someone who, during the Battle of France, had himself been in charge of Bomber Command and, like Harris, had done everything he could to ensure his bombers were used to bomb industrial targets in Germany rather than support Allied armies.[12] Portal was as convinced then as Harris was now that bombing Germany was the best way to support the troops on the ground.

Using bombers from other fronts to make good losses was not a sustainable solution. Somehow the loss rate had to be brought down. The only solutions seemed to be those that had been suggested and rejected countless times before. There were all the usual demands to reconsider heavier armament, with four-machine-gun dorsal turrets or cannon. The latter, with their high recoil, were no more practicable than they had ever been. Their introduction would require far sturdier and heavier aircraft structures. Heavier calibre machine guns or four-gun turrets were possible on existing aircraft but would reduce what the planes could carry. A four-gun dorsal turret would reduce Stirling and Lancaster bomb load by 500lb and the Halifax bomb load by 300lb.[13] Reduced bomb loads would make it even more difficult to achieve the bomb tonnage Portal believed was necessary to achieve decisive results. There were increasingly desperate Air Ministry efforts to persuade bomber crews that rifle-calibre machine guns were adequate to deal with cannon-armed night-fighters.[14]

The need to use older planes like the Wellington did not help. One-third of the forty-one Wellingtons employed in the 28/29 August Nuremburg raid were lost. However, even the new four-engined bombers were proving vulnerable. The proportion of these steadily increased during 1942, but this did not prevent losses rising. The Stirling and Halifax were proving particularly susceptible. The Stirling could not even fly high enough to avoid the worst of the German flak. The Halifaxes were not doing much better. From March to August the loss rate among the Halifax-equipped No. 4 Group was 6.2 per cent and squadrons had to be withdrawn from operations for the best part of a month to rest and refit.[15] The depressing conclusion was that 'the Stirling and probably the Halifax have not much more useful life in them'.[16]

The obvious solution was to switch Stirling and Halifax production to the Lancaster, but the switch-over would result in a catastrophic reduction in output. The MAP estimated that if the Stirling and Halifax were both abandoned in favour of the Lancaster, production would not recover until mid-1945. Nor were there enough Merlin XX engines to expand Lancaster production. The Stirling would have to go, but it would be replaced by a Hercules-powered version of the Lancaster. Any loss in production would have to be made good by ordering aircraft from the United States, a rather optimistic expectation given that the Americans wanted to build up their own bomber fleet as quickly as possible. However, Harris would not be satisfied until his entire bomber fleet was equipped with Merlin-powered Lancasters. It was an impossible demand that underlined the enormity of the task facing the Air Ministry and Bomber Command.

Whatever aircraft the squadrons were equipped with, they would never have the performance to evade German night-fighters. The Lancaster was an improvement on the Stirling and Halifax, and could carry more bombs further but was only marginally faster. Cruising at little more than 200 mph meant spending far too long in enemy air space. Bombers could make life difficult for the enemy by taking violent evasive action, but the crew needed to know the German fighter was there. The cover of darkness was very much a double-edged sword. It provided as much protection for the interceptor as it did for the bomber and, with radar, the night-fighters could see better.

Since the autumn of 1940, Bomber Command had been demanding that the radar technology night-fighters were using should be available to bomber crews to warn of approaching enemy fighters. This had led to the development of Monica, a rearward-pointing radar. Trials had taken place in December 1941 and these went sufficiently well for a recommendation to be made in January 1942 that it be fitted to all night bombers.[17] In March 1942, this became a priority, despite warnings from scientists that, as was the case with all devices that transmitted a signal, there was the danger that German night-fighters would lock on to the transmissions. Another system under development, Boozer, was safer in this respect. This picked up enemy radar transmissions and therefore did not betray its position but only warned that enemy fighters were in the approximate vicinity or ground-based radar was locking on to the bomber.

The Air Ministry was still hoping against hope that flak rather than night-fighters was the real problem. The Air Ministry had always preferred this explanation because it meant there was less point in increasing defensive armament at the expense of offensive bomb load. The fact that more bombers were returning home with flak damage rather than damage inflicted by night-fighters, was taken as evidence that, proportionally, flak was more of a threat. An alternative, and as it turned out correct, explanation was that bombers were more likely to survive a hit by anti-aircraft fire. Once a night-fighter made a contact with a bomber, the chances of the bomber surviving were slim. German night-fighters, equipped with *Lichtenstein BC* airborne radar, were indeed largely responsible for the increased losses.

There was an air of desperation about the simple instruction passed on to the scientists at the TRE. Their task was no less than to find a way of jamming the entire enemy radar early-warning and tracking system. There were two elements: the longer-range *Freya* early-warning stations and the more accurate shorter-range *Würzburg* stations. It seemed fairly straightforward to have some effect on the *Freya* radars. Transmitters in England and on board bombers were able to drown out the *Freya* emissions with electronic noise (Mandrel). This would in effect create an electronic smoke screen from which the bombers would emerge about 20 miles from the coast. This became operational in November 1942. *Würzburg* stations, however, seemed to be beyond the reach of electronic jamming.

At least the bombers seemed to be inflicting some serious damage to justify the losses being suffered. Photo-reconnaissance of targets revealed ever-increasing areas of flattened real estate and, although industry was not being specifically targeted, it seemed it must be suffering. The experts were convinced that the German economy was already seriously stretched by the demands of war and that any damage inflicted on industrial capacity must be having an effect. In fact, there was still considerable slack in the German economy and the production of non-essential items was still running at a relatively high level. The Air Ministry should also have been aware from Luftwaffe efforts that, immediately after an attack, a smashed factory looked like a complete write off but machine tools often survived and production was often underway again remarkably quickly. It was now the Germans' turn to be surprised. At Lübeck production was back to

80-90 per cent of capacity within a week. As for the global impact of the Allied bombing on the German economy, post-war studies would reveal that in 1942 the percentage effect on German armaments production at a national level was so small it was not measurable.[18]

Nor were there any signs that German morale was cracking. The savagery of the Lübeck raid shook the German leadership. However, once the initial shock had passed, German civilians showed every bit as much stoicism as their British counterparts had mustered during the Blitz. The bomber strategy had always relied on the belief that foreigners were less capable of taking hardship than Britons. In 1922, when Trenchard launched the policy Bomber Command was now pursuing, Lloyd George had doubted 'the wisdom of relying in so large a measure on the superiority of our race'.[19] It was still a poor basis for policy two decades later.

Harris, however, remained blissfully unaware of the futility of the task he had set himself. As far as he was concerned the momentum was with Bomber Command. New technology was being introduced which would make his bombing even more effective. The Lancaster bomber gave him a reliable means of delivering substantial bomb loads. Mandrel would help deal with German defensive efforts and Boozer would provide warning of attack.

Bombing accuracy was improving. On 20 December 1942 the Oboe blind-bombing marking system was used for the first time. Also by the end of the year H2S had overcome its technical problems. Coastal Command made a last-ditch effort to at least get sufficient delivered to enable the Command to take the U-boats by surprise and inflict a significant defeat on the enemy, before it was used over Germany. However, in December Churchill ruled that Bomber Command should begin using H2S before Coastal Command got any centimetric ASV Mark III sets.

Oboe, like GEE, relied on signals from the United Kingdom, so it could only be effective over western Germany. The H2S sets carried by bombers, however, were effective wherever the bombers were. Navigators would now have an image of the territory they were flying over, which, to the skilled operator at least, could provide the position of coastlines and built-up areas and other major geographical features. How long this would remain unaffected by German jamming was another matter; six months was considered the normal shelf-life for any jammable device. There were good and, as it turned out, justifiable reasons for believing H2S might last longer. Centimetric radar was so far in advance of anything the Germans had developed there was a good chance it would take German scientists some time to come up with ways of jamming it. Devising a device that could detect and home in on its signals might prove to be easier.

Harris was also encouraged by even more advanced projects in the pipeline. Blind-firing technology was on the way. AI Mark IX was not just capable of guiding the fighter to the bomber, it was hoped it would be accurate enough to take the plane into a firing position and decide when the guns should be fired. Defending RAF bombers was now a more urgent task than shooting down enemy bombers; Bomber Command gunners needed to be able to engage their unseen assailants, so TRE were told to focus their efforts on applying the principles of the system to develop a blind firing rear turret (codenamed Village Inn) for night bombers. Harris was expecting it to become operational in the first six months of 1944, with a cruder interim blind-firing system based on the metric Monica early-warning system perhaps arriving sooner.

In the meantime, equipment like Mandrel, Monica, Boozer, Oboe and H2S were enough to give Harris the belief that Bomber Command had the upper hand technically. Both Oboe and H2S were initially available in very small numbers and Oboe could only control one bomber at a time. To make best use of the available sets, it made sense to allow the best crews to use them. These could then mark the target for those following without these navigational aids. Harris was against the formation of elite formations in principle but was eventually forced to concede the point and No. 8 Group pathfinder force came into being.

Bomber Command had never had it so good. Ever more resources were going into bomber production. In terms of airframe weight, heavy and medium bomber production rose from half of the total weight of aircraft produced at the beginning of 1942 to two-thirds by the spring of 1943, with a rapidly increasing proportion of these bombers being four-engined.[20] Nobody could claim the bomber offensive was not being given every chance to succeed.

Early in 1943 the American Eighth Air Force carried out its first raid on a target inside Germany. How the two air forces should co-ordinate their efforts was one of the issues on the agenda at the January 1943 Casablanca conference. The different approaches and aims of the two air forces would generate some heated debate. Harris would not be there to put forward his views in person but Slessor accompanied Portal to the Casablanca conference in his role as Assistant Chief of Air Staff responsible for policy and he was the ideal delegate for Harris.

Before they departed Slessor had laid down his own views on the bomber issue. It was a powerful illustration of how the bomber strategy had re-asserted its grip on British policy in the preceding six months. No longer was Slessor suggesting that bombing was a fallback option, or that there should be any preparations for an invasion of France. Indeed, in his memoirs, Slessor would dismiss his views of just a few months before as an inexplicable aberration.[21] The Slessor of old had resurfaced and was in full cry. He lamented how the American Army, unlike their air force colleagues, 'find it almost impossible to think of Air Power as a war-winning factor in itself'.[22] The current muddled policy of trying to achieve victory by taking the offensive on land and in the air would just extend the war indefinitely and, Slessor feared, Britain would probably end up having to agree to an unsatisfactory compromise peace with Germany.

Abandoning the bomber strategy and focusing all effort on a victory on land was almost as unpromising, Slessor insisted. Assuming the Soviet Army was not defeated, a successful invasion of France 'before (underlined in the text) German industry and economic power was broken' would require thirty-five armoured divisions supported by eighty to one hundred infantry divisions, not to mention fleets of short- and long-range fighters and specialised ground attack planes. This prediction was about three times the number of divisions that would fight in Normandy. If the Soviet Union was defeated, this estimate would have to be 'vastly increased'. Even with these resources, Slessor doubted a landing would succeed. However, if all effort was put into creating a 6,000-strong fleet of heavy bombers to 'shatter' German industry, victory would soon follow, possibly in 1943, certainly in 1944. The return to Europe would be a simple policing operation.[23]

Portal was fully in tune with these conclusions. He told his fellow Chiefs of Staff that by the end of 1944, a four-to-six-thousand-strong Anglo-American bomber force could be dropping 90,000 tons of bombs on Germany each month. Using German results during the Blitz as a yardstick, 900,000 Germans would have been killed, a million seriously injured and twenty-five million rendered homeless. A third of German industry would be destroyed in the process and this would make an invasion of France 'practicable'. Indeed, so weakened would Germany be, it might only require 'relatively small land forces' to retake the occupied territories.[24]

At the Casablanca conference, Portal played down the possibility of a successful bombing offensive making a major military operation unnecessary and focused on selling the bomber strategy as just a necessary preliminary for successful ground operations. The question was how best the bomber could contribute. It was hardly surprising there was little agreement, given the differing attitudes in the two bomber forces. Harris had no intention of being part of any overall plan. Harris was not trying to make it easier for the Allied armies to win the war; he was still trying to win the war without the need for armies and so, in truth, was Portal.

Bomber policy was the last item on the Casablanca agenda. Slessor, just an observer at these proceedings, described how, on the last scheduled day of the conference, little progress could be made on how to integrate the British and American bombing policies and tempers were getting frayed. In the lunch break Slessor knocked up a compromise which listed the targets in order of priority. It described the role of the long-range bomber as 'the progressive reduction and dislocation of the German military, industrial and economic system and the undermining of the morale of the people to a point where their capacity for armed resistance was fatally weakened'. This essentially encompassed American plans for precision bombing to destroy industry and Harris's plans for area bombing to break German morale.

Priority was to go to U-boat construction yards, the German aircraft industry, transportation, oil and 'other targets in enemy war industry'. This left plenty of scope for Harris to attack what he liked. Wherever Harris bombed, there was bound to be some industry. To keep the army and naval commanders happy, Slessor conceded that 'If and when it is decided the Allied forces should re-enter the continent', air operations would focus on supporting the forces on land. With a few amendments Slessor's draft was accepted. One of the amendments was replacing 'If and when' with 'When'.

The bombing would just be a preparation, but the degree of destruction required to 'permit initiation of final combined operations on the Continent' was extraordinary. The expectation was that submarine construction could be reduced by 89 per cent, ball bearings by 76 per cent, bomber production by 65 per cent and fighter by 43 per cent. Fifty per cent of synthetic rubber production would also be destroyed as well as 'nearly all' tyre production. Insufficient data was available to make a realistic estimate of the percentage reduction in military transport production, but it was expected to be considerable.[25]

The preconditions for an invasion of France were extraordinary. The decimation of enemy industry was not a precondition for the amphibious assault on Sicily or the planned landings in Italy. It would not cross the mind of any Allied general, Soviet, British or American, even to suggest such stiff preconditions for taking the offensive on any other front. Elsewhere, the war would be fought as wars are always fought, with neither side waiting for the ideal circumstances and both sides doing the best they can with what is available. For the invasion of France it would be different.

The required level of destruction was scarcely any less ambitious than Harris's aim of achieving outright victory by bombing alone. If achieving these targets was really necessary before an invasion could go ahead then the operation might indeed never happen. The Germans were not aware of it, but the Allies were throwing their enemy a lifeline. As had happened in the Battle of Britain, relying on a pre-invasion bomber offensive simplified the task of the defending forces. If the Allies stuck to their policy, in order to delay or even prevent an invasion in the west, the Luftwaffe just had to make sure the Allied bombing offensive was not as effective as the Allies hoped. With its commitments on the Eastern Front, the Luftwaffe might struggle to meet the multiple needs of a German Army trying to repel an invading army in France, but it might be strong enough to defeat an invading bomber force with all the advantages of fighting over home territory.

The Casablanca directive was a victory for the bomber advocates. In truth, it was more a description of current policy rather than an instruction about how to proceed. It did not require Harris to change his approach in any way. However, in one way the conference was a setback for Harris's policy. One of the decisions made was that the Allies would demand unconditional surrender from its enemies. However heavily Harris's Bomber Command stick might beat the German people, there would be no carrot to encourage any thoughts of surrender. This would not have concerned Harris. He did not believe his strategy required any additional inducement.

The idea of the British bombing by night complementing American efforts by day gave the Allied campaign a superficial unity of purpose, but the reality was not so collaborative. It was more a competition between rival bomber forces with rival methods than a joint effort. Crucially, however, it had been established that without the bomber offensive, the war could not be won. Little more than twelve months before, Churchill's expectation of the bomber offensive was that it would be at best 'a seriously increasing annoyance'.[26] Now it was once more central to Allied victory.

On the night of 30/31 January, Harris was able to deploy the latest technical wizardry the scientists had come up with. The radar-mapping H2S was used for the first time on a raid on Hamburg. Three nights later, a Stirling carrying the device was shot down near Rotterdam and enough of the device survived for the Germans to learn that the British had mastered centimetric radar. A disconsolate Göring was horrified the enemy was so far ahead. 'I did hope that even if we were behind we could at least be in the same race,' he lamented.[27] German scientists immediately set to work on the passive receivers that could detect and home in on centimetric emissions.

As German scientists began unlocking the mysteries of centimetric radar, Harris was being prevented from making much use of it against targets in Germany. As much as Harris wanted to wage his own war against the German nation, the war raging across the globe continued to interfere with his plans. In the winter of 1942/3 the Allies were losing the Battle of the Atlantic. Convoy defences were struggling to deal with the U-boat wolfpacks operating from ports on the west coast of France and Bomber Command, and the US Eighth Air Force, were ordered to divert their efforts from Germany to the submarine bases. So great was the U-boat menace, a ban on the area bombing of built-up areas in occupied territories was lifted. French civilians were warned of the impending attacks in an attempt to keep casualties as low as possible. Eight area raids on Lorient in January and February were followed by three major raids in March on St Nazaire.

It was all to no avail. It soon become clear that, despite the general devastation in the surrounding town, the reinforced concrete U-boat pens remained intact. It was another reminder of the limitations of air attack. With Germany already considering underground bomb-proof factories, many more key targets might soon be beyond the reach of high explosives. The only consolation for Bomber Command was the lower losses inflicted by the relatively light defences the French ports had been provided with.

In March, the Air Staff called off the offensive and Harris was able to turn his bombers back on Germany. His first target was the Ruhr. The proximity of the target made it ideal for the shorter summer nights that were approaching. The Ruhr, with its permanent industrial haze, had always represented the most difficult of targets for Bomber Command and had been the scene of some of the most spectacular failures. Harris was determined to put this right and, with the target well within Oboe range, he believed he had the tools to do it.

The Battle of the Ruhr would last from March to July 1943. The series of raids began with an attack on Essen by some 442 bombers in which nearly 500 people were killed and over 3,000 houses destroyed. In the early stages of the campaign such heavy casualties were the exception rather than the rule. Civilian deaths in most raids ranged between 100 and 300. There were still some sensational failures. On 26/27 March, 455 bombers attacking Duisburg managed to destroy just fifteen houses and kill eleven people. In April results continued to be variable. Even in the successful raids it was not just German civilians who were suffering. On 14/15 April a raid on Stuttgart killed over 600, of whom 400 were French and Russian prisoners of war.

On the night of 16/17 May 1943, Lancasters of the specialist No. 617 Squadron destroyed the Möhne and Eder dams with Barnes Wallis's bouncing bombs. The Ruhr dams provided both power and water for Ruhr industries and were targets that had been attracting the attention of the Air Ministry since before the war.[28] Entire villages were washed away by the flooding that followed; the death toll reached 1,300, more than twice any previous raid. Two weeks later, on 29/30 May, a devastating raid on Wuppertal by over 700 bombers destroyed 1,000 acres of real estate and killed a staggering 4,000. In June, results continued to vary but the trend was clear. On four occasions, including a return to the already hard-hit Wuppertal, the death toll exceeded 1,000. On the night of 28/29 June, in a raid on Cologne, the death toll again exceeded 4,000. These were massive blows against the civil population and whether the German people could take it became a matter of grave concern for Hitler.

Energetic efforts to assist stricken cities did much to sustain morale. Mobile food kitchens, squads on standby to repair homes where possible and the rapid restoration of water and power supplies all helped sustain morale. Even so, as was the case in Britain, the fortitude of the population was remarkable. Despite the trauma and horror of bombing, there was little sign that Harris's attempt to break the German people was succeeding.

On the home front, however, Harris was succeeding. For the British public, the bombing of Germany was a very visual success. Newsreels were able to show cinema-goers dramatic footage of bombs raining down on the Ruhr and the explosions and fires below. Pictures of the smashed dams and the resultant flooding were particularly impressive. It all looked so easy. The government insisted that only military targets were being attacked and any civilian casualties in the vicinity of the target were just unfortunate. From the air, it looked like clinical destruction for minimum friendly casualties. On the ground it was as grim as, if not grimmer than, any other form of warfare, but this did not come over in the images. The dam-busters' raid was a brilliant example of daring and ingenuity that was bound to capture the imagination of the public. The RAF was having no difficulty winning the public relations war. However, bomber losses were steadily rising again: 4.5 per cent in April, 4.6 per cent in May, 4.7 per cent in June. It might look easy for the cheerful aircrews on cinema screens but the missions involved hours of numbing cold and constant fear.

By day, Eaker's VIII Bomber Command was also suffering heavy losses. The American day offensive against Germany seemed to get off to a reasonable start. The first target on German soil was the naval base at Wilhelmshaven, struck on 27 January 1943. Ninety-one bombers were despatched, fifty-five bombed the targets and only three were lost. However, losses were soon climbing. Although targets still did not require a deep penetration of German air space, American air force commanders were discovering that no matter how many guns a plane carried, bombers could not take on defending interceptors on equal terms. The true scale of the problem was concealed by the multiple claims made by gunners, all convinced that they were responsible for shooting down any fighter seen diving away. However, there was no concealing the number of bombers that were not making it back.

It was an unpleasant shock for Eaker and his bomber crews.

If the growth of the German fighter strength is not arrested quickly, it may become literally impossible to carry out the destruction planned and thus to create the conditions necessary for ultimate decisive action by our combined forces on the Continent.[29]

To get the bomber offensive back on track, the Pointblank Directive introduced the intermediate step of destroying the German fighter force before setting about the destruction of German industry.

This would not be achieved by Allied fighters. They had a part to play but, because of their limited range, they could only operate on the fringes. Nor at this time were there any plans to extend their range so that they could escort bombers all the way to their targets. The Americans were still convinced that once bombers were attacking in blocks of 200 they would overwhelm the defending interceptors. Air superiority would be achieved by bombing the key industries associated with fighter production. Futile attempts to intercept American bombers would only hasten the process. It was the bomber route to air superiority, which Billy Mitchell had preached in the United States and which had been the guiding principle behind Bomber Command's bombing strategy.

Initially, the American bomber force would not be strong enough to launch 200-strong bomber raids, but a start would be made on depleting the German fighter force by attacking targets within fighter escort range. During a second phase, from July to October 1943, the Eighth Air Force would have the numbers to penetrate unescorted deep inside German air space and these hammer blows would complete the destruction of the German fighter force. A third phase to January 1944 would see the bomber force turn its attention to the industrial targets outlined at the Casablanca conference. A fourth phase would see this process continue along with attacks on communications and other targets of immediate value to the invasion forces.[30]

The Pointblank directive was supposed to be applied by both air forces, but Harris made sure the final version of the directive emphasised the ultimate objective for Bomber Command remained the dislocation of German industry and 'the undermining of morale', as laid out in the Casablanca directive.[31] Harris could continue to make urban areas his primary target. As with all priorities his superiors came up with, if anyone questioned his targeting there would always be something related to fighter production in the areas he was bombing. There was not even the pretence that Bomber Command could defeat the German night-fighter force in combat. Since turning to night operations, the aim had been to avoid enemy fighters, not take them on and defeat them.

The photo-reconnaissance evidence might suggest Harris was winning but German armament production was still rising. Bombed factories were soon back in production, even if still roofless. Rather than build a new roof, black material below the height of the surrounding walls gave the impression of an abandoned factory to prying reconnaissance planes.[32] As in Britain, the bombing hastened the dispersion of industry. The breaching of the Möhne and Eder dams was every bit as devastating as it looked. Mines and factories were flooded and there was a loss of electricity and, just as significantly, water for the coking industry. However, the Eder dam was not particularly important and the Sorpe dam survived and continued to supply water and power. Water did have to be rationed until the dams were rebuilt but the Ruhr kept going. By September the dams were back in operation and things had returned to normal. The hope had been it would take the Germans years to recover from the raid. In fact it took months.

The speed of the recovery rather proved Harris's point. He had always insisted that precision bombing in general and the dam-busting raid in particular was a waste of time and effort. However, so successful was the attack on the dams, Harris had a partial change of heart. He allowed the specialist No. 617 Squadron to stay in existence to see what else could be achieved with precision bombing. For all the extraordinary precision and skill of the crews, the dams raid was by no means a surgical strike with no collateral damage. The result of the raid was still mass destruction and indiscriminate death; the 1,300 deaths included around 500 prisoners of war. It was the destruction caused rather than the precision employed which impressed Harris. In this respect this sort of operation fitted Harris's overall strategy perfectly.

The dam-busting raid underlined just how difficult it was for bombing to have a decisive influence on the course of the war. Economic systems are enormous beasts. There are too many ways of making good losses, too many alternative sources of supply. What can seem like devastating hammer blows to an economy can turn out to be just a major inconvenience in the overall scheme of things. This was particularly true of Harris's more indiscriminate approach where the overall levels of destruction were impressive but the effect on German industrial output was distinctly unimpressive.

Harris might be right in believing it was no good looking for panacea shortcuts; the entire beast would have to be fatally wounded but this was far more difficult than Harris imagined. There was no doubting the growing destructive capabilities of the Allied bomber fleet and it was beginning to have an effect. In the second quarter of 1943, German armaments production was still rising but, according to post-war surveys, for the first time it was not rising quite as fast as it would have done had there been no bombing. It was a small loss, less than one half of one per cent, but at least it was measurable.[33] Even so, it had taken three years of bombing to get this far. It was a very poor return on the enormous resources the country had invested in the bomber strategy over so many years, resources that might have been better employed elsewhere.

Harris believed he was doing much better than one half of one per cent. 'If we can keep this up it cannot fail to be lethal within a period of time which in my view will be surprisingly short,' he enthusiastically reported to Portal at the height of the Ruhr offensive.[34] By July Harris had decided that the Ruhr had been dealt with and he switched his attention to Hamburg, the second largest German city.

Chapter 15

Firestorm

Hamburg was outside Oboe range but it was on the coast and an ideal target for H2S to identify. Harris decided that the whole of Bomber Command would concentrate on this target until it was destroyed. The stakes were high. Hamburg required a deeper penetration of German air space than the Ruhr. The summer nights were still short and the German fighters were becoming ever more deadly.

One by one, the electronic counter-measures Harris had been relying on were proving disappointing. Mandrel did cause some initial confusion but the Germans soon countered by widening the range of frequencies being used and operators soon became adept at getting the best of their equipment by retuning. The bomber crews were aware that the Germans might be homing in on their transmissions, so continuous Mandrel jamming by any particular plane was unwise, which further reduced the overall effect. By July 1943 Mandrel had become so ineffective it was temporarily suspended. Boozer was also not as helpful as had been anticipated. The warning lights flashed on too often to be useful. Nor did a light going off necessarily mean the bomber had shaken off an enemy fighter; it could just be that the fighter had closed to visual range and had turned the radar off.[1] The rear-warning Monica radar also gave far too many false warnings as it picked up other bombers in the ever denser bomber stream.[2] Electronic wizardry was not proving to be the answer.

There was, though, a very simple, non-electronic means to jam enemy radar that had been known about and occasionally discussed since the very early days of radar research. Before the war, Lindemann had suggested that wires half the length of the wavelength radar was operating on would give similar reflections to aircraft and could make radar useless. Indeed there seemed to be no shortage of people with similar ideas. Even a lowly BBC engineer had contacted the Air Ministry with a suggestion that wire netting would interfere with radar emissions.[3] The TRE had, rather perversely, investigated the idea of RAF aircraft dropping silver strips to identify themselves as friendly. Lindemann suggested the navigational beams German bombers started using in 1940 might be upset by dropping metal strips into them. Somehow the possibility of using similar ideas to defeat the German radar defence system managed to get overlooked.

The possibility had, however, occurred to the crews of No. 148 Squadron in the Middle East. The Wellingtons of this squadron were engaged on gathering radio intelligence and the crews were convinced that the aerials their planes carried were attracting the attention of radar-guided flak. To confuse the enemy, the crew decided to drop metal strips. The idea was right but the number dropped was too small. The Germans did not notice and the accuracy of the German fire was unaffected. The Navy was also pondering the application of radar-generated decoys. In September 1941, the Admiralty Signals unit came up with a scheme whereby a balloon trailing chicken wire would be allowed to drift down the English Channel in the hope that German radar would identify it as a convoy and waste time looking for it.[4]

Robert Cockburn, Head of Counter Measures at TRE, got to hear about this scheme but again the full significance was not appreciated. Cockburn was working on a decoy system, Moonshine, which amplified and retransmitted German radar signals, allowing one aircraft to give the impression it was a large formation.[5] Cockburn's only interest in the Admiralty scheme was that it might interfere with his own plans. It was not until December 1941 that Cockburn suddenly remembered the Admiralty chicken-wire idea and realised that this could be used to confuse the German air defence system. TRE organised some trials in which 'precautions will be taken to avoid the course of experiments being observed by the enemy'.[6] Suddenly, security had become crucial. There was certainly no question of the Admiralty being allowed to give the Germans a public demonstration in the middle of the English Channel of a possible new jamming technique.

The trials proved surprisingly successful. Relatively small metal strips could produce a remarkably strong echo. It was cheap, simple and far more effective than any technologically sophisticated electronic alternative. Air Commodore Oswyn Lywood in the Signals Department was immediately impressed and thought the technique should be introduced without delay. Forty thousand metal strips would be required for each mission and they could even be dropped in the form of propaganda leaflets, thus disguising their real purpose, a rather optimistic expectation if they proved to be as effective as Lywood hoped.[7]

Indeed, it would be so obvious what the RAF was doing that the Luftwaffe would be bound to turn the technique on Britain. Lywood thought it wise to look into what effect metal strips would have on the British air defence system. The answer was mixed. RAF early-warning radars worked on much longer wavelengths and were therefore far less vulnerable. An equivalent German 'leaflet' would have to be 3–4 metres long![8] British anti-aircraft guns using centimetric radar would be more vulnerable. It was a question of balancing the offensive and defensive advantages and disadvantages.[9] It was believed German radar-guided flak was inflicting heavy losses on Bomber Command while German raids against the United Kingdom had been steadily declining in the second half of 1941 and at the beginning of 1942 had completely stopped. Existing German early-warning radar was very vulnerable. British radar was not. The case for using what had become known as Window seemed very strong.

In January 1942, Portal prepared a brief statement of the case for deploying Window for Tizard's RDF Policy sub-committee. (RDF or 'Radio Direction Finding' was still the official name for radar.) Portal expected approval to be a mere formality, but the committee felt that Portal's request was based on insufficient data and ordered comprehensive trials on the effects Window might have on British radar. Portal was not pleased. He insisted it was not Air Staff policy to refrain from using a device that might assist our bombers just because the enemy might use it in retaliation.[10] This might be an acceptable argument when the consequences might only be felt by military personnel, but it was not quite so persuasive if civilians of all ages suffered the consequences. It was even less persuasive at a time when the bomber offensive had been shown to be achieving very little.

With the air offensive struggling and temporarily on hold, Portal and the Air Staff were very much on the back foot and felt obliged to comply with Tizard's request. The trials carried out included using it against British airborne radar systems, something it had been assumed would not be a problem. It was believed that Window would only confuse ground-based radars, not short-range airborne equipment. In March 1942 rather perfunctory trials seemed to confirm this theory. A single batch of Window was ejected from a plane being pursued by a night-fighter equipped with metric AI Mark IV equipment. The rapidly decelerating metal strips did not have time to become sufficiently spread out to form a significant echo before the chasing night-fighter was through them. Centimetric radar (AI Mark VII and VIII) gave stronger readings but again trials revealed that the spoof readings rapidly disappeared as the fighter flew through the Window cloud.[11] There seemed to be no danger. It was even suggested that if a bomber released a series of bundles the effect would merely be to leave a trail for the radar-equipped fighter to follow. Indeed, so concerned did the Air Ministry become about this possibility that ways of launching the bundles ahead of RAF bombers were investigated.[12]

By March 1942 Air Ministry fortunes were on the rise. The Lübeck raid had demonstrated how destructive Bomber Command could be and the Air Staff were winning back Churchill's support. An emboldened Portal decided he could wait no longer. On 8 April 1942 Portal ruled that Harris could go ahead and deploy Window.[13] Tizard was not impressed by this unilateral decision. He pointed out that the committee had not reached a decision simply because it had not received any of the information it had asked for. Tizard wondered if Portal was fully aware of the repercussions of his decision. He doubted Window would make much difference to the bomber offensive. He claimed that most bombers shot down had been caught by searchlights and he did not think there was any convincing evidence that radar, rather than sound location, was being used to direct them. Portal was forced to back down and once again the decision to use Window was put on hold while Tizard's committee considered the matter.[14] The delay would prove crucial.

On 22 April 1942, Tizard's Radio Direction Finding Policy committee, presented with all the information, agreed with Portal that Window should be used. On the 28th Portal gave Harris the go ahead. The production process was by this time well advanced and the first batches of strips began arriving at bomber bases at the beginning of May. However, on the night of 23/24 April, as retaliation for the Lübeck raid, the Luftwaffe had launched the first of its Baedeker raids. As the targets chosen had little military or economic value and therefore fewer anti-aircraft defences and no barrage balloon cables to worry about, German bombers could bomb from as low as they liked. This was precisely where metric AI Mark IV did not work and the new centimetric AI sets did. With the civilian death toll rising rapidly and the first operational use of Window just days away, Lindemann intervened, insisting that insufficient research had been carried out to see precisely how vulnerable British centimetric radar might be. Bomber Command was hastily contacted and told to cancel any plans to use Window.[15]

Lindemann's suspicions that the Window/airborne-radar trials had not been sufficiently thorough proved correct. The initial trial had simply assumed a bomber being chased would eject a pack of metal foil as a decoy and releasing a series of bundles would only provide a trail for the fighter to follow. What the trials did not consider was the possibility of an entire bomber fleet dropping Window at regular intervals, as Bomber Command was planning to do. More trials were now ordered, this time run by Fighter Command to ensure nothing was overlooked.[16]

Initial trials seemed to confirm previous results. Metric radar would not be too badly affected but centimetric radars would suffer severely. Fighter Command, however, claimed that the length of strip being used was too short to affect the 1.5-metre AI Mark IV systems and ground-based radar. More trials took place with longer strips and, sure enough, the effects were catastrophic. The radar systems were paralysed. Metric AI Mark IV was badly affected, centimetric AI Mark VII and VIII were obliterated and the ground-based GCI stations that directed the night-fighters to their targets and early-warning radar were blanked out over large areas.[17] Douglas insisted using Window was out of the question; it had to be considered a secret that should be kept from the Germans at all costs, not something that should be scattered all over Germany. Despite these results, Portal still believed that, with American bomber forces arriving, the Allied bomber force was expanding faster than the German threat and Britain had more to gain than lose if both sets of defences were neutralised.

In terms of destruction and civilian casualties Portal's cold calculation was correct. Nevertheless, the Luftwaffe was still capable of delivering some telling blows. In response to the thousand-bomber raid on Cologne, the Luftwaffe could manage fewer than 100 sorties against Canterbury. Casualties were relatively low, just forty-three killed, but 20 per cent of the town was flattened. It was just enough to make the British think twice about using Window. The Luftwaffe was doing better than it imagined. A shadow bomber force, cobbled together from units normally engaged in more useful activities, was not just satisfying the German desire for revenge; it was delaying the introduction of Window.

By this time it was occurring to some that there might be no secret to keep. It had taken time for the British to appreciate how useful Window might be but, with hindsight, it all seemed so obvious that there was a growing conviction that the Germans must know about it. Even if they had not thought of it themselves, they would have had plenty of opportunities to hear about it. The previous May, Bomber Command had been on the point of deploying it. The Window strips had actually been delivered to airfields. It seemed inconceivable that aircrew had not got to hear about it, and speculated on what these strips were for. These were aircrew that by this time might well be prisoners in Germany. Loose talk from captured German airmen had been a priceless source of information for British intelligence officers in their investigations into German radio aids, and there was every reason to suppose British aircrew would be equally careless, especially as they were not even aware there was anything to keep secret.

In June 1942, the Air Ministry got to hear about the experiments No. 148 Squadron was carrying out in the Middle East and frantically issued orders that no further experiments should take place in any circumstances.[18] The idea was so simple that, to the horror of the Air Ministry, a *Daily Mirror* cartoonist had worked the concept into the exploits of his daredevil secret agent Buck Ryan. In his latest escapade, he had defeated a German attempt to conceal the landing of troops by confusing the defences with metal box kites pulled by cars. To some it seemed inconceivable the Germans did not know about it and, if they did and they were not using it, it must be because they feared the consequences on their own defence system. If so, then perhaps the RAF should start using it. The Germans had indeed known, since at least 1940, although, like the British, the full implications seemed to get overlooked. It was only trials much later in March 1943 that demonstrated the devastating effect on radar systems. Göring was so terrified that the British would discover the secret that any further trials were banned, lest news leak out.[19]

Lindemann fully supported Douglas's efforts to stop Window being used. Robert Watson-Watt, the British father of radar and the MAP's scientific adviser, also preached caution. Unless British scientists came up with an antidote, circumstances would have to be very special to justify its use. A major operation where Window might make the decisive difference between success and failure might be one justification or an alarming increase in RAF losses. At this time losses were indeed becoming alarming. Even the Air Ministry was beginning to concede that the radar-equipped night-fighter was now the principal enemy.

It was a stark choice. Either Bomber Command accepted heavy losses or Window was used and Fighter Command, and British civilians, would have to live with the consequences. The stakes for the bomber offensive were rising ever higher. Still the fear of a German knockout blow dominated British thinking. In the summer and autumn of 1942 the Red Army was fleeing towards Stalingrad and, if the Soviet Union were to collapse, the Luftwaffe would be able to turn its entire bomber might on the United Kingdom. It was decided to await developments on the Eastern Front before reconsidering the issue.[20]

This also gave the scientists more time to come up with possible counter-measures or at least something that would minimise the effects. It seemed no stone was being left unturned in the search for a solution. One possibility was that, given sufficient experience, operators would become much better at distinguishing between the real and spoof responses. Trials were conducted but the operators remained adamant that, no matter how much practice they had, they would never be able to distinguish.[21] It was perhaps a predictable response when nothing was at stake. Under the pressure of dealing with actual raids, radar operators of all nationalities became remarkably skilled at filtering out interference.

Any system that did not use airborne radar, or at least not the centimetric version, would be the ideal solution. Helmore's Turbinlite searchlight system was one such method. Even before the Window question arose, it was already thought of as a major advance in air defence technology. If the air defence of the UK could be built around the less vulnerable metric AI Mark IV and searchlight combination, it might be even more valuable. At the beginning of 1942 it was planned to have ten of Fighter Command's twenty-five night-fighter squadrons equipped with the Hurricane and Turbinlite Havocs. Confidence in the system was so high that the operational debut of the combination was delayed until a worthy German raid justified revealing the secret. Hitler's Baedeker raids provided the justification and the weapon was unleashed on the German bomber force.

It is surprising that there was so much faith in a method that seemed intrinsically rather complicated, and so it proved in combat. The batteries aboard the Havoc could only keep the searchlight going for a couple of minutes and it was far too easy for the German bombers to jink out of the narrow beam. The Hurricanes that accompanied the Havoc just got in each other's way when trying to take advantage of any bombers that were briefly caught.[22] So much had been expected from the system, and so much hope that it would allow Window to be used that it was not until the end of 1942 that the Air Ministry could bring itself to abandon the Turbinlite experiment.[23]

Ever more desperate alternatives to centimetric air defence were considered. It was suggested that Fighter Command might return to using sound location as the primary means of tracking bombers. Douglas began training operators just in case.[24] The next generation AI Mark IX Bernard Lovell and his team were working on was another possibility. It was argued the lock-on capability might make it easier to distinguish between the target and the Window cloud. Serious work on AI Mark IX had begun in the spring of 1941 and initially progress was rapid. A ground-based lock-on capability was functioning by May 1941 and there was talk of having fifty Beaufighters in service with the radar by the end of the year.[25] However, airborne trials did not go so well. Then the Butt report forced all effort to be focused on improving navigational aids for the bombers and Lovell was transferred to the H2S programme.[26] The Village Inn blind-firing turret system also had a higher priority.

The AI Mark IX programme recovered some of its priority when it was realised it might be able to deal with Window and, by October 1942, the equipment was successfully locking on to targets at a range of 5 miles. Tests with an AI Mark IX equipped Beaufighter attempting to deal with an opponent dropping Window began in December 1942 from Coltishall airfield in Norfolk. Initial tests were not promising, the radar preferring to lock on to the Window cloud rather than the plane releasing the Window. Dr Arthur Downing, who had taken over from Lovell, came up with some modifications which he hoped would solve the problem and further trials, with Downing on board, were set for 23 December.

It was perhaps not the wisest decision to test the new AI Mark IX first at Christchurch, near the TRE centre at Swanage, and later at Coltishall, both of which were in the front line of the United Kingdom's air defence system. The accident waiting to happen occurred on 23 December when Spitfires intercepted and shot down the Beaufighter, destroying its prototype AI Mark IX and killing Downing.[27] This tragedy effectively ended all hope of AI Mark IX arriving in time to resolve the Window dilemma. With no antidote to Window and the situation on the Eastern Front still not clear, its use remained on hold.

Harris did not seem too concerned by the delays and rarely attended conferences on the matter. With the longer winter nights, bomber losses were dropping and Harris was perfectly happy with the radar counter-measures being introduced.[28] However, in the spring of 1943, as these electronic-jamming devices proved increasingly ineffective and the shortening nights increased the vulnerability of his bombers, Harris needed alternative ways of protecting his crews if they were to strike deep inside Germany.

When Portal re-opened the Window debate in April 1943 all the arguments for not using Window had disappeared. The Luftwaffe was reduced to small-scale hit-and-run raids against the United Kingdom. With the defeat at Stalingrad, German armies were in full retreat, so there was no immediate prospect of a Luftwaffe revival in the west. There was also a new American airborne radar that seemed to offer hope that air defences would be able to cope if the Luftwaffe started using Window. The new centimetric SCR 720, the American equivalent of AI Mark VIII, seemed far less sensitive to Window jamming.[29] There were also plenty of sets available. The radar was in production but the fighter the radar was intended for, the Northrop P-61, was behind schedule, so the Americans had radar sets to spare. The first fifty were expected in the summer of 1943 with 200 by January 1944. This would become AI Mark X in British service. There were also still hopes that Britain's AI Mark IX would eventually provide an even better solution.[30]

By early 1943 it was known that the *Lichtenstein* airborne radar operated on more or less the same wavelength as the *Würzburg* ground radars, so the same length Window would disrupt both. With losses rising, it was time to play the Window card. Once again Harris was given the go-ahead, although not until after the invasion of Sicily, just in case the Germans had their own Window standing by, ready to disrupt Allied radar during the landings. It would, however, be available for his proposed assault on Hamburg.

Window was used for the first time on the night of 24/25 July 1943 as 791 bombers headed for the ill-fated city of Hamburg. The bundles of aluminium the bombers dropped had the desired effect. The confusion in the German air defence system was total. Ground controllers saw their screens filled with uncountable echoes. Airborne operators suddenly saw their target subdivide into many targets. The frustration was very apparent to the RAF personnel eavesdropping on German radio channels. No previous counter-measure had produced anything like this scale of confusion. Only twelve aircraft were lost, just 1.5 per cent of the attacking force. Window had worked. Over 2,000 tons of bombs were dropped in fifty minutes. Damage was extensive with some 1,500 civilians killed. It was not the first time casualties had been so high, but it was still relatively rare. Unfortunately for the citizens of Hamburg, it was just a foretaste of what was to come.

One hundred USAAF Fortresses bombed the Hamburg submarine construction yards on the afternoon of the 25th. However, it was the return of 787 RAF bombers three nights later that proved decisive. Again accuracy was high and several major fires were started. The weather had been very hot; there had been no rain for some time and water levels were low. Most of the fire appliances were still in other parts of the city dampening down areas struck by the first raid which, it was feared, might still re-ignite. The new fires rapidly expanded in the tinder-dry suburbs, joining to become one huge conflagration. An entirely new phenomenon emerged as the updraft of the fire caused a chimney effect. Air was sucked in to feed the fire and, as the heat grew more intense, so the air was sucked ever faster into the base of the rising column of hot air. Wind speeds eventually reached hurricane strength. Burning timbers were swept along streets like matchsticks. Roofs were torn off buildings, exposing more flammable objects for the falling incendiaries. The air became too hot to breathe. The central column of smoke rose to 20,000 feet. It was like an atomic bomb in slow motion. It was probably not the first time it had happened; the phenomenon may have occurred on a smaller scale in the Wuppertal bombing. However, this was on a completely different scale. Bomber Command had created its first firestorm.

Those sheltering in cellars escaped the effects of bomb blasts and fire, only to be suffocated as the oxygen was sucked from the air. Those who fled their shelters faced sheets of flame swept along by unimaginable winds. In the aftermath it was impossible to count how many died. Bodies were fused together in the heat or reduced to piles of ashes. The death toll probably reached a staggering 40,000, an unprecedented number of casualties. This was far worse than any of the pre-war scaremongering predictions. The bombers returned for a third time two days later causing devastation in the so far untouched northern and north-eastern suburbs and, though once again there were many fires, there was no firestorm. A fourth RAF raid was mercifully defeated by the weather.

Bomber Command could be well pleased with its work. Ten kilotons of bombs had been dropped on the city and photographic reconnaissance revealed 61 per cent of living accommodation in Hamburg had been destroyed. This time, however, the true scale of the disaster facing the Germans could not be fully appreciated from the photos of devastation. For once Bomber Command was underestimating the impact of a raid. Word of the disaster soon spread as refugees fleeing from the stricken city passed on the horrors of what had happened. Lübeck had caused indignation, the bombing of the Ruhr concern, but Hamburg shook the German military/ political leadership to its core. A large part of a major city had been wiped out. Albert Speer, responsible for military production, warned Hitler that six such similar attacks would bring Germany's armaments to a total halt.[31] Erhard Milch, in charge of aircraft production, believed more such raids would result in German workers throughout the country downing their tools.[32]

Hitler fumed that the only way to deal with terror was terror and ordered more reprisals, but the makeshift bomber forces the Luftwaffe could assemble were never going to match the fleet of dedicated heavy bombers the Allies were now pouring such huge resources into building. Seventy-one bombers attacked Plymouth on the night of 11/12 August, ninety-one hit Portsmouth four nights later and eighty-eight bombed Lincoln on the night of the 17/18th.[33] In the month, a total of just 300 sorties were flown over the United Kingdom.[34] In the same month Bomber Command flew nearly 8,000 sorties.[35] The German effort was sufficient for the German propaganda machine to claim retribution had been delivered, but that was all. Nor were German losses light. In the raid on Lincoln the defences accounted for eleven of the attackers, bringing the total to seventeen in the three attacks. There would be no more German raids until October.

However, Hitler now demanded that a concerted attempt should be made by the Luftwaffe to deliver a retaliatory offensive against London. In May 1940, Dowding had hoped bombing the Ruhr would force the Germans to switch the Luftwaffe from supporting the German Army in France to bombing British cities. Bomber Command could finally claim the tactic was working. Germany was being drawn into a pointless battle, wasting its resources on a struggle it could not win and one that could have no effect on the course of the war.

There was, however, no need to rely on conventional bombers. If all that was required was indiscriminate retaliation, then highly trained aircrews were not necessary to deliver it. As well as a manned bomber offensive, Hitler ordered development of the Fieseler Fi 103 flying bomb and von Braun's A-4 ballistic missile to be speeded up. Indeed, the day following the first Hamburg attack, Hitler signed an order for the mass production of the A-4 rocket.[36] Industrial as well as operational resources would now be poured into the effort to retaliate. It was a policy Germany could not afford to embark on although, in truth, even with the high technology A-4 project, it was still a small proportion of German resources compared to the huge proportion of British manpower, material resources and scientific effort that had been sunk into Bomber Command's offensive over many years.

British intelligence already had an idea of how Germany intended to strike back. Through the eyes of the Air Ministry and Arthur Harris the Germans were trying to match the RAF's bomber strategy with the next generation of indiscriminate weapons. Germany's political leaders might have placed great hope in the war-winning potential of indiscriminate unguided missiles – politicians of all nationalities tend to be far more impressed by weapons of mass destruction than the military – but few in German military circles held out such hopes. The names given to these new weapons perhaps indicated a more realistic appreciation of their value. They were not 'War Winners', they were Revenge Weapons 1 and 2. Revenge did not win wars but, as Britain had found during the Blitz, the ability to hit back helped maintain morale on the home front and it was a very spectacular way of hitting back. Harris would have approved and indeed in his post-war memoirs had no doubt these were the war-winning weapons of the future.[37]

Long-range indiscriminate bombing by any method was not going to win a war. As shocking as Hamburg was, it did not, as the Germans feared in the immediate aftermath, bring their country any closer to defeat. Despite the unprecedented loss of life and devastation there was no uprising against the government, no desire to surrender. The methods the Allies were using scarcely encouraged any soul-searching about the rights and wrongs of the policies of their own regime. Once again the authorities were astonished by the speed with which Hamburg returned to a degree of normality. The most devastated areas remained cordoned off for the rest of the war but, where the damage was manageable, some sort of order returned. Once again, and indeed even more dramatically than in the Blitz, the ability of society to maintain its cohesion in the face of such a traumatising catastrophe, would have astounded the pre-war bomber theorists. In restoring services, armaments production had priority; workers drifted back and production resumed. Output dropped by half in the month following the attack but then steadily rose, with key armament industries eventually returning to full output. The speed of the recovery astonished Speer.[38] The loss of life had been unprecedented, but the blow had not been fatal.

Harris did not know it but in July 1943 he lost his battle with the German people. An unusual combination of circumstances had enabled Bomber Command to deliver a scale of destruction that not even the Dresden raid in the closing stages of the war could match. Hamburg was not a success Bomber Command could reproduce at will. Despite the fears of German leaders, the people were able to pull through. It could get no worse; the German people had weathered the storm. The future was grim, more death and destruction was inevitable but, as had happened in London, Coventry and other towns and cities, in the war between the people and the bomber, the bomber had lost.

Once again the words of Alfred Mond come to mind. In 1909 the Zeppelin seemed to be heralding a new terrifying era of wars decided by indiscriminate mass destruction. The prospect provoked heated debate in Parliament. The Liberal MP attempted to calm his agitated colleagues by assuring them that 'No nation would make peace because the enemy was killing civilians'.[39] Mond could not have imagined the horrors of Hamburg, but he was right. Trenchard, Harris and Portal were wrong.

Harris still believed he was on the brink of victory. Window seemed to have provided a way of delivering mass destruction without suffering heavy losses However, as spectacularly successful as the introduction of Window had been, losses were soon rising once more. Indeed, the catastrophic effects proved surprisingly short-lived.

Even before the introduction of Window, the Germans had been considering alternatives to the rather tightly controlled system they used to direct individual fighters to particular bombers. There would always be a limit to the number of fighters the ground controllers could direct to targets, especially with the bombers arriving in a narrow stream that swamped the defence sector they were passing over. Above the burning cities there was no need for radar; the bombers were silhouetted by the fires raging below. On cloudy nights, searchlights could be used to add to the glow by lighting up the clouds, exposing the bombers to the fighters flying above them. Single-seater fighters could be used for these interceptions. Coincidentally, this was tried out for the first time during the first Hamburg raid.

The RAF bomber streams were now so densely packed with bombers, and with Window if anything even more clearly defined that, instead of directing fighters to a particular bomber, the ground controller provided a running commentary on the direction the bomber stream was taking and fed fighters into it. Once in the stream an RAF bomber would not be too far away. This was a tactic already being used in the second assault on Hamburg.[40] After suffering a 1.5 per cent loss rate on the first Hamburg raid, losses rose to 2.2 per cent on the second, 3.6 per cent on the third and 4.1 per cent on the fourth.

Nor was Window an insuperable problem for radar. On the very first night some radar operators were already picking out the bomber, which remained fairly stationary relative to the chasing fighter, from the decelerating metal strips which the night-fighter closed in on very quickly. German scientists may have been forbidden from conducting any trials but it did not stop them from thinking about the problem and coming up with possible solutions. One approach, which did not seem to attract much attention among their British counterparts, was to exploit the Doppler effect.

Radio waves bouncing off objects moving at different speeds will have different frequencies and filtering out the reflections from the slow-moving Window made it easier for radar operators.

Within three days of the Hamburg raid some basic anti-jamming aids based on the Doppler effect had been developed for the ground-based *Würzburg* radars.[41] It was not ideal; it was complicated to use and reduced range, but it lessened the advantage Window had temporarily given Bomber Command. Varying the wavelength also helped mitigate the effects of Window and, from August 1943, German radars were suitably modified. To be fully effective, the British had to know the wavelength the Luftwaffe was using. For short-range radars this involved clever guesswork, dangerous intelligence gathering in enemy air space or, best of all, the equipment fortuitously falling into friendly hands.

By the time Window was used, the British had found out all they needed to know about *Würzburg* ground and *Lichtenstein* airborne radar. The wavelength of future German radars would not always be known and indeed the Germans would make sure it could be varied. Window was a success but not a decisive turning point. In the electronic war neither side could stay ahead for long. Whatever jamming device or navigational aid Bomber Command introduced, it could only bring temporary relief for the bomber force. There was no substitute for actually defeating the enemy fighter force, and by night this was difficult, if not impossible.

In the same month that Bomber Command finally delivered terror on the scale it had for so long promised, at Kursk German forces lost their last chance to win a decisive victory and retake the initiative on the Eastern Front. Having blunted the German offensive, Soviet forces were soon driving westwards. For the German Army it was the beginning of a long retreat. The Soviets had turned the tide before Allied bombing could have any significant effect on German industrial output. With hindsight, July 1943 was the definitive turning point in the war. It was also the critical month for the two competing philosophies of war and the two methods by which Germany might be defeated. The Soviet Army broke the Wehrmacht at Kursk while at Hamburg the bomber had failed to break the German people.

Conclusion

The period 1942–1943 had seen a remarkable revival in the fortunes of the strategic bombing policy. The setbacks of 1941 and the mounting evidence that bombing alone was not the way to win wars seemed more than enough to put an end to the bomber experiment. German ground and air forces working together had won battles and wars whereas RAF heavy bombers trying to achieve results independently of the other services had so far failed to win anything. More than two years seemed long enough to establish which method of waging war was more effective. It seemed time to switch the resources being poured into the bomber offensive into more conventional strategies.

In the Middle East the Desert Air Force was showing the way. In Britain the RAF was lagging behind but here, too, the green shoots of a more flexible way of applying air power were appearing. Fighter squadrons were being trained in an army support ground attack role. Within the Air Ministry, as well as the War Office, there was talk of developing aircraft whose sole purpose would be to intervene on the battlefield. The importance of the air superiority fighter had been rediscovered. The War Office wanted a modern fleet of transport planes. A truly modern, agile, adaptable force was trying to break out of the Trenchardian bomber/interceptor straitjacket.

However, not only did the bomber strategy survive but, recast in Trenchard's original concept as a weapon of terror, the strategy was soon going from strength to strength. Arthur Harris was the man chosen to apply the indiscriminate area-bombing approach. Harris declared his first year in command to be merely a preparatory year. This in itself was a damning indictment of the bomber policy. The Air Staff had spent two decades preparing for the bomber war. More than two years of war should have been long enough to fine-tune the strategy. Yet all this effort had counted for nothing. In the same time span, air supported mechanised warfare had moved from tentative theory, through military exercises to a proven battle and war-winning strategy. The alternative bombing strategy was still on the starting line. This was not because of incompetence or a lack of resources; it was just that winning wars by bombing alone was vastly more difficult than anyone had imagined.

Yet Harris was convinced there was no alternative way for Britain to fight the war. In his book *Bomber Offensive*, Harris, with an air of resignation, insisted that 'the bomber offensive was at that time the only measurable help to our armies engaged in a desperate struggle in the Middle East'.[1] Allied commanders on the spot would no doubt have come up with more useful forms of 'measurable help'. Harris could not see beyond his own bomber strategy. For Harris it was perfectly logical to demand the Middle East return their bombers so his Bomber Command could provide the theatre with even more 'measurable help'.

In a way Harris's time had passed. His unwavering certainty that the bomber could win the war was what the country needed in 1940. In the desperate days following the defeat of France, there did indeed seem to be no other reasonably plausible way of defeating Hitler. By 1942 much had changed; Britain had new powerful allies to take the place of France and more conventional ways of winning the war were once again possible. In 1940 Britain needed leaders with Harris's steadfastness to ensure the nation survived. By 1942 the only contribution Harris could make was ensuring the bomber strategy survived.

The blind faith that sustained the country in 1940 was still sustaining the bomber strategy in 1942. Even in their darkest hour the Air Staff remained remarkably optimistic about the prospects of success. This confidence was in sharp contrast to the despondent attitude of army leaders who saw only problems in winning the war by more conventional methods. While naval and ground forces were suffering headline grabbing defeats the Air Ministry could parade images of devastated German cities.

The irony was that a major factor in the defeats on land and at sea was the lack of air support, which in turn was the inevitable result of the priority the bomber offensive was getting. Bomber Command might give the impression of being the only element of the armed services making a serious contribution to victory but, in reality, it was one of the reasons why the country was suffering so many defeats. The resources invested in Bomber Command were weakening Britain far more than RAF bombing was weakening Germany. None of this was apparent to the Air Staff. Through the Air Ministry prism it was a bomber war, not a tank war.

Instead of learning from the way the Wehrmacht forged ground and air forces into a single powerful, military force, German practice in its less successful air-only campaigns – the Battle of Britain, the Blitz – were held up as examples of how to use air power correctly.

It is perhaps ironic that a strategy designed to avoid the horrors of trench warfare ended up by replicating the plodding, staged approach that proved so costly and unproductive in the First World War. For most of the 1914–1918 conflict the strategy had been simple: first the artillery destroyed and then the infantry advanced. If enough artillery was assembled and if it fired for long enough, advancing troops would just be required to occupy devastated defences. When it did not work the solution was always more guns firing for longer.

In the Second World War, Air Staff thinking was along similar lines but on a grander scale. Once Europe had been devastated by bombing, the re-occupation of the conquered territories would not require any serious fighting. When bombing did not have the desired effect, no one in the Air Ministry questioned the basic strategy. The solution was to build more bombers and have them drop more bombs for longer. The Air Staff wanted 1,000, then 2,000, then 4,000, perhaps 6,000 bombers. There was no limit to the level of mass destruction they were willing to apply. For the generals of the First World War and the air marshals of the Second World War, once set on a particular course it was very difficult to turn back. Reputations were on the line. The more of their reputations the advocates of bombing invested in the theory the more difficult it became to concede it might be a mistake.

Attempts to make the bomber offensive work became ever more ruthless. Extraordinary risks were taken just to keep the strategy afloat. The radar secrets that Britain's air defences relied on and the campaign against the U-boats needed were risked over Germany in the certain knowledge they would fall into enemy hands. The inevitable retaliation against British civilians was part of the price the Air Staff were willing to pay to push their plans forward. Nothing would be allowed to stand in the way of the bomber policy succeeding. There was a grim determination to see the policy through, come what may.

It was not the image the RAF liked to portray. The service prided itself on its flexible, forward-thinking and modern approach, especially when compared to the supposedly archaic practices and attitudes of their sister services. In Parliament the Air Minister painted a glowing picture of the force. Its achievements were 'in no small part due to its youth, its freshness, its freedom from old, hampering prejudices and its receptiveness to new ideas. The achievements of the Royal Air Force do not spring from complacent adherence to old traditions and conventional methods.'[2]

In reality the opposite was the case. In its short existence the Air Ministry had created its own prejudices against the way warfare was evolving. This was in part due to the reasons behind the creation of the RAF. The force had not been set up to develop the combined arms approach that was re-emerging at the end of the First World War. The RAF had been created to develop the bomber as an alternative to the bloodletting on the Western Front. The military lessons of the First World War were ignored because the RAF was supposed to be replacing conventional land warfare. The only reason for mentioning the 1914–1918 conflict was to remind everyone about the horrors involved in that war, to discourage waverers from straying from the bomber path.

The separate and independent outlook the Air Ministry was so keen to foster was bound to create barriers that made it difficult to see how air power fitted into the way warfare as a whole was evolving in the twentieth century. As nation after nation succumbed to the Wehrmacht, the Air Staff failed to see that the methods used were an extension of the ideas that had been emerging in 1918. The Air Ministry and RAF were not set up to be receptive to new ideas that involved aspects of war outside the narrow bomber-orientated vision of future conflict. Mechanised warfare was seen as just another element of the failed First World War approach they had been asked to replace. To the Air Ministry, the methods the Wehrmacht had developed were just a short-term expedient the Nazi regime had been forced to resort to out of desperation; in reality it was a long-term revolution in the means used to wage war. Understanding the part air power had to play in this revolution was key to winning the conflict and would remain crucial long after Hitler was defeated. Instead of learning from the current conflict and adapting to the way war was evolving in the 1940s, the Air Staff retreated to the primitive bomber theories of the 1920s.

As 1942 wore on, the realities of war and the influence of a dominant new ally made it difficult to rely so completely on the bomber as a war-winning weapon. Trenchard, Harris and Slessor all spoke of Britain's air policy being at a crossroads. Britain had to choose between the bomber route and an army/air mechanised approach. They were right. Britain could not afford to develop both. Going down both routes might cripple the country financially. This, however, was what Britain found itself doing.

By 1942 no one outside air force circles still believed bombers could win wars. The only way the bomber could remain an important element of Allied war strategy was as a preparation for the invasion of France. In fact, the bomber advocates did even better than that; they managed to cement a successful bomber offensive into Allied policy as not just a useful contribution but as a necessary pre-condition for invasion. Nevertheless, armies preparing for the invasion of France, and those already fighting in other theatres, could not be denied the air resources they needed. Britain was being dragged into the economically ruinous policy of trying to build a huge, expensive heavy-bomber fleet and a conventional mechanised army with its associated tactical air force. Even with the United States providing a large number of the tactical aircraft required it was still a task that was beyond the means of the country.

The RAF was also at the crossroads in terms of its future equipment. The reality of war was forcing a rethink on the sort of aircraft the RAF needed. Air force commanders were beginning to appreciate that perhaps long-range bombers and short-range interceptors were not enough. For the first time, development programmes for a specialist ground attack plane, an air superiority fighter, even purpose built transports, were on the agenda. It was an opportunity for the RAF to change course and become a more versatile, flexible force, not just in the Second World War but in the years that would follow. This did not involve breaking new ground; it was simply returning to the sort of air force that existed in 1918. However, the specialist air superiority fighter and ground attack aircraft never got beyond the discussion stage. British air policy seemed trapped in its rigid bomber ideology.

Trenchardian dogma still dominated air policy. The idea that air forces would decide wars and ultimately replace armies and navies was never far below the surface, even amongst those with less extreme views. Too easily, air force commanders slipped back into thinking the other branches of the armed services were there to serve the needs of the Air Force. Ground forces existed solely to win the airfields the Air Force needed. The Soviet Army had to prevent Soviet aircraft factories falling into German hands and building bombers for the Luftwaffe. The British Army could be sacrificed in a doomed invasion of France to help the Soviets achieve this. For many in the Air Ministry, the entire war revolved around the needs of the bomber policy. Bomber Command was not there to help armies win the war, armies were there to help Bomber Command win the war. Army and Navy air requirements were an obstacle to overcome rather than a need that had to be met.

Even in the Middle East the move towards a more modern approach to air warfare seemed to be losing ground. Following the stunning breakthrough at Tebaga, RAF commanders in the Middle East began reverting to a more ponderous, methodical approach. Air commanders were distancing themselves from the need to combine with other arms on the battlefield. Preventing any movement behind the front was more important than helping the army break through enemy defences. Air superiority was won in the enemy rear, not over the front. The idea that without air superiority no military action was possible was gaining ground. The list of pre-conditions for an invasion of France was growing.

It was the re-entry into France that was always going to be the key battle on Germany's western front and setting stiff pre-conditions before embarking on the operation was bound to delay it. As soon as it became clear that the bulk of the German Army was enmeshed in the Soviet Union, opening a second front was more than just an option, it had become an opportunity. For a country with a proud naval tradition it might seem strange that a 100-mile stretch of water should be seen as such an insurmountable barrier. It was perhaps a convenient assumption in 1940, when it was necessary to believe the Germans would find it impossible to cross the Channel, but this judgement seemed to spill over into British thinking about an invasion in the opposite direction. For a country like Germany with only a small navy it might be a challenge, but it should not have posed the same problems for two major naval powers. The Americans certainly did not think it should. To the frustration of their generals, however, Britain deployed every conceivable argument – strategic, tactical, geopolitical, technical and industrial – to delay an invasion of France. While amphibious Allied assaults were taking place in North Africa, the Mediterranean and islands across the Pacific, the 100 miles across the Channel continued to be viewed, at least by the British, as almost an impossible undertaking.

An invasion of France would have failed in 1942, but this was not because two years was not long enough to move from a defensive to an offensive posture. It would have failed because for two decades the focus of British defence policy had been based on bombers winning wars rather than relying on the efforts of all three services acting as one. Britain had not even tried to create the joint force required. The British armed forces were as unprepared to free France in 1942 as they had been to support France in 1940.

The Air Staff have to bear much of the responsibility for allowing the bomber to become so dominant in Allied strategy. They were, after all, the experts who were supposed to get it right. However, others played their part. The War Office never effectively challenged the basic bomber premise. Although the Army was constantly demanding a powerful tactical air force for its forces in the UK it also believed a cross-Channel invasion was impossible until bombing had seriously weakened Germany's ability to resist. The War Office was effectively giving the strategic air offensive its stamp of approval. American support was also crucial. The USAAF might disagree with the method but American air force commanders were just as convinced as their RAF counterparts that the bomber was a war-winning weapon. Even American army generals were persuaded a bombing offensive was a necessary preliminary to an invasion.

Churchill also has to accept some of the responsibility. Although he no longer saw bombing as a war winner, the sight of devastated German towns was enough to revive his backing for the bombing policy. Politically it was useful; at the very least it demonstrated to Stalin that Britain was doing some fighting. Both Churchill and Brooke were quite happy to give Bomber Command the opportunity to prove it could seriously weaken Germany before attempting an invasion of France and neither seemed to mind how long it took. One suspects the longer it took the happier Brooke would be. The Air Ministry did not want a second front because their bomber offensive needed all the resources it could get. Hitler certainly did not want a second front in France. He needed time to win his war in the east. Rather bizarrely, in the summer of 1943, the War Office, the Air Ministry and Adolf Hitler all hoped an invasion of France would be put off for as long as possible.

It could, however, not be put off for ever. Soviet forces advancing on the Eastern Front would soon be closer to Berlin than the Allied armies sitting tight in the United Kingdom. In 1941 British armed forces had not even begun to prepare for a second front. In 1942 the Dieppe disaster demonstrated that there was little understanding of what such an operation entailed. In 1943 the British and Americans decided they needed more time before they embarked on decisive battle in northern France.

Would they be ready in 1944?

Notes

Chapter 1

1. NA WO233/60, p. 152
2. NA AIR39/16, 6 July 1941
3. NA CAB80/60, 22 October 1941
4. Baughen, *Blueprint for Victory*, pp 174-6
5. NA CAB80/60, 13 October 1941
6. NA WO193/679, 16 October 1941
7. NA WO193/679, 14 October 1941
8. NA WO193/679, 14 October 1941
9. NA WO193/679, October 1941
10. NA WO193/679, 14 October 1941
11. Postan, Appendices, Tables J, K; NA AIR20/3730, 27 December 1941
12. NA WO193/679, 14 October 1941
13. NA WO193/679, 13 October 1941
14. NA CAB80/60, 22 October 1941
15. NA AIR39/16, 2 November 1941
16. NA WO193/679, 14 October 1941
17. Hansard, 24 February 1942
18. NA CAB69/4/9, 1 April 1042
19. Arnold, p. 303
20. NA AIR41/25, p. 33
21. NA AIR41/26, p. 10
22. NA AIR41/25, p. 235
23. Shores, Ring, pp. 86-7
24. NA AIR41/26. pp. 16-17
25. NA AIR41/26, p. 19, Shores, Ring, p. 90
26. NA AIR41/25, p. 292
27. NA AIR41/25, 12 March 1942
28. NA AIR41/26, pp. 13-32
29. Hansard, 29 January 1942

30. Hansard, 25 February 1942
31. NA AIR8/899, 7 March 1942
32. NA AIR9/258, 7 March 1942
33. NA WO106/4174, 14 March 1942
34. NA AIR16/546, 24 March 1942
35. NA CAB80/62, 7 April 1942
36. NA CAB66/21/41, 5 February 1942
37. NA PREM3/8, 13 March 1942
38. NA PREM3/8, 7-16 March 1942
39. NA WO193/679, 10 March 1942
40. NA WO193/679, 7 March 1942
41. Probert, *The Forgotten Air Force,* pp. 95-6

Chapter 2

1. NA AIR8/258, 27 September 1941
2. Roskill, Vol. 2, p. 87
3. Arnold, p. 235
4. Craven, Cate, Vol. 1, pp. 148-9
5. FM 31-35 Basic Field Manual 1942
6. Webster, Frankland, Vol. IV, p. 144
7. NA AIR20/6112, 1, April 1941
8. NA AIR8/449, 8 April 1942
9. Baughen, *The Rise of the Bomber*, p. 24
10. Omissi, p.158.
11. Webster Frankland, Vol. 1, pp. 323-4
12. Baughen, *Blueprint for Victory*, pp. 213-14
13. NA AIR40/1926, 14 February 1942
14. Middlebrooke, Everitt, p. 248
15. NA AIR14/614, 17 August 1941
16. Hansard, 15 April 1942
17. Webster, Frankland, Vol. 1, pp. 331-2
18. Webster, Frankland, Vol. 1, pp. 334-5; Clarke, pp. 305-13
19. NA CAB69/4, 6 April 1942
20. NA AIR20/2810, 12 March 1942
21. NA AIR20/2810, 14 March 1942
22. NA CAB69/4/9, 1 April 1942
23. NA CAB69/4/9, 1 April 1942
24. NA WO193/679, 7 April 1942
25. NA WO193/679, 2 May 1942
26. NA WO193/679, 19 May 1942

Chapter 3

1. NA CAB69/4/3, 14 April 1942
2. NA CAB80/62, 13 April 1942
3. Baughen, *RAF on the Offensive*, p. 29
4. Baughen, *The RAF in the Battle of France and the Battle of Britain*, p. 121
5. NA AIR9/258, 29 April 1942
6. NA AIR9/258, 18 April 1942
7. NA AIR8/1063, 27 May 1942
8. NA CAB79/56/21, 8 April 1942
9. NA AIR9/159, 14 April 1942
10. NA WO 193/808, May 1942
11. NA WO193/808 8 April 1942, Churchill, *Hinge of Fate*, p. 364
12. NA AIR8/1251, July 1942
13. NA AIR8/1063, 21 May 1942
14. NA AIR9/258, 4 July 1942
15. NA AIR9/258, 26 May 1942
16. NA AIR9/258, 26 May 1942
17. NA CAB80/62, 7 April 1942
18. NA WO216/127, 25 May 1942; AIR10/5547, p. 32; WO233/60, p. 158
19. Carrington, p. 83
20. NA AIR10/5547, p. 34; WO233/60, p. 159
21. NA AIR20/4842, 21 May 1942
22. NA PREM3/85, October 1942
23. NA AIR16/776, January- February, 6 March, 1942
24. NA AIR16/776, 19 February
25. NA AIR16/552, Enc. 26B, 30 April 1942
26. NA AIR16/552, 1 June 1942
27. NA AIR16/552, 18 May 1942
28. NA AIR41/49, p. 9
29. NA WO233/60, p. 155, AIR16/552, June 1942
30. NA WO233/60, p. 160; AIR10/5547, pp. 33-4
31. NA WO193/679, 31 July 1942
32. NA AIR9/258, 1 July 1942

Chapter 4

1. NA AIR39/22, 15 November 1942
2. NA AIR39/22, 15 November 1942
3. NA WO233/60, p. 146
4. Parham, Belfield, p. 23
5. NA WO233/60, p. 146

6. NA AIR8/1251, 5 May 1942

7. NA AIR14/1140, 15 February 1942

8. Goulter, p. 140

9. NA AIR14/1140, 15 February 1942

10. NA AIR8/452, 24 August 1942

11. NA AVIA15/1583, 16 June 1942

12. NA AIR16/517, 29 October 1941, February 1942; AVIA46/120, Enc. 26A

13. NA AVIA15/1583, 24 February 1942; AIR20/4572, 30 June 1942

14. Alanbrooke, p. 231

15. NA AIR16/517, 19 March 1942

16. NA AVIA15/1640, 1 January 1942

17. NA AVIA15/1640, 1 January 1942

18. NA WO232/56, 6 August 1941

19. Baughen, *The RAF in the Battle of France and the Battle of Britain*, p. 57

20. NA AVIA15/1640, 3 January 1942

21. NA AVIA15/1583, 2 June 1942

22. NA AVIA15/1640, 7 March 1942

23. NA AVIA15/1640, 11 April, 16 May 1942

24. NA AVIA15/1640, 25 March 1942

25. NA AVIA15/1640, 18 April 1942

26. NA AVIA15/1640, 26 April 1942

Chapter 5

1. Baughen, *The Rise of the Bomber* pp. 178-9

2. Postan, Appendix 3

3. NA AVIA10/381, 23 December 1941

4. NA AVIA15/1583, 20 January 1942

5. NA AVIA10/381, 19 January 1942

6. NA AVIA15/1583, 24 February 1942

7. NA AIR20/3029, 12 March 1942

8. NA AIR20/3029, 14 March 1942

9. NA AVIA 15/1583, 16 March 1942

10. NA AIR20/3029, 10 February, 4 March, 30 September 1942

11. NA AIR41/49, p. 147

12. NA AIR20/3029, 1 April 1942

13. NA AIR9/258, 1, 11 May 1942

14. NA AIR20/3029, 27 April 1942

15. NA AIR41/49, p. 102

16. NA AIR41/49, p. 103

17. NA AIR41/26, p. 104
18. NA AIR41/26, p. 106
19. NA AIR41/49, p. 149
20. NA AIR41/26, April 1942
21. NA AIR41/49, pp. 107, 110
22. NA AIR16/546, 1 May 1942
23. NA AIR20/4842, 12 May 1942
24. NA AIR19/226, 22 May 1942
25. NA AIR41/49, p. 111
26. NA AVIA15/2601, 12, 18 August 1942
27. NA AVIA15/2601, August-December 1942
28. NA AVIA10/381, 3 April 1942
29. NA AIR20/3029, 3, 17 April 1942
30. NA AVIA9/24, March 1942
31. NA AIR20/3029, 31 July 1942
32. NA AVIA9/24, 22 May 1942
33. NA AVIA10/231, 8 April 1942; AVIA10/232, 2 April 1942
34. NA AVIA10/264, 23 January 1942
35. NA AIR2/1738, 24 March 1942
36. NA AVIA10/231, May/June 1942
37. NA AVIA15/1606, 3 February 1942
38. NA AVIA15/1606, January- February 1942
39. NA AVIA15/1667, 10, 13 April 1942
40. NA AVIA15/1667, April-May 1942
41. NA AVIA15/1527, 22, 30 March 1942
42. NA AVIA9/24, 4 May 1942
43. NA AVIA15/1667, 13 April 1942
44. NA AVIA15/1667, 23 April 1942
45. NA AVIA15/1478, 15 April 1942
46. NA AVIA9/24, 22 May 1942; NA AIR2/1738, 22 May 1942
47. NA AVIA 9/24, 22 May 1942
48. NA AVIA9/24, 26 May 1942
49. NA AVIA46/134, 28 January 1943; AVIA15/1478, 27 March 1942
50. NA AVIA46/261
51. NA AVIA10/381, 11 August 1942
52. NA AVIA15/1606, 28 May, 2, 11 June 1942
53. NA AVIA10/264, 7 September 1942
54. NA AVIA15/1478, 11, 13, 17 June 1942
55. NA AVIA15/1606, 1 August 1942

56. NA AVIA46/134, 6 August 1942
57. NA AVIA9/30, 16 June 1942
58. NA AIR20/3620, 5 May 1942
59. NA AVIA15/1717, 14 June 1942
60. NA AVIA15/1717, 4 June 1942
61. NA AIR15/1583, 6 August 1942
62. NA AVIA15/1583, 16, 28 August 1942
63. Harrison, p. 18
64. NA AIR37/159, 18 May 1942
65. Baughen, *The RAF in the Battle of France and the Battle of Britain*, pp. 29, 68-9
66. NA AVIA6/11516, May 1943
67. NA Air16/546, 24 March 1942; AIR16/327 26 January 1942
68. NA AIR37/166, 7 March 1942
69. NA AIR8/327, 22 February 1942
70. NA AIR8/327, 1 March 1942
71. NA AIR8/327, 15 March 1942
72. NA AIR8/327, 1, 15 March 1942
73. NA AIR8/327, March 1942
74. NA AIR8/327, 21 June 1942
75. NA AIR8/327, 3 March 1942
76. NA AIR8/327, 23 May, 30 June 1942
77. NA AIR16/556, 8 August 1942
78. NA AIR16/556, 19, 31 August 1942

Chapter 6

1. Webster, Frankland, Vol. 1, p. 366
2. Baughen, *Blueprint for Victory*, Chapter 1
3. Baughen, *The Rise of the Bomber*, Chapter 5
4. https://www.youtube.com/watch?v=xv3kAZkMzls
5. https://www.youtube.com/watch?v=CRYCx_G25ro
6. Collier, Appendix XXXVI
7. https://www.youtube.com/watch?v=FkLPpO6We-w
8. https://www.youtube.com/watch?v=FkLPpO6We-w
9. Baughen, *Blueprint for Victory*, chapters 14,15; *The Rise of the Bomber*, chapter 5
10. https://www.youtube.com/watch?v=FkLPpO6We-w&t=1s
11. NA AIR9/472, 17 June 1942.
12. NA AIR9/8, 15 Jan 1936, p. 10, Para. 36
13. NA AIR2/2673, 26 January 1937

14. NA AVIA15/1020, 9 January 1942. Buttler, pp. 121-2
15. Probert, Bomber Harris, p. 140
16. NA AIR14/3507, 17 June 1942
17. NA AIR14/3507, 17 June 1942
18. NA AIR14/3507, 17 June 1942
19. NA AIR14/3507, 17 June 1942
20. Webster, Frankland, Vol. 1, p. 239
21. Tedder, p. 253
22. Churchill, *The Hinge of Fate*, p. 445
23. Baughen, *RAF on the Offensive*, p. 218
24. Hancock, Table 131
25. Carrington, pp. 87-9
26. Probert, *Bomber Harris*, pp. 159-81
27. Carrington, pp. 108-9, 112,
28. Craven, Cate, Vol. 2 pp. 295-7

Chapter 7

1. NA AIR41/26, p. 134
2. Tedder, p. 226
3. Shores, Ring, p. 99
4. NA AIR41/26, p. 97
5. NA AIR41/26, p. 68
6. Sores, Cull, Malizia, p. 104
7. Shores, Ring, p. 120
8. Bateson, p. 50
9. NA AIR41/26, p. 155
10. NA AIR41/26, pp. 141-65
11. Gooderson, p. 105
12. NA AIR8/258, 29 June 1942
13. NA AIR41/26, pp. 163-91
14. NA AIR41/26, pp. 161, 224
15. NA AIR41/26, pp. 191-209
16. NA AIR41/50, pp. 22-41
17. NA AIR41/50, p. 19
18. NA AIR8/558, 1 June 1942
19. NA AIR8/558, 28 May 1942
20. NA AIR41/50, p. 12
21. NA AIR8/558, 30 July 1942
22. NA AIR41/50, pp. 64-5
23. Shores & Ring, p. 142

Chapter 8

1. NA AIR8/895, 27 June 1942
2. NA AIR8/895, 27 June 1942
3. NA AIR8/895, 26, 27, 29 May 1942
4. Air16/748, 5 September 1942
5. NA AIR16/746, July 1942 (undated)
6. NA AIR16/746, July 1942 (undated)
7. Franks, p. 27
8. NA AIR16/551, 26 May 1942
9. NA AIR16/746, 31 July 1942
10. Franks, pp. 39,48
11. NA AIR16/748, 5 September 1942
12. NA AIR16/765, Enclosure 3a, WO233/60, p. 162
13. NA AIR16/765, Enclosure 3a, 6a
14. NA AIR16/765, Enc 17A, AIR16/746, 31 July 1942
15. Franks, p. 58
16. Baughen, *The RAF in the Battle of France and the Battle of Britain,* p. 147
17. Craven, Cate, Vol. 2, p. 216, Franks, p. 99
18. Franks, p. 63
19. NA AIR16/765, 24 August 1942
20. Franks, p. 199
21. NA AIR16/748, 22 August 1942
22. NA AIR16/748, undated note
23. NA AIR8/883, 22 August 1942
24. NA WO233/60, p. 162
25. NA AIR16/765, Enc. 2a, 14a
26. NA WO233/60, p. 162
27. NA AIR16/765, Enc. 7a
28. NA AIR16/765, Enc. 27A
29. NA AIR16/ 748, 15 September 1942; Franks, p. 220
30. NA AIR16/765, Enc. 22A
31. NA AIR16/776, 27 September 1942
32. NA AIR16/552 September 1942
33. NA AVIA46/122, Para. 5
34. NA AVIA46/120, Enc. 26A
35. NA AVIA15/1800, November-December 1942; AIR20/889, 22 December 1942
36. NA AIR16/805, 10 August 1942
37. NA WO193/679, 17 September 1942

38. NA AIR20/4572, 30 June 1942
39. NA AVIA15/1640, 30 August 1942
40. Buttler, p. 73
41. NA AVIA15/1640, 19 December 1942; Buttler, p. 73
42. NA WO193/679, 26 September 1942

Chapter 9

1. NA AIR19/286, 17 July 1942
2. NA AIR19/286, 17, 21 July 1942
3. NA AIR16/805, 12 Sept 1942
4. NA AIR19/286, 17 July 1942
5. NA AVIA15/1583, 27 August 1942
6. NA AVIA15/2660, February-March 1943
7. Lloyd, Pugh, p. 122
8. Baughen, *The RAF in the Battle of France and the Battle of Britain*, p. 79
9. NA AIR19/286, 30 July 1942
10. NA AVIA10/381, 24 August 1942
11. NA AVIA15/1583, 16 August 1942
12. NA AIR19/286, 20 July 1942
13. NA AIR19/286, 31 July 1942
14. NA AVIA15/1731, 10 August 1942
15. NA AIR8/451, 13 November 1942
16. NA AVIA15/1731, 13 August 1942
17. NA AVIA15/1731, August-September 1942
18. NA AVIA15/1731, September-November 1942
19. NA AVIA15/1731, 20 November 1942
20. NA AIR16/329, 20 October 1942
21. NA AIR8/451, 13 November 1942
22. NA AVIA15/1667, 23 April 1942; AIR16/329, 14 October 1942; AIR20/3029, 12 December 1942
23. NA AIR8/451, 25 December 1942
24. NA AIR8/451, December 1942
25. NA AIR8/451, 19 December 1942
26. NA AVIA15/1771, 10 December 1942
27. NA AVIA15/1771, 29 December 1942
28. NA AVIA15/1747, 15 January 1943
29. NA AIR8/451, 6 January 1943
30. NA AIR8/451, 5 April 1943
31. NA AVIA15/1771, 10 December 1943

32. NA AVIA46/134, 3 February 1943
33. NA AIR16/630, September 1942
34. NA AIR19/286, 17 July 1942
35. Goulding, p. 146
36. NA AVIA15/1627, January-September 1942
37. NA AIR19/226, 26 June, 19 November 1942
38. NA AIR19/226, 9 November 1942; AIR16/558, December 1942
39. NA AVIA15/2601, 24, 25 October 1942
40. NA AVIA15/2601, 27, 29 October 1942
41. NA AVIA15/2601, August-December 1942
42. NA AVIA15/1583, September 1942 (undated)
43. NA AIR20/3090, 15 September 1942
44. NA AIR20/3029, 1 August 1942; Avia15/1583, 7 August 1942
45. NA AVIA46/120, Enc. 35A
46. NA AIR20/3029, 31 July 1942
47. NA AVIA15/1583, 2 June, Sept 1942
48. NA AVIA15/1583, 16 June 1942
49. NA AIR8/452, 24 August 1942
50. Maxwell Air War College AU/AWC/RWP067/96-04 *The P-51 Mustang as an Escort Fighter*, K. Daneu 1996 (unpublished)
51. NA AIR8/754, December 1942-March 1943
52. NA AVIA15/1717, 14 June 1942
53. NA AIR20/889, 15 May 1943
54. NA AIR16/558, 14 December 1942
55. NA AIR16/558, Enc. 5A
56. NA AVIA15/1606, 14 July 1943
57. NA AVIA15/1606, 3 February 1943
58. NA AVIA15/1583, September 1942
59. NA AVIA15/1583, 8 October 1942
60. NA AVIA8/714, 5 October 1942
61. NA AVIA9/44, 11 December 1942

Chapter 10

1. Orange, *Conningham*, pp. 221, 232
2. NA AIR19/286, 13 July 1942
3. NA AIR41/50, pp. 161-221
4. Churchill, Vol. 3, p. 393
5. NA AIR41/50, pp. 167-97
6. Hallion, p. 160

7. *History of Second World War* (Purnell) Vol. 3, no. 10, p. 1152

8. NA AIR41/50, p. 264

9. PRO AIR41/50, pp. 247-417

10. PRO AIR41/50, pp. 327-328

11. NA AIR41/50, pp. 272-328

12. *History of the Second World War* (Purnell), Vol. 3, No. 10, p. 1165

13. NA AIR41/50, pp. 412-14

14. NA AIR41/50, p. 356

Chapter 11

1. NA AIR41/33, p. 38

2. NA AIR41/33, p. 35

3. NA AIR41/33, pp. 34-5

4. Craven, Cate, Vol. 2, p. 51

5. NA AIR41/33, p. 80

6. Shores, Shores, Ring, Hess, pp. 6-7

7. Shores, Shores, Ring, Hess, Chapter 1

8. Shores, Shores, Ring, Hess, Chapter 1

9. Craven, Cate, Vol. 2, p. 89

10. Parham, Belfield, pp. 31-7

11. NA WO233/60, p. 148

12. NA AIR41/33, pp. 77-8

13. NA AIR41/33, p. 79

14. Shores, Ring, Hess, p. 117; NA AIR41/33, p. 81; WO32/10403, 9 January 1943

15. Craven, Cate, Vol. 2, p. 89

16. Shores, Ring, Hess, p. 397

17. Peret, p. 191

18. Baughen, *RAF on the Offensive*, pp. 67-70

19. NA AIR41/33, p. 79

20. NA AIR20/889, 15 November 1942

21. NA AIR20/4408, 22 January 1943

22. Shores, Ring, Hess, p. 186

23. NA AIR8/1063, 1 November 1942

24. Chruchill, *Hinge of Fate*, p. 599

25. Tedder, pp 369-71

26. NA AIR23/1709, 16 February 1943

27. Craven, Cate, Vol. 2, p. 139-40

28. Shores, Ring, Hess, p. 209

29. NA AIR41/33, p. 127

30. Shores, Ring, Hess, p. 212
31. Tedder, p. 400
32. NA WO193/679, 27 February 1943
33. NA AIR23/7772, 26 February 1943
34. NA AIR23/7772, 28 February 1943
35. Orange, *Coningham*, pp. 132, 136
36. Shores, Ring, Hess, p. 253
37. Tedder, p. 331
38. Tedder, p. 395
39. NA AIR20/2809, 15 June 1941
40. Tedder, p. 363
41. Tedder, p. 382
42. NA AIR23/7772, 18 February 1943
43. NA AIR41/50, pp. 478-9
44. NA AIR23/1709, 16 February 1943
45. NA AIR23/1709, 16 February 1943
46. Orange, *Coningham*, p. 137
47. Orange, *Coningham*, p. 144
48. NA AIR23/1709, 27 February 1943
49. Orange, *Coningham*, p. 137
50. NA AIR10/5547, p. 87
51. Baughen, *Blueprint for Victory*, Chapter 7
52. Baughen, *The Rise and Fall of the French Air Force*, p. 34
53. Terraine, p. 380
54. Terraine, p. 380
55. Orange, *Coningham*, p. 132
56. NA AIR23/7772, 17 April 1943, Orange, *Coningham* pp. 146-7, Tedder, p. 411
57. NA AIR23/7439, 22 May 1943

Chapter 12

1. NA AIR41/33, pp. 157-8
2. NA AIR41/50, pp. 432-3
3. NA AIR41/50, pp. 504-5
4. Montgomery, p. 163
5. NA AIR41/50, p. 505
6. NA AIR41/50, pp. 506-9
7. NA AIR41/50, pp. 504-10
8. Baughen, *Blueprint for Victory*, pp. 180-2
9. NA AIR41/50, p. 51

10. *The Times,* 29 March 1943

11. *The Times*, 31 March 1943

12. Orange, *Coningham*, p. 144

13. NA AIR23/1708, 26 March 1943

14. Gooderson, pp. 186-7

15. NA AIR2/3353, 12 May 1943

16. NA AIR20/889, 28 June 1943

17. Roskill. Vol 2, p. 342

18. Tedder, p. 440

19. Tedder, p. 442

20. Craven, Cate, Vol. 2, p. 432

21. Craven, Cate, Vol. 2, p. 439

22. Hooton, p. 227

23. Santoro, Vol. 2, p. 538

24. Santoro, Vol. 2, p. 533

25. Craven, Cate, Vol. 2, p. 445

26. NA AIR41/52, p. 54

27. NA AIR41/52, p. 52

28. Craven, Cate, Vol. 2, p. 452

29. NA AIR41/52, p. 66

30. NA AIR41/52, pp. 76-7

31. Playfair, Vol 5, p. 173; NA WO32/10403, 6 September 1943

32. Craven, Cate, Vol. 2, p. 469

Chapter 13

1. Churchill, *Hinge of Fate*, p. 755

2. Craven, Cate, Vol. 2, p. 301

3. Morgan, p. 154

4. NA AVIA10/232

5. NA AIR8/714, 12 October 1942

6. NA AIR8/714, 12 October 1942

7. NA AIR8/714, 12 October 1942

8. NA AIR41/49, 3 August 1942

9. NA AIR41/49, pp. 146-55

10. NA AIR41/49, p. 151

11. NA AIR41/49, p. 152

12. NA AIR41/49, p. 152

13. NA AIR20/3029, 5, 11 March 1943

14. NA AIR2/2833, 15 April 1943,

15. NA AIR20/889, 4 May 1943
16. NA AVIA15/2601, 18 January 1943
17. NA AIR41/49, p. 265
18. NA AIR41/49, pp. 260-1
19. Morgan, p. 51
20. NA AIR37/166, 20 April 1943
21. NA AIR37/159, 15 July 1943
22. NA AIR20/888, 20 August, 7 September 1943
23. NA AIR41/34, pp. 17-18
24. NA AIR37/633, 17 June 1943
25. NA AIR37/633, 4 June 1943
26. Horden, p. 52
27. NA AIR19/498, 14 December 1940
28. Probert, *The Forgotten Air Force*, p. 133
29. Hansard, 4 March 1942
30. NA AIR19/233, 19 February 1943
31. Hansard, 24 February 1943
32. NA AIR19/233, 19 February 1943
33. NA AIR19/233, 25 January 1943
34. NA AIR37/633, 20 June 1943
35. NA AIR19/233, 27 June 1943
36. NA AIR37/633,10, 22 July 1943
37. NA AIR19/233, 5 April, 30 June 1943
38. Probert, pp. 252, 259, 262
39. NA WO32/10403, May 1943
40. NA PREM3/8, September 1942; WO216/127, 31 August, 3, 7 September 1942
41. NA PREM3/8, Sept 1942
42. NA PREM3/8, 5 October 1942
43. Brooke, 12 Sept 1942
44. NA PREM3/8, 14 September 1942
45. NA PREM3/8, 14, September 1942
46. NA PREM3/8, 16, 19 September 1942
47. NA AIR10/5547, p. 36
48. NA WO205/567, 20 December 1942
49. NA AIR10/5447, p. 38
50. NA WO232/51, 3 February 1943
51. Baughen, *Blueprint for Victory*, pp. 180-1
52. NA WO232/51, 3 February 1943
53. NA WO232/51, 3 February 1943

54. NA WO232/51, 9 March 1943
55. NA WO205/567, 6 June 1943

Chapter 14

1. NA AIR20/2910, 28 September, 6 December 1941
2. Trevor-Roper, p. 102, Hitler's Directive No. 23
3. NA AIR20/2864, 11 July 1942
4. NA AIR8/714, 5, 10 October 1942
5. Craven, Cate, Vol. 2, p. 297
6. Craven, Cate, Vol. 2, p. 299
7. Hancock, Table 19
8. Webster, Frankland, Vol. 1, pp. 490-1; Hooton, p. 253
9. Price, *Blitz on Britain*, pp. 132, 145
10. Webster, Frankland, Vol. 1, p. 490, Vol. 2, p. 295
11. Probert, *Bomber Harris*, p. 143
12. Baughen, *The RAF in the Battle of France and the Battle of Britain*, pp. 72, 91-2
13. NA AIR2/3126, 5 April 1942
14. NA AIR2/3126, 23 October 1942, 4 January 1943
15. Middlebrook, Everitt, p. 300
16. NA AVIA 9/44, 18 October 1942; AVIA10/231, 29 December 1942
17. NA AIR14/614, Jan, March 1942
18. Webster, Frankland, Vol IV, p. 468
19. NA CAB2/3, 5 July 1922
20. Hancock, Table 131
21. Slessor, pp. 399-400
22. NA AIR75/11, 25 October 1942
23. NA AIR75/11, 9, 25 September 1942
24. Webster, Frankland, Vol. 1, p. 366, Vol. 4, Appendix 20
25. Webster, Frankland Vol. 4, Appendix 23
26. NA AIR8/258, 27 September 1941
27. Price, *Instruments of Darkness*, p. 137
28. Baughen, *The Rise of the Bomber*, p. 206
29. NA AIR20/2673, 18 May 1943
30. Webster, Frankland Vol. 4, Appendix 23
31. Webster, Frankland Vol. 2, pp. 28-31
32. Overy, p. 456
33. Webster, Frankland Vol 4, p. 468
34. Webster, Frankland Vol 2, p. 25

Chapter 15

1. NA AIR14/2003, March 1943; Price, *Instruments of Darkness*, p. 139-40
2. NA AIR2/5323, 3 August 1943
3. NA AIR20/1446, 13 August 1941
4. NA AIR20/1446, 23 Sept 1941
5. NA AIR20/1446, 23 Sept 1941
6. NA AVIA15/675, 7 December 1941
7. NA AIR20/1446, 2, 3 January 1942
8. NA AIR20/1446, 6 January 1942
9. NA AIR20/1446, 3 March 1942
10. NA AIR20/1446, 6 January 1942
11. NA AVIA7/3618, 31 March 1942
12. NA AIR41/13, p. 106
13. NA AIR20/5800, 4, 8 April 1942
14. NA AIR41/13, p. 101
15. NA AIR41/13, p. 106
16. NA AIR41/13, p. 107
17. NA AIR20/5800, 19 May 1942; AVIA7/3618, 7, September 1942
18. NA AIR41/13, pp. 98-9
19. Aders, pp. 80-1
20. NA AIR41/13, p. 110
21. NA AIR41/13, p. 111
22. NA AIR41/49, pp. 61-2
23. NA AIR16/441, 19, 22 November 1942
24. NA AIR41/13, p. 113
25. Lovell, pp. 69, 74
26. Lovell, p. 79
27. Lovell, pp. 80-1
28. Jones, p. 377
29. NA AIR14/1354, 4 November 1942
30. NA AIR20/2557, 28 March 1943
31. Speer, p. 389
32. Irving, p. 230
33. Collier, p. 515
34. Hooton, p. 274
35. Webster, Frankland, Vol. 4, p. 432
36. Price, *Instruments of Darkness*, p. 159
37. Harris, p. 216
38. Webster, Frankland, pp. 260-3

NOTES

39. Baughen, *Blueprint for Victory*, p. 16.

40. Jones, pp. 385-6

41. Aders, pp. 122-3

Conclusion

1. Harris, p. 74

2. Hansard, 4 March 1942

Appendix 1

Aircraft deliveries January 1942–July 1943

(A=airframe only, B=bomber, C=coastal, F=fighter)

Aircraft production January 1942–July 1943

	1942												1943						
	Jan	Feb	Mar	Apr	May	Jun	Jul	Aug	Sep	Oct	Nov	Dec	Jan	Feb	Mar	Apr	May	Jun	Jul
Albacore	34	30	36	33	25	19	15	10	7	10	3	3	-	-	-	-	-	-	-
Auster	-	-	-	-	2	2	9	18	15	23	18	13	23	21	37	56	54	46	46
Barracuda	-	-	-	-	-	-	1	1	0	12	8	27	26	24	27	34	48	42	58
Beaufighter (C)	-	-	36	44	55	60	67	62	76	95	87	52	84	81	69	16	0	0	0
Beaufighter(F)	123	137	93	92	87	69	59	50	54	49	49	83	51	46	78	113	140	132	131
Beaufort	28	22	28	27	29	27	23	22	27	31	24	29	26	26	42	28	34	34	30
Blenheim	42	53	56	66	72	70	60	49	60	59	51	45	30	40	23	22	20	12	0
Defiant	16	23	19	23	5	-	-	-	-	-	-	-	-	-	-	-	-	-	-
Fulmar	20	12	24	17	18	8	8	7	4	2	1	0	2	3	-	-	-	-	-
Halifax	28	34	41	48	56	67	66	73	79	109	99	102	121	137	153	155	180	159	156
Hampden	31	21	4	-	-	-	-	-	-	-	-	-	-	-	-	-	-	-	-
Hurricane	313	269	249	264	277	270	263	231	252	247	219	213	238	200	279	210	260	239	200
Lancaster	26	16	26	40	46	53	67	61	84	97	71	106	116	128	137	126	156	144	145
Mosquito (B)	1	1	0	3	4	10	11	15	20	24	24	18	21	40	32	26	30	28	12

	1942												1943						
	Jan	Feb	Mar	Apr	May	Jun	Jul	Aug	Sep	Oct	Nov	Dec	Jan	Feb	Mar	Apr	May	Jun	Jul
Mosquito (F)	8	16	19	7	22	25	19	27	36	39	47	32	41	48	56	52	70	77	77
Sea Hurricane	-	-	-	-	-	-	-	-	-	30	7	29	0	0	4	10	10	-	-
Seafire	-	-	-	-	-	10	3	4	57	30	35	30	41	25	26	30	23	17	23
Spitfire	300	287	354	379	369	338	363	348	363	380	343	310	347	372	374	335	380	364	292
Stirling	22	26	36	39	39	44	44	46	52	43	49	21	40	58	72	72	82	86	65
Sunderland	7	6	3	12	10	13	10	11	16	15	14	12	13	21	15	20	21	18	15
Swordfish	30	20	21	10	0	5	10	20	30	37	40	47	42	45	45	46	40	51	55
Typhoon	11	22	12	41	61	52	71	54	96	79	54	133	91	85	104	103	103	64	93
Warwick	-	-	-	-	-	-	2	2	0	0	1	4	5	7	10	11	16	10	2
Wellington	212	175	223	226	238	215	257	204	252	257	226	217	223	210	231	214	226	209	207
Whitley	41	57	45	51	65	53	46	42	40	39	32	29	25	23	16	14	12	5	-

US deliveries to UK January 1942–July 1943

	1942												1943						
	Jan	Feb	Mar	Apr	May	Jun	Jul	Aug	Sep	Oct	Nov	Dec	Jan	Feb	Mar	Apr	May	Jun	Jul
Airacobra	30	10	6	16	51	100	122	13	18	6	2	1	-	-	-	-	-	-	-
Baltimore	2	1	-	1	-	-	1	-	-	-	-	-	-	-	-	-	-	-	-
Bermuda	-	-	-	-	-	-	-	-	-	-	-	3	3	1	2	1	-	-	1
Boston	62	36	10	1	25	19	17	5	3	2	1	2	5	10	14	9	10	34	36
Catalina	-	3	2	3	12	7	6	7	22	20	26	9	14	17	17	11	3	8	9
Fortress	-	-	-	2	-	6	11	14	8	1	-	1	5	1	4	1	1	3	2
Hampden (A)	-	-	-	-	-	4	5	5	7	4	-	-	-	-	-	-	-	-	-
Hellcat	-	-	-	-	-	-	-	-	-	-	-	-	-	-	-	-	1	10	18
Hudson	22	13	9	43	103	35	46	13	5	15	1	5	21	5	2	3	14	7	48
Hurricane	54	48	20	50	87	81	90	61	33	19	15	13	-	-	-	16	40	38	45
Kittyhawk	3	1	-	4	-	-	-	-	2	-	-	-	-	-	-	-	-	-	-
Liberator	5	1	10	12	14	13	10	26	22	-	5	6	5	6	21	23	16	7	25
Lightning	-	-	-	2	1	-	-	-	-	-	-	-	-	-	-	-	-	-	-

	1942												1943						
	Jan	Feb	Mar	Apr	May	Jun	Jul	Aug	Sep	Oct	Nov	Dec	Jan	Feb	Mar	Apr	May	Jun	Jul
Mitchell	-	-	-	-	-	2	6	-	21	24	4	16	5	2	-	-	2	13	17
Mustang	6	14	20	52	57	76	130	68	84	62	4	32	7	4	50	13	1	-	2
Tomahawk	3	1	4	12	11	2	2	2	-	-	-	-	-	-	-	-	-	-	-
Vengeance	-	-	-	-	-	-	-	2	-	-	1	1	-	-	-	-	-	-	-
Ventura	-	-	-	-	5	31	50	38	4	14	-	2	2	-	-	-	-	8	2
Wildcat	32	-	-	-	-	1	-	-	41	7	35	35	2	7	7	-	1	10	20

American deliveries to overseas commands and Dominion governments direct January 1942–July 1943

	1942												1943						
	Jan	Feb	Mar	Apr	May	Jun	Jul	Aug	Sep	Oct	Nov	Dec	Jan	Feb	Mar	Apr	May	Jun	Jul
Baltimore	15	30	47	50	42	45	34	41	26	0	12	25	64	42	52	37	80	116	64
Hudson	67	35	65	48	43	31	11	79	14	5	41	32	14	7	9	0	1	-	-
Kittyhawk	116	42	118	51	118	128	29	81	143	50	119	28	10	39	100	5	91	8	18
Liberator	4	-	1	-	-	-	-	-	-	-	-	-	-	-	-	1	1	1	-
Marauders	-	-	-	-	-	-	19	-	11	-	1	1	2	2	-	-	-	-	-
Martlet	-	-	-	-	12	7	0	13	0	3	30	-	-	-	-	-	-	-	-
Mitchell	-	-	-	-	-	6	3	2	0	7	4	1	-	-	-	-	-	-	-
Vengeance	-	-	-	-	-	5	-	15	26	10	98	50	15	98	107	33	8	30	35
Ventura	-	-	2	6	0	11	18	84	12	0	10	20	7	14	4	0	1	10	11

Appendix 2

Aircraft Performance

(Unless otherwise stated, mg refers to 0.303 calibre machine guns)

Fighters

	First flight	Engine	Speed (mph)/ altitude (ft)	Range (miles)	Climb (ft/min-sec)	Ceiling (ft)	Empty Weight (lbs)	Loaded Weight (lbs)	Wing area (sq ft)	Armament
Bell Airacobra	06/04/1938	1,150hp Allison V-1710	358/15,000	1,100	10,000/ 3-54	35,000	5,360	7,380	213	6 mg, 1 x 20 mm cannon
Bristol Beaufighter	17/07/1939	2 x 1,590hp Hercules	323/15,000	1,500	20,000/ 14-6	28,900	14,069	20,800	503	6 mg, 4 x 20 mm cannon
Curtiss Kittyhawk I	22/05/1942	1,150hp Allison V-1710-39	362/15,000	700	15,000/ 6-22	29,000	6,350	8,280	236	700lb bombs 4 or 6 x 0.5 mg
Curtiss Tomahawk II	10/1938	1,150hp Allison V-1710-33	345/15,000	730	15,000/ 5-06	29,500	5,812	8,058	236	4 mg 2 x 0.5 mg
Dewoitine D.520	02/10/1938	910hp Hispano-Suiza 12Y45	329/19,685	777	13,120/ 4-0	36,090	4,608	6,129	172	4 mg, 1 x 20 mm cannon

Fighters

	First flight	Engine	Speed (mph)/ altitude (ft)	Range (miles)	Climb (ft/min-sec)	Ceiling (ft)	Empty Weight (lbs)	Loaded Weight (lbs)	Wing area (sq ft)	Armament
Focke-Wulf 190A-2	01/06/1939	1,360hp BMW 801	389/18,000	500	16,400/ 4-50	37,400	5,530	7,716	197	2 mg, 2 x 20 mm cannon
Gloster Gladiator II	09/1934	840hp Mercury IX	253/14,000	410	15,000/ 5-48	32,300	3,554	5,020	323	4 mg
Grumman F4F–4 Wildcat	02/09/1937	1,200hp Pratt & Whitney R-2800-86	318/19,400	770	1,950/ 1-00	39,400	5,758	7,406	260	6 x 0.5 mg 200lb bombs
Hawker Hurricane I	06/11/1935	1,030hp Merlin III	315/16,500	425	20,000/ 8-21	34,500	4,743	5,672	258	8 mg
Hawker Hurricane II	01/06/1940	1,460hp Merlin XX	342/22,000	460	20,000/ 8-24	36,500	5,500	7,000	258	12 mg or 4 x 20mm cannon
Hawker Typhoon	24/02/1940	2,180hp Sabre	405/18,000	610	15,000/ 6-12	34,000	8,800	11,400	279	12 mg or 4 x 20mm cannon
Macchi MC.202	10/09/1940	1,175hp Alfa Romeo R.A.1000	370/16,400	475	19,685/ 5-55	37,730	5,181	6,459	181	2 mg, 2 x 12.7mm mg
Messerschmitt Bf 109F	1940	1,300hp DB 601E	390/22,000	440	19,865/ 5-42	37,000	4,330	6,054	174	2 mg, 1 x 15mm cannon
Messerschmitt Bf 110C	12/05/1936	2 x 1,100hp DB 601A	349/22,965	565	18,000/ 8-30	32,000	11,466	14,884	413	5 mg, 2 x 20 mm cannon
North American P-51A Mustang	26/10/1940	1,200hp Allison V-1710-81	390/20,000	1,000	20,000/ 9-06	31,350	6,433	8,600	233	4 x 0.5 1,000lb bombs
Supermarine Spitfire V	20/02/1941	1,470hp Merlin 45	371/20,000	470	15,000/ 4-36	37,000	5,033	6,525	242	4 mg and 2 x 20mm cannon

Fighters

	First flight	Engine	Speed (mph)/ altitude (ft)	Range (miles)	Climb (ft/min-sec)	Ceiling (ft)	Empty Weight (lbs)	Loaded Weight (lbs)	Wing area (sq ft)	Armament
Supermarine Spitfire IX	04/1942	1,720hp Merlin 61	403/27,400	434	20,000/ 6-30	42,000	5,800	7,500	242	4 mg 2 x 20mm cannon
Supermarine Spitfire XII	27/11/1941	1,735 Griffon III	393/18,000	493	20,000/ 6-42	40,000	5,600	7,400	231	4 mg and 2 x 20mm cannon
Westland Whirlwind	11/10/1938	2 x 885hp Peregrine	360/15,000		15,000/ 5-48	30,000	7,840	10,270	250	4 x 20 mm cannon 1,000lb bombs

Bombers

	Prototype first flight	Engine	Speed (mph)/ altitude (ft)	Range (miles)	Ceiling (ft)	Empty Weight (lbs)	Loaded Weight (lbs)	Wing area (sq ft)	Bomb load (lbs) Armament
Avro Lancaster I	09/01/1941	4 x 1,460hp Merlin 22	281/11,000	2,250	20,000	36,900	68,000	1,297	14,000 8 mg
Bristol Blenheim IV	24/9/1937	2 x 920hp Mercury XV	266	1,460	22,000	8,700	13,400	469	1,000 4 mg
Bristol Blenheim V	24/02/1941	2 x 950hp Mercury XX	245/5,900	1,600	26,000	10,775	12,500	469	1,000 5 mg
de Havilland Mosquito	25/11/1940	2 x 1,250hp Merlin 21	380/17,000	1,795	33,000	13,400	21,462	454	2,000
Douglas Boston III	26/10/1938	2 x 1,600hp Wright Twin Cyclone	304/13,000	1,020	24,250	12,200	25,000	465	2,000 8 mg
Flying Fortress	28/07/1935	4 x 1,200hp Wright Cyclone 9	320/20,000	2,100	33,300	30,670	45,470	1,420	2,500 1 mg, 6 x 0.5 mg

Bombers

	Prototype first flight	Engine	Speed (mph) /altitude (ft)	Range (miles)	Ceiling (ft)	Empty Weight (lbs)	Loaded Weight (lbs)	Wing area (sq ft)	Bomb load (lbs) Armament
Handley Page Halifax I	25/10/1939	4 x 1,280hp Merlin X	265/17,500	2,400	18,000	34,500	59,000	1,250	13,000 6 mg
Lockheed Ventura	31/07/1941	2x2,000hp Pratt & Whitney R-2800	322	1,660	26,300	20,200	31,000	551	3,000 6-8 mg (2 x 0.5)
Martin 167 (Maryland)	14/03/1939	2 x 1,050hp Pratt & Whitney R-1830	294/13,000	1,870	27,200	11,000	17,890	452	1,800 6 mg (four fixed)
Martin B-26 Marauder	25/11/1939	2 x 1,850hp Pratt & Whitney R-2800	315/15,000	1,000	25,000	21,400	32,000	602	4,800 8 x 0.5 mg
North American Mitchell	01/1939	2 x 1,700hp Wright Twin Cyclone	284/15,000	1,500	21,200	20,300	34,000	610	3,000 5 mg (3 x 0.5)
Short Stirling III	14/05/1939	4 x 1,640hp Hercules VI	270/7,000	2,010	17,000	45,000	70,000	1,460	14,000 8 mg
Vickers Wellington III	15/06/1936	2 x 1,500hp Hercules XI	255/12,500	2,200	18,500	19,000	29,500	840	4,500 8 mg

Army co-operation/Naval/Ground attack									
	Prototype First flight	Engine	Speed (mph)/ altitude (ft)	Range (miles)/ Endurance (hrs)	Ceiling (ft)	Empty Weight (lbs)	Loaded Weight (lbs)	Wing Area (sq ft)	Bomb Load (lbs) Guns
Brewster Bermuda	17/06/1941	1,650hp Wright Twin Cyclone CR-2600	274	1,650 mi	23,000	9,920	12,240	379	1,000 6 mg
Fairey Albacore	12/12/1938	1,065hp Taurus II	161/4,000	930 mi	20,700	7,200	10,600	623	2,000 3 mg
Fairey Swordfish	17/04/1934	690hp Pegasus IIIM	139/4,750	546 mi	16,700	5,200	9,250	607	1,500 2 mg
Grumman TBF Avenger	07/08/1941	1,900hp Wright Twin Cyclone CR-2600-20	275	1,000 mi	30,100	10,545	17,890	490	2,000 2 mg 1 x 0.5 mg
Hawker Hurricane IV		1,640hp Merlin 24	284/13,500	470	32,600	5.900	8,500	258	1,000lbs or 8 rockets or 2 x 40mm cannon
Junkers Ju 87 D-2	1940	1,400hp Jumo 211D	255/13,500	510 mi	15,520	8,598	12,880	343	3,968 4 mg
Taylorcraft D Plus	1939	55hp Lycoming	110	275 mi	15,000	700	1,200	155	None
Vultee Vengeance	30/03/1941	1,650hp Wright Twin Cyclone CR-2600	275	1,500 mi	22,500	9,725	14,300	353	1,000 6 mg
Westland Lysander	16/06/1936	890hp Mercury XII	229/10,000	600 mi	26,000	4,065	5,920	260	500 3 mg
Westland Whirlwind	11/10/1938	2 x 885hp Peregrine	318/15,000		30,000	7,840	10,270	250	1,000 4 x 20 mm cannon

Bibliography

Aders, G., *History of the German Night Fighter Force 1917–1945*, (London: Janes, 1979)

Air of Authority, www.rafweb.org

Alanbrooke, Lord, *Alanbrooke War Diaries 1939–1945* (London: Weidenfeld & Nicolson, 2001)

Army Doctrine Publications – Land Operations (2005) https://vdocuments. mx/irectorate-general-evelopment-and-doctrinearmy-doctrine-publication-land-operations.html

Arnold H., *Global Mission*, (Blue Ridge Summit: TAB, 1989)

Bateson, R., *Stuka*, (London: Ducimus Books, 1972)

Baughen, G., *Blueprint for Victory* (Stroud: Fonthill, 2014)

, *The Rise of the Bomber* (Stroud: Fonthill, 2015)

, *The RAF in the Battle of France and the Battle of Britain* (Stroud: Fonthill, 2016)

, *RAF on the Offensive: The Rebirth of Tactical Air Power 1940–1941* (Barnsley: Frontline, 2018)

Bowater, R., *263 and 137 Squadrons* (Stroud: Fonthill, 2013)

Bowman, M., *USAAF Handbook 1939–1945*, (Stroud: Sutton Publishing, 1998)

Bowyer, M.J.F., *Aircraft for the Few* (Yeovil: Patrick Stephens, 1991)

, *Aircraft for the Many,* (Yeovil: Patrick Stephens, 1995)

, *No. 2 Group RAF* (London Faber and Faber, 1974)

Boyle, A., *Trenchard* (London: Collins, 1962)

Brookes, A., *Photo-Reconnaissance* (London: Ian Allan, 1975)

Budiansky, S., *Air Power* (London: Penguin, 2003)

Buttler, T., *British Secret Projects, Fighters and Bombers 1935–1950* (Hinckley: Midland, 2004)

Carrington, C., *Soldier at Bomber Command*, (London: Leo Cooper, 1987)

Churchill, W.S., *Grand Alliance* (London: Reprint Society, 1952)

Churchill, W.S., *The Hinge of Fate* (London: Reprint Society, 1952)

Clark, R., *Tizard* (London, Methuen, 1965)

Clarke, R., *British Aircraft Armament Vol. 2* (Sparkford: Patrick Stephens, 1994)

Collier, B., *The Defence of the United Kingdom* (London: IWM, 1995)

Craven, W. and Cate, J., *The Army Air Forces in World War II, Vols 1, 2* (Chicago: University of Chicago Press 1948, 1949)

Divine, D., *The Broken Wing* (London: Hutchinson, 1966)

Douglas, W., Wright, R., *Sholto Douglas* (London: Collins, 1966)

Embry, B., *Mission Accomplished* (London, Methuen, 1957)

Farrar-Hockley, A., *The Army in the Air* (Stroud: Alan Sutton Publishing, 1994)

Franks, N., *The Greatest Air Battle* (London: Grub Street, 1997)

Freeman, R., *The Mighty Eighth War Diary* (London: Jane's, 1981)
, *The Mighty Eighth* (London: Cassell, 2000)

Furse, A., *Wilfred Freeman* (Staplehurst: Spellmount, 1999)

Gooderson, I., *Air Power at the Battlefield* (London: Frank Cass, 1998)

Goulding, J., *Interceptor* (Shepperton: Ian Allan, 1986)

Goulter, C., *A Forgotten Offensive* (London: Frank Cass, 1995)

Green, W., *Warplanes of the Second World War Fighters Vol. 2, 4* (London: MacDonald, 1966)

Gunston, B., *Rolls-Royce Aero Engines* (Frome: PSL, 1989)

Hallion, R., *Strike from the Sky* (Shrewsbury, Airlife, 1989)

Hancock, W., *Statistical Digest of the War* (London: HMSO, 1951)

Hardy, M., *The North American Mustang* (London: David and Charles, 1979).

Harris, A., *Bomber Offensive* (London: Greenhill Books, 1990)

Harrison, G., *European Theater of Operations, Cross-Channel Attack* (Washington: Centre of Military History, 1951)

Hastings, M., *Bomber Command* (London: Pan Books, 1981)

Hill, A., *The Great Patriotic War of the Soviet Union*, 1941–45 (London:Routledge, 2009)

Hooton, E.R., *Eagle in Flames* (London: Arms and Armour Press, 1997)

Horden, B., *Shark Squadron* (Bromley: Independent Books, 2002)

Irving, D., *The Mare's Nest* (London: Corgi, 1966)
, *The Rise and Fall of the Luftwaffe* (London: Futura 1976)
, *The Trail of the Fox* (London: Futura 1978)

Jackson, B. and Bramall D., *The Chiefs* (London: Brassey's, 1992)

Johnson, J.E., *Full Circle* (London: Pan, 1969)

Jones, R.V., *Most Secret War* (London: Coronet 1981)

Kosin, R., *The German Fighter Since 1915* (London: Putnam, 1988)

Leasor, J., *War at the Top*, (London: Michael Joseph, 1959)

Lloyd, I. and Pugh, P., *Hives and the Merlin* (Cambridge: Icon Books, 2004)

Lovell, B., *Echoes of War* (Bristol: Adam Hilger, 1991)

Mead, P., *The Eye in the Sky* (London: HMSO, 1983)

Meekcoms, K.J. and Morgan, E.B., *The British Aircraft Specifications File* (Tonbridge: Air Britain Publication, 1994)

Mets, D., *Master of Airpower*, (Novata: Presidio Press, 1988)

Middlebrook, M. and Everitt, C. *The Bomber Command War Diaries* (London: Penguin, 1990)

Montgomery, B., *The Memoirs of Field Marshal the Viscount Montgomery of Alamein* (London: Collins, 1958)

Morgan, F., *Overture to Overlord* (London; Hodder and Stoughton, 1950)

Newton Dunn, B., *Big Wing* (Shrewsbury: Airlife 1992)

Omissi, D.E., *Airpower and Colonial Control* (Manchester: Manchester University Press, 1990)

Orange, V., *Coningham*, (London: Methuen, 1990)

, *Slessor Bomber Champion* (London: Grubb Street, 2006).

Overy, R., *The Bombing War* (London: Penguin, 2014)

Parham, H.J. and Belfield, E.M.G., *Unarmed into Battle* (Chippenham: Picton Publishing, 1986)

Peret, G., *Winged Victory*, (New York: Random House, 1993)

Playfair, I., *The Mediterranean and Middle East Vol. 2* (London: HMSO, 1956)

Postan, M., *British War Production*, (London HMSO, 1952)

Price, A., *Focke-Wulf 190 at War* (Shepperton: Ian Allan, 1977)

, *Instruments of Darkness*, (London: Macdonald and Jane's, 1977)

, *The Spitfire Story* (London: Jane's, 1982)

, *World War II Fighter Conflict* (London: MacDonald and Jane's, 1975)

Probert, H., *Bomber Harris* (London: Greenhill Books, 2001)

, *High Commanders of The Royal Air Force* (London: HMSO, 1991)

, *The Forgotten Air Force* (London: Brassey's, 1996)

Richards, D., *Portal of Hungerford* (London: Heinemann, 1977)

Roskill, S.W., *War at Sea*, Vol. 2, (London: HMSO, 1956)

Santoro, G., *L'Aeronautica Italiana Nella Seconda Guerra Mondiale Vols 1, 2* (Rome: Apollon, 1957)

Sharp, M. and Bowyer J.F., *Mosquito* (London: Faber and Faber, 1971)

Shores, C., *Second Tactical Air Force* (Oxford: Osprey, 1970)

, and Cull, B., Malizi, N., *Malta: The Spitfire Years* (London: Grub Street, 1991).

, *Malta: The Hurricane Years,* (London: Grubb Street, 1999)

Shores, C., *Ground Attack Aircraft of World War II*, (London: Macdonald and Jane's, 1977).

Shores, C. and Massimello, G., *A History of the Mediterranean Air War 1940–45 Vol. 4*, (London: Grub Street, 2018)

Shores, C. and Ring, H., *Fighters Over the Desert* (London: Neville Spearman, 1969)

Shores, C., Ring, H. and Hess, W., *Fighters Over Tunisia*, (London: Neville Spearman, 1975)

Slessor, J., *The Central Blue* (London: Cassell, 1956)

Speer, A., *Inside the Third Reich* (London: Sphere Books, 1975)

Tedder, Lord, *With Prejudice* (London: Cassell, 1966)

Terraine, J., *The Right of the Line* (Sevenoaks: Sceptre, 1988)

Trevor-Roper, H., *Hitler's War Directives 1939–1945* (London: Pan Books, 1973)

Webster, C. and Frankland N., *The Strategic Air Offensive Against Germany 1939–1945 Vol. 2, 4* (London: HMSO, 1961)

Wilson, T., *Churchill and the Prof.* (London: Cassell, 1995)

Index

AIR WORLD

ALSO BY GREG BAUGHAN
www.pen-and-sword.co.uk

RAF ON THE OFFENSIVE
The Rebirth of Tactical Air Power 1940–1941

Long before the start of the Second World War it had been believed that strategic bombing would be the deciding factor in any future conflict. Then Hitler launched the Blitzkrieg upon France and the Low Countries in 1940, and the much-vaunted French Army and the British Expeditionary Force were swept away in just six weeks.

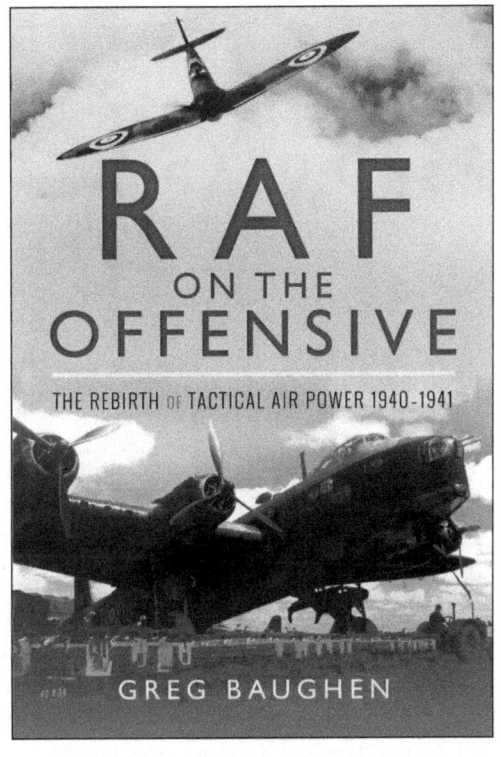

This new form of warfare shook the Air Ministry, but the expected invasion never came, and the Battle of Britain was fought in the air. It seemed that air forces operating independently could determine the course of the war; bombing Germany into defeat seemed Britain's only option. In North Africa, however, Commonwealth armies and air forces were demonstrating that they too could use blitzkrieg tactics to crush opponents. Britain was also no longer alone; Greece and then the Soviet Union joined the fight.

RAF on the Offensive explores how British air power developed after the Battle of Britain. Which direction, then, would the war take?

ISBN: 978-1-52673-515-7

AIR WORLD

BEST FOOT FORWARD
The Autobiography of the RAF's Other Legless Fighter Pilot

Colin Hodgkinson

In the whole of the Second World War, only two men succeeded as operational fighter pilots in the RAF after losing both legs. Douglas Bader was one, and his story is well-known indeed, he has been described as one of the Royal Air Force's most famous pilots. The other was Colin Hodgkinson.

Colin was injured in a flying accident whilst training with the Fleet Air Arm in 1939. He awoke in hospital to find that his right leg had been amputated at the thigh, whilst his left leg was severely injured. His face was also damaged and he had trouble with the sight in one eye. In the weeks that followed, Colin's remaining leg refused to heal. Coolly, calculatingly, he made his decision: Chop the damned thing off and lets be done with it.

Just nineteen at the time, Colin developed a burning determination to prove himself a normal man by becoming a fighter pilot and flying Spitfires. With Douglas Bader as his example, and brilliant surgeons such as Sir Archibald McIndoe treating him, Colin achieved his aim with a hand-tailored pair of tin legs. He proved himself as a fighter pilot many times over, until the war ended, for him at least, as a German prisoner of war.

ISBN: 978-1-47389-762-5

AIR WORLD

ALSO AVAILABLE
www.pen-and-sword.co.uk

BADER'S LAST FIGHT
An In-Depth Investigation of a Great WWII Mystery

Andy Saunders

On 9 August 1941, one of the greatest icons of the Second World War, Douglas Bader, was shot down, captured and later incarcerated. But by whom, and how? Was it by one of his deadly German opponents, as Douglas Bader himself maintained, or was it by one of his own side? There has been much debate and controversy among historians and in 2003 the author of this book revealed for the first time that Bader may have been victim to friendly fire.

That revelation was followed by interest in the national press and later by a TV documentary screened on Channel 4 in August 2006. In the book aviation historian Andy Saunders develops his hypothesis, backed up by strong evidence and a wealth of statistics, and separates fact from fiction. He expertly dissects all the material relating to the day itself, and subsequent events.

In this new, updated edition, Andy Saunders tells of his quest to find the legendary fighter pilots aircraft, which led to the remarkable discovery of a lost Spitfire which is being restored to flying condition.

ISBN: 978-1-47389-540-9

AIR WORLD

ALSO AVAILABLE
www.pen-and-sword.co.uk

Battle of Britain 1940
The Finest Hour's Human Cost

Dilip Sarkar MBE

The summer of 1940 remains a pivotal moment in modern British history – still inspiring immense national pride and a global fascination.

The Fall of France was catastrophic. Britain stood alone and within range of German air attack. America, with its vast resources was neutral, Hitler's forces unbeaten, the outlook for Britain bleak. As Britain's wartime leader, Winston Churchill, rightly predicted, 'the Battle of Britain is about to begin'. Churchill also immortalised Fighter Command's young aircrew as the 'Few' – to whom so many owed everything.

In this unique study, veteran historian and author Dilip Sarkar explores the individual stories of a wide selection of those who lost their lives during the 'Finest Hour', examining their all-too brief lives and sharing these tragic stories – told here, in full, for the first time. Also included is the story of a German fighter pilot, indicating the breadth of investigation involved.

Researched with the full cooperation of the families concerned, this work is a crucial contribution to the Battle of Britain's bibliography.

ISBN: 978-1-52677-593-1